GW01606585

Reason and Revolution

~~qu'elle les recevra avec joye et qu'elle s'empressera après la vérification de leurs pouvoirs, de partager avec eux les grands travaux qui doivent procurer la régénération de la France.~~ l'abbé Sieyes.

La dénomination d'assemblée nationale est la seule qui convienne à l'assemblée, dans l'état actuel des choses, soit parceque les membres qui la composent sont les seuls représentans connus et vérifiés, soit parcequ'ils sont envoyés directement par la presque totalité de la nation, soit enfin parceque la représentation nationale étant une et indivisible, aucun des députés dans quelque ordre ou classe qu'il soit choisi, n'a le droit d'exercer ses fonctions séparément de la présente assemblée.

Renvoi # La ditte assemblée nationale arrête ~~ordonne~~ que les motifs de la présente délibération seront incessamment rédigés, pour être présentés au roi et à la nation.

l'abbé Sieyes.

Reason and Revolution
The Political Thought of the Abbé Sieyes

Murray Forsyth

1987 Leicester University Press
Holmes & Meier Publishers, Inc., New York

First published in 1987 by Leicester University Press
First published in the U.S.A. in 1987 by
Holmes & Meier Publishers, Inc.
30 Irving Place
New York, NY 10003

Copyright © Leicester University Press 1987

All rights reserved. No part of this publication may be reproduced, stored in a retrieval system, or transmitted in any form or by any means, electronic, mechanical, photocopying, recording or otherwise, without the prior permission of the Leicester University Press.

Designed by Douglas Martin
Phototypeset in Linotron Sabon
Printed in Great Britain by
Redwood Burn Ltd, Trowbridge

British Library Cataloguing in Publication Data

Forsyth, Murray
Reason and revolution: the political thought
of the Abbé Sieyes.
1. Sieyes, Emmanuel Joseph, *Comte* –
Contributions in political science
2. Political science – France – History
I. Title
320'.01 JC179.S534
ISBN 0–7185–1222–7

Library of Congress Cataloging-in-Publication Data

Forsyth, Murray Greensmith.
Reason and revolution.
Bibliography: p.
Includes index.
1. Sieyes, Emmanuel Joseph, comte, 1784–1836 –
Contributions in political science. I. Title.
JC179.S534F67 1987 321.09 87–10854
ISBN 0–8419–1143–6 (Holmes & Meier)

Frontispiece

On 15 June 1789 Sieyes proposed in the chamber of the Third Estate that a new assembly, representative of the French nation, should be constituted forthwith. After a long debate it was decided that the new body should be called the 'National Assembly'. This note shows Sieyes amending his motion to incorporate the new name. (From the Sieyes Archives.)

Contents

For Anna, Deborah and Andrew Forsyth

Acknowledgments

My thanks are due in the first instance to the British Academy for the award of a Wolfson Fellowship which enabled me to visit the Sieyes Archives in Paris and to begin the research on which this study is based. I would also like to thank the Social Science Research Council (now the Economic and Social Research Council) and the Research Board at Leicester University for grants which enabled me to continue and complete this research. M. Robert Marquant, of the French National Archives, kindly helped me to decipher Sieyes' handwriting in the very early days. Mrs Dorothy Brydges in turn deciphered my own handwriting and typed the manuscript of the book with unfailing good humour. Finally I would like to thank my wife who has accompanied me on visits to the Sieyes Archives, to Sieyes' tomb in the cemetery of Père Lachaise, to the building (now very dilapidated) in Versailles where Sieyes delivered his historic speeches in June 1789, and indeed to Fréjus, where Sieyes was born – all as if it were the most natural thing to be doing in the world.

Uppingham
February 1987

Murray Forsyth

Introduction: the life, works and significance of the Abbé Sieyes

THE AIM OF THIS BOOK is to give a clear and comprehensive account of the political thought of one of the most important figures in the French Revolution, Emmanuel Sieyes. The exposition is based not only on Sieyes' published works, but also on his extensive unpublished papers which were rediscovered by a singular stroke of good fortune in 1967, after having disappeared from view for over a hundred years. It is hoped that the present study will help to restore Sieyes, at least in the English-speaking world, to the distinguished position in the history of political thought that is rightfully his.

It will perhaps be helpful to begin by removing any doubts about either the spelling or the pronunciation of his awkward name. As regards pronunciation the testimony of Sieyes' contemporaries is reasonably unambiguous. 'The French pronounce Sieyes, Sies', wrote the author of the *Revolutionary Plutarch*.[1] According to Camille Desmoulins, '*on prononce Syess*'.[2] There is much greater disagreement about the orthography, which has given rise to its own specialized literature.[3] Contemporaries used a very wide variety of forms ranging from Sieys and Syeyes to Syesse and even Scyès. The most common form was unquestionably the unaccented Sieyes, and this, together with its convenience for the English typesetter, is the reason why it has been adopted in the present study. The other form which has become legitimized by long usage, and by the aid it gives to pronunciation, is Sieyès. The irony is that Sieyes himself, so far as I have been able to observe, seems to have favoured the form Siéyes, which today finds no acceptance at all.[4]

Sieyes was not only a writer and thinker of quality, but also a statesman. He had the rare privilege of being able, on occasion, to transmute his own previously elaborated political ideas into practice. He held public office almost continuously during the revolutionary decade from 1789 to 1799, and although he lapsed at times into what he called 'philosophical silence' he was able at other times to intervene decisively in the course of events – the two most notable examples being the motions that he proposed in the chamber of the Third Estate in June 1789, and his elaboration of the *coup* of 18 Brumaire in 1799 which had the result of elevating Napoleon to power. By the first Sieyes opened the Revolution, by the second he closed it – or rather, as Sainte-Beuve remarks, it was closed on him.[5]

Almost all Sieyes' published writings were very closely related to political practice. They were written, that is to say, to guide or influence events in a very immediate way. He seems to have needed the spur of a possible practical result in order to finish a work. As he admitted in his autobiographical fragment (which itself had a practical purpose, though less direct than most of his other writings) he had the intellectual curiosity to enquire deeply into a subject, but he lacked the will to complete a work of purely scholarly enquiry.[6] As a result his works do not contain any substantial study of the state in the mode of Hobbes' *Leviathan* or Hegel's *Philosophy of Right.* Sieyes' writings were short and sharp. It is typical that the one text by him which is generally held to be a 'classic' – *What is the Third Estate?* – takes the form of a manifesto or programme of action, while his longest work – *Views on the means of execution* – contains only 168 pages.

Given the close correlation between thought and practice in Sieyes' writings it might appear that the only appropriate way of treating them was by integrating them into a biographical narrative, examining each of the products of his pen in chronological order, and in relation to the particular circumstances of his life and times in which they were produced. This was the way J.H. Clapham treated them in his excellent study published in 1912,[7] and clearly it has great merits from the point of view of the historian of the French Revolution.

From the point of view of the political theorist, however, the biographical treatment of political ideas is not usually the most illuminating. The political theorist is not so much concerned with ideas as forming part of the chronological narrative of a person's life as with the ideas themselves, their coherence, logic and consistency. Because of this he tends to divide up his material differently. Concepts, not time and circumstance, are the most important criterion influencing the shape of his exposition.

For these reasons the present account of Sieyes' ideas is moulded in a different way from Clapham's. It treats them not as a part of the biography of the man, but as a self-subsistent theory of politics or a system of ideas. This does not mean that they are treated in isolation from the historical context, but rather that the historical questions that are posed are different from those of the biographer. It is the historical origins of Sieyes' system of ideas, the historical development of his system and the historical impact of his system, that become of primary interest.

In treating Sieyes' ideas and his life separately the present volume has a formidable precursor in Paul Bastid's study *Sieyes et sa pensée,* first published in 1939, and republished in an expanded version in 1970.[8] The wealth of detail contained in Bastid's work make it indispensable to any student of Sieyes. At the same time the original impulse behind the present study came not from Bastid, but from a curiosity about what happened to the state in theory and practice at the end of the eighteenth century. It was largely because Bastid's work did not satisfy – or only partially satisfied – this curiosity, that the decision to embark upon a fresh reconstruction of Sieyes' system of ideas was made.

Mention of the reconstruction of Sieyes' system raises a further important issue. It may be conceded that it is valuable to look at a thinker's ideas in the round and as a unity, but it may still be asked if it is appropriate in Sieyes' particular case, given that his writings tended to be of such a short and practical nature. The chapters that follow will, it is hoped, remove any doubts on this matter, so I will confine myself here to making a few general observations.

I Sieyes' significance

Sieyes' writings may have been short and practical, but this does not mean that they were merely a heterogeneous bundle of reactions to events with no nerve of connection running through them. On the contrary one of the main characteristics of Sieyes' writings which marks them out from the others of his time, and makes them so interesting and rewarding to the political theorist, is precisely the unrelenting logic which pervades them and which, while certainly taking account of events and circumstances, refuses to capitulate to them. Sieyes' haughty, independent spirit, his fastidiousness about language and concepts, his so-called 'metaphysical' approach to the problems of the day – features which often incited amusement and sometimes irritation and hostility in his contemporaries – are precisely those which give his works a more lasting value than the more predictable, loosely constructed, and often merely rhetorical products of those same contemporaries.

Sieyes may have been unwilling or unable to write a sustained book of pure theory, but this does not mean that the theory was not there in his head. Each of his short works represents an excursion of theory, provoked by external events and the wish to mould them. Bit by bit, as his works succeed one another, overlapping and expanding on the themes already introduced, a real system of ideas presents itself. His rediscovered papers are of particular value because they reveal a little more of the hidden, inner side of this system, and of the way it crystallized well before the French Revolution took place.

Seen in its entirety Sieyes' system of political ideas is superior in originality, breadth and depth to that of any of his contemporaries, not excluding such well-known figures as Thomas Paine or Condorcet. He is, more than any other, the man who articulates the political theory of the French Revolution, by which is meant, not that he theorizes about the Revolution, but that his theory presents the idea of the Revolution itself in its first, momentous stages. Of course the French Revolution was not a single homogeneous movement, and in the period between 1792 and 1794 the original dominant impetus of 1789 was superseded by another movement that was radically opposed to it. Sieyes was not the theorist of this Second Revolution but of the First. When the Second Revolution brought Robespierre and his colleagues to power he retreated into silence. When Robespierre's regime disintegrated he came to the fore again. The *coup* of 18 Brumaire 1799 represented his final attempt to establish the French government on the basis of the original ideas of 1789.

Sieyes then is *the* man of 1789. Sainte-Beuve, who was marvellously attuned to Sieyes' character and talents, gave perhaps the best short statement of his central achievement. 'Sieyes,' wrote Sainte-Beuve, 'has genius. He was the first clearly to conceive and to invent, in an ideal and rather absolute form, the new order that was to replace the old one. He was the first to proclaim it, at the decisive moment, in his precise and luminous writings.'[9] Lord Acton was even briefer: 'I must speak of a man memorable far beyond Mirabeau in the history of political thought and political action, who is the most perfect representative of the Revolution. I mean the Abbé Sieyes.'[10]

As the most perfect representative in thought of the French Revolution of 1789 Sieyes is simultaneously the most perfect representative in thought of the ideas that that Revolution transmitted to Europe and to the rest of the world in the course of the nineteenth and twentieth centuries regarding the ends and organization of the state. In a study of the democratic constitutions of Europe, published in 1929, Agnes Headlam-Morley could write: 'Sieyes' original contribution to modern political thought consists in a theoretic justification of representative government.... These theories, first expounded during the era of the French Revolution, form the basis of all the democratic constitutions of the nineteenth and twentieth centuries.'[11] Even the halting and piecemeal modifications of the unwritten British constitution that have taken place in the course of the same two centuries may be said to have been in the direction of the ideas of 1789.

It will now be apparent why Sieyes is such a significant figure in the history of political thought. To omit him is to leave that history incomplete. It is to neglect a critical turning-point at which political ideas that had been germinating since the Reformation, ideas that had at their core the notion of the unique self-determining quality of the human being, were developed, synthesized and applied in a form in which we can recognize the main lineaments of the states in which we in the western world now actually live. This recognition is not there or only very partially there, when we read Rousseau, or Burke, or indeed large portions of Hegel. It is there when we read Sieyes. One of the purposes of this book is to fill this gap in the history of political thought.

In doing so it will follow a different course from those who see in the ideas of 1789 only the preface to the Terror, and condemn the whole revolutionary movement from 1789 to the fall of Robespierre in 1794 as a disastrous example of what happens when man attempts to shape his political destiny according to rational principles. Talmon's book on *The Origins of Totalitarian Democracy* has been perhaps the most popular and powerful expression of this standpoint in recent times. Sieyes is seen by Talmon as merely a herald of the storm, opening the floodgates to the totalitarian democracy of Robespierre and Saint-Just. His ideas 'marked a decisive advance in the direction of the totalitarianism of ideas based on an exclusive creed.'[12] Sieyes, according to Talmon, is saved from being completely totalitarian in outlook solely by his practical concern with the protection of property.

To the extent that the radical democratic movement that led to the Terror did indeed draw on principles and slogans that had first been enunciated in 1789 – the most obvious of these being the 'sovereignty of the people' – then it is right to see a continuity between 1789 and 1794. It is surely wrong though to conclude from this that 1789 produced only the materials for a later despotism, and that it did not simultaneously produce a coherent liberal doctrine that was completely at variance with the regime of Robespierre and Saint-Just, and not a stepping-stone to it. Sieyes more than any other elaborated this alternative doctrine.

Talmon's error is rooted in the rigid dualism that marks his work. Influenced by the political events of his own day he pitted 'liberal democracy' against 'totalitarian democracy'. The first he equated with a pragmatic, empirical Anglo-Saxon approach to politics. Liberal democracy arose from trial and error, and the slow, half-conscious processes of history. The second he equated with the assumption that there was a sole and exclusive truth in politics that ought to be applied. This rigid schema unfortunately has the effect of making anyone who attempts to base liberal democracy on rational principles, rather than merely on historical fact or pragmatism, a crypto-totalitarian. It precludes a serious and adequate consideration of the rational liberalism of a thinker like Sieyes.

In a similar way the traditional Marxist interpretation of the French Revolution also precludes a serious and adequate consideration of the rational liberalism of a thinker like Sieyes. This is because the traditional Marxist interpretation has tended to see the men of 1789 as representing merely a 'bourgeois revolution' that was destined to be overtaken by the altogether more advanced 'democratic revolution' led by Robespierre and his colleagues. As in the conservative view, the French Revolution is seen as culminating in 1794, and once again the men of 1789 are subjected to a schema which reduces them to a prelude to the 'real thing'.

In the case of Sieyes the Marxist approach has been taken recently to a novel extreme by Zapperi, in the introduction to his useful edition of *What is the Third Estate?*[13] Zapperi does not reduce Sieyes to a puppet of the 'bourgeois revolution', because he argues vehemently (like several historians of the Revolution in recent years) that 1789 was *not* a 'bourgeois revolution' in the traditional Marxist sense. However, this by no means exonerates Sieyes in Zapperi's eyes. The Abbé is now castigated for *failing* to inaugurate a 'bourgeois revolution'. More precisely Zapperi reduces Sieyes to a mere cipher, unable to understand what either capitalism or anti-capitalism required in France at the end of the eighteenth century. He failed to follow Quesnay, whom Zapperi (following Marx in a peculiarly literal fashion) believes showed the way to capitalist exploitation, and he failed to follow Rousseau, who indicated the route to true as distinct from degenerate democracy. Sieyes was hence both a fool and a knave, best classified as a conservative adhering blindly and indeed ideologically to the structures of the *ancien régime*. Clearly for Zapperi what took place in 1789 is of trivial importance compared with what ought to have taken place according to good Marxist logic. One is reminded irresistibly of one of Sieyes' own remarks: '*Combien des gens croyent savoir, qui ne font que vouloir!*'[14]

To reject such Marxist convolutions is not necessarily to reject the insights that Marx himself often offers in relation to Sieyes. These insights come (in my judgement) in Marx's very early writings when he was speculating on the nature of the French Revolution and in particular on the role of ideas and interests in its creation, and working his way towards his own theory of revolution.[15] Marx's remarks at this time seem far more helpful than the familiar mechanism of interpretation that is used over and again by his followers.

Sieyes' ideas will hence be studied in this volume not as a preface to some other system, but in their own right. It remains to say something more about his life.

2 Sieyes' life

Emmanuel Joseph Sieyes was born on 3 May 1748 in Fréjus, a small town in Provence. His father was an agent of royal administration in the town, and a man of modest wealth, who decided at an early point in Emmanuel's education that he should enter the Church, although his son seems to have felt no calling whatsoever for such a career. The young Sieyes was therefore sent from Fréjus to the seminary of Saint-Sulpice in Paris. He arrived in the capital in 1765 and was to remain there for ten years, reading theology at the Sorbonne as part of his religious training. The time he spent in Paris was particularly important in his intellectual development, as we shall see in chapter 2, for it was while he was there that he read widely and deeply beyond the bounds of the course on which he had been enrolled. Philosophy, political economy and politics were the three main areas to which he directed his intellectual energies, and his political radicalism is already apparent in these very early studies.

Ordained as a priest in 1772, Sieyes was able, three years later, through patronage secured by his father, to become secretary to Lubersac, the newly appointed Bishop of Tréguier in Brittany. He departed from Paris to Brittany and stayed there for five years. They do not seem to have been happy ones. Then, in 1780, Lubersac was appointed Bishop of Chartres and Sieyes duly followed him to his new diocese and became vicar-general. He now began to enjoy some advancement in the administrative hierarchy of the Church. In 1783 he became a canon. In 1786 he attended the sovereign chamber of the clergy of France as a councillor. In 1787 he was appointed a representative of the clergy in the Provincial Assembly of Orléans. In 1788 he became chancellor of the chapter at Chartres.

Then, in August 1788, Sieyes' career as a revolutionary writer began. As the financial and political crisis of the *ancien régime* deepened, and the date was fixed for the summoning of the Estates-General, he wrote his first tract, setting out his views on the strategy that the future assembly ought to follow. This work was followed by three more (one of them part of a joint work commissioned by the Duke of Orléans) in the winter of 1788–89. All of them were uncompromisingly radical, and all of them made an impact, but none more than *What is the Third Estate?*, which was published in January 1789.

As a result of these writings Sieyes suddenly became famous. He was elected to the Estates-General by the Third Estate of Paris, and took his seat on 25 May 1789. On 10 June and 15 June he presented in the chamber of the Third Estate the two motions that brought about the transformation of the Estates-General into the National Assembly. It was undoubtedly his greatest single political achievement. Shortly afterwards, on 14 July, he was elected to the Assembly's Committee of Eight, charged with drafting a constitution, and was immediately assigned the task of drawing up a declaration of rights. This formed the subject of his next important publication.

Sieyes lost some of his popularity as a result of his stand on the question of tithes in August 1789, but he continued to work energetically on the creation of a new political order throughout the remainder of 1789 and the early part of 1790. During these months perhaps his most significant achievement was his plan for the territorial redivision of France for administrative and electoral purposes. It was largely accepted, and led to the creation of the modern departmental system. He also spoke out against the proposals of those who wanted to give France an English-type constitution and presented his opinions on the reorganization of the law and of the Church, and on the regulation of the press.

Early in 1790 Sieyes and Condorcet founded the *Société de 1789*, partly in order to provide a political alternative to the Jacobin Club which was at that time dominated by the Duport–Lameth–Barnave group, and partly as a forum for the impartial discussion of social and political ideas. The new society flourished briefly. Then, from about the middle of 1790, to some extent disillusioned with the progress of the Revolution, Sieyes receded from the mainstream of events. He did not truly re-emerge until April 1791 when, as a member of the Directory of the Department of Paris, he took vigorous measures to protect liberty of worship in the capital, and defended the action of the Directory in the National Assembly.

In June 1791 came the crisis provoked by Louis XVI's flight to Varennes. This act destroyed Sieyes' belief that the new constitution, to which he had contributed so much, could be made to work while Louis was on the throne, though it did not turn him into a republican (in the sense of an anti-monarchist). He played little part in the final revision of the constitution in 1791, and when the National Assembly concluded its business and dissolved he retired to the village of Auteuil not far from Paris. He remained there during the life of the Legislative Assembly (1791–92), watching political events, but not directly participating in them.

Sieyes welcomed the overthrow of Louis XVI by the insurrection of 10 August 1792, but at the same time he had grave reservations about the new political forces that had been unleashed in Paris. He was elected to the National Convention and privately advised the Girondins to take strong action against the popular, agitatory bodies in the capital that threatened the Convention's independence. They did not listen to him, however, and he appears to have gradually distanced himself from them in the first half of 1793. He voted for the death of the king in January, but subsequently he seems to have deliberately moved on to the periphery of the political stage. While the final battle between the Girondins and the Mountain was being fought out, he busied himself with education and briefly edited a journal with Condorcet.

The victory of Robespierre and the Mountain over the Girondins drove Sieyes to retreat completely from active politics. From the middle of July 1793 until several months after Robespierre's overthrow in July 1794 he became scarcely visible. When he reappeared he threw his energies into a new field, that of foreign affairs. For the greater part of 1795 this was his main preoccupation, and he soon became one of the main moulders of French foreign policy. Not least among his achievements was the negotiation and signature of the Franco–Dutch Treaty in May 1795. He also found time to propose a law providing protection for the National Convention and to deliver two outstanding speeches on the new constitution that was being drafted. His constitutional proposals were not, however, accepted.

With the establishment of the Directorate at the end of October 1795 the pace of Sieyes' political career began to slow down again. He was elected to the new legislature and took his seat in the Council of Five Hundred. He was also elected a member of the new collegiate executive – the Directory – but declined the post, as well as that of foreign minister. He seems to have been content with a leisurely life during 1796, but a moment of excitement occurred in the spring of the following year when an attempt was made on his life by a demented priest. Fortunately it did him little harm.

Sieyes regarded with deep suspicion the increase in the strength of rightist and royalist tendencies within and outside the legislature during 1797 and he was a firm supporter of the *coup* carried out by the Executive Directory on 18 Fructidor (4 September 1797) which effectively checked them. After the *coup* he was active in devising punitive measures against the right.

In May 1798 Sieyes was appointed special envoy to the court of Berlin. The main aim of his mission was to try and persuade Prussia to enter into an alliance or pact with France. Sieyes stayed in Berlin for almost a year. He was unable to move the Prussian king or his ministers in the direction of a positive arrangement with France, but he may possibly, towards the end, have helped to keep the country neutral in the struggle that was then looming between France and the Second Coalition.

The last phase in Sieyes' political career opened in the spring of 1799 when he was elected to fill a vacancy in the Executive Directory, and returned from Berlin to Paris to take up his duties. The Executive Directory had by this time lost most of its authority, not only because of the mediocrity of its members but because of the repeated acts of force to which it had been driven to ward off its internal enemies on the left and on the right. The external situation of France had also become highly critical. A significant body of opinion in Paris thought that a reform of the constitution was essential and that only Sieyes could effect it. Sieyes too believed that a constitutional change was necessary, and when his friends and supporters in Paris organized his election to the Directory he was ready to accept it as a means to this end.

A few days after his arrival back in Paris the Directory was purged and Sieyes became its president (18 June 1799). He was then faced with the danger that threatened from resurgent Jacobinism, and it was only after he had successfully fended off this danger that he was able to proceed with his own *coup*. He needed a general to guarantee its success and he had some difficulty in finding one. Then in October Bonaparte returned unexpectedly to France from Egypt, receiving a hero's welcome. After some wariness on the part of both men, Bonaparte agreed to work with Sieyes in overturning the existing regime. The *coup* was carried out on 9 and 10 November (18 and 19 Brumaire Year VIII). Power was surrendered by the existing legislature into the hands of a provisional Consulate consisting of Sieyes, Bonaparte and Ducos, and work was started on a new constitution. It was during this provisional regime that Bonaparte, through a combination of factors – the mood of the country, his immense popularity and his own shrewd tactics – succeeded in outmanoeuvring Sieyes, and ensuring that the new constitution would reflect his own ideas as much as those of his colleague. By the time the constitution was promulgated at the end of 1799, and the Consulate formally established with Bonaparte at its head, Sieyes had decided once again to beat a retreat from the political scene. This time it was to be final. He was granted an estate in recompense for his public services and this ensured that his retirement was a comfortable one. He was appointed the first president of the new Senate, and indeed remained a senator throughout the Napoleonic period, but he never spoke there or played any significant role. As a final irony, when Bonaparte decided to elevate the status of the senators, Sieyes was made a count (1808).

The defeat of Bonaparte at Waterloo and the restoration of the Bourbons drove Sieyes, a regicide, into exile in Brussels. He stayed there until 1830, when the July Revolution allowed him to return to Paris. He was now a very old man, living an isolated, vegetative existence. He died on 20 June 1836, at the age of eighty-eight, one of the last survivors of the great revolutionary generation of 1789.

3 Sieyes' works

Such, in outline, was the life of the man whose political ideas form the subject of this study. It is necessary now to provide an account of his numerous writings, on which the present study is based. Sieyes' published works are listed below, followed by a description of his unpublished writings which are housed in the Sieyes Archives.

The list of published works does not include everything that Sieyes produced, but only those works that are of relevance to his political thought. Details are given of the first edition of each work and it is indicated which text has been used where this differs from the first edition. English titles have been given of the various works, and these are used throughout the volume, either in full or abbreviated form. Citations from the works, and from the unpublished writings, are also in English for the most part. It was not easy to decide which language to use predominantly, where the use of both equally would have made the book inordinately long. In the end English was chosen because the study is largely aimed at making Sieyes' ideas more familiar to the English-speaking world. All translations, both of Sieyes' works and of those by other writers, unless otherwise indicated, are by the author.

In the case of many of Sieyes' speeches and interventions in parliament, and some of his other pronouncements, reference has been made to the *Moniteur* (*Réimpression de l'ancien Moniteur depuis la réunion des Etats-Généraux jusqu'au Consulat*, 30 vols, Paris, 1840–45) and to the *Archives parlementaires* (*Archives parlementaires de 1787 à 1860 ...* 1ere serie, 1787 à 1799, Paris, 1879–present).

Published works by Sieyes

1. *Vues sur les moyens d'exécution dont les représentants de la France pourront disposer en 1789* [*Views on the means of execution which the representatives of France will have at their disposal in 1789*]. Anonymous

(1789), 161pp. The first of Sieyes' published works to be written, but not published until after the *Essay on Privileges*. Also the longest of his works. It was written in August 1788, and appeared probably at the very start of 1789. The text of the second edition, which has 168 pages, has been used.

2. *Essai sur les privilèges* [*Essay on Privileges*]. Anonymous [November 1788], 48pp. The critical edition in Edme Champion (ed.), *Qu'est-ce que le Tiers état?* (Paris, 1888) has been used.

3. *Qu'est-ce que le Tiers état?* [*What is the Third Estate?*]. Anonymous (1789) [January], 127pp. The critical edition by Roberto Zapperi (Geneva, 1970) has been used.

4. *Instructions envoyées par S.A.S. Monseigneur le duc d'Orléans* [*Instructions sent by S.A.S. Monseigneur the Duke of Orléans*]. Anonymous [1789, February], 66pp. This text includes both the *Instructions* proper (10pp.) which were addressed to the duke's representatives in the assemblies of the Bailiwicks, and related to the forthcoming meeting of the Estates-General, and the much longer *Délibérations à prendre dans les assemblées de bailliages* [*Deliberations to be taken in the assemblies of the Bailiwicks*]. The latter is by Sieyes. The authorship of the *Instructions* has been debated. Amongst Sieyes' papers there is a copy of this text in which he has filled in the name 'Laclos' in the attribution of the *Instructions* and his own name in the attribution of the *Délibérations* (284 AP 18.2). This would seem to settle the debate in favour of Choderlos de Laclos, the duke's private secretary and the author of *Les Liaisons dangereuses*.

5. *Motion of 10 June 1789*, presented in the chamber of the Communes or Third Estate. *Arch. parl.*, VIII, 85. The original text of this motion is to be found in the Sieyes Archives under 284 AP 4.1. It has recently been published in Emmanuel Joseph Sieyes, *Politische Schriften 1788–1790*, edited by Eberhard Schmitt and Rolf Reichardt (Darmstadt, 1975) pp. 230–2.

6. *Motion of 15 June 1789*, presented in the chamber of the Communes or Third Estate. *Arch. parl.*, VIII, 127. The original version of this motion, with the later amendments penned in by Sieyes, is also to be found in the Sieyes Archives under 284 AP 4.1. The two original versions of the motions of 10 and 15 June are the most remarkable and dramatic documents in the Sieyes Archives.

7. *Préliminaire de la Constitution; reconnaissance et exposition raisonnée des droits de l'homme et du citoyen* [*Preliminary of the Constitution: recognition and reasoned exposition of the rights of man and citizen*]. Paris (1789) [July], 21pp. Several variations of this work appeared in 1789. Some consisted solely of Sieyes' 'Declaration of rights' detached from his introductory essay. The length of the Declaration itself varied. The version dated simply 1789, which consists of 52 pages, and in which the Declaration contains 42 Articles, has been used.

8. *Quelques idées de Constitution applicables à la ville de Paris en juillet 1789* [*Some constitutional ideas applicable to the town of Paris in July 1789*]. Versailles [September, 1789], 38pp.

9. and 10. *Observations sommaires sur les biens ecclésiastiques, du 10 août 1789* [*Summary observations on ecclesiastical goods, 10 August 1789*]. Versailles, 48pp. This text incorporates also: *Opinion de M. l'Abbé Sieyes, sur l'arrêté du 4, relatif aux dîmes, prononcé le 10 août, à la séance du soir* [*The Abbé Sieyes' opinion on the decree of 4* [*August*] *relating to tithes, delivered on 10 August, during the evening session*].

11. *Dire de l'abbé Sieyes sur la question du veto royal à la séance du 7 septembre 1789* [*Speech by the Abbé Sieyes on the question of the royal veto in the session of 7 September 1789*]. Versailles [1789], 30pp. The copy in the Sieyes Archives contains Sieyes' marginal notes. 284 AP 18.2.

12. *Rapport du nouveau comité de Constitution fait à l'Assemblée nationale, le mardi 29 septembre 1789, sur l'établissement des bases de la représentation proportionelle* [*Report of the new Constitutional Committee made to the National Assembly on Tuesday 29 September 1789, on the establishment of the bases of proportional representation*]. Versailles (1789), 24pp. Although presented by Thouret this report strongly reflects Sieyes' ideas.

13. *Seconde partie du rapport du nouveau comité de Constitution fait à l'Assemblée nationale, le mardi 29 septembre 1789, sur l'établissement des Assemblées administratives et des nouvelles municipalités* [*Second part of the report of the new Constitutional Committee made to the National Assembly on Tuesday 29 September 1789, on the establishment of administrative Assemblies and new municipalities*]. Versailles (1789), 24pp. This again reflects Sieyes' ideas though presented by Thouret.

14. *Observations sur le rapport du comité de Constitution concernant la nouvelle organisation de la France* [*Observations on the report of the Constitutional Committee concerning the new organization of France*]. Anonymous, Versailles (1789) [October], 53pp.

15. *Rapport sur un projet de loi contre les délits qui peuvent se commetre par le voie de l'impression et par la publication des écrits et gravures* [*Report on a draft law against crimes committed through the printing and publication of writings and engravings*]. 20 January 1790, *Arch. parl.*, XI, 259–64.

16. *Projet d'un décret provisoire sur le clergé, etc., du 12 février 1790* [*Draft of a provisional decree on the clergy, etc., 12 February 1790*]. Paris (1790), 40pp.

17. *Opinion d'un député sur le clergé, cette opinion doit être incessamment proposée à l'Assemblée nationale* [*Opinion of a deputy on the clergy: this opinion should be proposed forthwith in the National Assembly*].

Anonymous, 12pp. Sieyes ascribes this text to himself (284 AP 18.2) Although undated it may be placed in the early part of 1790 before the Civil Constitution of the Clergy had been decided.

18. *Aperçu d'une nouvelle organisation de la justice et de la police en France* [*Outline of a new organization for justice and the police in France*]. March 1790 Paris, 62pp. The version published in *Arch. parl.*, XII, 249–58 (19 March 1790) has been used.

19. *Opinion de M. l'Abbé Sieyes. Suite de la discussion sur l'ordre judiciaire.* [*Opinion of the Abbé Sieyes. Continuation of the discussion of the judicial order*]. *Arch. parl.*, XII, 582–4 (8 April 1790).

20. *Arrêté du directoire du département de Paris concernant les églises paroissiales, les chapelles et autres édifices de la ville de Paris* [*Decree of the Departmental Directory of Paris concerning the parish churches, chapels and other buildings of the town of Paris*]. *Arch. parl.*, XXV, 179–80. Although issued under the name of the president of the departmental directory (La Rochefoucauld) this decree was largely if not wholly Sieyes' work.

21. *First intervention* in the National Assembly on the freedom of religious worship, 18 April 1791. *Arch. parl.*, XXV, 184–7.

22. *Second intervention* in the National Assembly on the freedom of religious worship, 7 May 1791. *Arch. parl.*, XXV, 646–50.

23. *La déclaration volontaire proposée aux patriotes des 83 departéments ce 17 juin 1791* [*Voluntary declaration proposed to the patriots of 83 departments on 17 June 1791*]. Paris (June 1791), 16pp. Only a few copies of this joint work by Sieyes and Condorcet were printed before it was withdrawn. The copy in the British Museum bears Sieyes' own handwritten corrections.

24. *Letter* rebutting accusations of republicanism, published in the *Moniteur*, IX, 46–7 (6 July 1791).

25. *Note explicative* replying to Thomas Paine on the subject of republicanism, in the *Moniteur*, IX, 137–9 (16 July 1791).

26. *Projet de loi pour faire cesser les troubles religieux* [*Draft law to put an end to religious troubles*]. Anonymous, *Chronique de Paris*, 18 November 1791, pp. 1296–7. A copy of this draft is to be found amongst Sieyes' private papers (284 AP 4.9), corrected and with an insertion in his own hand. It is undoubtedly by him.

27. *Pour l'organisation du ministère de la guerre. Rapport fait au comité de défense générale, le 13 janvier, l'an IIe de la République* [*On the organization of the War Ministry. Report presented to the Committee of General Defence – 13 January, year II of the Republic*]. *Arch. parl.*, LVII, 644–53.

28. *Journal d'instruction sociale: Prospectus*. It is impossible to be certain that Sieyes wrote the Prospectus of the *Journal* that he, Condorcet and Duhamel wrote, and of which five issues appeared between 1 June and 6 July 1793. The content suggests he had at least a part in it. For this, and the next two texts the reprinted *Journal* (EDHIS, Paris, 1981) has been used. The Prospectus is on pp. 1–11.

29. *Des intérêts de la liberté dans l'état social et dans le système représentatif* [*The benefits of liberty in the social state and the representative system*]. Published in the second issue of the *Journal d'instruction sociale*, 8 June 1793, 33–48.

30 *Du nouvel établissement public de l'instruction en France* [*Concerning the new public establishment of instruction in France*]. Published in issues 3, 4, 5 and 6 of the *Journal d'instruction sociale*, 22 June–6 July 1793, 81–96, 97–104, 145–60, 161–5. It contains Sieyes' plan for education, which was presented by Lakanal in the National Convention.

31. *Notice sur la vie de Sieyes, membre de la première Assemblée nationale et de la Convention, écrite a Paris, en messidor, deuzième année de l'ère républicaine (vieux style: juin 1794)* [*Notice on the life of Sieyes, member of first National Assembly and of the Convention, written in Paris, in Messidor, second year of the republican era (old style: June 1794)*]. Paris, Year III, 66pp. Published early in 1795. Another French edition was published at about the same time in Switzerland. The *Notice*, written in the third person, was put together by Sieyes' German friend, K.E. Oelsner, from notes sent to him by Sieyes. It is hence the closest that we have to an autobiography of him. The text reprinted in *La Révolution française*, XXIII (1892), 161–81, 257–78 has been used.

32. *Opinion de Sieyes sur plusieurs articles des titres IV et V du projet de Constitution* [*Opinion of Sieyes on several articles in Titles IV and V of the draft Constitution*]. Printed by order of the National Convention, 24pp. The text of Sieyes' speech of 20 July 1795 in the Convention. The text in the *Moniteur*, XXV, 291–7 has been used.

33. *Opinion de Sieyes sur les attributions et l'organisation du jury constitutionnaire proposé le 2 thermidor* [*Opinion of Sieyes on the attributes and organization of the constitutional jury proposed on 2 Thermidor*]. Printed by order of the National Convention, 24pp. The text of Sieyes' speech of 5 August 1795 in the Convention.

Unpublished writings by Sieyes

Sieyes' unpublished writings are to be found in the Sieyes Archives which are lodged in the National Archives in Paris. The indispensable guide to the writings is Robert Marquant's *Les Archives Sieyes* (Paris, Imprimierie nationale, 1970).

The papers are contained in nineteen boxes or cartons numbered from 284 AP 1 to 284 AP 19. Each carton is divided into dossiers, and these again into smaller folders or sections. In the references in the present study the carton number will be given, and then the dossier number. In some instances the section within the dossier is also indicated.

For the student of Sieyes' ideas the most important cartons are the first five which contain Sieyes' handwritten notes on politics, constitutional matters, political economy, metaphysics, language, music, etc., written before, during and after the revolutionary decade 1789–99, as well as his drafts for speeches and published works during the revolutionary decade. Marquant classifies them as follows:

284 AP 1: Notes on music and bibliography.
284 AP 2: Notes on philosophy, economics and politics before the Revolution.
284 AP 3: Notes on philosophy, economics and politics before the Revolution.
284 AP 4: Political notes during the Constituent Assembly.
284 AP 5: Notes during the Legislative Assembly, the Convention, the Directorate, the Consulate and the Empire.

Most of the other cartons contain Sieyes' official correspondence and documentation accumulated by Sieyes in the course of his political career. There is, however, some interesting private correspondence contained in 284 AP 17, and 284 AP 18 contains a useful collection of printed works by and about Sieyes.

Three unpublished texts by Sieyes, contained in the Archives, deserve to be mentioned separately. They are relatively complete and finished works of great relevance to his political and economic ideas:

1. 'Lettres aux économistes sur leur système de politique et de morale. Première lettre. Sur les Richesses' ['Letters to the Economists [i.e. Physiocrats] on their political and moral system. First letter. On Wealth'], 23pp. This text 'transcribed in January 1775', was approved for publication in the following month, but was destined never to appear 'because of the dismissal of M. Turgot'. It was the nearest Sieyes came to publication before 1788. 284 AP 2.10.

2. 'Bases de l'ordre social ou série raisonnée de quelques idées fondamentales de l'état social et politique: an III' ['Bases of the social order or a reasoned series of certain fundamental ideas concerning the social and political state: year III'], 16pp. Written by Sieyes probably late in 1794 or early in 1795, it anticipates some of the ideas in his speech to the Convention in 20 July 1795. 284 AP 5.1 (sixth section).

3. 'Observations constitutionelles dictées au citoyen Boulay (de la Meurthe), membre de la Commission législative des Cinq-Cents dans les derniers jours de brumaire de l'an VIII et qu'il m'a rendues après les avoir fait transcrire ... *Nota* – Rien n'est plus incomplet et fautif que ce canevas dicté à la hâte' ['Constitutional observations dictated to citizen Boulay (de la Meurthe), member of the Legislative Committee of the Five Hundred, in the last days of Brumaire in the year VIII, and which he returned to me after having them

transcribed ... *Note* – Nothing is more incomplete and faulty than this hastily dictated outline']. 22pp. 284 AP 5.7 (seventh section). This is the original text of the manuscript from which Boulay de la Meurthe cites in his *Théorie constitutionnelle de Sieyes, Constitution de l'an VIII* (Paris, 1836). It has been heavily overwritten by Sieyes.

The list of Sieyes' published works gives some indication of the scope of his ideas and interests. In the pages that follow these ideas will be systematically examined, beginning with his concept of the nation and of the national seizure of power in 1789, moving from there to his conception of the ends and means of the new state that was to be founded by the nation, and ending with a discussion of his specific proposals for the organization of different aspects of the public power in France. A preliminary discussion of some general aspects of his mode of thought, and of the origins of his ideas, will set the scene.

1 Sieyes' mode of thought: a general perspective

> Au reste, quand on veut décider une question comme celle-ci, il ne faut pas se contenter, comme on le fait trop souvent, de donner son désir, ou son volonté, ou l'usage, pour des raison; il faut remonter aux principes.
>
> Sieyes, *What is the Third Estate?* (1789), 145.

SIEYES BECAME FAMOUS at the age of forty as a result of writing four revolutionary tracts. They were produced in the period that immediately preceded the meeting of the Estates-General in May 1789, a period of great intellectual excitement and fermentation, of which the momentous events of June 1789 were in one sense the culmination. The period opened in the summer of 1788 when the king's minister, Brienne, invited people to submit their opinions on how the Estates-General – which had not met since 1614 – should be composed and organized, and when, a month later, he finally fixed the date on which the Estates-General should meet. In the months that followed an intense political debate was joined, pamphlets and brochures poured in ever increasing numbers from the presses, political clubs began to open, and that mysterious force, public opinion, sprang into life.

Sieyes' first tract was written in August 1788 and bore the unwieldy title *Views on the means of execution which the representatives of France will have at their disposal in 1789*. In it Sieyes addressed himself to the problem of how the future Estates-General should see itself, organize itself, and act in the coming year. At this time he seems to have envisaged all three Estates – the clergy, the nobility and the Third Estate – as working together to force through the political changes that he favoured. Only the non-elected members of the nobility in the Estates-General were regarded by him as being precluded by their very status from taking part in the work of radical reform that had to be done.

Sieyes' second composition, the *Essay on Privileges,* was rushed out before the first had been published, and was far more ferocious in tone. It appeared in November 1788, and it reflected Sieyes' bitter reaction to the nobility's express refusal to contemplate any changes in the traditional, ancient forms in which the Estates-General held its meetings. The nobility's attitude had revealed itself in a decision by the *Parlement* of Paris on 25 September, and in the meeting of the second Assembly of Notables that sat between 6 November and 12 December. The *Essay* attacked privilege in general, and the aristocracy in particular with logic and venom. It was followed, early in January 1789, by *What is the Third Estate?* which was to achieve the greatest fame of all Sieyes' writings. In this tract Sieyes unequivocally equated the cause of political justice and the political future of France with the cause of the Third Estate. Finally, in the *Deliberations,* which appeared in February 1789, he pressed home this doctrine by giving detailed practical advice to the electors of the Third Estate within the domain of the Duke of Orléans.

Sieyes' four pamphlets stood out from the mass of publications that were produced at this time, and were all of them republished in the course of 1789. Two editions appeared of the *Views* and the *Essay*; three of *What is the Third Estate?;* and no less than four of the *Deliberations*. The reputation they gave him was instrumental in securing his own election to the Estates-General in May 1789 and thus starting his political career.

It seems appropriate therefore to begin a study of his political ideas by considering, in quite general terms, the qualities that stamp these early products of his pen. What is distinctive about them? Why did they strike the public's eye? Having suggested an answer to these questions it will then be possible to probe a little deeper and to see what were Sieyes' basic presuppositions about the way politics should be studied, about political theory and political practice, and about language and style. Finally, because a thinker's assumptions about ultimate questions inevitably form the underpinning of all his other ideas, the chapter will discuss Sieyes' religious beliefs.

1 The distinctive features of Sieyes' revolutionary tracts

The most striking feature of Sieyes' early tracts is the intensity with which they concentrate on principles. Sieyes took as his yardstick for judging the course of political events in 1788–89 what to-day would be called the theory of the body politic, but what he himself most usually termed the principles of the 'social art'.[1] Once he referred more explicitly to the principles 'which form the science of the social order',[2] on another occasion to the 'true science of the state of society',[3] and on a third to the 'natural and essential order of social truths'.[4] Whatever the name, he meant that the criterion for measuring advance and regression in the political manoeuvrings that took place in the period preceding the meeting of the Estates-General and, more importantly, the criterion for deciding what ought to be done in the Estates-General once it had assembled, was the rational or scientific conception of the body politic, or the body politic as it ought to be. Whatever advanced the realization of such a conception was good; whatever contradicted or obstructed it was bad.

Sieyes' characteristic method of launching a discussion of a political issue at this time was hence not to survey the factual data of the problem, or to engage in a lengthy historical disquisition, but to move directly, even abruptly, to a consideration of the principles involved. Having defined and related these, he would draw from them the consequences for the conduct of affairs. In the *Views,* for example, the first section began with a theoretical analysis of the ends or purpose of a legislative body, from which Sieyes demonstrated that a general assembly of elected representatives was the legitimate organ of the national will. From there he proceeded to deduce how the Estates-General, as such an assembly, should organize itself once it met in May 1789. Towards the end of the same work he posed the question: What is a constitution? (This kind of rhetorical question was a favourite Sieyesian device for moving directly to the essence of the matter.) The answer he gave provided in turn the guideline for the constructive work that he believed the Estates-General ought to undertake once it had suitably organized itself. In the *Essay on Privileges* he announced boldly at the very start that he was not going to get involved in an interminable 'discussion about facts'.[5] Instead he gave a concise definition of the essence of privilege and then measured it against the norm of genuine law. Needless to say privilege stood condemned. In *What is the Third Estate?* he began by defining the essence of the Third Estate, its real meaning, which he saw as being identical with the essence of a nation. From there he judged the empirical demands that were being made by the members of the Third Estate, and found them to be wanting. Later he engaged, as in the *Views,* in a theoretical discussion of the way a body politic ought to be constituted and deduced the practical steps that were required by the Third Estate in order to realize this idea. Finally, in the *Deliberations,* he refused at the outset to talk in the traditional terms of *doléances, griefs, cahiers,* and so on, and focused instead on the logical order of discussion that a deliberating electoral assembly ought to follow, once again taking as his guiding thread the conception of a rightly ordered body politic.

In saying that Sieyes began with ideas or principles and then moved to practice, we are simultaneously saying that his tracts were peculiarly and intensely radical. He did not gradually develop, like some of the other writers – for example Rabaut Saint-Etienne[6] – from a moderate to a radical position under the pressure of the events of the winter of 1788. Sieyes was radical in all four of his writings; he changed only in the sense that he came to realize that the driving force for implementing his radical objectives could not be, as he had originally believed, the three Estates acting together, but the Third Estate acting on its own initiative. Very few of the other tracts produced during this period – Pétion's *Avis aux Français sur le salut de la patrie* of 1788 is one of the rarities – could match the radicalism that infused all those of Sieyes.

Sieyes' approach, his belief that the summoning of the Estates-General provided a unique opportunity to implement the principles of political science, which demonstrated how a body politic ought to be constituted, was most obviously opposed to that of the pamphleteers who argued in historical terms, and saw in the meeting of the Estates-General in 1789 a chance for restoring or reviving an earlier form of French constitution dating from feudal or even pre-feudal times. It was opposed also to the ideas of those who wanted merely to import into France the constitutions that other countries – notably England – had evolved. It was opposed finally to the ideas of those who found inspiration, Rousseau-like, in the ways of primitive societies.

The opening page of the *Views* expresses Sieyes' impatience with all these alternative approaches:

> There are more than enough people who think that the laws of civilized nations are to be derived from barbarous ages. We will not lose ourselves in an uncertain research into ancient institutions and errors. Reason is for all time; it is made for man; and it is above all when it speaks of his deepest interest that it should be listened to with confidence and respect.

> When it is a question of satisfying the needs of life are we going to disdain the recent products of a perfected art, and search for models in Tahiti or amongst the ancient Germans?[7]

The reference to a 'perfected art' should be noted here. This is precisely the 'social art' that Sieyes took as his own guideline.

Did Sieyes' radical, rational approach to politics mean that he completely despised history and its lessons? It has often been suggested that it did, but this conclusion seems much too extreme. In a footnote to the *Views* he explained that his opposition to the historical approach to the central political issues of the time was directed against the passive 'spirit of imitation', the lazy monkey-like mentality that did not attempt to think things through but merely borrowed from the past. It was not directed against the usefulness of meditating on history as such.[8] In *What is the Third Estate?* there are in fact several occasions on which Sieyes reflected on historical developments, most notably on the historical development of the Third Estate itself.[9] Although he clearly did not believe that historical facts in themselves could demonstrate what was right, he does seem to have believed that the study of history could illuminate the growth of what was right.

Sieyes' skill at connecting the principles that he set out in his early tracts deserves to be emphasized next. It would be seriously misleading to give the impression that he enunciated principles in the form of detached and isolated slogans – such as were to become the mode as the Revolution progressed. On the contrary, he always stressed the interlocking nature of political principles, the need to comprehend the way all the different elements in the body politic were related, and the need to act systematically, with a full awareness of these interconnections, and not in a piecemeal, haphazard fashion. *Tout se tient dans l'ordre social*[10] was one of his profoundest convictions. People mistakenly imagine, he wrote in the *Views*, 'that a little bit of good achieved to-day, a little tomorrow, and a little on another favourable occasion will enable us to advance towards the establishment of a good order. When a system is laid hold of by only one of its elements, nothing has been achieved. If you build on one side, you will destroy on another; to-day you will make one or two steps towards a useful goal, tomorrow you will have to start again in a different direction.'[11] It was precisely the lack of the faculty of *combinaison*, or the capacity to relate their demands together, that Sieyes criticized in the other pamphleteers of the time.[12] For him rational change meant coherently interrelated changes.

Sieyes himself was particularly adept at combining the principles of the political economist with those of the constitutionalist in his early tracts. He reinforced – in the *Essay on Privileges* and *What is the Third Estate?* – arguments about political structures with arguments about productivity. He wished to demonstrate that existing social and political practices were wrong not only in terms of political right but in terms of utility. The nobility was savaged by him from both these angles simultaneously and the Third Estate was correspondingly lauded from both angles. As will be shown later, he had studied political economy intensively in his youth. Nothing is more misleading than to think of him as concerned only with political 'superstructures'.

Sieyes not only asserted that rationally deduced principles were far better than any historical or foreign model as a guide to France's political future, he also insisted that rationally deduced principles ought to take precedence over particular group interests as a guide to political action in the troubled period through which the country was passing. Interests could not be ignored, and Sieyes was skilful at dissecting and assessing them, but interests were not in the last resort the most important thing, which was the harnessing of interests to principle, or more accurately, of raising interest to the level of principle by a process of enlightenment. It was not enough, he abjured the Third Estate in his most famous pamphlet, to argue simply on the basis of what one wanted or desired; 'it is necessary to ascend to principles.'[13] *Il faut remonter aux principes*. Further on in the same work he made the same point again:

> We can consider this question in three ways: after the manner of the Third [Estate], following the interests of the privileged orders, and finally according to good principles.[14]

This distinction is typical of Sieyes, and a little later he expanded on what he meant by the 'third way':

> If we now wish to consider the same subject, independently of all particular interest and in accordance with principles designed to enlighten it, that is to say in accordance with those that form the science of the social order, we will see this question take on a novel aspect.[15]

In similar vein, after demonstrating that the Third Estate might legitimately take the initiative in the Estates-General, he wrote:

> I know that such principles will not be to the taste even of those members of the Third [Estate] who are most skilful at defending its interests. So be it: provided you agree that I have set out from true principles and proceed only with the support of good logic.[16]

Another argument is justified in the same way: 'I know that such principles are going to appear *extravagant* to the majority of readers. Truth must appear as strange to prejudice as the latter is to truth. All is relative. It suffices for me that my principles are unquestionable and that my conclusions well deduced.'[17]

In these passages we can hear Sieyes quite distinctly trying to persuade the Third Estate to look beyond its particular interests, to raise itself to the level of principles, to act in the name of what was necessary and right rather than of what was merely to its own immediate advantage.

There is a further, very important feature of Sieyes' early tracts that requires to be stressed: their programmatic nature. They defined in some detail the practical steps that were required to be taken. This may seem at first sight to stand at variance with the emphasis on principles to which attention has so far been drawn. In reality, however, it was the combination of these two characteristics that lay at the very heart of Sieyes' originality. On the one hand he wanted to raise the struggle of group interests to a new, higher level, the level of social and political principle, and on the other he wanted to indicate clearly and realistically the steps that had to be taken if such principles were to be realized. Practice into principle: principle into practice; that was the double-edged transformation which Sieyes sought to implement in his early tracts, and it is nowhere better expressed than in the motto which he placed at the head of the *Views*: 'One can, indeed one must raise one's wishes to the level of one's rights; but it is essential to relate ends to means.'[18]

Sieyes' belief that one had not only to enunciate principles but to show in some detail how they could be translated into reality, is evident from the introduction to his first tract, the *Views,* in which he emphasized that he did not want to be a mere philosopher, but what he called an administrator:

> [H]owever beautiful, however complete the plan may be that one wishes to establish in the interest of the peoples, it is still only the work of the *philosophe*; it is still only a project. The view of the administrator seeks for means of implementation. It takes into account in advance the possibility of realizing the good ideas of the *philosophe,* and these are two distinct kinds of meditation. Will the Estates-General have sufficient means of implementing its designs? Will it take hold of them firmly? That is the largely practical question to which I shall confine myself here. This publication can hence be seen as a supplement to the large number of theoretical works which circumstances are going to produce.[19]

Sieyes' practical recommendations may be divided into two kinds. First, he always indicated in some detail the kind of institutional or organizational mechanisms that were required if what was right in principle was to be made effective. This is particularly evident in the *Views* and the *Deliberations* where he discussed at some length the form and internal organization that the Estates-General would have to adopt in order to become a genuine 'national assembly'. Sieyes himself seems to have recognized his own talent for going beyond abstractions to mechanisms, for he wrote some years later: 'If anything distinguishes me from ancient and modern publicists, it is the importance that I attach in politics to organization and the rarity with which I produce abstractions or eternal phrases drawn from morality or philosophy, etc., when it is a matter of constructing wheels and getting them to mesh together to produce a real effect.'[20]

Sieyes' second kind of practical recommendation was to indicate the tactics and strategy that should be employed in the existing political struggle in order to ensure that the cause of political right triumphed. In the *Views* he emphasized particularly that the use of the fiscal lever by the Estates-General – more specifically, the provisional suspension of all taxes – would be crucial in neutralizing ministerial opposition to change, and this lever was in fact used in June 1789. More importantly, in the concluding chapters of *What is the Third Estate?* he defined the tactics that the Third Estate should – and did – adopt in order to transform the Estates-General into a genuine 'national assembly'.

It was Sieyes' talent for tactics that Mallet du Pan seemed to have had particularly in mind when he wrote of him:

> Those who have considered him merely in the light of a political metaphysician and a manufacturer of constitutions, only know one side of him. Fertile in inventing means of execution, capable of holding his tongue and waiting, not given to conceiving chimerical plans and combining dexterity with firmness, no man is better able, when a great interest demands it, to keep command over himself and gain it over others. [21]

Having described the leading features of the contents of Sieyes' early tracts, it remains to say something of their style, for this too was unusual. Sieyes' writing was intense, nervous, compressed, resolving itself constantly into terse contrasts and categorizations, as if the whole end and purpose was to convey the truth in the shortest and most pointed way. There was little ornamentation, no purple passages, no 'fine writing'. The message was all. Passion too was there. It is a mistake to think of Sieyes as a calm, detached scholar. He was cerebral but he was also intensely passionate. In the *Views* the cerebral side of him seems to predominate and the argument is calm and measured, but in the *Essay on Privileges* and *What is the Third Estate?* the passion breaks through, chiefly the passion of intense indignation and of scorn bordering on hatred. The only light relief comes from his mordant and ironic sense of humour which also rises to the surface from time to time and gives a further edge to his logic.

Sieyes' style is not to everyone's taste. Rivarol thought it 'barbaric', and accused Sieyes of sinning against the French language.[22] This may be contrasted with Marie-Joseph Chénier's later verdict. Sieyes, he wrote, 'thinks with energy, with depth, with originality; in each phrase he says something, almost always something new; and, without appearing to think of style, he is a writer of quality, for his frank and rapid mode of expression has all the qualities of his thought.'[23] Wilhelm von Humboldt was equally impressed when he read Sieyes' tracts in 1798. 'The style', he wrote, 'is very good, searching and yet not dry, pure reasoning, never superficial, never epigrammatic and merely witty, short and above all precise and pertinent.' Interestingly he thought Sieyes' 'method of pure inquiry' was 'not at all French.'[24]

In sum then, the distinctive features of Sieyes' revolutionary tracts were the uncompromising assertion that the great crisis of the day had to be treated in terms of scientific principle, the systematic presentation of those principles, the precision of the practical programme designed to implement them, and an arresting style. It was little wonder that they made an impact.

2 Reason, system and science

Having described the characteristics of the writings that made Sieyes famous, it is time to look a little more deeply at the intellectual assumptions that lay behind them. What exactly was the 'social art' that he esteemed so highly? What was the method by which he reached the principles which he sought so vigorously to implement? What did he mean by reason?

Let it be said immediately that Sieyes' writings, and particularly the early tracts, are infused with the terminology that is regarded as typical of the Enlightenment. There are constant references to the progress of the 'lights of reason', *les lumières*, and the need to increase them, consult them and apply them still further. The 'empire of reason spreads further every day' he wrote characteristically in *What is the Third Estate?*[25] The assumption throughout is that at long last truth was beginning to penetrate the mass of the French people, that a splendid dawn was breaking, and that the task of the patriotic writer was to hurry on this process of illumination with all the means at his disposal.

Sieyes, however, drew some interesting distinctions when he described more closely the nature of the intellectual renaissance that he wished to accelerate.

He took it for granted that huge progress had taken place in recent times in natural science, and in the mechanical and commercial arts. In social and political science, or what he referred to as the 'social art', however, he believed that progress had been comparatively slow. It was not that no advances had been made in this field; he was quite convinced that they had. But, for a variety of reasons, they had been late in coming, and had not been as widely recognized and appreciated, and certainly not as widely put into practical operation as those in other areas of knowledge. Sieyes saw himself as rectifying this particular imbalance and introducing to the reading public the methods and fruits of a newly emerging political science.

In the *Views* Sieyes argued the case for consulting this new science in the following terms:

> Order a clock from a clockmaker and see if he bothers to consult the history of clockmaking, true or false, about the different ways the early industry used to measure time. Quite rightly he considers that the prolonged groping of the human mind during the centuries of ignorance is far less suited to guide his craft than that branch of mechanics in which the laws and ideas of modern genius are expressed.
>
> Social mechanics has been equally enriched in our own day by the long creative nights of genius. Why then do we refuse to consult it over the true means of satisfying the great needs of political societies?
>
> We are always quick to profit in terms of enjoyment from the least progress that has been made in the arts of commerce and luxury – must we always retreat into a shameful indifference when it is a question of the progress of the *social art,* the premier art, whose wise combinations divulge the happiness of the human race?[26]

In *What is the Third Estate?* the same point was made slightly differently:

> No people, they say, has done better [in terms of political constitutions] than the English. If this is so, then the products of the political art ought to be the same at the end of the eighteenth century as they were in the seventeenth century! The English did not lag behind the enlightenment [*lumières*] of their time; let us not lag behind the enlightenment of our own. Above all let us not get discouraged by seeing nothing in the past that is suited to our condition. The true science of the state of society does not date from very far back. People built cottages for a long time before they were able to raise palaces. Surely it is evident that the progress of social architecture had to be slower still, because although it is the most important art of all it does not – understandably – receive any encouragement from despots and aristocrats.[27]

It was not merely despotism that had led to the comparative stunting of the social and political sciences. In the *Views* Sieyes pointed to a further factor. The very progress that had been made in the natural sciences had given an unfortunate bias to the moral sciences. In his own words:

> The deplorable course of events has gradually come to make us disbelieve that any importance attaches to the simple power of truth. It is seen as an ideal thing without force, and its light as alien to the affairs of peoples. It has become accepted that nothing is to be decided except by facts. This is because despotism has everywhere begun with facts, and because it is necessary for it always to offer this false model, which is at its service, rather than the truth, which is independent and condemns it.

> Every day we see a foolish form of pedantry endeavouring confidently to deny the philosopher who goes back to the principles of the social art. Useful and fruitful meditation appears to the ponderous scholar simply as the work of idleness, and when the man of superior talents has abandoned, with disgust as much as with wisdom, the sad story of the errors of our forefathers, mediocrity throws itself into the task of industriously annotating every page of history. It sees in the mere talent of reading and transcribing the merit *par excellence*, and the answer to every question.
>
> Unfortunately, the very philosophers who, in the course of the present century, have rendered such signal services to the physical sciences, seem to authorize this ridiculous confidence, and to lend the force of their genius to these blind declamations. Rightly disgusted with the systematic mania of their predecessors, they devoted themselves to the study of facts, and proscribed all other methods. Up to this point, they deserve only praise. But when, leaving the physical order they wished to employ and to recommend the same method in the moral order too, they were wrong. Before prescribing the same course for every science, the difference in their object and genius should have been considered.
>
> Nothing is more sensible than that the physicist should content himself with observing and gathering facts and grasping the relationships between them. His object is to understand nature, and since he has not been called upon to assist either with his counsel or with his hand, the plan of the world's system, since the physical universe exists and maintains itself independently of his corrective meditations, it is indeed necessary that he restricts himself to the experience of facts. Physics can be nothing else than the knowledge of *what is*.
>
> Art, bolder in its flight, sets out to bend and accommodate the facts to our needs and enjoyments; it asks what *ought to be* for the utility of man. Art is ours; speculation, combination and operation belong to us equally. Well, of all the arts indubitably the first is that concerned with arranging men in relationship to one another according to a plan which is most favourable to all. And I ask, is it necessary here to consult facts in the manner of the physicist? What ought to be the true science, that of facts or that of principles?[28]

Here we begin to see the root of Sieyes' hostility to the grubbers in archives, and also perhaps why he preferred to speak of the social 'art' rather than of social 'science'. He wanted to distinguish it from *physical* science.

A little later he returned to the same theme:

> Be very wary of the influence ... of the idea which has already been too widely spread abroad by scholars, of founding morals like physics on the basis of experience. During this century men have been recalled to reason by way of the natural sciences. It is a real service. But let us beware of a false gratitude which keeps us in the narrow circle of imitation, or which, barring the way, prohibits us from wanting to make a new order in the end.
>
> Undoubtedly, true politics combines facts and not chimeras, but it combines; and like the architect who prepares and realizes his plan in his imagination before executing it, the legislator conceives and realizes in his mind the totality and the details of the social order that fits the peoples. When he offers us the fruit of his meditations, let us judge its utility and receive the benefits of his genius, without asking him for proofs of fact; for nothing would be, if it could not present itself to existence – if you will pardon the expression – except with proofs of fact. Never has it been more urgent to restore to reason all its force, and to remove from facts all that they have usurped for the unhappiness of the human species.[29]

Notable here is the Rousseau-like reference to the 'legislator' and the tacit self-identification of Sieyes with this role. As we shall see in the next chapter, Rousseau unquestionably influenced Sieyes, though the political systems of the two men differed not merely in detail but in fundamentals.

For Sieyes the respect for 'facts' which he saw in his contemporaries amounted to a superstition, a 'confused sentiment of faith dominating our souls' that inspired a 'horror of the profane councils of reason and good sense in legislative matters'.[30] It was, so to speak, the last superstition that the age of enlightenment had to destroy, a last ignominious method of warding off 'the enlightenment that presses in on us from all sides.'[31]

Undoubtedly the main antagonists that Sieyes had in mind when he launched his attack on facts in the name of reason and principle were those who searched amongst the facts of history to try and establish the right form of government for France at the end of the eighteenth century. A closer look at his words, however, reveals that he had also another opponent in mind: those who attempted to demonstrate the kind of government France ought to have, not by an appeal to historical facts but by treating man himself as a purely physical fact or phenomenon, and by making political deductions on the basis of the supposed physical inexorabilities of his nature. Who were these men? There can be little doubt that Sieyes was attacking the political physics of the Physiocrats, the school of writers who had wielded so much influence in France in the 1770s, when he was a student in Paris. Their views will be discussed more fully in the next chapter.

From his early handwritten notes we can see that Sieyes came to grasp the distinction between the moral and the physical sciences only after a process of trial and error. In a fragment on 'method' he wrote:

> Why has no progress been made in the moral sciences? It is because people have wanted to reason, prove, demonstrate, when it is only a question of exposition. Man's first act is linked to the second and so on. It is a question of observing this sequence, of extending it by analogy, and then, calling the preceding term cause and the succeeding one effect, of working to procure what one wants and does not have by means of what one has.
>
> When I wanted to explain the principles of natural law I thought that my labours would finally enable me to demonstrate the truth. I carried over into nature the absurdity of scholastic research, and did not know by which end to get hold of what I was looking for. I heard people say that one had to proceed with the baton of observation in one's hand, but, for the metaphysician all these maxims are like the grand principles of morality for the politician – we all know that we must do what is good. Even if I were endlessly battered with these trivial maxims I would still make no progress, for the essential thing is to know how good is done, how one observes, what has to be observed, and what observation is. It was only after I had talked nonsense on all these things that I began to see that the science of qualities was fundamentally different from that of quantities and that their methods were as different as their objectives.[32]

This citation is important because in it we begin to see what Sieyes meant by the use of reason in political science. It was patently not a matter of accumulating facts, imitating or copying facts, trying to 'prove' things by reference to facts, or approaching political matters with the methods of natural science. It was a question of analysing human relationships, of reaching back, using hypothesis (analogy) where necessary, not to what was historically prior, but to what was *logically* prior in such relationships, and then of rebuilding social reality on the basis of the logical sequence. Analysis and synthesis, resolution and composition, logical reconstruction – the names are old and various for this classic mode of procedure that Sieyes adopted as the true method of reason. He said of himself in his autobiography that when he took hold of a subject, he was not satisfied 'until he has deepened it, analysed in all its parts, and then reconstructed it in its totality.'[33] It is a good summary of his method.

Sieyes can be seen using this method in the first section of the *Views* where he took apart and reconstructed the body politic as a logical totality, starting with a contract. He used it again, even more explicitly, in *What is the Third Estate?* when he announced: 'The social mechanism will never be understood unless one undertakes to analyse society like an ordinary machine, to consider each part separately, and then to rejoin them all in the mind, one after the other, in order to grasp their congruence and to understand the general harmony that ought to result from them.'[34] His analytical method was perhaps most fully and successfully employed in his study of the *Rights of man and citizen* that was published in the summer of 1789. The chain of reasoning that he used in this study reappeared in part in his essay on *Liberty* published in 1793. Finally, in late 1794 or 1795, Sieyes again analysed and recomposed society in his unpublished text: *Bases of the social order or a reasoned series of some fundamental ideas concerning the social and political state.* Always we can see him using the same approach.

Right reasoning about the social world was hence a question of digging below the factitious surface of things to get at necessary and essential relationships, the relationships which, as he wrote once, determined the place of each part of the social mechanism but 'which did not depend on the mere will of the mechanic.'[35] Sieyes clearly believed that, although this kind of reasoning was a science in which progress had only recently been made, it could in principle be applied at any time and without the aid of voluminous information about the human world. This was because it was really directed towards understanding man's nature, and this was not, by definition, something extraneous or alien, to be studied as a strange object, but something each person could observe in himself, something he 'carried' with him, and could consult if and when he so wished. This was the point that Sieyes made with particular force in the *Views,* after his long diatribe against the fetishism of facts. It was, he said, senseless to look for 'right' in archives:

> Your rights are in yourselves, they are all there, they are imprescriptible, an all-powerful hand has etched them there in deathless characters; and you want to compromise them, to reduce them so that they depend on a chance discovery or a point of erudition:[36]

And again:

> When injustice presides over events and changes societies into a confused mixture of oppressors and oppressed, reason watches over all; it never tires of presenting them with a faithful picture of their rights and duties for the sake of happier times.[37]

In the *Essay on Privileges* he used once more the analogy of truths etched for ever: 'Let me take heed not to violate the sublime relationships of humanity that nature has been careful to engrave on the bottom of our hearts.'[38]

And in 1793, when Robespierre and the Jacobins were about to seize power, he stressed that the corrupting influence of centuries of unreason was no excuse for ignoring the voice of reason:

> No: I can neither defend nor conceal the innumerable evils that prejudice and anti-social vanity impose on enslaved generations. Let me appeal from ignorance to enlightenment, from errors to philosophy; allow me to make the assumption of a tolerable social state, without which the only resort is silence.[39]

Not only did Sieyes emphasize that the science of society involved an examination of man's own being, he also stressed that true reasoning about the nature of society led necessarily to the development of an interlocking totality of ideas or, in other words, a 'system'. True knowledge, true science was systematic. We have already noted as one of the distinctive features of the tracts that made his name, his constant insistence that piecemeal reform was dangerous and self-defeating, and that 'everything holds together in the social order.' When we look at his more abstract remarks on method, we find that his hostility to a piecemeal approach and his advocacy of 'system' was very deeply rooted:

> *Unity – compared with systems.*
>
> The law of unity embraces all the arts, all the sciences, all the relationships of man. The last details ought to be *one* taken separately, and they ought to form a collectivity that is *one*; this results from the method, so essential to the human mind, of classifying ideas and of generalizing them more and more in the process of analysing them.
>
> Not only should all the ideas relative to one science be ordered in a united way, but also all the objects that we know, in a word, the overall form of the knowledge of each particular should be placed within a single order. Without this we have only unstitched brains, whose knowledge does not hold together and is of no use. They know nothing, although they have much in their memory. Such brains resemble exactly those pieces of music which lack the unity of method that Rousseau *felt* strongly without *seeing*. Those who submit themselves to unity are called *gens systématiques*, and whatever the *peuple des lettres* may say, they alone know how to study nature, to reproduce it, and to be useful. They have but one fault to avoid, and that is not to rush to build when they do not yet have sufficient materials to unite, or bind together all the parts of the building. A piece of music must be a unity, but not every piece that is *a unity* deserves for that reason *to be a piece of music. Unity is the daughter of liaison* without which there is no world for man, without which he is no longer anything. The *gens de lettres* are too akin to music without unity.[40]

Sieyes thus did not share the widespread hostility to 'systems' that existed in eighteenth-century France. While he acknowledged that there could be faulty and inadequate systems, the notion of system was not for this reason to be jettisoned, for it was conterminous with scientific knowledge. In this respect his opinion came close to that of Turgot. In his *Eloge de Gournay* (1759) the latter had noted the tendency of recent philosophers to inveigh against *l'esprit de système*. He continued:

> It is nonetheless true that every man who thinks has a *system,* that a man who did not have a system or logical sequence (*enchaînement*) in his ideas could only be an imbecile or a madman. – No matter. The two senses of the word system become confused and the person who has a system in the sense of men of the world, that is a fixed opinion based on a sequence of observations, excites the reproaches made by philosophers against the spirit of system used in a quite different sense, namely as an opinion which is not founded on sufficient observations.[41]

Sieyes unfortunately never sketched a complete map of the intellectual world, showing the overall system that embraced the different sciences. However, in the Prospectus of the Journal that he helped to establish in 1793 there is an interesting schema which probably reflects his views. Here it must be explained that on two occasions, after the outbreak of the Revolution, Sieyes attempted to place the discussion and dissemination of the 'social art' on a more regular and systematic basis. The first was when he and Condorcet established the *Société de 1789* early in 1790. As the Prospectus to the Journal of this club indicates very clearly, one of the objectives of the new body was to foster the impartial discussion of the 'social art', the latter being defined very broadly as the overarching science that was directed towards maintaining and extending the felicity of nations. The Journal of the 1789 Club appeared between June and September 1790, the Club itself lingered on until the spring of 1791.[42]

The second occasion was when Sieyes, again working with Condorcet (and a third partner, Duhamel), set up the short-lived *Journal of Social Instruction* which appeared in June and July 1793. This close co-operation between Sieyes and Condorcet should not incidentally deceive one into thinking that the two men thought alike on the question of the study of society; Condorcet was by background a mathematician and was keen to apply mathematical calculation to the facts of society, whereas Sieyes' emphasis, as we have seen, was quite different.[43]

The Prospectus of this second Journal was more precise in its definition of the 'social art'. Although it was anonymous it can with some confidence be taken to embody Sieyes' views. This is how it classified the different branches of the scientific study of man in society:

> Individuals, as men, as members of a political society, have relationships between themselves, from which their rights and duties spring. There are other relationships between individuals and the society of which they are a part. Finally the needs of men and their industry have given rise to new relationships between them and the things they can produce, perfect, consume and employ.
>
> From these are derived the three branches of a single science, which has as its general object the knowledge of the rights, duties and interests of man in the state of society.
>
> We will adopt, in order to distinguish them, the names of natural law, political right, and public economy.
>
> All the sciences have a practical part. From each of them is derived an art, the rules of which follow from the principles of the science. The purpose of this art is to combine and select the means for implementing soundly what the principles have shown to be true, just, and useful.

> Thus morality or the art of proper conduct is derived from natural law; the social art is derived from political right; and the art of administration has as its basis the science of public economy.[44]

Sieyes did not always follow the strict terminology that is employed here: for example, he often used the word 'administrator' to mean something more than simply the practitioner of public economy. Nonetheless this schema is of some importance in indicating what he meant by the 'social art'. It was patently not the reverse of a 'science', but rather the constructive or reconstructive part of the analytical science of political right, the part that indicated the institutional mechanisms by which right was to be realized.

Noticeable too in this passage is the close connection that Sieyes saw between political economy and the science of political right: they were both branches of a single science. We have already seen how closely they were linked together in his early pamphlets.

There can be little doubt that the method which Sieyes deemed proper for political science, namely the analysis and systematic reconstruction of relationships in accordance with strict logical necessity, was 'metaphysical' in nature. And in fact Sieyes had no qualms about describing himself as a practitioner of metaphysics. In doing so he ran counter to a current of ideas that was strong both in France and in Britain in the eighteenth century, one that dismissed metaphysics as otherworldly dreaming with no strict scientific status. Sieyes paid the penalty for this, and was repeatedly denounced in his own time – as well as subsequently – simply for being 'metaphysical'. That he considered this kind of attack reflected solely the crass ignorance of those who made it is plain from the scornful peroration at the start of his exposition of the *Rights of man and citizen*, a work written after the first major steps in the Revolution had been taken:

> There is no act of patient endeavour from which the Frenchman is more skilled at insulating himself, than that of devoting attention to matters which do not affect his pleasures or his particular affairs. Beyond his private likes and habits everything seems to him *metaphysical*. Try and prove to him that men have only been able to make progress because they have listened to and appropriated new ideas – this kind of reasoning itself seems to him *metaphysical*. For this is the name the general public gives to the most useful truths until the moment when, whether they like it or not, they dawn on every class of citizen. The small number of people who can read and listen are scarcely more reasonable at the start. *Amour-propre* has to have its revenge, so every new truth is opposed as *premature*. People forget, or pretend to forget, that reason itself must *mature*, and that to prepare the season of enlightenment, it must precede it.
>
> All the least disputed and most widespread truths of to-day endured this reproach or would-be insult when they began. Then, little by little, they became principles believed in by some, and ignored or rejected by others. Finally they joined the mass of general ideas, and became no more than common sense for everyone. Such is the fate of truth, and so invariable is its passage through these three stages that our most trivial ideas still seem like transcendental metaphysics to the greater part of the people spread around the world. Even without moving beyond Europe, was not the political catechism of England little other than metaphysics to the Frenchman a few years ago? Though if one reflects that at

the very same time our own opinions were still too strong, too *metaphysical* for the Spanish, then one can perhaps reconcile oneself to the unhappiness of receiving a bit of metaphysics.

After all, we can reassure ourselves by what we find around us. For example, when people first spoke of giving France a national constitution, it was metaphysics. When it was demonstrated that the legislative power belonged to the nation and not to the king, it was metaphysics. When people wanted to have real *representatives* as deputies to the Estates-General, and the most useful truths had been drawn from this most fecund word, it was metaphysics. When for the first time the constituent power was distinguished from the constituted powers, and in particular, the legislative power, it was metaphysics....

On the other hand I willingly accept that if nothing is more metaphysical than a principle, nothing is less so than dispensing with one. When the notables tried to keep the nation impotent, this was not metaphysics. When the *Parlement* [of Paris] wanted to make us start again at 1614, that was not metaphysics. The eloquent speeches and peremptory decrees of the privileged orders, before they joined the National Assembly, did not resemble metaphysics at all.

The neglect of principles! Surely that is what the neglect of metaphysics means? And yet we must expect to see political metaphysics treated for some years to come in the same way that moral philosophy has been for half a century, and for the same reasons. Anyone who abandons conventional ideas and makes a few steps forward will be greeted with the title of *metaphysician*.[45]

Sieyes' refutation of those who ridiculed him for being metaphysical was very similar to his refutation of those who ridiculed him for being a mere theorist remote from practical matters. He did not argue that theory was on a completely different, higher plane from practice. He argued rather that even those who most preened themselves on being practical were in fact governed by theory, however thin and inadequate their theory might be. In other words it was not a question of theory *versus* practice but of practice governed by sound, articulate, reasoned theory, *versus* practice governed by theory that was unacknowledged, obscure and feeble:

The babblers without ideas continually spout miserable statements about what they call the importance of practice and the uselessness or danger of theory. I will say only one thing: assume whatever sequence you like of the wisest, most useful, most excellent *facts*. Well! Do you not believe that there exists on the theoretical plane a sequence of ideas or truths that corresponds exactly with your practical sequence? If you are not completely without reason it [i.e. the theoretical sequence] follows you, or let us say rather it precedes you. For what is theory, may I ask, if it is not this corresponding sequence of truths that you are incapable of perceiving before *it is realized,* but which it is nonetheless essential that someone perceives, unless everybody is acting without knowing what they are doing. The people who in the ordinary way belabour conversation with the kind of nonsense I have just mentioned, are in truth neither theoretical nor practical. Why do they not follow the wisest, the most *practical* path, and enlighten themselves, if they can, about the one, so that they can profit from the other, and keep silent over questions about which they can console themselves that they know nothing?[46]

Roederer mentions another occasion on which Sieyes made the same point with even more biting brevity: 'Someone was speaking to Sieyes of the scorn that his detractors endlessly affected for what they called grand theories.

"Theories", he said, "are the practice of centuries; and their practice is the theory of the passing moment".'[47] It is a brilliant reply.

While Sieyes hence did not pit theory against practice, as if they were mutually exclusive, he did draw a sharp distinction between the philosopher and what he called the 'administrator'. The philosopher pursued theory *à l'outrance,* unchecked by anything except the requirements of truth. The administrator, while he had always to be guided by theory, was also obliged to take into account the resistance, so to speak, of the concrete situation.

The administrator, wrote Sieyes,

> advances as he can; provided that he does not leave the right road, he deserves nothing but praise. But this road must have been cut through to the end by the philosopher. He must have reached the end, because otherwise he cannot guarantee that it really is the right road....
>
> When the philosopher cuts a road, he is concerned only with *errors*; if he wishes to advance he has to clear them aside ruthlessly. The administrator follows; he comes up against *interests,* which I agree are more difficult to tackle. Hence a new talent is needed, a rarer science, different from the solitary meditations of the study, but – let us not deceive ourselves – far more different from the art of those ministers who believed they were administrators simply because they were not philosophers.[48]

As we noted earlier, Sieyes saw himself as both a philosopher and an administrator, as both cutting the path, and showing the way that obstacles in the path could be removed.

3 Language and style

What were Sieyes' assumptions about language and style? His interest in the former dated from an early age. Amongst some unpublished writings, dated by him 1773, we find him engaged in the quest for 'a philosophical, universal, melodious, harmonious, and instrumental language'![49] Naïve as the title is, it indicates a concern that remained with him throughout his writing career. He regarded the language of ordinary, everyday speech as unsuitable for serious scientific or philosophical discussion. It had been formed to express the common needs of society, and not for the sake of precise intellectual enquiry. It tended to mislead and confuse when devoted to the latter task. Undoubtedly in his younger days he favoured the formation of some kind of new vocabulary. 'Ideas', he once wrote, 'are simple, reasoning not difficult; it is language that obscures them and makes labyrinths out of ways that are perfectly straight. The reform of language and that of society are the two greatest needs of man in the present epoch.'[50]

In keeping with this belief during his political career he had a penchant for inventing new words to express his ideas: *adunation, ré-totale, excession de pouvoirs* are good examples. But he also recognized, at least by 1793, that there was a limit to the creation of new words, and that it was 'barbarous to create technical terms to express simple and common ideas.'[51] The true answer hence lay in the realization that words were strictly secondary and instrumental to the analysis of ideas. 'In effect, a definition, when it is possible, is only the result of an analysis that it presupposes and recalls. Before attaching a word to a complex idea, it is necessary to have developed and circumscribed it; it is necessary that those who agree in pronouncing the same word, receive the same idea; and analysis alone can fulfil this condition.'[52]

In his essay on *Liberty* he emphasized again the priority of analysis:

> Instead of lending an ear to analysis, many people only focus their attention on words. They search them for what one has just said and do not find it; which is quite natural. The words have not fallen from heaven with an inherent and divine virtue. They do not contain human science in advance. It is not by excavating them that one discovers what has not been put into them. Words are only what men make them. They do not contain any other ideas than those which people wished to attach to them; and it is reasonable to assume that man has not yet put into any language ideas which he has not yet had. As analysis progresses, so language will improve more and more. In the meantime let us draw from it what we can.[53]

From his view on language as the instrument of analysis followed his views on style both literary and oratorical. The clear communication of ideas was for him the crux, and hence that style was best which was the most transparent, allowing content to occupy the centre of the stage:

> The most reasonable language should be that which makes the least show, which allows *the coup d'oeil of the understanding a free passage* and enables it to be occupied purely with things; and certainly not that coquettish language which seeks to attract attention. Or, if you prefer, language, in so far as it ought only to be the *servant* of ideas should not try to assume the part of the *master*. Why then these long dissertations on harmony, period, and all the qualities of style? There is much that is false in all these pretensions.[54]

In a later note, written after he had had experience of the conduct of the parliamentary assemblies that had been created by the Revolution, Sieyes expressed himself as follows:

> Why is our oratorical and academic style so studied? ... Truly we no longer have an object; the audience to whom my speech is addressed assist at a game in which they have no interest. ... They are ready to examine the form and to judge talent. That is all. I should like to know whether in Greece or free Rome orators concerned themselves with any other art than that of getting to their objective. We, who do not have one, we embellish, we make music for the senses, make images, etc. We have some fine techniques, we produce sensuous affects, we communicate vague or particular emotions, but we ignore the art of illuminating a course of action and of urging its adoption. ... Speeches in the English Parliament have an objective; they do not resemble our oratorical style; they do not have our magniloquence, our lofty tone. ... They are men who do business; we are idle and stop to put on airs. They walk, we dance; we have fine artifices but neglect the *art*, because we have no use for it.[55]

At about the same time he pointed out the dangers of 'imagery' by way of an amusing anecdote. It referred to his life before the Revolution when he had attended a lecture on animal magnetism in the house of Dr Mesmer. 'There were many women present', he recalled,

> and I have too high an opinion of their natural wit to believe that they were able to understand anything in what was being said. The professor chose to use an

extremely familiar image. He compared something or other to the panes of glass in a window. The audience was dead, but at the word 'window' I saw everyone turn gently and gravely towards the one in the room. Minds which had up to that moment been empty though intent, were suddenly filled, for everyone was thinking of their windows, and what connections there are between a window and thousands of ideas! Nothing wrong with that, of course, but from that moment farewell silence and attention. There was not a woman who did not have twenty objections, twenty remarks to make all equally foreign to the matter in hand, all relating solely to the glass and windows of her home. That is the danger of images.[56]

4 Sieyes' religious views

It remains to say something of Sieyes' ideas about religion. During his lifetime he was accused of atheism by those who detested the Revolution, and of being too loyal to his own order, the clergy, by many who ardently supported the Revolution. What is the truth about his convictions in this fundamental area?

There can be little doubt that Sieyes was not by temperament a religious man, in the sense of being preoccupied with his personal relationship with the deity, or with his own posthumous salvation. There is no indication in his writings or speeches of an inner intimacy between himself and the will of the deity, or of providence, such as there was for example in the outpourings of Robespierre.

There can be little doubt too that Sieyes believed that organized religion, and in particular the Catholic Church, had been responsible historically for obstructing the progress of the human mind. It had decoyed man from his true vocation. As he wrote in an early fragment:

> Man appears on earth and observes in order to enjoy. He begins to develop the science of causes. Religion arrives and blocks his enquiries by placing causes in heaven. From this moment the perfectibility of man is halted, and his efforts are diverted. Instead of increasing his knowledge and enjoyment on earth, they are transposed and dissipated in the heavens. Religion was hence the first enemy of man.[57]

And again: 'Superstition detaches causes from effects, and, removing them from the combined efforts of curiosity and hope, *places them in heaven*.'[58]

Religion and superstition in this sense, as the paralysis of man's reason through the creation of another, supraterrestrial order, in the name of which the things of this world are explained, met with Sieyes' profound hostility. It was a system of what he repeatedly called 'theocracy'. In one of his unpublished notes he suggested, briefly but interestingly, that the hold of theocracy over politics had been broken by the emergence of a *classe disponible* – a leisured, educated class – who were able to develop a system of genuine, independent political and moral 'science', but then theocracy had reappeared in the form of superstition.[59]

In another passage written in 1788, he clearly endorsed the attack on religious prejudice that had taken place in the eighteenth century, but stressed that the time had come to go forward from the struggle against religious prejudice to the struggle against political prejudice:

> In our youth we saw the *hommes des lettres* distinguish themselves by their courage in attacking opinions that were as powerful as they were pernicious to humanity. To-day, they are content to repeat the old arguments against prejudices which no longer exist. The prejudice of privilege is perhaps the most dangerous that has ever existed; it is more intimately connected with social organization; it corrupts it more deeply; it is defended by more interests. Reasons enough, surely, to arouse the zeal of true patriots, and to cool that of the *gens de lettres*.[60]

Sieyes' rejection of religion in its historically evolved form is evident not only in his theoretical ideas but in many of the events and episodes of his own life. He found the ecclesiastical career his father had chosen for him intensely repugnant, and in his autobiography reflected bitterly on the generations of young men who had been annually denied a career or profession in society by being drafted into the Church. 'As if God had need of man's services, as if he could want a house or seraglio established for him like those for earthly kings!'[61] His lack of affinity with his original career is shown by his readiness to stand for the Third Estate instead of the clergy in 1789 and by his refusal to be a candidate for the bishopric of Paris when the election took place early in 1791. Finally, in his deposition to the National Convention in 1793 he announced that he knew 'no other worship than that of liberty and equality, no other religion than the love of humanity and of my country.'[62]

Was Sieyes then an atheist, who believed that all forms of religion – in the sense of the worship of God – should be abolished or allowed to wither away? Fortunately one of his unpublished writings allows us to answer this question with rather greater precision than before. It is entitled *On God the Immeasurable and the religious strain in man*, and it was written in 1780.[63] The preface gives the clue to the tendency of the whole:

> Since I cannot *comprehend* God, nor give myself any idea of him, I must enquire if it is possible to get to him by *sentiment*.
>
> It is unquestionable and accepted that no human idea, however exalted, is applicable to God.... They are two heterogeneous natures. It is a question of proving the existence not only of the unknown but the unknowable.

The first question that Sieyes poses in the main text is: 'Are you an atheist?' Sieyes answers this by picturing man as standing at the centre of a number of concentric circles, which represent the ever-expanding limits of his activities intellectual and practical. God, he writes, 'is nothing, unless he is that which is *beyond*, and forever beyond anything that I can know.' He is 'always beyond reason' and hence '*ultra mètre,* beyond human measure.' In a footnote, which may have been added at a later date, Sieyes gives greater precision to his notion:

> The idea of an *ultra mètre* is not simply the conjecture (*soupçon*) of an *ultra mètre,* because after having had many such conjectures which have ceased to exist as a result of our own progress, we have abstracted from all discovered measurables, the *idea* of a *future reality* to be discovered.

God then for Sieyes was the incomprehensible but thinkable idea of a reality 'beyond', posited by man's active nature. His status was similar to that of a Kantian 'regulative idea'.

The next question in Sieyes' text is: 'Can that which is beyond be of use to us?' And Sieyes answered: Yes, it answers to a human need, it soothes our 'active anxiety'. Man's desires always carry him beyond the outer circle; he is never satisfied with what he has achieved. This desire, illuminated by the idea of God, becomes hope. 'He *hopes*! – that is the great point; he is hence less unhappy.' God is thus the '*ultimate need of man*'.

It followed that for Sieyes religion, in the sense of the worship of God, was something deeply rooted in man; we cannot avoid being religious. At the same time religion belonged to the sphere, not of knowledge or dogma, but of feeling. '*Elle restera purement sentimentale.*' It was the sentimental or instinctive part of man that was the mainspring of religion.

The religious instinct, Sieyes proceeded to argue, is potentially dangerous. Unregulated and unchecked it could undermine man's true vocation, and turn him into the resigned instrument of God's will. It could also endanger the political organization of society. It must therefore be rationally regulated. The following passage gives a clear idea of what Sieyes meant by this:

> How can one prevent a religion common to a great number of people from being politically dangerous? Forbid it any kind of public organization and all connections with any other religious assembly. Do not permit the existence of a clergy, by which I mean a corporation, for all corporations other than the public establishment within the great national association, are a vice in the social machine. Each place of worship (*temple*) must remain isolated, without any relationship, whether of inferiority or superiority or of dependence, with any other place of worship. No place of worship must have anything in common with those who live elsewhere, for if, as with the Jews, the whole nation recognizes the single place of worship, then the whole nation will regard itself from this point of view as a second corporation which will sooner or later be harmful to the political association. Ther must be no religious corporation, but the most complete freedom for local, independent assemblies.

Sieyes' views on the relationship of church and state will be discussed further in relation to the tracts that he published on this crucial matter during the revolutionary period. The unpublished paper of 1780, however, has the advantage of allowing us to see at a glance the main parameters of his thought on God and religion. He was patently hostile to all forms of dogmatic religion that kept man from using his rational faculties to understand and change the world. At heart he was hostile to the way the Catholic Church operated in France, and was hostile to the idea of an established national church. On the other hand he was not an atheist, and not against all forms of organized religion. He considered that man as an active, striving knower and transformer of this world still had need of God, and was propelled by instinct to worship God. God was a focus of hope. As regards the organization of religious worship Sieyes came closest to what in England would be called Independency.

5 Conclusion

This chapter has been concerned to present some of the leading features of Sieyes' mode of thought, features that will become less abstract and more concrete as the study proceeds to explore the substance of his political ideas.

The feature that perhaps deserves to be stressed most of all is that Sieyes, when he started on his political career in 1788, did not see himself as a mere critic of existing structures, seeking to repel oppression here and to introduce reform there. He saw himself as expounding the principles of a recently developed science of politics and as drawing the practical consequences from these principles. This science was different in kind from natural science, but had close links with the science of political economy. It was a moral science.

2 The influences on Sieyes' thought

...mes recherches et mes résultats ont précédé la révolution.

Sieyes, replying to Thomas Paine (16 July 1791)

HAVING OUTLINED some of the general features of Sieyes' thought it is necessary to consider more closely the influences that helped to mould it. This task is of broader significance than might appear at first sight. It is one of the major contentions of this study that Sieyes was the pre-eminent exponent of the 'ideas of 1789', articulating more clearly than any of his contemporaries the original aims of the French Revolution. To trace the influences on his thought, therefore, is not merely to engage in intellectual biography. It serves also to indicate how far the 'ideas of 1789' were related to earlier ideas, to the Enlightenment, to the teaching of the *philosophes*. This is a problem that has preoccupied students of the Revolution almost from the moment it occurred, and has given rise to a vast body of literature. Despite the volume of the literature, however, there remains much to be said about the specific connections between the leading actors of the French Revolution, particularly those who were active before Robespierre and the Jacobins took power, and the ideas of earlier writers and thinkers. Sieyes offers an admirable opportunity to investigate such connections.

To make an accurate assessment of the influences on a particular writer or thinker it is essential to possess a firm grasp not only of his views on individual topics, but of the way these views interlock, and of the whole tenor or spirit of his thought. Without this there is a serious danger of misjudging or exaggerating influences. A particular passage is found to coincide with that of another writer and immediately it is concluded that this other writer is the 'hidden inspiration' of all that the first has done, regardless of the overall dissimilarity between their outlooks. For this reason it is arguably more sensible to discuss 'influences' *after* one has made a complete exposition of a particular thinker's system of ideas, and not before. Although the more conventional order has been followed here, the discussion will inevitably have to take for granted much that will be more fully explained in the chapters that follow.

Another, perhaps obvious, *caveat* about 'influences' is worth making. A person may be 'influenced' by another writer, in the sense of being provoked or challenged by him to think through a particular problem, but this does not necessarily mean that he finishes by agreeing with him. Kant may have been woken from his dogmatic slumber by Hume, but he did not become a 'Humean'. He was influenced but not convinced. This distinction is crucial in the Sieyesian context. He was not the kind of man who became the disciple or follower of another. On the contrary, he had disciples.

The wide, even bizarre divergence of views regarding the sources from which Sieyes drew his intellectual inspiration inspires a certain caution in assessing them. Néton, for example, whose biography was the standard one in French before that of Bastid, seemed almost casual in his attribution of influences. Sieyes was the 'son of Voltaire and the disciple of Diderot', but at the same time he 'borrowed from Montesquieu the theory of the separation of powers' and 'drew almost all his ideas from Mably, whose most ardent popularist he became'.[1] Pariset, writing shortly afterwards, argued that Spinoza was a major influence on Sieyes' constitutional doctrines.[2] Sieyes' first English biographer, Clapham, argued cogently that Néton exaggerated the dependence of Sieyes on Mably. He emphasized rather the general influence of Condillac, and the specific influence of Locke and Harrington. Sieyes, he wrote, 'was in substantial agreement with Locke' in his 'views on the seat of authority in the State and on the origin and end of society', while his 'scheme of highly organized representative government has more points of contact with the Constitution of the Commonwealth of Harrington's Oceana than with any plan put forward in the eighteenth century'.[3] Subsequent writings on Sieyes in English, notably those of Liljegren and Trevor, have stressed the links between Harrington and Sieyes.[4]

It must be remembered that none of these commentators and biographers had the advantage of seeing Sieyes' unpublished manuscripts. Bastid did have this advantage, and was able to incorporate his findings in the second edition of his work on Sieyes. In his chapter on Sieyes' 'spiritual affiliation' Bastid emphasized the pervasive influence of Descartes. Sainte-Beuve, in his celebrated essay on Sieyes written in 1851, had already made the analogy between Descartes' radicalism and that of Sieyes, but Bastid went much further. It was no mere figure of speech, he argued, to call Sieyes *'un Descartes de la politique'*. He 'really wished to apply the rules of the *Discourse on Method* to the organization of societies', and his 'radical and insolent' attitude towards history was derived directly from his seventeenth-century mentor. Yet curiously Bastid gave no hard evidence for this connection and admitted that we are 'badly informed about the ways in which Sieyes received the teaching of Descartes.'

Bastid convincingly dismissed the argument that Spinoza was a major influence on Sieyes. The resemblances, he wrote, were 'fortuitous and vague'. Locke, Condillac and Bonnet undoubtedly influenced Sieyes' purely philosophical speculations, and Locke in particular influenced his social and political philosophy also. It was to the Lockean tradition of the *'Etat gendarme'* rather than to the Rousseauan tradition of '*aliénation totale*' that Sieyes' political thought belonged, though Bastid nevertheless recognized certain affinities between Rousseau's ideas and those of Sieyes. Interestingly Bastid believed that Voltaire exercised a permanent influence on Sieyes. Montesquieu and Mably by contrast were not significant influences; Sieyes' thought diverged markedly from that of both. Finally Bastid recognized several points of contact between Sieyes' ideas and those of the Physiocrats, and a certain affinity between him and the Encyclopaedists and Helvétius.[5]

As might be expected, Zapperi's interpretation of the influences that helped to shape Sieyes' thought differs markedly from that of Bastid. For Zapperi Sieyes was a 'neo-mercantilist' follower of Condillac as regards economic theory; he was 'faithful to Lockean dogma' as regards property; and he 'pillaged' Rousseau for his doctrine of political organization without in any way understanding him![6] Roels, by contrast, returns to the old idea that Sieyes stood in direct line of descent from Montesquieu and Mably, and remained 'faithful to the ideology of Spinoza'.[7] Finally Schmitt breaks fresh ground by drawing attention to the link between the article on 'Representatives' in the *Encyclopédie* and Sieyes' ideas on this subject.[8]

This brief survey illustrates the rich variety of interpretations that have been made of Sieyes' intellectual forebears. The analysis that follows will attempt to sift the genuine affiliations from the purely hypothetical, beginning with some general observations, and moving on to a more detailed examination of particular thinkers.

1 Some general observations

In his published works Sieyes very rarely referred explicitly to other writers. He praises Adam Smith on one occasion, he scorns Montesquieu on another, and he mentions his youthful approval for the works of Locke, Condillac and Bonnet in his autobiography. Apart from this there are a handful of references to other writers. This lack of references does not seem accidental. Sieyes saw no merit in basing his ideas on the authority of others. He remarked on one occasion that only what was known by reason was truly known, and on another that 'truths belong only to those who demonstrate them'.[9] Logical demonstration, in other words, was what mattered to him; it was the only true authority.

This lack of reference to other writers does not mean that he had ignored them. All the evidence indicates that he had read voraciously as a young man. In particular the ten years that he spent in Paris between his arrival there as a young theological student in 1765 and his departure for Brittany on his first ecclesiastical appointment in 1775 were ones in which he explored a vast range of literature reaching far beyond what was required for his course of studies at the Sorbonne. Partly this exploration was a distraction from the theological training in which his father had placed him and for which he felt no sympathy. Partly it answered to a genuine and intense intellectual curiosity. Even at a later date, in the 1780s, when he was vicar-general at Chartres, and when Dumont wrote that 'he read little and meditated much' his letters show him ordering and receiving books from Paris, books by Necker, La Harpe and Linguet, and doubtless many others.[10]

The best indication there is of the scope of Sieyes' reading in his earliest years is his 'project for a library or bibliography', a catalogue of books which he intended to put in his library 'were he ever rich enough to form one for himself'.[11] This project was begun in 1770, when Sieyes was only twenty-two years old. It is an unfinished work, that was probably composed intermittently over a year or possibly more. The list of authors begins rather incoherently, then starts again in alphabetical order, and then starts again classified under subject headings. Sieyes clearly had difficulty in deciding what classification to adopt. In a preface to the work he explained that he first considered the order in which the *encyclopédistes* had ranged human knowledge but found it difficult to implement. He also stressed that his list was confined to 'truly useful' books, that he would like to acquire, and was not concerned with those 'rare and ancient' volumes with which libraries built their reputations. In fact the works of classical antiquity and of medieval scholarship are conspicuously absent from his catalogue. From the start Sieyes was emphatically on the side of the 'moderns'.

The range of subjects covered in the catalogue is vast. Following the schema he eventually adopted it included philosophy, logic and grammar, metaphysics, ethics and theology, natural law, positive law both divine and human, politics, physics, natural history and anatomy, the physico-mathematical sciences and geography, geometry, numerical calculation, French history, foreign history, *belles-lettres,* translations and varia. We need not assume that Sieyes had read all the books listed, but we may assume that he had read a great number of them, for his criticisms and comments are interspersed with many of the titles.

What particular interests does the list reveal? First, the strong impact of English, or perhaps more accurately, of British ideas and culture on eighteenth-century France is vividly reflected. The number of works by English or Scottish authors is almost equal to that of French. Sieyes obviously learnt English at an early date, perhaps by way of Dyche's *Guide to the English Tongue* (1743) which is included in his list. A surprising number of purely literary works by English authors are included – the works of Shakespeare, Milton, Pope, Addison, Dryden, Swift and so on – and Sieyes probably began his English studies with them. Then it is clear that in his early years he was strongly (and understandably) interested in the arguments for and against natural religion and the authenticity of revelation, for the works of Herbert of Cherbury, Anthony Collins, Samuel Clarke, Andrew Ramsay, Richard Price (Sieyes called his *Review of the Principal Questions in Morals* of 1758 'excellent'), Matthew Tindal and Thomas Woolston feature prominently. Turning to the broader field of philosophy it is clear that Sieyes was familiar with the materialist writings of La Mettrie, and had begun on those of Holbach – the latter's *Système de la Nature* (1770), published under the pseudonym of Mirabaud – comes near the start of the catalogue. The works of Hobbes, Spinoza and Bayle are listed with conspicuous thoroughness and completeness. Locke is treated more summarily, but his treatises on *Civil Government* are included. Malebranche and Leibniz are mentioned under 'metaphysics', and Sieyes spent a long time discussing the works of Formey, the French expositor of Wolff's philosophy. Other British thinkers mentioned include Bacon, Cumberland, Cudworth, Shaftesbury, Bolingbroke, Mandeville, Hutcheson and Berkeley. Hume's *History* is mentioned, and his essay on the *Populousness of ancient nations,* but not his main philosophical works, and there is nothing to suggest that Sieyes was ever familiar with these. Another conspicuous absentee from the philosophical sections is Descartes, and there is no evidence, in any of Sieyes' writings, of a link between the two thinkers. Amongst the French writers and books included mention may be made of Maupertuis, Boulanger, Robinet, Bonnet, Condillac's *Traité des animaux,* Helvétius' *De l'esprit,* Rousseau's discourse on *L'origine de l'inégalité,* the *Encyclopédie,* and

Quesnay on *Despotisme de la Chine* and *L'économie animale*. Under 'politics' we find the Abbé Saint Pierre, Davenant on trade, Forbonnais on commerce and finance, and several works by Mably, as well as Hume's essay, already mentioned. Sir James Steuart's *Inquiry into the principles of political economy* (1767) is listed in an earlier section, while a title-heading 'works for and against the economists' [i.e. the Physiocrats] is mentioned at the outset but not actually filled.

It can be seen that the twenty-two-year-old Sieyes spread his net very widely. In the years between 1770 and 1776 he continued to read intensively, and his thoughts began to crystallize around certain themes, most notably the theory of knowledge expounded by Condillac and others, and the economic and social doctrines of the Physiocrats. On the latter subject he came very close to publication in 1775. In the pages that follow we shall examine more closely the writers that interested him in these years, and indeed in the whole period up to 1789.

2 The influence of Locke, Condillac and Bonnet on Sieyes' ideas about knowledge, scientific method and the human personality

There are three direct testimonials regarding the books that most influenced Sieyes in the years before the Revolution. The first came from Sieyes himself in his autobiography. Referring to his youthful studies in Paris he wrote: 'He studied the works of metaphysics and morals. He often confessed that no books gave him keener satisfaction than those of Locke, Condillac, Bonnet; he encountered in them men having the same interest, the same instinct, and preoccupied with the same need.'[12] Then there is Dumont's account of Sieyes' habits when he was at Chartres in the years immediately preceding the Revolution: 'He read little and meditated much; the works that he liked the most were Rousseau's *Social Contract*, the writings of Condillac and Smith's *Treatise on the Wealth of Nations*.'[13] Finally there are the words of Sieyes' German friend Oelsner, who wrote that 'the book that he read the most and which had shaped him, was Condillac's *Researches on the origin of human knowledge*.'[14]

The persistence of Condillac's name in these three accounts leaves little doubt about the deep impression he made on Sieyes, and his impact is further confirmed by Sieyes' unpublished papers. It was above all Condillac's ideas on the problem of the source and nature of human knowledge that absorbed the young Sieyes. This was the problem to which he was referring when he wrote that Locke, Condillac and Bonnet all shared a common preoccupation. Locke's epistemological writings are in fact rarely mentioned in Sieyes' papers, but those of Condillac and Bonnet are intensively examined.

Sieyes' interest in the epistemological problem developed early. He once wrote that he first read Condillac's *Traité des sensations* in 1765, which was the year that he arrived in Paris as a young student.[15] His interest reached a climax during the last of his student years in Paris. Between 1773 and 1775 he wrote a bulky text which he called *le grand cahier métaphysique*.[16] Here he concentrated his attention on the celebrated hypothesis which both Condillac and Bonnet used in order to explain the origin and development of human understanding, the hypothesis namely of a statue endowed with senses that are opened one after another. Condillac used this hypothesis in his *Traité des sensations* and Bonnet in his *Essai analytique sur les facultés de l'âme.*

At one point in the *cahier* Sieyes wrote that Condillac's *Traité des sensations,* from the second part onwards, seemed to him a *vrai chef-d'oeuvre.* He was obviously fascinated by the argument that Condillac displayed. But was he convinced by it? That seems to be the real question that has to be answered. It is tempting, because of Sieyes' deep interest in Condillac, to conclude that he became a follower of Condillac, and that his theory of knowledge, like that of Condillac, was a 'sensualist' or 'sensationalist' one. This temptation is strengthened by the fact that Condillac's philosophy, unlike that of most of the thinkers of the Enlightenment, generated a 'school' in France, the school of the *Idéologues,* which flourished in the decade from 1794 to 1804. Cabanis, Destutt de Tracy, Laromiguière, Garat and Volney were the leading members of this school, and Sieyes knew most of them well. Nothing would therefore seem more obvious than to classify him as a sensualist and an *Idéologue.*

The obvious path does not, however, seem the right one in this instance. Wilhelm von Humboldt, who met Sieyes and several of the *Idéologues* in 1798, and discussed metaphysics with them, placed Sieyes in a separate category from the others. He recognized that there were elements in Sieyes' approach which distinguished it from the prevailing sensualism and brought it closer to the idealism of Kant and Fichte. Others too appear to have seen a resemblance at this time between Sieyes' ideas and those of Kant.[17]

Humboldt's assessment is confirmed by Sieyes' unpublished writings on metaphysics. To understand their significance it is necessary to say something first about Condillac. He stands out as one of the small number of genuinely systematic thinkers that were produced during the period of the French Enlightenment. One of the main goals of his epistemological writings was to reduce Locke's theory of knowledge to consistency, order and unity. It was precisely the systematic character of Condillac's thought that made it capable of inspiring a school of followers later in the century, and it was probably this aspect too that first attracted Sieyes to it. As we shall see his attention was probably attracted to the Physiocrats for the same reason; whatever their faults the Physiocrats were, like Condillac, not mere *gens de lettres* (a term which Sieyes used contemptuously) but genuine thinkers, *gens systématiques,* trying to weld their ideas into a reasoned whole.

Sainte-Beuve defined the doctrine of the eighteenth century as being 'basically materialism, or pantheism, or naturalism'.[18] His words succinctly identify the centre of gravity of the great outpouring of ideas that began in earnest in the middle of the 1740s and continued unabated for the next thirty or forty years, to which the name of the French Enlightenment is usually attached. Condillac's writings spanned the whole of this period, and were heavily impregnated with the naturalism that was the spirit of the age. Turning his back on what he regarded as the 'false', 'abstract', 'hypothetical' philosophical systems of Descartes, Leibniz, Spinoza and Malebranche, Condillac sought to construct instead a true philosophical system which would rise up from the firm foundations of the observable workings of the natural physical world. Nature for him as for so many of his contemporaries was the pure and infallible lodestone for philosophical reasoning.

Condillac's theory of knowledge, which was first developed in his *Essai sur l'origine des connaissances humaines* of 1746, and came to full fruition in the *Traité des sensations* of 1754, reflected this naturalism. His aim was to demonstrate that all the operations of the human will and understanding were resolvable into, and reconstructable out of, the sensations transmitted to the human soul by the organs of sense, and the pleasure and pain that man's natural organs attached to these sensations. Through 'experience' – by which Condillac meant the mutual 'instruction' of the senses, and the development of 'associations of ideas' and 'contracted habits', spurred on by the impulse to find pleasure and avoid pain – the basic, rudimentary components of the human system produced a more complex and sophisticated being. In his own words: 'Judgement, reflection, desires, passions etc., are only sensation itself transforming itself differently.'[19] And summing up his demonstration in the *Traité des sensations,* he wrote: 'one sees how man, having at first been but a feeling animal, becomes a reflecting animal, capable of looking after its own preservation by itself.'[20]

Man as conceived by Condillac in the *Traité* may be called an active being in the sense that his knowledge and ideas had always a very practical source, the attainment of pleasure and the avoidance of pain, or as Condillac often described it, the satisfaction of 'need'. In another sense, however, Condillac's man was extraordinarily passive, for his activity was but the product of impressions and impulses aggregating and disaggregating within him. Man did not transform anything; he was but an arena where transformations occurred. The 'self' or *moi* became a paltry manifestation in Condillac's scheme. At one point he called it 'only a collection of sensations that it [i.e. the statue] experiences, and of those that memory recalls to it. In a word, it is simultaneously the consciousness of what it is and the memory of what it has been.'[21] The 'self' was in other words the co-existence of past and present sensations. When Condillac attempted to explain how the statue gained a consciousness of externality, or developed a sense that there were things outside its 'self' he relied on the sense of touch. The statue's body experienced a particular sensation of solidity when it touched something that was not its own body, and this was the seed of its consciousness of an outside world, the sense of touch 'instructing' the other senses of its discovery.

When we turn to Sieyes' observations on the epistemological theories of Condillac and Bonnet we find that he placed a far greater emphasis than them on the activity of the human self or *moi.* His ideas, he explained a long time afterwards, in 1798, were founded on the principle of 'action and reaction', and sure enough, amongst his early notes there is one with this very heading.[22] It begins: 'For us there is initially only *reaction* analogous to *action.* It [i.e. reaction] is the response to the impression, the one doubtless determined by the other, and that is all. But when does the directing *moi* arise? Well, in steering, fortifying the reaction it masters in some fashion the sensation, without changing its nature.' Sieyes continued by saying that it might appear as if action was in the soul and reaction in the external object. 'On the contrary, in the first impressions, action was in the external bodies, and reaction in the soul.' He went on:

> In any whole subjected to the action of beings around it and capable of reaction, it is impossible for it not to form a centre for all the actions that it experiences. It is there that I establish the source of reaction. Out of this single point I constitute the soul of all. Beforehand there had been as many souls as parts, now there is a *moi* to which all responds, all is subordinated.

This account of the self or *moi* as a unity asserting itself against multiple impressions is taken up again and again in the metaphysical notebook where Sieyes examined the 'statue' analogy. Sensations alone, he argued, could not provide an adequate account of the development of human faculties. 'The work of *sensations*, and that of *perceptions* are two separate works.' 'A concrete *perception* ... posits several sensations regarded as forming an image.' '*Judgement* is to the perceptions, what feeling is to the sensations.' 'Extension is not a sensation, it is a judgement. It is the *local liaison* of our sensations.' Turning to the question of 'self' Sieyes argued that as soon as the statue said *moi,* something had altered: 'the verb *have* takes the place of the word *be*.' In other words, the moment at which the statue took possession of its sensations, and saw them as happening to it, had a significance which Condillac and Bonnet completely overlooked. Sieyes deepened this point in a rhetorical passage towards the end of his notebook:

> Is sensing oneself recognition of oneself? How could the mere vision of the mind (*esprit*) produce space, which is more independent of the mind and its vision than the body itself? Produce is not the word, one has to say *recognize,* going beyond first sensations, which are merely indications without recognition, and arriving at the faculty which discovers *it is me, it is not me,* the faculty which puts one sensation outside another, which distinguishes *several,* which develops the idea of unity. It is necessary to attribute to this faculty not exactly the *sensation* of solidity, but the recognition *of the solid thing* felt, or of bodies, [of] the difference between fugitive sensations and permanent ones, [and] which confirms recognition outside, or the placing outside that recognition effects, by positing that the *subject outside* has its own reality in the same way as the *subject inside.*'

In another note written about the same time Sieyes elaborated this moment of self-identification with a paradoxical flourish:

> When man has put his sensations outside himself, and *when he has formed nature,* i.e. the assemblage of what is and what will be in relationship to him, he divides the principle of the forces of nature in two. All that takes place independently of him he attributes to an agent that he calls *nature* and all that is done by himself or by actions produced by the efforts of men and animals he attributes to *art.* Art like nature is a principle of action personified, and at the end of the day these two words art and nature are rather useless. If all the aggregates of forces and even if each force could become aware of itself, it would attribute *all it did* to art in opposition to nature. But this would be a vain enterprise, one cannot escape the forces of nature and all that happens only operates through her. Human art can only be that part of the forces of nature

which develops in man; it takes possession of another part of the forces of nature in order to subdue a third part of the forces of nature which is good or bad towards him. It is always nature that acts and even she is here only a poetic expression which illuminates nothing, teaches nothing, and cannot teach anything.[23]

Final confirmation of the distance between Sieyes and sensualist philosophy comes in the notes that he penned after his political career was over and his thoughts had returned once again to his first love, metaphysics. The statue of Condillac and Bonnet, he wrote then,

would never start to distinguish between sensations, and would be content to feel and nothing more, not knowing if it felt nor what it felt, if it had not been endowed in advance with the *recognition of self* and hence of a *not-self*, i.e. the external world. *I* presupposes *other*.... The *moi* which has detached itself from its sensations and its external relations, detaches itself also from everything that comes to it from within, distinguishing its details, and placing it outside.[24]

In another note Sieyes pronounced a kind of epitaph on all attempts – like those of Condillac – to reduce the workings of the mind and will to a single self-less process:

The metaphysicians, above all since Locke, emulate one another in composing and decomposing what they call the understanding and the will. After reading their different analyses one asks: what have I learnt? These analyses lead to nothing more than an arrangement in different words of what can already be found in them in another manner. The real, that which exists, has not moved. Everything proceeds independently of our thoughts. The questions posed are usually *false suppositions*. They do not aim at, they do not lead to instruction. What does it matter that seeing, comparing, judging, recalling, reflecting etc. are always *feeling*? A futile, arbitrary decision! You make *sensation* the generic word and you conclude that the mind, in all its operations, does nothing other than feel. That is not well done. Someone else prefers 'attention' or some other generic word, and he has just as much right to say that all can be reduced to attention etc. These general expressions are our invention, with no counterpart in nature, and remote from reality. There is nothing real but our particular intellectual acts....

We concur in the formation of our concrete ideas. Their liaisons of fact, the perception of their relationships, and dare I say, the organization of their mass, make up the notion that we express with the word *mind (esprit)*. We do not know reality in itself. The ideal world is the real world for us, always observing that this ideal reality is only certain through the verification of a constant experience.'[25]

There is one significant new development in the conception of man's self that Sieyes presented in his later notes. In his early years he appeared content to describe the *moi* as a 'single point' or 'centre' to which all impressions were related. In his later years he vigorously attacked physiologists such as Bichat who were seeking for a 'central point' in the 'human system'. This, he said, was to import visual preconceptions into an area where they were quite inappropriate. There was no central point round which all human faculties revolved:

The whole *(ensemble)* of man is an harmonic combination composed of several distinct systems, which are in turn composed of several organs concurring in the same goal in each system. To seek for the central point, whether of the whole, or

> of each part of this very complicated organization is an expression devoid of sense. What are you trying to say with your *point* coupled with the epithet *central*? You are looking for the central point![26]

Everything, Sieyes stressed, concurred in or towards the same goal in the human system, but this unity was a 'final cause' rather than 'a principle'. 'There is here concurrence of powers, an admirable equilibrium, it is a federated republic, not a monarchy.' It was also not a machine, nor a materialist system, but 'elasticity, life, and animality'. He went on:

> You seek the central *moi*! Take care, it is everywhere. There is not a faculty which does not say 'I'. *I* feel, *I* think, *I* judge, *I* imagine, *I* wish, *I* move, etc. Add, and this is important, that often all these *moi* scarcely agree, that one wants what the other refuses.
>
> Is it not clear that if *unity of the system* or rather *general harmony* is necessary in the human whole, under penalty of death, or at least of illness, depending on the nature of the derangement, it is not necessary at all to find there a *single moi*. The ancients and the moralists recognized *several* men within us. They touched on the truth without knowing it. We have taken a few more steps, not many.[27]

Sieyes' final vision of the human self as being not a single point, but rather a striving towards unity, in which several selves concurred, each, he stressed, with 'its special functions, which could not be usurped by any other', is interesting primarily because it tallies so closely with his final vision of the representative political system, a system in which each part of the public establishment, each institution, had its own function, and all combined or 'concurred' to produce action towards the overriding goal of preserving and enhancing individual liberty, a goal which he expressly called the 'final cause' of the social order.[28] Almost inevitably, in the ideas of every great political theorist from Plato onwards, the thinker's conception of the human person and his soul runs parallel with, and is analogous to his conception of the great public person, the state, and its soul. The two *personae* embody the same principles. Sieyes' ideas were no exception.

This survey has attempted to show that Sieyes, while powerfully stirred by the writings of Condillac and Bonnet to reflect upon the nature of man's mind and its workings, developed a quite distinctive philosophy which went well beyond theirs. He cannot be classified as either a sensualist or an *Idéologue*. Instead his conceptions come close to the kind of idealism that is expressed most completely in the writings of Kant and Fichte. (The latter's reflections on the 'ego' and the 'non-ego' come particularly to mind.) This affinity need not cause us surprise. The idealist philosophy of Kant and Fichte has often been seen as the metaphysical counterpart of the French Revolution of 1789. Sieyes played a leading role in making that Revolution. It is somehow fitting that his own metaphysical system should in turn run parallel with that of the two great speculative revolutionaries.

It would be wrong, however, to conclude from this that Condillac was but a stimulus to Sieyes' own distinctive philosophical development, and that none of his ideas became incorporated in the mental outlook of his younger contemporary. Even if we ignore for the moment Condillac's economic ideas, there are elements of his thought that are recognizable in that of the mature Sieyes. For the most part they pertain to Condillac's theories of logic and method rather than to his doctrine of sensualism.

There was, for example, Condillac's insistence that science and systematic knowledge were synonymous.[29] Condillac rejected, as we have seen, the false systems of thinkers like Descartes and Leibniz, but he did not reject the idea of system itself, the idea that genuine knowledge took the form of an ordered unity, in which all the parts were linked together in a mutually explanatory manner. Moreover he expressly rebutted the popular notion that politics was not a proper area for the construction of such a system of knowledge. Sieyes shared these ideas. As has been suggested, he was probably attracted to Condillac in the first place by the systematic quality of his thought, but he no doubt learnt from him in turn the justification for system.

Then there was Condillac's argument that analysis, or decomposition and recomposition, the taking apart and putting together of things in an orderly manner, was the sole method of finding the truth, the 'lever of the mind' as he put it.[30] Analysis began with what was known and worked back from there into the unknown, pressing on until it reached a first principle or first fact from which the work of reconstruction could begin and a 'system' developed. Sieyes may have disagreed with the way in which Condillac employed analysis in the concrete instance, as for example in his examination of the human faculties of understanding and will, but he never doubted throughout his life that analysis was the true scientific method. 'Analysis will always be', he wrote in one of his later notes, 'the great instrument of our intellectual and industrial perfectibility and indirectly of all perfectibility.'[31] The echo of Condillac is unmistakable.

It is unmistakable too in Sieyes' conception of words and language. In his *Essai* – though not in the *Traité des sensations* – Condillac insisted with unusual vigour that the development of language was the decisive stage in the growth of man's power to know and understand the world about him. The use of signs for things gave reasoning crucial independence and flexibility of action. Unfortunately it also led to the error of mistaking words for things. In the course of history the instrumental nature of words had been lost sight of, they had become in large measure divorced from the reality they were originally intended to denote, and had been invested with arbitrary meanings and significance. For Condillac the future development of true knowledge was synonymous with the purification of language, the restoration to words of their clear and precise reference to reality. He was accustomed to say that a properly developed science was the same as a well-made language.

Sieyes shared this view. As shown in the last chapter, for him words were emphatically counters, instruments the function of which was to convey as precisely and directly as possible the nature of things beyond them. They must not distract from reality. He was in favour of purifying language, and was not averse to inventing new words where he thought it necessary for precision's sake. Even his thoughts on style were foreshadowed by Condillac.[32]

There is a final, highly important affinity between the two men. Condillac repeatedly stressed that the growth of human knowledge and indeed the development of all man's faculties were initiated by 'need', which was his way of abbreviating man's inherent impulse to avoid or diminish painful sensations and to maximize pleasurable or enjoyable ones.[33] Everything elevated in man had a practical root. Sieyes too embraced this view, as can be seen most clearly by the way he begins his *Reasoned exposition of the rights of man and citizen*. To suggest that Condillac alone inspired his attitude would probably be an oversimplification. The close attention accorded to man's material or physical needs and their gratification was a distinguishing mark of the writings of many Enlightenment thinkers. It grew out of the general emphasis on 'nature' and what was 'natural' that characterized the whole movement. The modern science of economics can be seen developing out of it. Condillac must hence be seen as only one influence amongst others behind the great importance that Sieyes attached to the way in which man satisfied his needs and maximized his enjoyment. His vision of man was, as we have tried to show, an 'idealist' one: he saw man as self-determining, and not as a mere prolongation of nature. At the same time he recognized that it was material need that spurred man to self-determining activity and provided the first impulse that led to the creation of the political order. This leads us on to a consideration of the origins of his economic ideas.

3 Sieyes' economic ideas: an assessment of the influence of the Physiocrats, and of Turgot, Condillac and Adam Smith

Like his interest in the problem of human understanding, Sieyes' interest in political economy began very early. The plan for a library that he began in 1770 indicated that his curiosity had been drawn to this subject. In the next few years, that is to say between 1771 and 1776, he intensified his enquiries into it. As these were the years in which the fame and influence of the teaching of Quesnay and his followers – the 'Economists' or 'Physiocrats' – reached its zenith, it was natural that Sieyes' studies should gravitate towards the works of these writers, and all the more so because here again, as in the writings of Condillac, there were not merely random opinions, but a system of ideas that challenged the mind.

During the period from 1771 to 1776 Sieyes read and annotated the leading writings of the Physiocrats: the works of Quesnay, Mercier de la Rivières' *L'Ordre naturel et essentiel des sociétés politiques* (published in 1767), the Abbé Baudeau's *Première introduction à la philosophie économique* (1771) and the elder Mirabeau's *Philosophie rurale* (written in collaboration with Quesnay and published in 1763). He also made a thorough study of at least two important non-Physiocratic (or partially Physiocratic) works: Turgot's *Réflexions sur la formation et la distribution des richesses* (1769) and Condillac's *Le Commerce et le gouvernement considérés relativement l'un à l'autre* (1776), as well as developing his own ideas in a mass of notes.

In his autobiographical fragment Sieyes described his intellectual encounter with the Physiocrats, and placed it in the broader context of his other interests, and his method of work. It is worth citing in full:

> He [Sieyes] passed a part of the years 1773 and 1774, either in cultivating music (in which a revolution was taking place at this time in Paris) or in refuting the

> political system of the Economists which he found rigid and thin but a hundred times better than miserable routine, which as usual took fright at it, without in any way understanding it. He made or thought he made, in these two years, important research on the wayward march of the human mind in philosophy, and on the metaphysics of language and intellectual method. He published nothing. The dominant quality of his spirit is the passion for truth, the search for which absorbs him almost involuntarily. He is not content, when he takes up a subject, until he has deepened it, analysed it in all its parts and then reconstructed it as a totality. But the need to know once satisfied, he remains with his notes and analytical tables, which exist solely for him. The tidying up, the filling of gaps, and that kind of *toilette,* which even authors who are little interested in the bouquet *(fumée)* of literature feel compelled to accord to writings which are destined to see the light of day, are intolerable to him. He has already moved on to other meditations. If he sometimes betrayed this laziness it was only brought on by a feeling of the great public interest, and at moments when he hoped that he might possibly be useful.[34]

One of these moments when Sieyes 'betrayed his laziness' came undoubtedly when he wrote a *Letter on wealth* and transcribed it into publishable form in January 1775. It was intended to be the first of several letters addressed to the Economists, examining their doctrines. Officially approved for publication in February, the *Letter* was destined never to appear because of the dismissal of Turgot. It was the nearest that Sieyes came to publication before 1788.

The *Letter* gives a clear insight into Sieyes' views on Physiocracy and on certain central economic topics.[35] For this reason it is worth examining. In his opening paragraphs he made it clear that he thought the adherents of Physiocracy had fallen victim to that overweening self-confidence that the *esprit de système* generated in those who abandoned themselves to it without moderation. In the main text he looked first at the physiocratic notion of wealth. For them all that was fit to give enjoyment to man was called a 'good', and wealth consisted of all those goods that it was possible to exchange.

The fault with this definition, Sieyes wrote, was that it did not analyse deeply enough the nature of goods, and the factors that made them exchangeable.

> Amongst goods capable of giving enjoyment, some are *common,* like the air, sunshine, water, etc. These do not exchange since everyone enjoys them. Others are *particular (propres),* they belong to one, or several individuals. Where does property of a good come from? Surely from the *labour (travail)* that it has cost. To create a good, one adds one's labour to a common good, which is to appropriate it. *In society,* these properties are reciprocally recognized, and evaluated according to laws that I need not expound here. It is natural that one is unwilling to yield what one has acquired by labour without indemnification or recompense. That is the origin of exchange.

From here Sieyes proceeded to make some interesting subdivisions. First, when speaking of goods acquired by labour, the term 'labour' had to be taken 'in a generic sense, and for all the titles by which it has pleased us to represent it'. Second, only some goods were possessed by particular individuals. There were also 'common enjoyments, acquired at great cost by public works', enjoyments which no one could appropriate exclusively. Finally it had to be recognized that even particular goods were not always exchangeable, and that those that were susceptible to exchange could not always be exchanged in present circumstances because of lack of commerce, and so on.

By this means Sieyes had shown that by calling wealth the 'sum of exchangeable goods', the Physiocrats had left out of account a prodigious number of goods that enriched both nations and individuals. To this he added the argument that the phrase 'exchangeable goods' was too vague and general to be useful. For example the gold scorned by savages in America would count as part of their wealth according to the Physiocrats simply because it was 'exchangeable'.

Rejecting the Physiocrats' definition of wealth, Sieyes concluded that *'c'est le travail qui forme la richesse'*. All those goods that men were obliged to acquire by labour, or by the title that represented it, were wealth, whether they were exchangeable or not, public or private, appreciable or non-appreciable. From this basis Sieyes proceeded to draw some important general consequences about the nature of society:

> Every man wishes to be happy, i.e. to enjoy things in his own way. Enjoyment consumes goods; there is need therefore for a constantly acting force to produce them anew. Nature herself offers us what we have called simple goods, she alone bears the cost of their reproduction; it would be useless for us to concern ourselves with it. But we have to employ all our efforts to ensure and to increase the reproduction of goods which require the conjunction *(concours)* of our labours to come into being. This, the goal of each individual, becomes that of all society, could it have another end than that of its members. An association is nothing other than a more perfect means of obtaining with greater abundance and greater security, that which everyone desires, namely wealth. It is therefore necessary that, independently of the power of nature that is productive of goods, society should possess a *vital force* that is co-productive of wealth, and it is necessary that the elements of this force, united by society, produce more than they would if they remained isolated. The sum of the works of all the citizens forms the vital force. If a citizen withdraws his portion of activity, he renounces his rights. No man ought to enjoy the labour of another without exchange. General work is hence the foundation of society and the social order is nothing but the best possible order of works.
>
> The order develops like this. At first each man acquires all his enjoyments alone. Their number increases with the means [to acquire them], and as they become more complex, divisions of labour take place. The common advantage requires it, because workers less distracted by cares of the same kind than by occupations of different kinds always tend to produce greater effects with less means. The divisions multiply continuously in accordance with this law of all work: improve the effect and diminish the cost.
>
> I need not follow the development of this order. But I must stress the main division between productive works and co-productive works in order to forestall the embarrassment that certain readers may find themselves when regarding political and public works. How, it will be asked, do these produce wealth? By assuring the fruits of work, and by reducing the need for means, they are co-productive, in the same way as traders, carriers, citizens engaged in useful sciences, educators, etc., etc. The works of these classes, which we have no intention of confusing together in terms of dignity, have been separated from the general mass of productive works which they encumber, and which they serve much better in this state of separation. The aim of all these divisions is always to produce a greater sum of enjoyments, and their order, as we have said above, follows the general law: improve the effect and diminish the cost.

The Physiocrats' definition of wealth as 'exchangeable goods', Sieyes concluded, had dangerous consequences. By adopting it, he wrote,

> it will appear that you incite governments to think of exchange rather than of enjoyments, and to multiply the former at the expense of the latter. I do not accuse you of this, but that is the consequence of a bad definition, which makes you speak in a manner opposed to your feelings. When I hear you maintain that the administration ought to concern itself with increasing the sum of wealth, I seem to hear you exhorting it to abandon great public works, because the goods that these produce are not exchangeable. Let us not forget that it is work that produces wealth, and that in order to multiply the effect, it is necessary to perfect the cause. Consequently let us remember to mention the cause whenever we explain the nature of the effect.

Such was the argument of the first part of Sieyes' *Letter*. In the second part he turned his fire on the Physiocrats' theory of the 'sources of wealth'. This is of course the best known part of their doctrine, the area in which their brand of 'naturalism', which was every bit as intense as that of Condillac in his theory of knowledge, manifested itself most obviously: Physiocracy indeed meant the 'rule of nature'. For the Physiocrats the land was 'the source of wealth'. They argued that only when man was working in direct collusion with nature, either in the cultivation of crops or in the production of raw materials, did the amount of wealth produced exceed that which was consumed in its production. Here alone was there a 'net product'. This was because in this form of production 'nature' added *her* productive power to that of man. The surplus value created by work on the land sustained all the other branches of production, which did not create a surplus, but only added together or juxtaposed values already created. Industrial production was hence 'sterile' in comparison with agricultural production.

It would be tedious to follow in detail Sieyes' rebuttal of this long-rejected doctrine, because much of his argument will seem obvious. The main thrust of his refutation was that, while it could be said that work on the land produced the 'matter' which industry or art 'fashioned', nevertheless both forms of production represented the interaction of labour with nature, and each form was necessary to the other if man was not to lead a completely primitive existence. It was hence purely arbitrary for the Physiocrats to separate them into 'productive' and 'sterile' activities.

Perhaps the most interesting element in Sieyes' argument was the alternative explanation that he put forward to account for the 'net product' of agricultural production, or the surplus value that it created over and above the payment made for the work of the cultivators of the soil. Sieyes ascribed it to the dividing up of the land into exclusive properties and the lack of free competition that resulted. If a similar lack of competition existed in the industrial sector, if for example particular manufacturers had exclusive property in the 'natural laws' that governed their own forms of production, then a 'net product' would appear there too. In Sieyes' words, it was 'the lack of competition caused by landed property or exclusive privilege over the land that leads the evaluation of raw materials far beyond the payment made for the work of the cultivator, and if the same phenomenon does not always appear in the arts [industry] it is because there it is not possible completely to hinder this competition.' It is not difficult to see in this argument the germs of a theory of rent.

The third and last section of Sieyes' *Letter* was on the 'total sum of wealth'. It was short and to the point. The Physiocrats defined the annual sum of wealth as the reproduction of the land; the true principle, said Sieyes, was that 'all labour that produces a good produces wealth'. In well-organized labour lay the key to the increase of wealth, in agriculture as well as every other sphere.

Such was Sieyes' refutation of the economic doctrines of the Physiocrats, and it can be seen that his insistence on labour as the true source of wealth is a remarkable prefiguration of Adam Smith's similar insistence in *The Wealth of Nations* which was published in 1776. Sieyes' standpoint against the Physiocrats was also strikingly similar to the one he upheld against Condillac's philosophy. In each case Sieyes attacked naturalism, the characteristic doctrine of the Enlightenment, and asserted that man's active powers were as important as the automatic or quasi-automatic processes of the physical world. Against Condillac's notion that 'sensation transforming itself' accounted for all operations of the human spirit, Sieyes argued that '*we* concur in the formation of our concrete ideas'. Against the physiocratic doctrine that organic processes within the soil were the true source of wealth, Sieyes argued that 'in the art of production as in all others, man takes possession of one part of the forces of nature with which he subdues another part.'

What of the political teaching of the Physiocrats, or the way they wanted the state to be ordered and run? Sieyes unfortunately never made such a sustained critique of this as he did of their economic doctrines, but it is plain from his incidental remarks that he strongly opposed its overall tenor. To understand the significance of his opposition it is necessary to make a brief sketch of the political theory of the Physiocrats.

Mercier de la Rivière's work on *L'Ordre naturel et essentiel des sociétés politiques*, which Sieyes knew well, provides the best basis for such a sketch. Mercier's aim was a radical one: to bring the positive laws of the social and political order into accordance with the natural laws of the natural order. By natural laws he and the other Physiocrats did not mean the laws of a moral order different in kind from the physical order, but rather the laws of the physical order that demonstrated or revealed the laws of the moral order. More precisely the natural laws were the physical necessities that governed the optimum production of wealth by human beings, or led to the optimum satisfaction of their needs. These natural laws could be discerned by human beings when they cleared their minds of preconceived ideas and allowed the light of 'evidence' to shine in on their reason. From these laws could be deduced the rights and duties of man and government.

The fundamental law of nature was that which established the absolute right of property. Man when considered in his original, natural state was driven imperiously to conserve himself, and to make use of things about him in order to do so. This necessity provided in itself the title to property in one's person and in things. Such property was thus an absolute right, its only counterpart being the duty to respect the property of others. (In some ways the Physiocrats did for Locke's theory of the origins of society what Condillac did for his theory of knowledge: reduced it to a system.)

Men in their original nature-governed condition thus formed a universal tacit society of property owners. Pressure of population on resources then led to property being extended from persons and movable things to the land. Once again this necessity created an absolute right, the right of landed property. The appropriation and cultivation of the land marked a decisive stage in the development of humanity. It made possible a real multiplication of wealth, as a result of the famous 'net product', which has already been discussed. It led to the formation of particular, political societies in place of the universal, natural one. The division of the land and its cultivation caused the owners of property in its three forms – personal, movable and landed – to make 'conventions' amongst themselves to secure their property vis-à-vis one another and vis-à-vis outsiders. These 'conventions' led to the establishment of a 'tutelary authority' with the power to guard the natural order of absolute property.

This then was the Physiocrat's vision of the just political order, or the political order attuned to the physical necessities of the natural order. The task of the tutelary authority was really but one: to secure to property owners, and especially the owners of landed property, the full original, absolute right of property that was theirs. This in turn had powerful implications in France of the eighteenth century. It meant that all the 'artificial' restrictions that had crept up in the course of history and confined the original 'natural' right of property had to be swept aside. *Laisser passer, laisser faire*: that was the message of the Physiocrats to the government of the day. Competition must become the sole regulator of economic interaction. All forms of corporate privilege, restrictions on trade, and so on, had to be removed.

The 'tutelary authority' of the body politic, the Physiocrats argued, had necessarily to be one and indivisible. This was fundamentally because there was no need for divisions of power, bargains and compromises when the purpose was to apply a single, evident scientific truth. The Physiocrats thus favoured absolute monarchy or, as they often expressed it, a system of 'legal despotism', that is to say the rule of one man exercised in accordance with the natural laws for the production of wealth. Their arguments about the proper and just tax system to support such an authority need not concern us here.

The Physiocrats attempted to ensure that the monarch would identify his own personal interests with that of the maintenance of the natural order by making the monarchy hereditary, and by providing that the monarch would be entitled to a share in the 'net product' of the land. They also attached great importance to the creation of a system of national education. In this way an enlightened public opinion would be created, able to recognize the 'evidence' of the natural laws, and to keep the monarch from straying from them.

Sieyes expressed his opinion on the political theory of the Physiocrats in a trenchant note in which he equated their views with that of one of their leading opponents:

> The Economists are wrong to rail so strongly against Linguet. At bottom they think alike. They all want the citizens to be *the well-administered property* of an all-powerful *master* who *recognizes his own interests*, and to think of themselves as such. It is a far cry from this to the feeling of liberty and to the enjoyment of an infallible protection that the citizen himself establishes through his representatives

> in a society of which he is a member, and where the government exists for those who are governed. That is what makes a republican monarchy or a monarchical republic, for if in place of this you have only a private thing (*ré privée*), it scarcely matters if this private thing is owned by one or by many. Is aristocracy less anti-republican than royal despotism?[36]

With this statement Sieyes laid his axe to the root of the Physiocratic political idea. For him the ordering of a political body could not be equated with the application of a natural science to a natural body. Men were not passive objects. They had *themselves* to make the order of which they were a part.

In similar vein he attacked the Physiocratic doctrine of *laisser aller*. The principle of getting rid of all 'artificial' (*factice*) encouragements or discouragements to economic activity and of allowing the 'natural' course of affairs free rein, he argued, was when taken to an extreme, absurd. For what of roads, canals, bridges, security, etc. – were they to be condemned as 'artificial'? The distinction had therefore to be abandoned. The proper way ahead was to consider the goal one wished to attain and then to consider the 'natural' means of achieving it. If the goal could not be attained by private means (*moyens particuliers*) then 'in that case, and if public means are necessary, it is up to the sovereign to employ the means that the Economists are pleased to call artificial.'[37]

Sieyes' intensive studies of the ideas of the Physiocrats thus led him to reject both their strictly economic reasoning and their broader political and social programme. To conclude that this intellectual encounter left no lasting effects on him would, however, be the very reverse of the truth. In the course of analysing the works of the Physiocrats Sieyes was driven to work out his own ideas on how society as a whole was made up, to distinguish the various component elements and to see how they fitted together. Time and again in his early notes he experimented with different classifications of these components. This experimentation was emphatically not confined to what to-day would be called the economy; it was broader than that. It encompassed the overall division and combination of labour of a politically organized society, including not only the division and combination of labour within the economic sphere but also the division and combination of labour between the economic sphere and the political sphere.

In most of his notes he can be seen working towards a recognizably modern division of labour, consisting of those who produced the 'matter' of production, or what we would call to-day the primary producers; those who 'formed' or 'fashioned' this 'matter', or what to-day would be called the secondary sector; those who 'communicated' the products of the first two sectors and who performed 'services', or what is now called the tertiary sector; and then set over against all these forms of work, the public or political order. Here for example is his:

Tableau d'une société politique, dated 1772:

Productive economy	the gainful art of producing matter the gainful art of producing form the gainful art of commerce personal industry: liberal, agreeable, service

Social order

Tutelary regime	make laws ensure their observation fulfil public economic needs watch over external affairs[38]

Sieyes' encounter with the Physiocrats hence led him to clarify his thoughts on the organization of the body politic seen as a division of labour, and his thoughts led him to a conception which was very different from the confused mélange of public and private activities, of 'orders' and 'estates', that existed in the *ancien régime*. As will be seen this conception played an important role in his revolutionary doctrine.

Sieyes' use of the term 'tutelary regime' in the diagram above indicates another of his debts to the Physiocrats. He adopted much of their terminology, even if he usually invested it with a different meaning. 'Tutelary regime' or 'tutelary authority' is one example. Sieyes used it in many of his published writings to mean, broadly, the governmental or administrative power, without any connotation of 'legal despotism'. More significantly Sieyes always used the term 'social art' to mean the systematic ordering of society in accordance with political right – the very science that he wished to put into practice in France in 1789. This term came undoubtedly from the physiocratic writer the Abbé Baudeau, who used it in his *Première introduction à la philosophie économique*.[39]

Sieyes also adopted Mercier de la Rivière's tripartite division of property: personal property, movable property and landed property. He believed most strongly that it was the aim of the body politic to protect such property and to give it greater scope. (Men enter society for 'a greater energy of property and happiness' he once wrote.[40]) But he did not share the Physiocratic dogma that the task of government was to secure the absolute right of property that individuals possessed before forming the body politic, with its implication that government could not alter or extinguish property rights. In this as in all the other instances he was not prepared to subordinate the public power to the supposed necessities of the physical world. The public power, for him, served the common will, and this signified more than merely the protection of absolute rights.[41]

Another important concept used by Sieyes was that of the 'disposable class' (*la classe disponible*) or the 'disposable classes', by which he meant those 'in which a certain ease allows men to receive a liberal education, to cultivate their reason, and finally to interest themselves in public affairs.'[42] This concept came unquestionably from Turgot's *Réflexions sur la formation et la distribution des richesses* with which he was thoroughly familiar.[43]

Sieyes studied Condillac's *Le Commerce et le gouvernement* when it appeared in 1776 and his notes show that he accepted Condillac's path-breaking analysis of the relationship of value and price according to which price served to commensurate or equate the different values that partners to an exchange placed on the same things.[44] There is no need, however, to conclude that he was a disciple of Condillac in economic matters. Not only had he developed his own critique of Physiocracy well before Condillac's book was published, his notes also show that he was by no means uncritical of the book itself.[45]

The final thinker who deserves to be taken into account as an influence on Sieyes' economic ideas is Adam Smith. Sieyes studied *The Wealth of Nations* when he was at Chartres in the 1780s, well after his first intensive bout of research into economic matters was over, and when he was studying England's financial and economic structures with some interest (doubtless with one eye on France's financial difficulties). He had a high regard for the work. Not only do we have Dumont's testimony to this effect but Sieyes himself referred to the book approvingly in his published and unpublished writings.[46] At the same time it is probably truer to say that Smith's book confirmed and deepened Sieyes' already existing convictions, rather than that it caused him to move in a new direction. It has been shown that his conviction that labour was the true source of wealth anticipated Smith, and in an important note that he wrote in the 1780s he actually claimed to have gone further than Smith before 1776:

> The part of Smith's work that seems to receive the most applause in France is his first chapter on the *division of labour*. There is however nothing in his ideas that had not become common among all our fellow citizens who occupied themselves with economic matters. It seems that Smith's work appeared in England in 1776. It was announced in the *Journal des savants* ... in February 1777 ... the first translation ... was made in 1781.
>
> In my own case I had gone further than Smith from 1770 onwards. Not only did I regard the division of labour *within the same craft*, that is to say, under the same *superior direction*, as the surest means to reduce costs and to increase production, I had also considered the *distribution* of the main professions or crafts as the true principle of progress in the social state. All that is but a part of my *representative order* regarding relations between individuals. To allow oneself to be represented is the *sole* source of civil prosperity. Let us begin with the first occupation, that of agriculture. Taking the natural law of territorial fertility as given amongst us, and as being for example 1 for 10, that is to say, one family produces enough subsistence for ten, it is clear that if the land-holding of such a farming family is divided between ten families, not only will nine industrial works be lost, but the ten families will die of hunger on their respective territorial share.
>
> Multiply { *the means* / the power to satisfy our *needs* }
>
> enjoy more, work less. That is the natural growth of liberty in the social state. Now this progress of liberty follows naturally from the establishment of *representative work*.[47]

Brief as it is this note is of crucial importance because it indicates that Sieyes' central idea of a representative system of government grew out of his broader idea that by specialization and separation, or by one group of people doing things 'on behalf of' another group and vice versa, all the main functions of society could be done more effectively, and more freedom be generated. To be sure, he believed that the specialization and separation of the political function had unique characteristics. He believed that it had to be deliberately constituted by the people; it could not be left to evolve spontaneously out of human interaction. Nonetheless it was an expression of the broader principle of division of labour by which society progressed.

This discussion has amply demonstrated that Sieyes, while firmly convinced of the need to separate private and public functions, was not for that reason a believer in *laisser faire*. The public power had positive economic functions to perform; there could be no blanket rule of non-intervention, or of leaving exchange to adjust everything. Sieyes maintained this view throughout his life. In an important note written during the Directorate or the Consulate he criticized the conception of economic science that was being developed by J.B. Say. Say wanted to systematize the insights that had been made by Adam Smith regarding the workings of an exchanging or commercial society. He thought the term 'political economy' was no longer adequate for a science that was concerned first and foremost with analysing the operations of the price mechanism, and not with government or its activities. Say proposed the rather pedantic alternative title of *onéologie* – roughly, the 'science of buying' – to describe the new discipline.

Sieyes strongly disagreed, in words that recalled his earlier strictures on the Physiocrats. 'Industry and human nature', he wrote, 'seem to me to be extremely restricted if one considers only their exchangeable product.' He continued:

> Viewed from the perspective of general welfare a human society seems to me extremely miserable when its individual members are represented simply as a multitude of agents or instruments of exchangeable production, as if a political association was nothing but the formation of a huge manufactory, where three classes of individuals – idle rentiers, active entrepreneurs and the instruments of labour – are engaged in a constant veiled war to possess the major part of the social product. Production and consumption are correlative things, though rarely equal; riches destined for sale, even those that are susceptible of sale without actually being sold, comprise only the smallest portion of consumption and production in the general movement. *Onéologie* thus has not yet been extended to the extent that it ought to be as a *political science*. I occupied myself systematically with this viewpoint in 1774 and the years following. It led me into the project for establishing public fêtes that I presented to the committee for public instruction in 1793 etc. *Fata negarunt*.[48]

If one is looking, not for an influence on Sieyes' ideas about political economy, but rather for an analogy with them, then possibly the most accurate choice would be the theories of Friedrich List – not List as the popular imagination sees him, or as a mere protagonist of tariff protection for nascent industries, but the List who obstinately maintained that the science of prices and economic exchange needed to be supplemented by a broader 'national political economy' that looked at the balance between the main components of the division and combination of labour that made up a given politically organized people, a balance that could not be left to the spontaneous workings of the market, but demanded the constant attention of the public power.

4 The influence of Voltaire, Montesquieu, Helvétius, Rousseau, and other French writers

It is clear from his unpublished notes that Sieyes as a young man had little respect for the *gens de lettres*. What attracted him was systematic, rigorous thought, not stylish badinage. Moreover in his first published work – the *Essay on Privileges* – he stated that it was time to go beyond the kind of campaigns that had been waged by the *hommes de lettres* in the past and to attack more relevant targets, by which he meant that it was the political problem and not the problem of religious dogma and persecution that now demanded attention.[49]

It might have been assumed therefore that he would have had little time for Voltaire, who could scarcely be called a systematic thinker, who preferred irony and ridicule to logical demonstrations, and who directed his fury chiefly at the Church. Yet there is sufficient evidence to suggest that Sieyes had a strong liking for Voltaire's writings. He referred to them quite spontaneously in his notes, perhaps most significantly during the crucial month of June 1789 when he was pondering on the name to be adopted by the Third Estate in its reconstituted form, and recalled Voltaire's use of the term 'national assembly'.[50] Daunou, although not entirely a reliable witness, stated that Sieyes was fond of reading and rereading Voltaire's works and was wont to say that *tous les résultats étaient là* – an enigmatic judgement that is probably best left as it is.[51] It is also perhaps not without significance that a portrait of Voltaire, badly executed to be sure, hung in Sieyes' room in the 1790s.[52]

To understand the attraction of Voltaire for Sieyes one has to remember that the latter not only liked the rigours of analysis but had himself a dry, biting wit, an eye for irony, and a talent for the arresting and sharply cutting phrase that he used to great effect in his pamphlets. It was probably this side of Sieyes' character that found Voltaire's spirit so congenial.

By contrast Sieyes did not have a high opinion of Montesquieu. He attacked the leading ideas of the *Esprit des lois* in a very interesting early fragment dated 1772.[53] It began: 'Montesquieu was wrong (1) in badly classifying the different governments, (2) in classifying them under names which do not indicate their *nature*, and (3) in having systematically believed each of them to be reducible to a single principle.' Sieyes went on to refute Montesquieu's claim that 'honour' was the 'principle' of monarchy. Honour in the sense of 'a love of distinctions and a jealousy of rank' was not an inherent part of monarchy but a part of the 'feudal and aristocratic system'. This system was reflected in the manners of much of France, but there was, Sieyes observed, a 'considerable, self-subsistent mass of the Third Estate' that had grown up 'beyond the chain' of feudal honour. From this Sieyes concluded that all of them could liberate themselves from it, and that France, instead of being, as Montesquieu thought, the home of so-called 'monarchical honour', would be the 'first to free herself from it.'

The germs of the revolutionary doctrines that Sieyes propounded in 1789 can be seen very clearly in this remarkable note of 1772, and they spring not out of Montesquieu's teaching but in direct, explicit antagonism to it. It was totally in the spirit of this note that Sieyes wrote in his revolutionary tract

What is the Third Estate? that the privileged orders shielded their selfish claims behind 'the imposing authority of the aristocratic Montesquieu.'[54] If it is recalled that Sieyes was also a persistent opponent of the English model of government with its upper and lower Houses of Parliament and its 'balance of powers' then the idea that he was a 'follower' of Montesquieu becomes completely untenable.

It would be rash though to conclude that Sieyes gleaned nothing at all from the vast repertoire of the *Esprit des lois*. If we consider Montesquieu's discussion and endorsement of representation, for example, we find echoes of Sieyes' later ideas – even if he disagreed in 1795 with a particular sentence in it.[55]

Helvétius is worth mentioning here primarily because Sieyes' critique of his book *De l'esprit* which dates from the years 1771–75 reveals so clearly that side of his mind which we have already detected in his critique of Condillac and Bonnet. Sieyes rejected entirely Helvétius' declared ambition to '*faire une morale comm' une physique expérimentale*'. 'You wish,' Sieyes wrote, 'to deduce principles from facts; it would be far better to consult the nature of man, to observe what his end is, to seek the means by which to procure it, and then to frame the laws which should guide him. Those are the sole principles of morality.' If, Sieyes continued, man merely obeys 'the impression of nature like celestial bodies' he could never stray from his allotted path. But 'if he can, if, in a word we give him back his liberty, it is necessary to use a quite different method to discover his laws and to form the principles which can guide him.'[56]

These words, which are reminiscent of Rousseau's rejection of Helvétius' doctrines, lead us on to consider the relationship of the author of the *Contrat social* to Sieyes. It is perhaps the most interesting problem posed by an analysis of the origin of Sieyes' thought, and it does not seem possible to answer it except in a qualified manner. On the one hand there was unquestionably an important element or characteristic of Sieyes' thought that coincided with an element in Rousseau's – quite apart from any particular details about the organization of government that Sieyes may have derived from Rousseau. On the other hand the overall thrust of Sieyes' thought ran in a quite different direction from that of Rousseau.

Sieyes mentions Rousseau or his works by name only a handful of times in his unpublished notes, and he refers to him only once, without actually naming him, in his published writings. Despite this disappointing paucity of direct references, and the lack of any sustained analysis by him of Rousseau's writings, there can be little doubt that Sieyes was thoroughly familiar with them. This is obvious not only from the style of the notes – in one of them Sieyes refers simply to 'J.J.',[57] in another he refers *en passant* to Rousseau's ideas on music,[58] while in two others he cites a Latin tag taken from Rousseau's *Discours sur l'inégalité*[59]– but also from Dumont's observation that the *Contrat social* was one of Sieyes' favourite books when he was living in Chartres, and from the strong echo of Rousseau's words that are to be found in some of the products of Sieyes' pen.[60]

The most detailed and informative of Sieyes' references to Rousseau are sharply critical of him and date from the time of the Jacobin dictatorship or shortly after. Sieyes clearly thought that the movement that created this dictatorship had been largely inspired by Rousseau's ideas. Thus in one of his notes he criticizes those who thought that a study of early societies could serve as a guide for present reforms. 'Philosophy', Sieyes wrote, 'did not preside at the birth of societies', though if men wished to know how to develop a 'good social state' then they should consult philosophy. In France, he went on, a terrible degeneration had taken place: 'People thought they were getting closer to nature by dedicating themselves to all man's native crudity. Rousseau, you provoked this feeling. It is by nature indefinite; it has no stopping-point in the multitude. If you had spoken reason you would only have done good. Reason limits itself. Ideas have but a restricted sphere.'[61]

In his autobiography Sieyes took his critique of Rousseau further. The passage below comes at the end of a swingeing attack on the way the Revolution of 1789 had been deformed and distorted by the men who had come to power in the wake of the Second Revolution in 1792.

> How many words have sprung from the abuse that these miserable people [i.e. the Jacobins and their followers] made of the terms *revolution, revolutionary!* To take them as meaning a political mutation, a change of constitution or government, and the ensuing advantages of good legislation, was [in their view] to identify oneself with the *traitors* who had sworn the oath of the Tennis Court and undermined royalty in 1789, and the moderates who had conquered the tyrant and proclaimed the Republic in 1792. A true revolution, such as they wanted to make, had to be a general overthrow, and the complete ruin of all the links that bind men and things together in the civil order and the economic order. That was what they called the complete regeneration of a people corrupted by the aristocracy of intelligence, commerce, and wealth.
>
> Alas! Has not a justly celebrated writer [i.e. Rousseau] who would have died of sorrow if he had known his disciples, a philosopher as perfect in sentiment as he is weak in vision, has he not himself, in his eloquent pages, so rich in accessory detail, so poor at root, confused the *principles* of the social art with the *beginnings* of human society? What would one say if, in another sphere of mechanics, one saw people undertaking to repair or construct a ship of the line with only the theory and only the resources of savages making canoes?[62]

There is one other express reference by Sieyes to Rousseau that deserves to be mentioned. It comes in an unpublished paper of his entitled *Bases of the social order*, written in late 1794 or early 1795. In it Sieyes developed once again his own conception of the social and political order, stressing the benefits and the necessity of representation, which he said had 'taken hold of almost all the actions of men'. He continued: 'An unhappy phrase by J[ean] J[acques] alone opposes this unanimous concert. "The will", he says, "cannot be represented". Why not? It is not a question here of the whole will of man, and there are numerous examples of private people and of powers who treat of this or that matter by way of procuration. Besides, in the social state with which we are concerned, it is always possible for the man who refuses to submit to the decision taken by his representative to quit the association.'[63]

These fragments by Sieyes help us to build up a general picture of his attitude towards Rousseau. Clearly this attitude was not entirely negative. He thought Rousseau was 'justly celebrated', 'perfect in sentiment', the composer of 'eloquent pages, rich in accessory detail'. At the same time there was patently a great gulf between them.

If one stands further back so that the overall contours of each man's ideas come into perspective, the points of overlap and distinction become clearer. The comparison can perhaps best be made by concentrating on three of the main themes in Rousseau's thought, and by considering Sieyes' position in the light of them.

The first theme, and the one which in the popular mind is most closely identified with Rousseau, is his determination to uncover the 'natural man' that had been overlaid and obscured by historical man. For Rousseau it was essential, if one was to get a clear picture of what man's goal and vocation was in this world, to get back to man as he first emerged from nature's hands, or in other words to strip away all that was artificial or man-made in his character. The result of this process of scouring away all the accumulated layers of artificiality was Rousseau's famous hypothetical picture of pre-historical man living a simple, spontaneous, immediate, unreflective and repetitive, day-to-day, hand-to-mouth existence. This innocent hypothetical world provided Rousseau with the benchmark by which he could assess the course of history. To be sure, he accepted that man necessarily had to move out of the 'state of nature', that man was more than a mere animal; that he had potentialities within him that were unique. Nevertheless he argued that, except for a short early period when, as he put it, a 'just mean' was established between 'the indolence of the primitive state and the petulant activity of our egoism,' the process by which man had in fact moved beyond the primitive state had been disastrous for the development of the human species.[64]

The course of human history, in other words, stood condemned by Rousseau. It had been a grotesque error. In struggling to develop the natural world by a process of division of labour, in creating wealth, commerce, letters, the liberal and mechanical arts, in founding bodies politic, man had enslaved himself to his fellow man, and to nature, and to his wants. He had constructed for himself a wholly corrupt world of inequality, ambition, competition and greed. Instead of elevating himself he had degraded himself.

In reasoning in this way Rousseau was not so much opposing the 'naturalism' that was so strong a feature of Enlightenment thought, as taking it to a novel extreme. He pitted 'nature' against 'art' with a real vengeance.

Needless to say such an antithesis found little or no echo in Sieyes' mind. As we have seen from his reactions to Condillac, to the Physiocrats, and to Helvétius, Sieyes rejected naturalism completely. In subjecting the social world to his favoured method of analysis and recomposition he did not assume that what was 'natural', in the sense of being spontaneous, involuntary, immediate, unsullied by 'art' or 'artifice', was the yardstick by which all was to be measured. Clearly he did not believe that all that man had made historically was perfect, but he did not believe that the way to orientate oneself in order to reform corruption was to construct a hypothetical counter-world of 'pure nature'. Man was not 'pure nature'.

This brings us to the second main theme in Rousseau's thought, where he and Sieyes were in much greater accord. Rousseau was not only convinced that the first, pure impulses of nature were the one safe starting-point for assessing what man was meant to be, he was also firmly convinced that man was not a mere animal mechanism, that he possessed a soul, a *moi*, an active 'immaterial substance' (to use his words) within him.[65] Man in a word was a free being. This may seem paradoxical, and to accord ill with his naturalism, but Rousseau himself did not mind the paradox or see a contradiction. He sought out 'natural man' to contrast him with historical man and to point up the decline of the species but he did not believe in a return to 'natural man'. Man was destined to go beyond the animalic however much he had hitherto failed to do so.

This emphasis on man's liberty of course played a decisive role in Rousseau's theory of how the reformed and authentic body politic should be constituted, the theory which he outlined so forcibly in the early chapters of the *Contrat social*. Given man's freedom, the only obligatory form of rule was, in Rousseau's eyes, one which was made by those who were to be subject to it. In his own words, 'We must always go back to an original covenant.'[66]

With this theme in Rousseau's thought Sieyes was almost entirely in agreement, indeed his concern to uphold man's quality as a free agency against Condillac's sensationalist theories runs strikingly parallel to the argument about man's soul that Rousseau conducted in the *Profession de foi du vicaire savoyard*. Sieyes' doctrine of political rule was based unequivocally on the idea that it had to be constituted from below, and that it could not be legitimated by 'nature' or 'God' or some other source independent of the will of the people. Finally Sieyes' theory, like Rousseau's, was based on the idea of an original contract between those who sought to establish a form of political rule.

This area of convergence between Sieyes and Rousseau leads directly on to a further area of profound divergence. Rousseau's view of the form and function of the properly constituted state was far removed from that of Sieyes. The difference was not merely that they had a preference for different organizational techniques; that Sieyes approved of representation and Rousseau did not. It went deeper and related to Rousseau's *Weltanschauung*, his vision of man's historical corruption, a vision that Sieyes rejected. For Rousseau the creation of the authentic body politic was essentially the restoration of man to his true vocation on earth, a vocation which he had historically betrayed. This vocation was a moral one; it consisted in man subjecting himself unconditionally to the moral law or the voice of duty. It was to this end that man, in Rousseau's eyes, ought to have used his freedom in moving beyond the state of nature.

The creation of the Rousseauan body politic was hence in a sense a restarting of history at the point at which it had gone wrong. The 'social contract' by which it was founded was a mutual agreement by a group of people in which they bound themselves to be governed in future by the general will or the law, which Rousseau saw as substantive unchanging rectitude, a celestial voice that spoke to each man from the bottom of his heart if only he took the pains to listen to it in the silence of his passions. It was obvious to him that such moral self-government could only be done by the citizens themselves – it could not be done 'on their behalf' by 'representatives' without losing precisely its moral quality. Similarly the authentic body politic had to be carefully moulded so as to shut out or root out all those baneful influences that in the course of history had led man away from his original moral purpose. Rousseau's austere, rural, directly self-governing polity, engineered to give man a moral and communal existence, was a quasi-religious renunciation of the existing political, economic and social world. It was political theology.

Sieyes' revolutionary aims contained nothing as total or transcendent as this. He worked within the co-ordinates of history. He saw man's development of the earth and its resources, the division of labour, the multiplication of wealth, the growth of the arts and sciences, not as a denial but as a part of man's vocation on earth. He was a revolutionary because he saw in the Third Estate in France the embodiment or prefiguration of a new, just and efficient division of economic and political labour that was destined to replace the corrupt and inefficient one that had congealed in France since the medieval period. He had no moral qualms about the representation of man's will; on the contrary representation was the very essence of social life. To be sure he saw the need for the genuine state to express and give effect to the 'common' or 'general will', which was more than merely 'what the majority wants. But he did not invest this will with the quasi-religious significance that Rousseau gave it. In one of his unpublished notes Sieyes wrote:

> The *end* of the political order is individual liberty, the private weal (*la chose privée*).
>
> Those people who think of it as an abstract thing, a public happiness that belongs to no one, deceive themselves. Almost all so called republican systems go wrong on this point. For them the public weal is nothing but an abstract being, a superstition, an idol to which one offers victims. Mark well: the only real happiness is that of individuals.[67]

In another note he contrasted his own system with that of the 'moralists':

> In my system obligation derives from engagement. In that of the moralists they presuppose a higher authority, a will that has the right to command. Thus they all go back to the will of God, or alternatively, in their metaphysical reveries on the authority of reason, of an absolute reason, anterior to that of man, which ought to serve as a model, they do nothing other than deify this abstraction, and rejoin the ranks of the theocrats.[68]

These notes indicate the gap that separated Sieyes from Rousseau, though it has to be emphasized that they were written when Sieyes had had experience of the policies of Rousseau's fanatical followers. It is highly unlikely that he believed before 1789, or even before 1792, that men would actually seek to implement to the full Rousseau's doctrine of the complete regeneration of man. His close colleague, Lakanal, remarked that '*C'est en quelque sort la Révolution qui nous a expliqué le Contrat social.*'[69] Sieyes would probably have agreed.

Our conclusion is that the main thrust of Rousseau's reasoning about the state was quite different from that of Sieyes. The two men agreed that man was by definition a free being, and that the legitimate body politic had hence to be created from below, by the members of the political association, united by an engagement or contract. But on the form and end of the body politic, indeed on the form of the engagement, the gap between them was profound, and such inspiration as Sieyes may have derived from Rousseau regarding the concrete organization of public powers was related to details, not to fundamentals. Thus it is likely that Rousseau's discussion of kingship in his *Considérations sur le gouvernement de Pologne* influenced Sieyes' ideas on the same subject. Perhaps Sieyes' views on the separation of the legislative and executive powers, at least in his early published writings, derived in part from Rousseau. These borrowings do not affect the overall picture. Sieyes, it will be recalled, expressly said that Rousseau's doctrine, while 'poor at root', was 'rich in accessory details'.

Our conclusion accords with the broader thesis that Roger Barny has developed regarding Rousseau's influence on the French Revolution as a whole.[70] Barny reaffirms – in the face of a tendency by certain modern scholars to minimize it – the strong and continuous influence of Rousseau's ideas on the revolutionary movement from 1788 onwards, while at the same time he emphasizes that different aspects of Rousseau's teaching were taken up and came to the fore at different phases of the movement. Thus the Rousseauism of the early years, up until 1791, was rather different from that of the period after August 1792. This seems to be borne out by a consideration of Sieyes' case. A leader of the early movement, his ideas undeniably contained a Rousseauan element. But it was only an element. After the Second Revolution of 1792 men came to power whose ideas did not merely contain an element of Rousseauism but who were Rousseauans through and through, embracing his principles like true disciples. Robespierre was their leader. To these men, as we have already seen, Sieyes was completely opposed. They wanted, as he graphically put it, not a *ré-publique* but a *ré-totale*.[71]

Of the influence of other French writers and thinkers on Sieyes little requires to be said. He was obviously familiar with all the main works produced by his fellow countrymen on politics and economics in the half-century before the Revolution. Beyond the ones already mentioned, however, there seems to be little reason to select one or other of them as having influenced him significantly. We can be sure that he had read Mably and Holbach, for example, but there is little indeed in Sieyes' writings, published and unpublished, that justifies us in marking them out specially as 'influences'.

Eberhard Schmitt has recently drawn attention to the article (which he ascribes to Diderot, but which has been shown to be by Holbach) on *Représentants* in the *Encylopédie*, and suggested that there are links between it and Sieyes' doctrine of representation.[72] This is an interesting proposition. Sieyes must certainly have read the article and some of the ideas in it are reflected in those he later expressed. But it would be wrong to say that his concept of the representative system is to be found there. Holbach, progressive as he was, was chiefly concerned to recommend that all the main 'orders' or 'classes' of society ought to be represented in a modern political regime, while Sieyes went well beyond this.

There is also the problem that there were other writers who at this time were in favour of representation in government in more or less general terms. Montesquieu was one. Another good example is Chastellux, whose *De la Félicité publique* was published in 1772. Sieyes was so fired by this book that he had the idea of writing a sequel to it, but only got as far as a few rousing paragraphs directed against tyranny and superstition.[73] Chastellux attacked Rousseau's conception of the small state with no representation. 'For me,' he wrote,

> I think that there will only be solid and durable liberty, and above all felicity, amongst people where everything is done by representations ... a vast society, united by the same interests, and under the same laws, finds its repose in the division that it makes of its labours ... and in the same way that internal affairs are dealt with by representations, so war-like disputes are handled by representatives charged with settling them.[74]

Brief as Chastellux's discussion of representation is, it breathes a similar spirit to that of Sieyes.

Broad resemblances regarding general subjects such as representation, or property or liberty, between Sieyes and other French Enlightenment writers are hence not too difficult to find. It seems unprofitable to wander further in this direction, but better rather to restrict oneself to those areas and authors already discussed, where there is real evidence of a specific connection.

5 Possible English influences on Sieyes' political ideas: Locke, Hobbes, Harrington

Of the foreign influences on Sieyes' ideas only the English ones require to be discussed since Bastid has convincingly refuted the claims put forward on behalf of Spinoza. Adam Smith's influence has already been examined. Here we will consider at some of the other English names associated with Sieyes.

Was Sieyes the French counterpart of Locke? Several commentators have emphasized the parallels between the political ideas of the two thinkers. Unfortunately there is no evidence that Sieyes had a high esteem for Locke's political ideas, as distinct from his epistemological theories. Certainly there are areas of broad similarity. Sieyes saw property in things as an extension of property of one's faculties and placed great emphasis on the state's duty to guarantee property. Like Locke, he saw the people as the founding power of the body politic and an elected parliamentary assembly as a necessary part of the public establishment.

In this sense Sieyes was a 'Lockean'. But the value of such a categorization is seriously weakened by two considerations. First, there is no reason why Sieyes should have derived these ideas from Locke; in so far as they were derived, they could with equal and indeed more likelihood have emerged from Sieyes' intellectual encounter with the Physiocrats and Rousseau. The terminology which Sieyes used to discuss property has in fact more in common with that of the Physiocrat writer Mercier de la Rivière than that of Locke.

Secondly, to call Sieyes a 'Lockean' is to suggest that his political standpoint in 1789 was the same as that which Locke was attempting to justify in his *Two Treatises of Government* of 1790, when in fact there were considerable differences between the two. Locke was attempting to demonstrate that absolute monarchy was not a genuine form of political or civil society at all, and that a prince whose policies tended to the establishment of such a system could rightfully be resisted. He was also trying to demonstrate that if any government, no matter what its form, tampered with the property rights of the subjects then resistance was justified. His demonstration of the legitimacy of resistance rested on his conception of man's subjection to God's natural laws in a society that was prior to, and in a sense higher than the political association. This idea of the rightness of defending a natural God-given order against abuse by government was of course of decisive importance in the American Revolution.

Sieyes, by contrast, in 1789 was not concerned primarily with defending a natural God-given order against political abuse, but with *creating* a just and effective political order where none in his view existed. His goal was not resistance but inauguration; he wanted to found a political system that was positive, coherent and effective, not to restrain a government that was tending towards tyranny and arbitrariness. Here indeed lies the main difference between 1689 and 1789, and it shows why it is not always helpful to see Sieyes as being a 'French Locke'.

Hobbes is perhaps a surprising name to link with that of Sieyes. Surely the spiritual father of enlightened absolutism has little in common with the theorist of 1789? Yet it has to be remembered that Hobbes – unlike Locke – was concerned first and foremost with constructing an effective, rational and just political order in place of what he regarded as an irrational shambles. For this reason Sieyes might well have found a measure of inspiration in him, and there is indeed one brief reference that suggests that he did. It comes at the end of an early unpublished note which is worth quoting in full because it gives an interesting insight into Sieyes' conception of the historical foundation of states:

> The first feeling of man as he seeks to satisfy his needs is to treat as an enemy every living being that is capable of obstructing this end. It is in this spirit that he distinguishes harmful things, indifferent things, and all those things that can procure him enjoyment. But man, who of all beings is the most harmful and the most helpful to man, multiplies to the point where an isolated individual can no longer count on getting rid of this enemy. It is then that he has to capitulate and to form an association with him. That is the first step towards society, the true origin of social *dependence*. It is this word that changes his whole manner of being.
>
> Nonetheless man's end is still preserved. The earth is vast enough and produces enough for several men who have made a pact not to harm one another to find sufficient to satisfy their appetites. Then it is realized that the social bond itself is a very abundant source of wealth or enjoyment, that it is the true means to multiply them to the point where there is no longer any comparison to be made between the natural primitive state, which is a true state of war, and the state of association. The latter only suffers by comparison because ignorance and passions cause legitimate dependence to degenerate into tyranny. Such is the history of all nations.
>
> These are the ideas of dependence that it is essential to impart to children. Man of all the beings who can harm us is the only one who requires to be treated with tact. For the greater good it has become necessary to share the cake and to introduce the ideas of just and unjust. On this subject I cannot help laughing at the stupidity of all those pedants who because they cannot see the point of what is being said continually rail against Hobbes and all the authors who have thought. Every man who has thought about what he says, every original author, is right at least in his principles. It is the doctors and compilers who have perverted everything.[75]

Sieyes thus looked back not to an original idyll, but to an original warlike state, and did not pronounce the conventional anathema on Hobbes. The distance between the two thinkers is less than one might have imagined.

Finally there is the link between Sieyes and James Harrington, something which English commentators on Sieyes have understandably highlighted, and French commentators have tended to ignore. Undoubtedly a link existed. There is a tiny piece of paper amongst Sieyes' unpublished notes, which is undated, but can be assigned with reasonable confidence to the period 1792–95. It consists simply of a few quotations from Harrington including his famous analogy of two girls sharing a cake, the one dividing and the other choosing.[76] Liljgren tells us that a Harringtonian tract was presented to the Convention in November 1792, and Harrington's *Works* were translated into French in 1795, so Sieyes' interest in the English author may have been stimulated by either or both of these events.[77]

It is possible that Sieyes had become acquainted with Harrington before this time. The name 'Harrington' is included in a long list of authors under the heading 'Translations' in his draft bibliography of 1770. Clapham suggests that the idea of rotation which formed part of Sieyes' electoral proposals for the legislature in 1789 may have come from Harrington, as well as his concept of redividing France territorially.[78] But the idea of rotation had been incorporated into the constitutions of some of the American states well before the French Revolution, and Sieyes' thoughts on the redivision of France are more convincingly explained in the context of the successive schemes for the reorganization of local administration in France that appeared in the years preceding the Revolution, in the last of which Sieyes himself was personally involved (the provincial assemblies).

Other attempts, such as that of Liljgren, to demonstrate that Harrington's influence was a far-reaching one, seem equally dubious. It has to be stressed that Harrington's schema of government, in its fundamentals, was quite different from that of Sieyes. Harrington had no conception of the people or nation as one constituent power establishing a unified structure of functionally differentiated political institutions. Harrington still thought of political institutions incorporating specific estates or orders. He saw the task of the rationally inspired ruler as being that of fixing the balance of land ownership within the community he ruled, and of constructing legislative institutions to reflect this underlying balance of land ownership. Such a conception was far removed from Sieyes' political vision.

Where then did the influence of Harrington lie? The evidence indicates that it was limited to one specific constitutional technique: that of giving one part of the legislature the power to propose, and another the power to decide. This technique is to be found in Sieyes' constitutional proposals in 1795 and 1799 but not in his earlier proposals. It sprang undoubtedly from his study of Harrington at some time between 1792 and 1795, of which his unpublished note is the record.

6 Conclusion

This chapter has necessarily been far-ranging. Its main aim has been to bring some precision into the discussion of the shaping forces behind Sieyes' political thought. As a young, intellectually enquiring man, imprisoned in an ecclesiastical career that he had not chosen and that he found profoundly unpalatable, his mind was stimulated and absorbed by the 'alternative literature' of the Enlightenment that he found about him, and it is difficult to envisage him becoming a revolutionary without the aid of this intellectual environment. Yet at the same time he had a powerful mind that did not passively accept what it read. He was no mere transmitter and applier of the ideas of the others. He formed his own synthesis, and it was this synthesis that he attempted to apply in 1789.

As has been shown, he quickly broke with what was perhaps the most characteristic trend of Enlightenment thought, the trend of naturalism, or the tendency to see in the unconscious, unreflective mechanisms of the natural world the key to an understanding of man. For Sieyes, by contrast, man was a self-willed agency, whose very essence was to distinguish himself from the world of 'nature' and to use it for his own ends. His doctrine of the formation and end of the state was based unequivocally on this idealist notion of personality. In this respect it was at once a product of the Enlightenment and a move beyond it.

In asserting man's inherent liberty Sieyes' intellectual development ran parallel with Rousseau. But Rousseau, as we have seen, placed man's freedom in a wholly different context from that of Sieyes. Rousseau wanted man to use his freedom to slough off all the corrupting influences that sprang from his historical struggle with nature and to submit himself unreservedly to the moral law, which was his original vocation. Sieyes wanted man to use his freedom to create a new framework within which his historical struggle with nature could be conducted both justly and fruitfully. They envisaged different revolutions, and both were to be attempted in the revolutionary epoch.

Of all the influences on Sieyes' thought the most important would appear to have been three encounters. There was the encounter with Condillac's philosophy, which stirred him to develop his own concept of man's essential character, and which also gave him a method – analysis – of understanding society scientifically. There was the encounter with the Physiocrats and Turgot which stirred him to reconstruct society as a productive conjunction of public and private labour, in contrast to the confused, unproductive mélange of the *ancien régime*. In these speculations about the division of labour in society Sieyes' guiding idea of representation had its most important root. Finally, there was the encounter with Rousseau–an encounter less well documented than the others but still, one senses, of decisive importance. From this Sieyes developed a clearer vision of the way free men came together to constitute the body politic.

3 The revolutionary principle: the nation repossesses itself

All emancipation is a *leading back* of the human world, of relationships, to *men themselves*.

Karl Marx, 'Zur Judenfrage', in *Die Frühschriften*, ed. S. Landshut (Stuttgart, 1968), 199.

SIEYES' POLITICAL THOUGHT contained both a revolutionary doctrine and a constitutional doctrine. On the one hand he sought to demonstrate how and why a complete break should be made with the *ancien régime*. On the other he sought to map out the kind of political system that ought to be established in France to replace the chaos that existed. It is now time to explore the substance of these two doctrines, and there can be no better place to start that than with Sieyes' concept of the nation, for this was at once the heart of his revolutionary doctrine and the basis or point of departure for his constitutional theory.

'Already', Sieyes wrote in August 1788, 'the patriotic and enlightened citizens, who for so long have looked with sadness and indignation upon all these millions of men heaped together without order and without design, give themselves some hope. They believe in the power of circumstances; they finally see the moment arrive for us to become a *nation*.'[1]

These sentences provide the theme of the four great revolutionary tracts by Sieyes that were published between November 1788 and February 1789. The 'moment' that he saw coming was of course the meeting of the Estates-General which had been fixed for May 1789. It was crucial, in his eyes, that this moment should be seized firmly. The first priority was for the nation to use the occasion to reassert itself, to take back its rights, and then to make a constitution. It was no use, in his view, tinkering with the existing superstructure, or trying to mend the roof before the foundations were laid. It was no use seeking merely to obtain the redress of a bundle of grievances, or taking steps to adjust the balance of power between the three orders in the Estates-General so that the 'people' carried more weight than in the old days when the assembly last met.

The real task lay much deeper than this. It consisted in replacing a confused and fortuitous assortment of political institutions by a public order consciously fashioned to achieve the true ends of a body politic or, as Sieyes wrote, in raising 'the edifice of a human society organized finally for the utility and happiness of the members who compose it.'[2] The fortuitously 'given' had now to be deliberately 'made'. But who was to make or build this edifice? For Sieyes there could be only one answer: the nation. This was why the first priority had to be for this maker or creator to manifest itself, to appear. Everything was secondary to bringing about the crystallization of the nation as an active, independent power.

For Sieyes this process of national self-assertion was intrinsically an act of separation and repulsion. The nation could become itself only by distinguishing itself from what was alien to it and by sloughing off this foreign element. It had to recognize that entities closely enmeshed with it were wholly extraneous to it. It had to withdraw itself from the adventitious historical structures in which it had been dispersed, subjugated and paralysed. The rootless and unbounded power of royal ministers was only the first of such alien powers; beyond this lay the division into orders, corporate distinctions, provincial barriers, privileges of every kind and above all, the heart and soul of privilege, the nobility. Sieyes, in 1788 and the early months of 1789, saw himself as guiding the nation in its task of self-identification. Assuredly he could not himself 'create' the nation, but as a writer and thinker he could assist it to become itself; he could 'enlighten' it as to its true friends, its true enemies, and its true mission. His four great tracts were devoted to this task. Then, in June 1789, he moved even closer to the great act of self-identification. As a duly accredited representative of the Third Estate, he put forward the motion which enabled the 'nation' formally to 'recognize itself' as a self-subsistent political reality, capable of constituting a new political structure for the country. Out of the Estates-General a national constituent assembly was born.

It was because Sieyes thought in this way, because he thought not in terms of particular changes in the political structure of the country, but of establishing a completely new source from which the whole political structure would henceforth emanate as a deliberate, rational totality that he was, from the start, a revolutionary. And it was because a significant portion of the Estates-General followed in practice the path that he had sketched in his writings, and because the people at large then massively endorsed the steps that had been taken, that the French Revolution *was* a Revolution.

Let us now explore further the nature of this radical act of national self-appropriation which was both the first presupposition of Sieyes' thought, and the inception of the Revolution. How precisely did Sieyes envisage the nation? Was it an ideal, a reality, or both together? From what had the nation to distinguish itself?

Two possible misunderstandings may be forestalled at the outset. Sieyes wrote in terms of a 'restoration' of the nation and the 'restitution' of its rights.[3] It was not only a question of the French people acquiring or becoming something new, but of recovering what had been 'usurped',[4] of clearing away political 'superstition' so that the body it degraded might reappear 'in all its natural force and beauty.'[5] This did not mean, however, that Sieyes believed that the way forward in 1788 and 1789 lay in a search for historical evidence about the nature of early, unvitiated political communities and an attempt to imitate them. It has been stressed sufficiently in previous chapters that Sieyes did not think in this kind of historical or anthropological manner, and was particularly scathing about those who did. His talk of 'restoration', 'regeneration' and 'restitution' signified his more general belief that in the course of history, and more especially since the establishment of feudalism, the nation had not been allowed to enter into its political inheritance. Its rights had been usurped by other bodies, in particular the aristocracy or nobility. There is no sense in Sieyes of a specific historical time at which what was pure had become corrupted, and certainly no sense, as there was in Rousseau, of a pre-historical idyll which history itself had destroyed. There is, however, in Sieyes a strong sense that man's free essence which, as will be shown, was intimately bound up with his concept of the nation, had been historically prevented from finding its proper outlet in the political organization of the country, that feudalism both authentic and decadent was a monstrous barbarism, and that the time was ripe at the end of the eighteenth century for this grotesque historical aberration to be corrected.

Sieyes' nation was thus not tied to a past image of purity. Neither was it an ethnic concept, founded on such non-rational or pre-rational elements as blood, race or the possession of a particular 'tongue'. He did not, in other words, argue that there existed a racially and linguistically authentic French nation which ought to separate itself from those who were not authentically French in this sense. At the start of his essay on the Third Estate he briefly considered the argument that the special position of the French aristocracy was justified by the fact that they were the descendants of a Germanic race of conquerors. He mocked this argument by saying that, by the same token, the non-Germanic race of the Third Estate could argue that it was justified in conquering the invaders and becoming an aristocracy in its turn. In reality the races were mixed and the blood of the Germans and non-Germans had become mingled, so the argument based on race was, in his eyes, completely irrelevant.[6] Having swept it aside he proceeded with his own argument about nationhood which was based, as will be shown, emphatically on rational principles.

Instead of saying that the nation was an ethnic entity, Sieyes said that those who did not form an integral part of the French nation on other grounds, that is to say because of the divisive system of political and civil privileges, could be *compared* to those who were 'foreign' in the more conventional sense of being ethnically and linguistically distinct. Thus he once likened the aristocrats to the 'Algerians' of France[7], and on another occasion he wrote that each of the three orders of clergy, nobility and communes in the Estates-General was 'a distinct nation, no more able to mix in the affairs of the others than the Estates-General of Holland or the Council of Venice, for example, could vote in the deliberations of the English Parliament.'[8]

Having stressed that Sieyes' concept of the nation was not an ethnic one, it has to be recognized that there was a small but interesting linguistic side to his 'nationalism'. He was at once repelled and fascinated by the subtle, arcane language that the nobility used, which he said needed its own special dictionary. He saw the Revolution as abolishing for ever words like *taille*, *franc-fief*, *ustensiles*, *roturiers*, and so on. And as has already been mentioned, he himself had a propensity for inventing new words to express the new order: *adunation* is perhaps the best example. This linguistic 'struggle' was however only a by-product of the central one.

If we try to identify the positive features of Sieyes' concept of the nation we are led not to one simple idea, but to a combination of ideas. This combination was not accidental. It was not a confusion. On the contrary, it was a conjunction of the ideal and the real, and the right and the useful, in a way that gave the whole concept tremendous power. If we pick apart the meanings that are fused together, we find that there are three. First and foremost, the nation was a moral necessity, the equal union of individuals which lay at the foundation of every properly constituted political order. Second, the nation was a politico-economic necessity, a union of private works and public functions, something capable of satisfying man's needs more comprehensively and effectively than anything else. Lastly, the nation was an historical entity, a reality growing up within the very interstices of the *ancien régime*, in the form of the Third Estate. In sum, the nation for Sieyes was the Third Estate as the historical embodiment or carrier of a new political unity, one that answered to the demands both of political right and of politico-economic utility.

1 The nation as an equal union of individuals that constitutes the public establishment

Let us look in turn at the three ingredients of Sieyes' concept of the nation. First, there is his idea of the nation as an equal union of individuals. France, as an authentic political body, he was arguing, was at root such a union. It was not a union of corporations, or of provinces, or of estates. These were all 'multiple' unions, or unions of unions. The essence of nationhood was to be *one* union, a union of the very components out of which all other unities were made. Sieyes endlessly repeated the two words in conjunction – *une* nation, une nation *une*[9] – to emphasize their strict correlation. The concept was basically an assertion of individual equality, of *l'égalité du civisme*[10] as he expressed it at the end of *What is the Third Estate?*

Where did this idea of the nation as the union of individuals that lay at the foundation of the political order come from? The answer is that it came from Sieyes' analytical investigation of the body politic. It was a product of political theorizing in the modern contractual style that had been inaugurated by Hobbes. Here we link up directly with the account that was given in chapter 1 of Sieyes' method of reasoning. As this account showed, he regarded the meeting of the Estates-General as a unique opportunity for implementing the principles of political science or what he called the 'social art'. What was the method of this science? Analysis and reconstruction. In Sieyes' words (which could have been written by Hobbes): 'The social mechanism will never be understood unless one undertakes to analyse society like an ordinary machine, to consider each part separately, and then to rejoin them all in the mind, one after the other, in order to grasp their congruence and to understand the general harmony that ought to result from them.'[11] By employing this analytical method it could be demonstrated that the nation was the basis of all rightfully organized political bodies, or what Sieyes called the constituent power.

To what indissoluble primary element was one driven when one took political society apart in this fashion? For Sieyes the answer was plain: the individual human being as inherently a free, that is to say a self-determining being. 'Each man ... has the innate right to deliberate and to will for himself, to oblige himself, to make contracts with others, and consequently to impose laws on himself.'[12] 'It is necessary always to go back to the will free by essence as the unique source from which all laws which strike man with a genuine obligation are directly or indirectly derived.'[13] It was impossible for force to bind men together in any genuine way. Force was the constraint to which natural objects were subject, 'a mechanical compression which produces *effects* without producing obligation.'[14] Men were not natural objects. A genuine political order had to *oblige*, and it could not oblige if the constraint inherent in it was mediated by the free will that was characteristic of man.

To reconstruct the body politic in its rightful, logical order one had therefore to posit, as the first stage, a society formed by an 'engagement' between each and every individual, or at least between every 'head of family', for Sieyes was not prepared to quibble over such details.[15] 'A man can offer and *exchange* something for something, engagement for engagement. All is exchange amongst men; and in every act of exchange there is necessarily a free act of the will on either side; but no man has the right to *dominate* another; a maxim to the contrary would open the door to every crime, to every horror, and to the crushing of all rights.'[16]

This first engagement formed the nation. As Sieyes wrote in *What is the Third Estate?* in the first hypothetical 'epoch' of the body politic we must conceive of a more or less considerable number of individuals who wish to unite. 'By this fact alone they already form a nation: they have all the rights of one; it only remains to exercise them. This first epoch is characterized by the play of *individual* wills. The association is their work; they are the origin of all power.'[17] The first stage of political society or the 'social contract' was hence not an engagement between a number of individuals to decide what they would give to society and what they would retain. It was an engagement to form a union, to act together, to act as one. On the other hand this formation of a union, or society, or nation, had a purpose. It was not an *acte gratuit*. It was precisely the need to enable society to fulfil its purpose that led to what Sieyes called the second 'epoch' in the construction of the political order.

> The second epoch is characterized by the *common* will. The associates wish to give their union consistency; they want it to fulfil its purpose. They therefore confer and agree amongst themselves on the public needs and the means to provide for them. Hence power can be seen to belong to the public. To be sure individual wills are always the origin of it, and they form its essential elements; but considered separately their power is nil. It resides only in the whole. The community must have a common will; without *unity* of will it would not form a willing and acting totality. Clearly too this totality possesses no right that does not belong to the common will.[18]

This account of the first and second stages in the creation of a political order in *What is the Third Estate?* needs to be supplemented by the account given of this same initial process in the *Views*:

> As soon as we posit an association, it requires freedom to will and to make contracts, be it with other associates, or its own members, or foreign individuals. To fulfil its common needs it needs a *common* will. This will must naturally be the general product of all the particular wills, and doubtless the

> first common will of a number of men who are posited as unity in political society is exactly the sum of all the individual wills. But to insist that the common will was always precisely the sum of all wills would be to renounce the possibility of willing in common in the future, it would be to dissolve the social union. It is therefore absolutely necessary to resolve to recognize all the characters of the common will in a common majority [which Sieyes remarks in a footnote could take any of a number of forms]. And do not imagine that by making such an agreement, society is only governed at the base by an incomplete will. Each member, by his act of union, makes a permanent contract to regard himself as bound by the opinion of the majority, even when his particular will should form part of the minority. He submits to it, we say, in advance by a free act of his will, and he only reserves the right to leave the association, to go abroad, if the laws that are being made fail to suit him; so that his continued residence becomes a voluntary acquiescence in the majority, a tacit but positive confirmation of the first agreement by which he imposed on himself the obligation to regard the common will as his own. But always this common will, in whatever way it is formed, is made up solely of the individual wills of the citizens, this alone entitles it to impose a genuine obligation on all and makes law for the whole community.[19]

It is clear that there is a slight divergence between this account and that provided in *What is the Third Estate?* In the latter a nation is formed out of a union of individual wills (first stage) and then by an agreement to form a single common will for public matters (second stage). There is no explicit discussion of the way this common will emerges. In the *Views*, by contrast, the very formation of the nation is by definition the formation of a body which acts by some kind of majority decision. The omission of an explicit reference to the origins of the majority principle in *What is the Third Estate?* must surely be seen as purely accidental, a product of the speed at which Sieyes composed the work. In fact, in the rest of the essay, it is taken for granted that the will of a nation, the common will, as it expresses itself before any constitution has been made, can be expressed only by the will of the majority. He writes for example that 'a nation can never decree that the rights inherent in the common will, that is to say in the plurality, can pass to the minority.'[20] The maxim that the common will and the will of the majority are the same he describes as 'incontestable'.[21]

This interpretation is confirmed by Sieyes' words in his exposition of the *Rights of man and citizen* written a few months after the essay on the Third Estate. Here he reverts, in his account of the formation of a body politic, to the language of the *Views*, and develops the concept of 'mediate unanimity' to express the kind of original contract between individuals that stands at the basis of the rightfully ordered state. The passage is worth quoting in full:

> A political association is the work of the unanimous will of the associates.
>
> Its public establishment is the result of the majority will of the associates. Unanimity being a very difficult thing to achieve in the smallest of communities, it is clear that it becomes impossible in a society of several million individuals. The social union has its ends; it is necessary therefore to use such means as are possible to achieve them; it is necessary therefore to be satisfied with the majority. But it is worth observing that even then there is a kind of mediate unanimity, for those who have unanimously willed to unite to enjoy the advantages of society, have unanimously willed all the means necessary to

> procure these advantages. The choice of the means alone is delivered over to the majority, and all those who have their wish to express, agree in advance to abide constantly by this majority. Hence two respects in which the majority rightly substitutes itself for the right of unanimity. The general will is thus formed by the will of the majority.
>
> All public powers without distinction are an emanation of the general will, all come from the People, that is to say, the Nation. These two terms ought to be synonymous.[22]

Thus far we have covered only the first stages in Sieyes' analysis and logical reconstruction of the body politic. The final stage is yet to come, and it consists of the creation by the nation, acting by a common or majority will, of a representative system of government. Sieyes actually describes two alternative paths by which this final stage is reached.

According to the first path, which is described in the *Views*, the original (i.e. logically prior) small nation, acting by a majority will, is seen as growing in numbers to such an extent that it has to subdivide into a number of districts or cantons. Each of these subdivisions sends some of its members to carry the result of its majority decision to a common *rendez-vous*. In other words the original community transforms itself into a confederal structure. This system, however, soon reveals its inadequacy. Each deputy at the central *rendez-vous* being bound by the decision of his particular district, or in other words, being bound by an imperative mandate, it often becomes impossible to form a common will. In 'trying to reserve too immediately the exercise of their will, the associated members prevent it from acting.'[23] There is also the problem that, in counting votes at the common *rendez-vous* by districts, the will of all the individuals of the whole community will not be accurately expressed.

To obviate these difficulties, and to create for itself an effective and genuine common will, the community is driven to place greater confidence in its deputies. 'It confers on them power of attorney, so that they can meet, deliberate, reconcile their differences, and will in common: thus, instead of simple carriers of votes, it has genuine representatives.'[24] This does not mean that the latter can do what they like. That would simply be alienation. The overall extent of their powers – in the sense of the range of business they can treat – must logically be marked out and limited by the community. But 'the *power* or the right to propose, to deliberate and to decide within the framework of the function entrusted to the deputies, is necessarily unlimited. for it is essential that they are free to act and to act well, provided that they do not go beyond their mission.'[25]

It was also essential in this last stage to respect the maxim that 'each deputy represents the totality of the association.' In other words the various confederal districts or divisions would have to cease regarding themselves as separate wholes sending their own exclusive representatives to the centre, and would have to start regarding themselves as subdivisions of one whole, designed to elect the representatives of this one whole.[26]

In the *Views* the route from the small original democratic community to the large representative one passes by way of a confederal union based on regional imperative mandates. In *What is the Third Estate?* the route is much more direct, and the confederal stage is omitted. Here the first stage or 'epoch' is simply an act of union between a small group of individuals. The second stage is this union, or nation, acting by majority. Finally, in the third stage, the nation grows too numerous and extensive to exercise its common will directly. What do the members then do?

> They detach from it [i.e. the common will] all that is necessary to watch over and provide for public needs; and the exercise of this part of the national will and consequently of power is conferred on some of their members. Thus we arrive at the third epoch, that is to say a *government exercised by proxy*. Note several truths relating to it. 1. The community does not strip itself of the right to will; that is its inalienable property; it can only commit the exercise of this right. ... 2. The corps of delegates do not even have the plenitude of this exercise. The community has only conferred on them that portion of its total power that is necessary to maintain good order. In these matters one does not go beyond what is necessary. 3. The corps of delegates thus does not have the right to alter the boundaries of the power with which it has been entrusted. This faculty would plainly be self-contradictory.
>
> I distinguish the third epoch from the second, because here it is no longer the *real* common will that acts, but a *representative* common will. It has two ineradicable characteristics which must be repeated. 1. This will does not lie fully and unrestrainedly in the corps of representatives; it is only a portion of the great national common will. 2. The delegates do not exercise it by their own right, it is the right of others; the common will is only there in commission.[27]

The nature of Sieyes' analysis and reconstruction of the body politic, and the place in it of the 'nation' will by now be clear. The nation was the underlying compacted unity of free individuals that established or constituted a public order. As a community formed exclusively by and between individuals, and capable of acting by majority decisions, it was the constituent power. The social contract hence did not create a public order, it created the body of the people or nation, that created a public order. In Sieyes' words, the social contract could only be understood in the sense that 'it binds associates to one another.' It was 'a false and dangerous idea to suppose a contract between a people and its government. The nation does not contract with its mandatories, it *commits* the exercise of its powers.'[28]

It followed conversely that the nation could not itself be the *object* of a constitution. It was wrong to think of the nation as constituted, or to think of the relationship between different parts of a nation as *being* the constitution. This was the old idea, the idea that the historically evolved relationship or balance of power between kings, lords, clergy, and commoners *was* the constitution of the nation. The 'real way to misunderstanding', wrote Sieyes, 'is to confound all the parts of the social order under the name of constitution.'[29] The logic of this old system was that the constitution was made by the 'partners to it'. The constitution was a species of treaty. This again was a misunderstanding. A constitution, properly speaking, was a totality created by a single will anterior to it:

> The nation exists before everything, it is the object of everything. Its will is always legal, it is the law itself. Before it and above it there is nothing but *natural* law. If we wish to form a correct idea of the order of succession of the *positive* laws that emanate from its will, we see in first place the *constitutional*

> laws, which are divided into two parts: the ones regulate the organization and functions of the different *active* bodies. These laws are called *fundamental*, not in the sense that they can become independent of the national will, but because the bodies that exist and act through them cannot touch them. In each part the constitution is not the work of the constituted power but of the constituent power.[30]

It is clear, Sieyes continued, that the constitution related only to the government.

> It would be ridiculous to suppose the nation itself tied by the formalities of the constitution to which it has subjected its mandatories. If it had had to wait upon some way of being *positive* before it became a nation, it would never have existed. The nation forms itself solely by *natural* law. The government on the contrary can only belong to *positive* law. The nation is all that it can be by the sole fact that it exists. ... The national will ... need only be real to be always legal, it is the origin of all legality. ... Is there any authority which could have said to a multitude of individuals: 'I unite you under such and such laws; you will form a nation on the conditions that I prescribe to you'? We are talking here not of brigandage and domination, but of legitimate association, that is, voluntary and free.[31]

Sieyes used a further argument to demonstrate that it was logically impossible for the nation as the constituent power to be itself subject to a constitution. 'Perhaps it will be said', he wrote,

> that a nation can, by an original act of its will, independent as a matter of fact of all form, bind itself not to will in the future except in a particular way. But in the first place, a nation can neither alienate nor forbid itself the right of willing; and whatever its will may be, it cannot lose the right to change it when its interest demands. In the second place, to whom would the nation be bound? I can see how it can *oblige* its members, its mandatories, and all who belong to it; but how can it in any way impose duties on itself? What is a contract with oneself? The two sides being the same will, it is obvious that it can always free itself from the supposed contract.[32]

Not only was it impossible to think of the nation, *qua* constituent power, as subject to a positive constitution, it was wrong for it even to attempt so to subject itself:

> [A] nation *ought* not to place itself within the shackles of a positive form. This would expose it to the risk of losing its liberty irrevocably, for tyranny would only have to triumph for a moment to sacrifice the people, under the pretext of a constitution, to a *form* in which it would no longer be able to express its will freely, and hence to shake off the chains of despotism. One must regard the nations of the earth as individuals outside the social tie, or, in common parlance, in the state of nature. The exercise of their will is free and independent of civil forms. Existing only in the natural order, their will, to carry full effect, has only to carry the *natural* characteristics of a will. In whatever way a nation wills, it suffices that it wills; all forms are good, and its will is always the supreme law. If, in order to imagine a legitimate society, we have to presuppose that purely natural individual wills have the moral power to form an association, how can we refuse to recognize a similar force in the *common* will, equally natural? A nation never leaves the state of nature, and however many dangers surround it, it never has too many ways in which it can express its will. Let us not shrink from repeating: A nation is independent of all form; and,

> however it wills, it suffices that its will manifests itself, for all positive law to cease before it, as before the source and supreme master of all positive law.[33]

Here is Sieyes at his most revolutionary. The nation, as the community of individuals acting by majority, that is the source and fount of all positive political institutions, has an inalienable will, a will that it cannot 'sign away' by any positive arrangement, any more than an individual can 'sign away' his freedom by any positive arrangement. The will of the community only needed to be 'manifest' for it to be the supreme power. Sieyes was never to go this far again in emphasizing the inextinguishable residuum of freedom – the sovereignty, though he did not actually use this word – that dwelt in the nation.

In *What is the Third Estate?* Sieyes put forward one final argument to justify his proposition that the nation was the only rightful authority to pronounce on the bitter political struggle that was taking place in France. His final argument rested on the proposition that in any constituted government there had to be some power capable of terminating a dispute over the nature of the constitution itself. Normally the legislature, amongst a 'free people', is the proper place for this kind of ultimate decision to be taken. 'But what if the legislature itself, if the different parts of this first constitution do not agree amongst themselves – who then will be the supreme judge? For there must be one or anarchy will replace order.'[34]

Sieyes was here placing his finger on the central problem of the traditional 'mixed constitution' in which the legislature was formed of three 'estates' of the realm each of which possessed a veto power. Or, to put it another way, he was exposing the fundamental difficulty involved in a constitution that was formed by a pact or treaty between different parts of the community. He continued:

> One or more integral parts of a moral body are nothing separately. Power belongs only to the whole. As soon as one party appeals against a decision (*réclame*), the whole no longer exists; and if it no longer exists how can it judge? Thus we can understand that there would be no constitution in a country as soon as the slightest trouble arose between its parts, unless the nation existed independently of all rule and of all constitutional form.[35]

A 'mixed constitution' thus presupposed, for its peaceful continuity, a totality which was superior to the parts that formed the mixture. Sieyes passed from here directly to the situation early in 1789.

> It is patent that the parts of what you believe to be the French constitution [note the careful wording here: Sieyes was following through the assumptions of those who maintained that France already possessed a constitution prior to the Revolution, but he did not actually endorse this assumption himself] are in disagreement. Who has the right to decide? The nation, independent as it is necessarily of all positive form. Even if the nation had its regular Estates-General, it would not be for this constituted body to pronounce on a difference relating to the constitution. That would be a begging of principles, a vicious circle.[36]

It is clear from these words, and from all his other arguments, that well before the Estates-General met in May 1789, Sieyes was convinced that France required a constitution, and that the Estates-General, in its tripartite order-based form, could not make a decision about this matter. For him the question of the correct balancing of the component orders of the Estates-General, which exercised so many minds, was already an obsolete one. The only way forward was for the Estates-General to transform itself into – or be replaced by – a body that represented the nation as the constituent power, or the nation as a unity of equal individuals deciding by majority vote. Chapter 6 of *What is the Third Estate?* proceeded to sketch out the practical alternatives that followed from this crucial principle, and to indicate how, once the Estates-General had met, the nation as the constituent power could 'manifest itself'. These practical alternatives will be discussed later.

2 The nation as a totality of private works and public functions

Sieyes' concept of the nation as a totality of private works and public functions is a kind of politico-economic parallel to his concept of the nation as the constituent power. It does not require such extended treatment. In this second guise the nation is seen not as the community of individuals that form the basis of political power, but as the structured, differentiated unity that appears when a society is considered as a rationally organized, productive combination of labour. It would probably be more normal nowadays to call this structured whole the state, but Sieyes himself refers to it, in one of the most important passages in which he discusses it, as the '*nation complette*'.[37]

The 'private works' that formed an essential component of the 'complete nation' were examined by Sieyes on numerous occasions. As the previous chapter has shown, his unpublished notes written well before the Revolution indicate that he had long been preoccupied with the socio-economic composition of the body politic and that he had long seen labour as the key source of wealth. Just as in his more purely political speculations he was concerned to get back behind the system of 'estates' and 'orders' to the single nation as the constituent power, so in his studies in political economy he was concerned to get back behind the system of 'estates' and 'orders' to the truly useful and productive forms of labour that made up the nation. As described earlier, time and again, in the 1770s and 1780s, he anatomized society in an effort to show the logical concatenation of the various kinds of labour that together formed the whole. The opening paragraph of the first chapter of *What is the Third Estate?*, where he sketched the '*travaux particuliers*' that '*soutiennent la société*' may be seen as the culmination of these earlier efforts.

Sieyes divided the private works, on this occasion, into four 'classes', which he defined as follows:

> 1. Land and water providing the primary materials of human needs, the first class, in the order or ideas, is formed by those families devoted to work in the countryside. 2. Between the first sale of these materials and their consumption or usage, stands a second kind of labour, more or less multiplied, which adds a second value, more or less composite, to them. Human industry thus suceeds in perfecting the gifts of nature, and the raw product goes up one, ten, or a hundred times in value. Such are the works of the second class. 3. Between production and consumption, as between the different stages of production, stand a mass of intermediary agents, useful both to producers and consumers. These are the merchants and traders. The traders, ceaselessly comparing the needs of different times and places, speculate on the profit of storage and transport; the merchants devote themselves, in the last analysis, to selling either wholesale or retail. This type of utility characterizes the third class. 4. Apart

from these three classes of labouring and useful citizens, who concern themselves with *objects* appropriate for consumption and usage, it is necessary for a society to have a mass of private works and tasks that are *directly* useful or agreeable to *persons*. This fourth class embraces the most distinguished scientific and liberal professions as well as the lowliest domestic services.[38]

Agriculture, manufacturing, commerce and services: these were the four basic divisions of private labour that went to make up the 'complete nation' in Sieyes' eyes. On the composition of the public functions that co-existed with these private activities he was much less specific in the opening pages of *What is the Third Estate?* He was content there to say that, according to current usage, they were divided into four branches, namely the army, the law, the church and the administration. What he particularly stressed was that recruitment to these public functions ought to be free from monopolistic restrictions. 'Are not the effects of monopoly known?' he asked. 'If it discourages those it excludes, does it not also render those it favours less efficient? Is it not known that any work protected from free competition will be done less well and more expensively?'[39] The significance of these words will become more apparent when we consider the third sense in which Sieyes conceived the nation.

3 The nation as the Third Estate

The previous sections have shown that Sieyes saw the nation as first and foremost the unity of individuals that was the constituent power of the body politic, and secondly as the combination of labour that made up a rationally organized society. Now comes the concrete historical reality that Sieyes saw as the prefiguration of the nation in both these senses, namely the Third Estate. Here, within the *ancien régime* itself, lay the potential nation as constituent power, and the potential nation as a rationally organized combination of labour.

It is true that in the first revolutionary tract that he wrote – the *Views on the means of execution* which was composed in August 1788 – Sieyes did not place great stress on the Third Estate as the embodiment of the nation. In this tract he clearly hoped that, united by their hostility to 'ministerial despotism', all three Estates or orders of the realm or at least the bulk of them would work together to transform the forthcoming Estates-General into a single assembly, deciding by majority vote, which would authentically represent the nation as the constituent power, and which could then proceed to the framing of a constitution. The only persons whom he thought it would be logically necessary to exclude from such an assembly were all those who had not been elected, namely crown officials, dukes and peers, and princes of the blood.[40]

According to the *Views*, therefore, the nation would take possession of itself at one fell swoop, as soon as the Estates-General met. It was not until a few weeks after he had written this first pamphlet that Sieyes came to realize that his hopes of united action were based on a false premiss and that the nobility was going to hold fast to its traditional privileges and refuse to co-operate with the Third Estate in the work of national regeneration. In his own words, he came to see that 'it was no longer the entire nation wishing to recover its rights from the absolute power of the royalty; it was the *noblesse* ... seeking purely to assert its interests against those of the people, and hoping to ensure that its past and present claims would be accepted by the ministry simply by frightening it.'[41] Sieyes was here referring to the intransigent attitude adopted by the nobility between September and December, 1788.

It was from this moment onwards that Sieyes threw his whole weight behind the Third Estate, identifying its cause with that of the nation. In his *Essay on Privileges*, published in November 1788, he contented himself with a searing attack on the nobility. In *What is the Third Estate?* and the *Deliberations*, both published early in 1789, he equated the nation unequivocally with the Third Estate. As he wrote in the *Deliberations*: 'It is but improperly that the Third [Estate] is called an order; it is the nation; it has no corporate interest to defend; its unique object is the national interest. The Third Estate, or rather the nation, demands nothing less than to make the totality (*ensemble*) of citizens a *single* social body.'[42]

Sieyes' identification of the Third Estate with the nation can perhaps be illuminated by recalling the words of a later thinker, whose ideas owed not a little to his study of the French Revolution. When Marx wrote that Communism was not an ideal, or a state of affairs to be established, but rather 'the *real* movement that abolishes the present state of affairs'[43] and when he simultaneously defined the proletariat as being itself the 'dissolution' of existing society,[44] he was expressing almost exactly the same viewpoint that Sieyes had adopted in 1789 towards the nation *qua* Third Estate. And in the same way that Marx devoted himself to raising the proletariat to a true understanding of its historical mission as the dissolvent of existing society and the harbinger of Communism, so Sieyes saw his task as raising the Third Estate to a true understanding of its historical mission as the dissolvent of existing political society and the embodiment of the nation. 'It does not suffice', Marx wrote, 'for thought to press towards realization, reality must itself press towards thought.'[45] Sieyes would have agreed.

The problem was that the Third Estate, like Marx's proletariat, tended not to see beyond its own particular interests. It showed no real grasp of its true historic role as the nation. Its political demands were, as Sieyes repeatedly said, 'insufficient'.[46] Only if we realize this can we understand the irony of the last of the three resounding rhetorical questions with which Sieyes opened his most famous tract early in 1789:

1. What is the Third Estate? – *Everything.*
2. What has it been up till now in the political order? – *Nothing.*
3. What does it demand? – *To be something.*[47]

Sieyes' whole argument was that the Third Estate must – to quote the motto of his first written work – 'raise its desires to the level of its rights.' It must not merely demand to be 'something', it must see itself as the whole, and act accordingly. Why then was Sieyes convinced that this equation existed? Why did the Third Estate always 'blend in his mind' with the idea of a nation?[48]

There were many reasons. First of all there was the quantitative and qualitative transformation of the Third Estate which had taken place since the medieval period, that is to say since the ending of genuine feudalism. Sieyes, as noted earlier, was not only the man of reason; he was prepared to cite historical facts in their proper context. They could not in themselves determine what was 'right' but they could help to indicate that right was imminent in the concrete situation, that it was not merely a fanciful idea. This can be seen most strongly in a lengthy passage at the end of chapter 3 of *What is the Third Estate?* which is worth citing here in its entirety.

> The very people who invoke against the Third the authority of facts, could read in them their own rule of conduct if they were honest with themselves. A few good towns sufficed to form the Chamber of Communes of the Estates General under Philip the Fair.
>
> Since that time feudal service has disappeared, and the countryside has come to support a numerous population of *new citizens*. Towns have multiplied and grown larger. Commerce and the arts have created, so to speak, a multitude of new classes, amongst whom there are a large number of well-to-do families, filled with well educated men concerned with the public weal. Why has this double growth, far more important than that of the old towns in the balance of the nation, not led the same authority to create two new chambers in favour of the Third? Equity and good policy combine to pose the question.
>
> No one has dared to be so unreasonable with regard to a second kind of growth that has taken place in France; I mean that of the new provinces which have been united since the last session of the Estates-General. No one dares to say that these new provinces should not have their own representatives in addition to those at the Estates of 1614. But surely manufactures and arts, like territory, contribute new wealth, new sources of taxation, and a new population? Why then, since this kind of growth is so easy to compare to that of territory, why I say do they refuse to accord it representatives in addition to those at the Estates of 1614?
>
> But I use reason against people who are unable to understand anything beyond their own interests. Let us present them with the sort of consideration that touches them more closely. Is it fitting for the nobility of to-day to retain the language and attitudes of the gothic era? And is it fitting for the Third Estate to languish at the end of the eighteenth century in the sad and cowardly habits of former servitude? If the Third Estate recognized and respected itself then undoubtedly the others would respect it too! Remember that the old relationship between the orders has changed in two directions simultaneously. The Third, which had been reduced to nothing, has reacquired by its own industry some of the things which had been taken from it by the assault of the stronger. Instead of demanding its rights back, it has consented to pay for them; they have not been restored but sold; and it has acquiesced in buying them. But in the end, in one way or another, it is capable of taking possession of them. It must not forget that it is to-day the national reality, of which it was formerly a shadow; that during this long transformation, the nobility has ceased to be the monstrous feudal reality that could oppress with impunity; that it is now no more than a shadow and that this shadow will seek in vain to terrify a whole nation, unless this nation wants to be regarded as the vilest in the world.[49]

In a later chapter of *What is the Third Estate?* Sieyes returned to this theme:

> In vain the people of privilege close their eyes to the revolution that time and the force of the things has brought about; it is real none the less. Formerly the Third was serf, the noble order was everything. To-day the Third is everything, the nobility but a word; but under this word has crept illegally, through the

influence of false opinion alone, a new and intolerable aristocracy; and the people has every reason not to want aristocrats.[50]

It is plain from these words that Sieyes did not think that real or genuine feudalism existed any longer in France in the eighteenth century. Genuine feudalism had disappeared long ago, by the end of the medieval period. The problem was that the aristocracy or nobility had been able, out of the remnants of feudalism, to weave for itself a new form of domination over the country. This domination was not based any longer on anything real – the performance of specific military functions by the nobility – but on what Sieyes called 'a shapeless remnant of feudal opinions which are no longer based on anything real,' the 'debris' of a genuine form of hierarchy.[51] For Sieyes the most alarming aspect of the developments of late 1788 and early 1789 was that there remained a possibility that the informal, shapeless, unconstituted kind of hierarchy that had emerged in the seventeenth and eighteenth centuries would be formally recognized and sanctioned. One's blood boils, he wrote, 'at the very idea that it might be possible at the end of the eighteenth century to *consecrate legally* the abominable products of an abominable feudalism.'[52]

The historical growth of the Third Estate meant that it now contained within itself most of the hallmarks of what Sieyes called the 'complete nation', that is to say the combination of public functions and private works that he believed characterized a rationally ordered society. In France in 1789, the members of the Third Estate, Sieyes argued, carried out all four categories of labour – agriculture, manufacturing, commerce and services – that made up the 'private works' of a 'complete nation'. Its members also carried out nineteen-twentieths of all 'public functions' too, and in particular all those that involved the most hardships and labour. Only the lucrative and honorific public places were reserved to the privileged order, and this shameful monopoly, as we have seen, he utterly condemned.[53]

Sieyes laid particular stress on the fact that the Third Estate possessed within itself a considerable number of men able to devote themselves disinterestedly to the public good; in other words men capable of holding public office:

Consider the *disposable* classes (*les classes disponibles*) of the Third Estate; and here, like everyone else, I call those classes disposable in which a kind of ease enables men to receive a liberal education, to cultivate their reason, and to interest themselves in public affairs. These classes have no other interest than that of the rest of the people. See if they do not contain enough citizens who are knowledgeable, honest, and worthy in every respect to be good representatives of the people.[54]

The Third Estate thus had its own intellectual elite, men who possessed enlightenment (*lumières*). But Sieyes was honest enough to acknowledge that the Third Estate did not have a monopoly of enlightenment. He paid tribute to the writers of the other two orders (which of course included himself) who had shown themselves to be 'defenders of justice and humanity'. He even hinted that the occupations in which the bulk of the Third Estate were absorbed was not very conducive to the production of enlightenment.

I am not at all astonished that the first two orders have provided the first defenders of justice and humanity. For if *talents* are connected to the exclusive

> employment of the intelligence, and to long practice, and if the members of the Third order tend to distinguish themselves, for a thousand reasons, in this kind of career, *enlightenment* regarding the public good tends to be more evident amongst men better placed to grasp the overall relations of society, and amongst whom the original mainspring has been less frequently broken. For it must be said, it is a science that relates as much to the soul as to the intelligence.[55]

The economic activities typical of the Third Estate thus tended to snap the 'original mainspring', and to detach men from a true, moral consideration of the public good. This critique should be seen in the context of Sieyes' more serious criticism of the Third Estate, already discussed, namely that its demands in 1788 and 1789 were not adequate to the situation. The demands of the Third Estate, he wrote,

> must not be judged by the isolated observations of certain authors who are more or less instructed in the rights of man. The Third Estate is still very backward in this respect, not only in comparison with the enlightenment of those who have studied the social order, but even in comparison with that mass of common ideas that form public opinion. The real petitions of the Third can only be appreciated in the form of the genuine complaints which the large townships have addressed to the government. What do we see in them? That the people want to be *something*, and in truth the least thing possible. It wishes to have 1. Genuine representatives in the Estates General, that is to say, deputies *drawn from its own order*.... 2. A number of representatives equal to those of the other two orders together.... Finally.... The Third demands 3. That votes are taken *by head and not by order*. Such is the sum of the complaints which seem to have caused alarm amongst the people of privilege; they believed that by this alone the reform of abuses would be firmly secured.[56]

It was these demands that Sieyes condemned so vigorously as being insufficient. Their ultimate inadequacy rested on the fact that they accepted the tripartite order-based organization of the Estates-General and attempted only to modify and improve it. In his view it was 'perfectly useless to seek for the relationship or the *proportion* according to which each order should participate in the formation of the general will. This will cannot be *one* as long as you leave three orders and three representatives.'[57]

So far we have traced the socio-economic factors that led Sieyes to equate the Third Estate with the nation, namely the massive expansion of the activities of the Third Estate, which made it reasonable to identify it with the 'complete nation'. But what of the Third Estate as the prefiguration or embodiment of the nation as constituent power?

The first and most obvious feature which made it possible to think of the Third Estate as the constituent power was the sheer size of its numbers. Sieyes estimated that in 1789 the clergy and nobility combined numbered roughly 200,000 persons while the Third Estate numbered between 25 and 26 million.[58] If the constituent power of the properly constituted state was the nation as an assemblage of individuals acting or deciding by majority, then the Third Estate could, with only a very slight exaggeration, be called the constituent power. In *What is the Third Estate?* Sieyes did not shrink from making this equation. 'We have demonstrated ... the necessity of recognizing the *common* will solely in the opinion of the majority. This maxim is incontestable. It follows that in

France the representatives of the Third are the true depositories of the national will. They can without error speak in the name of the whole nation.'[59]

The Third Estate was not, however, a prefiguration of the national constituent power solely because of its numbers. Equally important, perhaps more so, was its special position in the existing social structure. The status of the Third Estate was peculiar precisely because it was not a positively privileged order, standing alongside two other privileged orders, but because it was the residuum or 'common order' from which the two other orders distinguished themselves *by* their privileges. As the 'common order' subject to the 'common law' the Third Estate bore a unique resemblance to the equal union of individuals that stood at the basis of the rightly constituted state.

Privileges, by contrast, were the radical negation of a state based on an equal union of individuals and Sieyes set out to demonstrate this *more geometrico* at the start of his *Essay on Privileges*. All privileges, he wrote, were either a *dispensation* from the law, or the grant of an *exclusive right* to something not forbidden by the law. 'The hall-mark of privilege is to be outside the common law, and one cannot move outside it except by one of these two ways.'[60] But what was the purpose of the law of a political community? It was surely to prevent the liberty and property of each individual from being infringed. It was, more abstractly, the positive realization of the natural law that one person should not harm another. Law in fact, was not there to *grant* or to *dispense* liberty; it was there to secure and enhance it. In Sieyes' words:

> People believe almost in good faith that they only have a right to what is expressly permitted them by the laws. They seem to forget that liberty is anterior to all society, and to every legislator; that men only unite in order to protect their rights from the designs of the wicked, and in order to devote themselves, in the shelter of this security, to a more extensive, more energetic and more rewarding development of their moral and physical faculties. The legislator is established not to accord but to protect our rights. If he limits our liberty, it can only be in relation to acts that are harmful to society, and for this reason civil liberty extends to everything that the law does not forbid.[61]

Sieyes was here restating the Copernican social principle first clearly enunciated by Hobbes that man is free unless and until the law speaks, and that where the laws are silent freedom reigns. By the aid of it he was able to conclude that all privileges were unjust. When they exempted people from the law they by definition gave them a right to harm others; when they granted people an exclusive right to something not forbidden by the law, they by definition infringed the freedom of others. 'All privileges are hence, by the nature of things, unjust, odious and contradictory to the supreme end of all political society.'[62]

In stark contrast to the world of privilege stood the Third Estate, the order which was not really 'an order' alongside the others, but the common order, prefiguring a world in which there would not be any orders at all, because all would be equally under one common law. Sieyes' definition of the Third Estate turned on this distinction. 'We must understand by the Third Estate the totality (*ensemble*) of citizens who belong to the common order. All who are privileged by the law, in whatever manner it may be, pass outside the common order, form an exception to the common law and as a result do not belong to the Third Estate.'[63]

Sieyes was well aware that in defining the Third Estate as the common order, free from all privilege, he was defining the essence of the Third Estate, or what he called the '*véritable Tiers*'.[64] The empirical reality, he recognized, was rather different. The upper echelons of the Third Estate had become closely enmeshed with the people of privilege, seeking advancement and preferment from them, and seeking indeed to become privileged like them. 'To prevent himself from being completely crushed,' wrote Sieyes, 'what is left for the unhappy non-privileged person? The art of attaching himself by all sorts of servilities to a great man; at the price of his morals and his dignity as a man he buys the faculty of being able, on occasion, to call upon *someone*.'[65] And in a more extensive passage he described graphically how the life of the nation becomes distorted by the constant efforts of the non-privileged to ingratiate themselves with the privileged:

> Are not the non-privileged who seem most fitted by their talents to uphold the interests of their order brought up with a superstitious or forced respect for the nobility? We know how ready men in general are to conform to whatever practices are useful to them. They are constantly pre-occupied with improving their lot, and when personal industry cannot advance them by honest means they set out on false paths. We read that among the ancients children were accustomed not to receive their food until they had engaged in violent or skilful exercises. It was a way of making them excel. Amongst us the most able class of the Third Estate is forced, in order to obtain its necessities, to exercise itself in flattery, and to devote itself to the service of powerful men, a kind of education that is less honourable, less social, but equally effective. This unhappy part of the nation has come to resemble a huge antechamber, where it is constantly preoccupied with what its masters are saying or doing, and where it is always ready to sacrifice everything for the benefits it expects should it give pleasure. Faced with such habits is it not natural to fear that the qualities most suited to the defence of the national interest have been prostituted to outdated ideas? The most resolute defenders of the aristocracy will be found in the Third Estate, and amongst men born with much *esprit* but little soul, who are as greedy for riches, power, and the caresses of the great as they are incapable of sensing the price of freedom.[66]

Conscious of the magnetic attraction that the privileged order exercised over those below them, Sieyes stood firmly by the principle that no one who enjoyed any privileges whatsoever ought to be regarded as belonging to the Third Estate. The 'newly ennobled', those who had recently succeeded in entering the aristocracy, were no exception despite the fact that the old *noblesse* regarded them as still a part of the Third. Neither were the so-called *privilégiés à terme*, those who had managed to obtain 'life honours', although public opinion regarded them as belonging to the Third. Sieyes recognized that his principle meant the exclusion of some very enlightened and highly esteemed men from the Third, but this did not deflect him. 'Does the fact that an army has had the misfortune to see its best troops desert, mean that it has still to use them to defend its camp?'[67] The proper remedy was for those with privileges who nevertheless regarded themselves as belonging to the Third Estate, to 'purge themselves of them immediately and completely.'[68]

These sentences serve to remind us, in conclusion, how intensely polemical Sieyes' identification of the Third Estate with the nation was. In pointing out that it was uniquely qualified by its special characteristics to speak and act on behalf of the nation, and in urging it to raise its demands in accordance with its unique role, he was simultaneously urging it to dissociate itself from those sections of the population who were not a genuine part of the nation, who were alien to it, who were 'nothing'. He was drawing a line between the friends of the nation and its enemies, and urging men to choose unequivocally on which side they stood. It is now time to look more closely at the other side of the equation, at the enemy against whom Sieyes saw the Third Estate asserting itself.

4 The enemy: the nobility as the embodiment of caste-rule

... jamais une nation coupée par ordres n'aura vien de commun avec une nation *une*.

Sieyes, *What is the Third Estate?* (1789), 168–9

THE THIRD ESTATE, as the positive force to whom the future belonged, was constantly contrasted by Sieyes with a negative force to whom the past belonged. This contrast was not accidental. By seeing what it was *not* the Third Estate came to see what it *was*. As Marx aptly observed: 'In order that *one* estate can become *par excellence* the estate of liberation, another estate must conversely become the estate of subjugation. The negative-universal significance of the French nobility and clergy conditioned the positive-universal significance of the nascent self-distinguishing and opposed class of the *bourgeoisie*.'[1] Marx's identification here of the Third Estate with the class of the bourgeoisie cannot be ascribed to Sieyes, who did not refer to the Third Estate as a class but rather as the union of all the non-privileged classes. Marx's main thesis about the way the 'negative-universal' conditioned the 'positive-universal' in the making of the Revolution is, however, particularly pertinent to Sieyes' mode of argument.

The enemy of the Third Estate, the enemy against whose oppression, as Sieyes wrote himself, 'all the classes of the Third Estate are bound by a common interest,'[2], was most usually described by him as *les privilégiés*, but also as *l'aristocratie, l'aristocratisme, la noblesse, l'ordre noble, la caste des nobles*, or, more abstractly, *un ordre* or *une classe privilégiaire*.[3] There can be little doubt that what he meant in concrete, historical terms was the nobility, and that what he meant in terms of principle was the idea of caste. The French nobility as the embodiment of the irrational principle of caste-rule was the negation of the Third Estate as the embodiment of the rational idea of the nation.

Does this mean that Sieyes had no objections to the order of the clergy? Not at all. It is plain, above all from his published and unpublished writings during the years 1790 and 1791, that Sieyes considered a radical restructuring of the clergy was necessary. The reason he did not concentrate his attack on the clergy in 1789 was not because he thought they needed no reform, but because he did not think they were inherently and intrinsically opposed to the principles of political order in the way the nobility was. This was because they possessed, even in their unreformed state, the elements of a public function. '*Qu'est-ce que le clergé?*' Sieyes asked in a footnote to his tract '*Qu'est-ce que le Tiers état?*'. He replied:

> A body of agents charged with the public functions of instruction and worship. Change its internal administration; reform it more or less; but it is necessary under one form or another. This body is not an exclusive caste, but open to all the citizens; this body is constituted in a way that costs nothing to the state.... This body cannot finally form a *body*; it stands within the hierarchy of government. The nobility by contrast is an exclusive caste separated from the Third which it scorns. It is not a body of public functionaries; its privileges relate to the person independently of any employment; nothing can justify its existence except the right of the stronger. While the clergy are continuously losing their privileges, the nobility conserve theirs; what am I saying? they increase them.[4]

Earlier in the same tract he made the distinction between the clergy and the nobility even more sharply:

> The fact that one has to go through a long succession of tests before one can become a member of the clergy is no reason for considering this body as a separate *caste*. The latter word can only mean a class of men who, having neither functions not utility, and by the sole fact that they exist, enjoy privileges attached to their person. They are truly a separate people, a false people, who are unable to exist by themselves through the lack of useful organs, and who therefore attach themselves to the real nation like vegetable growths which cannot live except on the sap of plants they exhaust and wither. The *Clergé*, the *Robe*, the *Epée* and the *Administration* are four classes of public agent who are always necessary. Why are they accused in France of being *aristocratisme*? Because the noble caste has usurped all the good places; it has treated them as its patrimony, exploiting them not in the spirit of the social law, but for its own particular profit.[5]

Sieyes, incidentally, was fond of the analogy between the noble order and a kind of fungoid growth on the body politic. On one occasion he went yet further and compared the existence of a privileged class within the nation to 'a frightful malady' that battens on the body of its unfortunate victim and 'devours his living flesh.'[6]

What has been said of Sieyes' attitude to the clergy in 1789 may also be said of his attitude to the monarchy. He never directly attacked the monarchy or proposed changes in its status in his early tracts. This does not mean, however, that he accepted the monarchy in the form in which it existed. On the contrary his remorseless insistence on the need to re-establish the French body politic on the basis of the nation necessarily implied a radical change in the status of the monarchy. Any claim to rule by divine right was patently incompatible with such a notion. In other words, it was inevitable once Sieyes' early arguments about the nation as constituent power were accepted, that the king would be transformed into the holder of a duly constituted public office, or become a 'public functionary'.

If this was the logical implication of Sieyes' early proposals, why did he not direct his fire against the king? The most probable answer is once again that while he thought the monarchy would have to change he did not see it as inherently and intrinsically in contradiction with a properly constituted state. As his subsequent constitutional proposals as well as his polemics against Thomas Paine in 1791 show, Sieyes always believed that there was a legitimate place for a monarch, in the specific sense of a single individual making decisions within the public establishment, in a nationally constituted government.

The 'monarchical principle' was not anathema to him. The 'caste principle' however, *was* anathema to him, because it was irreconcilable with the idea of a nationally constituted political order.

The *noblesse* thus received the full brunt of Sieyes' attack in the closing months of 1788 and the early part of 1789. The arguments he deployed against them were the exact obverse of those he used in favour of the Third Estate. The latter, it will be recalled, not only embodied the idea of the nation as a single unity of equal individuals, but performed all the necessary private works and nearly all the public functions that together made up a rationally ordered society. The *noblesse*, conversely, not only negated the principle of an equal union of citizens, but sinned against the principle of a rational division of labour. They were illegitimate *and* useless. They offended against the nation by their privileges and by their *fainéantise*.[7]

The ways in which the noblesse contravened the idea of an equal union will by now be fairly obvious. Their privileges were by definition the negation of the idea of one people existing under a common law. Their privileges were also the negation of the idea of a rational distinction between public functions and private work. On the one hand the *civil* privileges of the *noblesse* gave them power and authority over their fellow citizens where none should be permitted, and all should be regulated by free exchange. On the other hand, the *political* privileges of the *noblesse* made public functions into a kind of private property. The two worlds were hopelessly confused.

Sieyes' attack on privilege was conspicuous by being total. It was senseless, in his view, to dispense with the political privileges relating to the position of the nobility in the Estates-General, and at the same time to leave their civil privileges standing. Those who favoured the 'English solution', and thought that the French nobility could simply be placed in an upper legislative chamber like the English House of Lords, while the rest of the population could be represented in a lower legislative chamber like the House of Commons, made this error. They overlooked the profound differences between the French and English nobility.

> In England the only privileged nobility are those to whom the constitution accords a place in the legislative power. All the other citizens are blended in the same interest; there are no privileges which make them distinct orders. If therefore in France we want to assemble the three orders as one, it will be essential to abolish all kinds of privilege beforehand. It will be essential for the noble and the priest to have no other interest than the common interest, and for them to have no other rights by law than those of the simple citizen. Unless this is done you may well be able to bring together the three orders under the same denomination, but they will always form three heterogeneous substances impossible to amalgamate. I cannot be accused of wishing to uphold the distinction between orders, which I regard as an invention that has been most harmful to social good. I know only one misfortune which is worse and that is to blend the three orders *nominally* while leaving them *really* separate through the maintenance of privileges. This would be to consecrate for ever their triumph over the nation.[8]

The civil and political privileges of the French nobility were thus linked together, and stood or fell together. Neither were purely 'honorary' privileges exempt from proscription in Sieyes' view – though there were many who favoured such moderation. His argument on this matter pivoted on the distinction between the idea of 'privilege' and that of 'recompense'. Recompense he defined as a just and reasonable elevation of those who had served their country and the public well. Privilege by contrast debased the mass of the citizens before the person rewarded. 'Recompense the member who has deserved well of the body; but do not engage in the absurd folly of belittling the body vis-à-vis the member.'[9] What forms of recompense did Sieyes regard as legitimate for outstanding services? Rapid promotion, appointment to distinguished office and, in exceptional cases, the award of a pension met with his approval. Beyond this he thought that the unrestricted play of public esteem, welling up fully and spontaneously from the people, would suffice to reward the outstanding and he indulged in an almost lyrical eulogy of this form of *laisser faire*, contrasting it with the terrible results that followed when the court monopolized the dispensation of honour and directed it towards totally unworthy objects. When this happened: 'For the minority of enlightened men esteem retreats into the depths of the soul, indignant at the shame to which it is being subjected. Real esteem therefore no longer exists, although its language and mien continues to appear in society, prostituting itself with intriguers, favourites and often the guiltiest of men through false public honours.'[10] There is a strong hint of personal bitterness here.

The nobility of course wallowed in this polluted, monopolized form of honour, and Sieyes savaged them mercilessly: 'I see that you ask less to be distinguished *by* your fellow citizens than to be distinguished *from* your fellow citizens.' And again: 'In the depths of your soul you reproach nature for not having made your fellow citizens into inferior species destined solely to serve you.'[11]

What is particularly interesting in Sieyes' discussion of 'honorific' privilege is that he did not say that honour had no role to play in the society of the future, but rather that honour, freed from the distortion of privilege, had a very necessary role to play in the society of the future. In other words he did not see the 'money principle' as replacing the 'honour principle' but expressly argued that the 'honour principle' should balance the 'money principle':

> The two great motive forces of society are: *money* and *honour*. It is from the need for one or the other that it sustains itself, and the one should not exist without the other in a nation which knows the price of good customs. The desire to merit public esteem, and it exists in each profession, is a necessary brake on the passion for wealth.[12]

Let us turn from Sieyes' attack on the nobility as the embodiment of an unjust, because unequal order to his attack on them as useless and unproductive, indeed as positively damaging to the productivity of the country. Once again he used a succession of arguments to prove his case. As regards the exercise of public functions the nobility's monopoly of the lucrative and honorary posts was quite unnecessary. There were plenty of able men in the Third Estate who could perform these tasks successfully, and free competition was a far better regulative principle for recruitment than monopoly.[13] At the same time the performance of public functions by a caste was outrageously expensive because one had not only to pay those individuals who were actually employed, but also their families and the families of other members of the caste who were not employed. The number of posts and places thus became artificially inflated. While people affected to despise this overblown system when they read about it in the history of ancient Egypt or in books such as the Abbé Raynal's on the Indies, it was precisely this system that obtained in France. The utility of a noble order for the performance of public functions was but a 'chimera'.[14]

It was the same when one looked at the mass of private employments that together made up society. Here a 'whole class of citizens counted it their glory to remain static in the midst of the general movement, and was able to consume the better part of the product without having contributed anything to its creation.'[15] What kind of society was it, exploded Sieyes a little later, 'where work *demeaned*; where the painful professions are called *vile*; as if anything could be vile except vice, and as if this kind of vileness, which is the only real kind, was to be found chiefly amongst the working classes!'[16]

In the *Essay on Privileges* Sieyes examined at some length the ways in which the nobility extracted wealth from the social system. It was not that they were satisfied with honour and eschewed the search for money. On the contrary they were acutely conscious of the need for money:

> They are even more disposed to abandon themselves to the impulse of this burning passion because the conceit of their own superiority constantly incites them to overspend, and because in overspending they do not, like others, fear the loss of all honour and consideration.
>
> But by a bizarre contradiction, the very conceit (*préjugé*) of status which constantly pushes the person of privilege to mismanage his finances, bars him categorically from almost all the honest routes by which he could remedy this disorder.
>
> What ways remain then for the people of privilege to satisfy that love of money which dominates them more than others? *Intrigue* and *mendicancy*. These two occupations become the particular *industry* of this class of citizens. Devoting themselves exclusively to them, they come to excel; and wherever these two talents can be exercised with profit, they establish themselves in a way that sweeps aside all competition from the non-privileged.
>
> They fill the court, they lay siege to the ministers, they corner all the graces, the pensions, the livings. *Intrigue* casts its universal eye over the *Eglise*, the *Robe*, the *Epée*. It sees a considerable income, or rather a power which leads these, attached to a vast mass of places, and soon it comes to see these places as moneyed posts, established not in order to fulfil functions which demand talents, but to assure a *fitting* way of life for privileged families....
>
> In this way the state is subjected to principles that are completely destructive of all public economy. In vain the latter proscribes that preference should be given to the most skilful and the least costly servants; monopoly commands that those who are chosen are the most costly and necessarily the least skilful, since the well-known effect of monopoly is to prevent the emergence of those who could have shown their talents in free competition.
>
> The *mendicancy* of persons of privilege is less destructive of the public weal. It is a greedy growth, that desiccates as much as it can, but at least it does not attempt to replace healthy limbs. It consists, like all mendicancy, in extending the hand in an attempt to arouse compassion and to receive gratuitously; only

> the posture is less humiliating and it seems, when necessary, to dictate a duty rather than to implore help. ...
>
> This type of mendicancy is exercised principally at the Court, where the richest and most powerful men draw from it the first and greatest share.
>
> From there this fertile example proceeds to arouse, down to the very remotest corner of the provinces, the honourable pretension of living in idleness and at the expense of the public.[17]

Sieyes proceeded from this point to launch into a fierce attack on the special care and attention that was lavished on *les pauvres privilégiés*. It is a bitter diatribe, undoubtedly coloured by a sense of personal grievance. He compared the cushioned youth and early career of the *jeune privilégié* with the far more arduous lot of the *non-privilégié* of the same age. There is no need to enter into the details of this particular *cri de coeur*. At the end he returned once again to his main theme of the unproductive, parasitical character of the nobility, using the Physiocratic term 'sterility' to describe them.

> It is quite useless for agriculture, manufacturing, commerce and all the arts to lay claim to a part of the immense capitals that they have served to form in order to maintain themselves, to grow, and for the public prosperity; the people of privilege swallow up both capitals and persons; and all is condemned irrevocably to privileged sterility.[18]

We have now followed the full circle of Sieyes' two-pronged attack on the noblesse, which as can be seen, is the precise counterpart of his two-pronged support of the Third Estate. Justice and utility on one side were opposed by injustice and disutility on the other. Before concluding this discussion of the 'enemy', however, it is worth pausing to notice some of the observations and reflections on the nobility that Sieyes, so to speak, scattered along the way of his main argument. They may not be strictly relevant to this argument – they take the form rather of parentheses in or footnotes to it – but they are nonetheless illuminating not only with regard to Sieyes' outlook, but also with regard to the character of the French nobility itself, of which he was a shrewd and subtle observer. As a young clergyman he had spent five years in the remote province of Brittany and this undoubtedly had given him the opportunity to study at first hand the peculiar habits of the French provincial nobility in particular.

To begin with one of his remarks on the history of France. It was wrong, in Sieyes' view, to see France as having been subject to a monarchical regime. If you removed from the country's records, he wrote,

> certain years of Louis XI, of Richelieu, and certain moments of Louis XIV, when despotism pure and simple is visible, you would think you were reading the history of an *aulic* aristocracy. It is the court that reigns and not the monarch. It is the court that makes and unmakes, that names and dismisses ministers, that creates and distributes places, etc. And what is the court if it is not the head of that immense aristocracy which covers every part of France, and which through its members seizes and exercises everything of real importance in all areas of the public realm?[19]

When the people voiced its grievances, Sieyes added, it recognized the true situation by separating the monarch from the 'motors of power', and regarding the king as a man entrapped and deceived in the midst of an all-powerful court.

What of the ethos of this ramifying aristocratic network? Sieyes, as has already been noted, was fascinated by the arcane language used by the nobility. In a passage added to the second edition of the *Essay on Privileges* he commented at length on this language and the hierarchical vision of society that was embedded in it:

> I shall not try and catch all the nuances, all the finesses of the customary language of the privileged. It would need a special language which would be new in more than one way; for instead of giving the proper or metaphorical meaning of words, it would be a question of detaching words from their true meaning so as to leave nothing but a void for reason, though splendid depths for prejudice. We would read in it what it means to be privileged with a privilege that has not *commencé*. Those who possess privileges of this nature are *des bons*. They are, by the *grâce* of God, quite different from the mass of newly privileged, who exist by the *grâce* of the prince. Those citizens who do not aspire to exist by *grâce*, and are reduced to appearing only through their personal qualities, can be ignored; they are unimportant; they are the nation.
>
> We would learn in this new dictionary that *naissance* only exists for those who have no *origine*. Even those who are privileged by the prince dare not assume that they have more than a *demi-naissance*, while the nation has none. It is superfluous to comment that *naissance* here has nothing to do with the sort that comes from a father and a mother, but the kind that the prince gives with a brevet and a signature, or better still the kind that comes from nowhere at all – which is the most esteemed. If, for example, you thought that everyone has a father, grandfather, ancestors, etc., you would be mistaken. In this instance physical certainty is not enough; all that counts is the attestation of M. Cherin. To be *ancien* you must be *des bons*, as we have said. The newly privileged are *des hommes d'hier*, while I am not sure what to say about the non-privileged citizens except that apparently they have not yet been born.
>
> I am amazed, I must confess, by the skill with which the privileged pursue to infinity, without ever losing themselves, these sublime though ceaseless discussions. The most curious, in my view, are those who are constantly on their knees before their own *honneur* and their own pretensions, but who nevertheless laugh wholeheartedly at the same pretensions in others. I believe that the opinions of the privileged match their feelings, and to give fresh proof of this I will sketch what they take to be the true picture of political society.
>
> They see it as formed out of six or seven classes subordinated to one another. In the first come the *grands seigneurs*, or that part of court society in which birth, a high position, and wealth are combined. The second class consists of the known *présentés*, those who *paraissent*: these are the people of *qualité*. In third place come the unknown *présentés*, those who sought only to gain the honours of the gazette: these are the people with *quelque chose*. 4. In the class of the *non-présentés*, but who may nevertheless be deemed *bons*, come all the *gentillâtres* of the provinces: that is the expression they use. In the fifth class must be placed those who have been *anoblis* in the not very distant past, or the people with *néant*. In the sixth come, or rather are relegated, the newly *anoblis*, or those with *moins que rien*. Finally, lest we leave anyone out, all the rest of the citizens come in the seventh category, which it is not possible to define except by insults. Such is the social order according to the ruling prejudice, and it will not come as a surprise except to those who are not of this world.[20]

Sieyes pointed out the connection between the hierarchical social outlook of the nobility and the boredom that so often afflicted them, particularly in the provinces. True felicity, he argued, lay in the spontaneous interchange of equals, unencumbered by any considerations other than the purpose or end that drew men into company together. The *privilégié*, however, debarred himself by his obsession with rank from such felicity. His much vaunted *politesse*, even towards those who were not of his rank, made no difference in this respect. For what was this *politesse*? 'The Frenchman of privilege is not polite because he owes it to others, but because he thinks it a *duty* to himself. It is not the rights of others that he respects but rather himself, his own dignity. He does not want his own manners to be confused with what is called *mauvaise compagnie*. How shall I put it? He fears that the object of his politeness will take him for a *non-privilégié* like himself.'[21]

However much persons of privilege affected to despise equality they nevertheless felt its necessity. Drawing expressly on his own personal experiences, Sieyes considered the lot of those men of rank who enjoyed the supposed charms of superiority in the provinces. 'It is everything to them, this superiority; but they find themselves alone, boredom wearies their soul and avenges the rights of nature. See how ardently impatient they are to return to find their equals in the capital, how senseless it is to sow continuously the seeds of vanity when one can only reap from them the thorns of pride and the poppies of boredom.'[22] And in what was perhaps another observation born from personal experience, Sieyes wrote: 'How many ladies of the house are forced to distance themselves from the men who interest them the most out of a regard for the persons of high rank who bore them!'[23]

Sieyes not only regarded the nobility as having a distinctive vision of society and a distinctive language in which they expressed this vision, he also saw them as possessing a distinctive credo or, as one might say to-day, an ideology by which they justified their position in the political structure of society. As he had already seen in his early years as a student in Paris, this ideology was borrowed from Montesquieu. It maintained that a privileged order was necessary as an 'intermediary power' within a monarchical form of government. Those who are privileged, wrote Sieyes, think 'that they are necessary to any society with a monarchical regime. If they speak to the heads of government, or to the monarch himself, they present themselves as the support of the throne and its natural defenders against the people; if, on the other hand, they speak to the nation, they become the true defenders of the people who, without them, would soon be crushed by despotism.'[24] Sieyes had of course watched the *noblesse* play this two-faced role in the period from the First Assembly of the Notables in 1787 to the Second Assembly of the Notables in November 1788.

What lay at the root of this idea that rule by one stratum or class of citizens over the others was justified because it was 'necessary' or fulfilled a 'need'? Sieyes saw conquest as one source. 'To conceive of a subordination amongst the governed, we must imagine an armed band seizing a country, making themselves proprietors of it, and keeping, for the sake of common defence, the same relationships of military discipline. In this case the government is blended with the civil condition. It is not distinguished from it.'[25]

The military attitude, however, had a parallel in the monastic one. Here was a second source of the idea of direct rule by one group over others.

> When the military spirit wishes to assess civil relationships it sees the nation simply as a great barracks. The author of a recent brochure has dared to compare the relationship of the privileged and non-privileged to that between officers and men! If you consult the monastic spirit, which has so much kinship with the military, it too replies that there is no real order in a nation unless it is subjected to the same kind of regulations by which its own numerous victims are governed. The monastic spirit retains amongst us, under another less debased name, more favour than you might imagine.[26]

This description by Sieyes of the military and monastic spirits as the twin sources of the idea of direct rule by one class over another in the name of 'need' or what he termed 'false hierarchy', was made by him in his first published work, the *Essay on Privileges*. It is of particular significance because, as we can see now, and as Sieyes himself to some extent saw, it was precisely the resurgence of these two spirits, the monastic and the military, during the course of the Revolution, that was chiefly responsible for the shipwreck of his own idea concerning a nationally constituted, indirect or representative government. The form of rule exercised by Robespierre and the Jacobins was – as Sieyes himself said in 1795 – a resurgence of the monastic spirit.[27] The form of rule exercised by Napoleon could with equal validity be called a resurgence of the military spirit. The struggle between them and Sieyes' system has a lasting significance because the monastic and military spirits continue to exist to-day as perhaps the most potent antagonists of the idea and practice of the representative form of government.

This leads us to the last of Sieyes' *aperçus* regarding the nobility. He did not merely see the 'false hierarchy' that they stood for as a species of oligarchy. He also saw it paradoxically as a species of democracy. It was oligarchic in that it embodied the rule of the few over the many. But it was democratic in the sense that it was direct and unmediated rule, as distinct from roundabout or representative rule. This was how he argued:

> *No aristocracy* ought to be the rallying cry of all the friends of the nation and of good order. The aristocrats think they can reply by saying: *No democracy*. But we repeat with them and *against them* no democracy. These people forget that representatives are not democrats; that true democracy being impossible amongst a numerous people it is senseless to believe in it or to feign to fear it. But false democracy is alas! only too possible; it consists in a caste that claims by right of birth or by some other title equally ridiculous and independent of the procuration of the people, the *powers* that the body of the citizens would exercise in a true democracy. This false democracy, with all the evils that come in its train, exists in a country which is called and believed to be monarchical, but in which a privileged caste has appropriated to itself a monoply of government, of powers and of all places. It is this feudal democracy that you have to fear, which does not cease to stir up unreal terrors in order to preserve its great importance, and which conceals its incapacity for good under the term *intermediary body* and its capacity for evil under the imposing authority of the aristocrat Montesquieu. It is plain to anyone who reflects that a caste of aristocrats, although decked out with the stupidest prejudice, is as contrary to the authority of the monarch as it is to the interests of the people.[28]

Sieyes' account of 'false' or 'feudal' democracy here bears a curious resemblance to Marx's description of the Middle Ages as the 'democracy of unfreedom'.[29] What both men were saying was that the direct unmediated rule of the few over the many has this in common with democracy, and in opposition to representative government, that it is direct and unmediated. The few appropriate to themselves the right to govern in the name of all.

5 The revolutionary act: June 1789

Sieyes proposa de se constituer purement et simplement l'assemblée nationale de France, et d'inviter les membres des deux ordres à se reunir à cette assemblée: ce décret passa, et ce décret étoit la révolution elle-même.

Madame de Staël, *Considérations sur la Révolution française*, ch. XVIII.

FROM THE SUMMER OF 1788 onwards Sieyes had seen the meeting of the Estates-General in 1789 as presenting a unique opportunity to bring about a radical transformation in the political structure of France, a transformation in which the first step had to be the crystallization of the nation as a single, active, independent power, capable of making a constitution. From the end of 1788 onwards he had come to realize that the Third Estate was to be the motor of this transformation; that its cause was that of the nation; and that the nobility were the enemy of the nation. The crucial thing now was to raise the level of consciousness of the Third Estate, so that it became aware of its epochal role, and did not let a splendid opportunity slip by engaging in petty partisan battles to enhance its particular interests vis-à-vis those of the other orders.

The problem, however, remained: how in concrete terms was the Third Estate to act once the Estates-General met? What strategy ought it to adopt? Sieyes put the fundamental issue thus:

> Are the changes that we are going to experience to be the bitter fruit of a civil war, disastrous in every way for all three orders, and profitable solely to ministerial power, or are they going to be the natural, deliberate and well governed result of a simple and just view, of a happy concurrence, favoured by powerful circumstances and promoted candidly by all interested classes?[1]

In the next few pages Sieyes' overall strategy for action will be described. One of the outstanding features of his writings was, as we have seen, that they did not restrict themselves to an exposition of principles but showed how principles could be transformed into practice. The last two chapters of *What is the Third Estate?* were fundamental in this respect. They presented a programme of action for the Third Estate. It is on these chapters that the discussion will concentrate.

In chapter 5 of *What is the Third Estate?* Sieyes set the context for resolving the practical question by first asking what the king and his ministers *should have done* in the period before the Estates-General were due to meet. They should not have manoeuvred between the interested parties trying to get each to cede a little. They should not have resummoned the Notables. They should instead have summoned the nation as the constituent power. The Estates-General were, to him, the wrong body to resolve the 'terrible struggle'[2] that had erupted between the orders. They were incapable of resolving it. This was because the crisis, the fundamental opposition, lay between the parts that conjointly made up the Estates-General, and concerned the whole structure of the Estates-General. The Estates-General, as the arena and object of the dispute, could not sit in judgement on the dispute. Conversely, if the opposed parts decided to act as judges in their own cause, the Estates-General as a conjoint body would be *ipso facto* dissolved. The only way of forestalling the *debâcle* that was bound to occur when the Estates-General met would have been to summon a third force, capable of acting as an arbiter of the dispute, and this arbiter could not have been anything other than the nation as the constituent power. 'It is patent that the parts of what you believe to be the French constitution are in disagreement. Who has the right to decide? The nation, independent as it is necessarily of all positive form.'[3]

Sieyes proceeded to describe the proper mode of summoning the nation as the constituent power. Obviously there could be no question of the nation literally meeting together as one gigantic assemblage of individuals. There would have to be representation. An assembly elected specifically to represent all the people as the constituent power, and to carry out the work of constitution, would have to be summoned. It was of the utmost importance to keep this *extraordinary* constituent assembly distinct from the *ordinary* legislative assembly of the people. The constituent assembly would be appointed 'for only one business and one period of time.'[4] Its members would 'will in the same way as individuals in the state of nature; however they were appointed, however they assembled and deliberated, provided that they could not be ignored (and how could the nation that committed them ignore them?) and that they acted by virtue of an extraordinary commission of the people, their common will would be the same as that of the nation itself.'[5]

By whom would the constituent assembly be elected? Sieyes' answer showed that he was already thinking in terms of the territorial reorganization of the country. The electoral basis would have to be formed by the 40,000 parishes which 'embrace all the territory, all the inhabitants, all the contributors (*tributaires*) to the public weal (*chose*)'[6] The deputies elected by these would come together in *arrondissements* formed out of twenty to thirty parishes; the *arrondissements* in turn would come together to form provinces; and the latter would send representatives to the capital to decide on the constitution. Voting would be by majority – there would be no question of the 'orders' playing any role whatsoever at any level.

Who had the right to summon such an assembly? For Sieyes the question, in the current crisis, had to be reformulated. Who did *not* have the right? It was the 'sacred *duty*' of all who could bring it about. But he thought that the king was the most appropriate person to issue the summons. 'Certainly the prince in his quality as first citizen is more interested than any other in convoking the peoples. If he is incompetent to decide upon the constitution, it cannot be said that he is incompetent to bring about this decision.'[7]

In all this, it must be remembered, Sieyes was describing what *ought to have been* done, or the proper sequence that *should have been* observed in the latter part of 1788 and the early part of 1789. The fact remained, however, that no constituent assembly had been summoned, and the Estates-General was about to meet. What was the correct way forward in these circumstances? In the final chapter of *What is the Third Estate?* Sieyes sketched two alternative paths, both of which were based on the assumption that it was now up to the representatives of the Third Estate to take the initiative in bringing about the establishment of the nation as the constituent power.

By the first, and more radical alternative, the representatives of the Third Estate in the Estates-General would meet separately from the nobility and clergy and would vote with them neither by order nor by head. Returning to his main theme of the total, qualitative distinction between the Third Estate and the other two, Sieyes argued:

> I beg you to note the enormous difference there is between the assembly of the Third Estate and those of the other two orders. The first represents twenty-five million men and deliberates on the interests of the nation. The two others, should they unite, have only the powers of about two hundred thousand individuals and think only of their privileges. The Third alone, you will say, cannot form the *Estates-General*. Well, so much the better! It will form a *National Assembly*![8]

In following this alternative the will of the majority of the nation, represented by the Third Estate in the Estates-General, would simply be equated with the majority will of the nation as constituent power. The minority could simply be ignored because they were the minority. In Sieyes' words: 'We have demonstrated ... the necessity of recognizing the *common* will solely in the opinion of the majority. This maxim is incontestable. It follows that in France the representatives of the Third are the true depositories of the national will. They can therefore speak without error in the name of the whole nation.'[9]

Sieyes recognized, however, that his strategy might seem 'a little too brusque'.[10] In particular it might be thought that since the rights of the nation were still disputed 'even by the smallest number',[11] it was necessary for there to be a kind of legal judgement which fixed them finally and irrevocably. Sieyes said he sympathized with this view, and suggested therefore, as a second possibility, that the Third Estate in the Estates-General should take the lead in summoning an 'extraordinary representation'[12] of the nation. The Third Estate would thus do what he believed the king ought to have done before the Estates-General met.

Following this alternative the Third Estate would suspend its activities within the Estates-General, until the nation had judged the great issue that divided the three orders. 'Such is, I argue, the frankest and most generous course, and accordingly the one that is most in keeping with the dignity of the Third Estate.'[13]

Thus according to the second alternative the Third Estate would continue to see itself as an order, until the supreme judge – the nation – had pronounced. According to the first it would recognize itself as the nation and would therefore have no need to appeal to the nation for a ruling. To be sure the representatives making up the National Assembly formed out of the Third Estate in pursuance of the first alternative would always be 'ready to submit themselves to such laws as the nation would be pleased to give them',[14] but they would not be bound to consult it on questions relating to the plurality of orders. In the last resort Sieyes appears to have preferred the second alternative. This is how he concluded his discussion:

> The sending of an *extraordinary* deputation or at least the concession of a new special power, as has been explained above, to settle before everything else the great business of the constitution, is thus the true means to put an end to the actual dissension and the possible future troubles of the nation.[15]

As we know, it was Sieyes' first and more radical alternative that was actually followed in June 1789, and he himself played a decisive role in securing its implementation. It would be inappropriate here to enter into a detailed historical account of the developments that took place within the Estates-General in May and June 1789, as this study is concerned primarily with Sieyes' ideas and their interrelationship. For this reason it will be sufficient to say that as soon as the Estates-General met there was a deadlock between the *noblesse* and the Third Estate over the question of whether the orders should proceed to organize themselves as if they formed one assembly, or as if they formed three distinct assemblies. Sieyes was elected a representative of the Third Estate of Paris and joined the Estates-General on 25 May. On 10 June he proposed a motion within the chamber of the Third Estate – or of the 'Communes' as it had decided to call itself – which was designed to break the continuing deadlock. His motion made a last appeal to the members of the other two orders to join with the deputies of the Third Estate in 'recognizing themselves' as 'representatives of the nation' by means of a common verification of powers, and added that such a common verification of powers would be carried out forthwith, regardless of whether the members of the other orders were present when the roll-call was made or not. The motion was carried after a debate lasting well into the night, and following its adoption the common verification of the powers of the deputies of the Estates-General was set on foot in the chamber of the Communes, although only a tiny number of the deputies of the other two orders – all from the clergy – actually responded to the invitation that had been made in the motion and took part in the proceedings.

Once the common verification of powers had been completed, on 15 June, Sieyes promptly presented a second motion which declared that the assembly – that is to say the new single assembly that was in the process of being formed out of the common verification of powers – in so far as it was already composed of representatives sent directly by at least 96 per cent of the nation, was capable of acting, and that it alone had the right to interpret and to present the 'general will' of the nation. Sieyes' notes show that he wanted to give the new body the name of the 'national assembly', but as 'proof of the spirit of conciliation' he proposed instead the more modest title of 'assembly of the known and verified representatives of the French nation.'[16] In the course of the long debate that raged round Sieyes' second motion it was decided that the bolder name of the 'National Assembly' was more appropriate, and this was incorporated into the final text of the motion, which was passed on 17 June by a majority of 491 votes to 90.

In this fastidiously correct manner the very thing that Sieyes had argued for in his pre-revolutionary tracts, the crystallization of the nation as an active, independent, and above all single unity, capable of creating a constitution, was effected, and it was effected largely by his own efforts and following his own practical recommendations. In the following fortnight the deputies of the Third Estate successfully resisted the efforts of the king and his ministers to win back the initiative that they had lost. Then in July and August, the nation at large, the empirical, real nation, so to speak, as distinct from the represented nation in Versailles, demonstrated in an unmistakable and often alarmingly ferocious manner that it completely endorsed the momentous step that had been taken.

Yet was the process by which the nation as constituent power emerged entirely in accordance with the strict logic of Sieyes' own reasoning? It will be remembered that he had argued in *What is the Third Estate?* that a national constituent assembly should be elected in a proportional, uniform fashion so that it genuinely reflected the will of the nation as an equal union of individuals, and that it should be specifically and exclusively entrusted with the mission of making a constitution. Could it be said that the National Assembly that emerged from the Estates-General and continued to sit until 1791 fulfilled these requirements?

It is interesting that Sieyes was not very happy about the way the newly established National Assembly proceeded, without any reform of its composition or any fresh mandate, to carry out the work of framing a constitution. His doubts are expressed in the opening paragraphs of his essay on the *Rights of man and citizen* which was written in July after the revolutionary transformation of the Estates-General into the National Assembly had taken place:

> The representatives of the French nation, united in a *National Assembly*, recognize that they have, by their mandates, the special charge of regenerating the constitution of the state.
>
> In consequence they are going, by virtue of this title, to exercise the *Constituent Power*.
>
> However, considering that the present representation is not rigorously in conformity with true social principles, be it because it is neither common, nor equal, nor general, nor perfectly free, or because it is not limited solely to the functions of the constituent power: the National Assembly declares that the Constitution that it is going to give to France, and which the necessity of circumstances must render provisionally obligatory on all, will not however be definitive until new deputies, regularly delegated to exercise solely the constituent power, will have reviewed it, revised it where necessary, and will have given national consent to it in conformity with the rigour of principles.[17]

In a footnote Sieyes added that the 'imperious law of circumstance' was no reason for not following the procedure he outlined. The danger presented by the prospect of a new national convention, he argued, was outweighed by the danger of dividing the nation into the contented and the discontented from whom all means of obtaining justice would have been removed, save that of force. A new, fairly elected, deputation to approve the constitution was required precisely in order not to drive those who opposed the present course to violent measures. It was essential 'to give them a simple, legal way of redressing the wrongs of which they complain.'[18]

Needless to say Sieyes' demand for a new deputation to approve the constitution was not implemented, and he did not voice it again. In the end the work of making a constitution became so involved and prolonged that the suggestion became completely unrealistic. The 'force of circumstances' prevailed.

As E. H. Carr has observed, there is not much to be gained by speculating upon what 'might have happened' in history. Nevertheless it is difficult not to wonder what would have occurred if the less radical of the two alternative courses that Sieyes presented to the Third Estate in his tract *What is the Third Estate?* had been adopted in June 1789 in place of the more radical one. Perhaps – who knows? – some of the bitter hostility of the minority would have been assuaged, and the immense changes that took place might have been effected without provoking the terrible antagonisms that did in fact emerge.

It remains only to add that Sieyes always saw in the achievements of the deputies of the Third Estate in the months of May, June and July 1789, or to put it more broadly, in the decisive, opening stage of the French Revolution, the work not of selfish interest or petty materialist calculations, but of something higher and nobler. The Third Estate *had* raised its interests to the level of principles. It *had* gone beyond mere bargaining for particular advantages. Later of course other, less savoury forces were to push into the foreground, but that, in Sieyes' eyes, was no cause to disbelieve in the power of reason to move people, and its power in those crucial days in 1789. When, one year later, he was trying to steer the National Assembly away from the petty temptations of anti-clericalism he reminded the deputies of this fact.

> If the Revolution which is taking place bears no resemblance to any other, it is because it has as its first and true cause the progress of reason. It is by the force of principles that we have been victorious.... It is reason, yes reason which has ripened us for liberty, and which ought to have the whole honour of the Revolution. When it is a question of completing and consolidating it, and of assuring the people of all its advantages, let us not become ungrateful; let us take care not to disdain the force of principles, and to spoil, to dishonour our work.[19]

Later still, in the autobiographical fragment that he wrote after he witnessed and endured the Terror he was more bitter:

> The influence of *reason* is a phenomenon that few people know how to appreciate. We have been forced to take note of it, above all at the beginning of the Revolution, when it exercised a powerful influence on public affairs. We have seen the *gens du monde*, astonished by its effects, attribute them, and being unable to do anything else but attribute them to *intrigue*, other ideas being as foreign to their outlook, as it would be to decide on something without following one's personal interest. We have seen them smile, out of pity, or incredulity, at the idea of a person charged with legislation raising himself above the sphere of passions, weighing, without becoming involved in, the various interests, suppressing some and conciliating the others with equity. Could they believe such a portrait, when they heard it, they would take it for that of a fool, or of a man who will never be of any use to himself or others; this reflection conveys best their character. Reason, which is the morality of the head, as justice is the morality of the heart, is for them like colours to blind people. The love of humanity, the desire for social perfection, the passionate attachment of an upright mind to such great objects, go beyond their morality; they cannot believe in them. They do not have even an inkling that the *social art* can really absorb and enthuse its philosopher practitioners, in the same way that the

> attraction of a painting, the taste for beautiful architecture, or the search for a beautiful harmony can take hold of a musician, a painter, or an architect. But they believe in ambition, in vanity, and always in immoral motives for every action in life. We have seen these uneasy guardians of their own ignorance, their little corruptions, their miserable daily round, take fright at the searchers after truth as if they were enemy spies, distrust the intellectual work which resolves a political problem as if it were a dangerous machination, and regard a scientific association as if it were a conspiracy. If these would-be Athenians had caught sight of the philosophers walking in the groves of Academe, they would have taken them for thieves hiding in a wood.[20]

There is bitterness in these lines, but also a message that goes beyond the time in which they were composed.

6 The ends of the new state: securing and furthering personal liberty

J'ai souvent entendu parler de la cause finale du monde et de tout ce qu'il renferme; il est bien plus vrai de dire que la cause finale de tout le monde social doit être la liberté individuelle.

Sieyes, *Opinion on the constitutional jury* (1795)

IT IS TIME TO MOVE from Sieyes' theory of revolution to his theory of the state that the revolution was designed to create. He had argued in his early tracts that a complete break with existing political structures was necessary. He had simultaneously indicated the way in which the nation as the constituent power of a new body politic could be brought into existence. By June 1789 the revolution he had urged had taken place, and the national constituent power had assumed an active, independent institutional form. Now the creative constitutional work could begin, and France could be provided with a political structure based firmly on the principles of what Sieyes called the 'social art'. It was to this task that he bent his energies from July onwards, as a member of the Constituent Assembly's Constitutional Committee, and it is to his vision of the proper and right ordering of the body politic attention must now be directed.

Needless to say, in the tracts written before the Revolution Sieyes had already given plentiful indications of the kind of order that ought to be established in France. In the *Views* he had discussed at some length the way in which the legislative and 'active' powers of government ought to be organized. In *What is the Third Estate?* he had sketched his conception of the 'complete nation', in which there was a firm division between 'public functions' and 'private works'. In the *Deliberations* he had set out programmatically the first steps that ought to be taken in creating what he called a 'representative constitution'.

But what was the end or goal of the order that Sieyes wanted to see established? What did he regard as the purpose of the political union that formed the nation? What was the end which it attempted to realize in making a constitution and creating a public establishment? In the *Deliberations* Sieyes significantly indicated that he believed that one of the first priorities in the work of constitution-making should be to draft a declaration of rights. Why was a declaration important? Because, Sieyes argued, a declaration 'indicates to the legislative body the social *goal* for which it has been created and organized.'[1]

These questions – and this answer – provide the theme of the present chapter. It will be concerned with Sieyes' conception of rights, of the common will, and perhaps above all, of liberty. The centrepiece of the discussion, the text round which the analysis will revolve, will be Sieyes' *Preliminary of the Constitution: recognition and reasoned exposition of the rights of man and citizen*. It was the first work that he produced after the Revolution of June 1789 had occurred.

Before examining Sieyes' argument in the *Exposition*, however, it is worth studying a little more closely what Sieyes had said about the ends of the body politic in his pre-revolutionary publications.

1 Sieyes' early ideas on the ends of the body politic

At the start of the *Views* Sieyes had been typically brief and categorical about what he took to be the purpose of political union:

> Let us enter into the subject, and form first of all an idea of the *end* of all legislation. . . . The liberty of the citizen consists in the assurance that he will be neither hindered nor troubled in the exercise of his personal property and in the use of his real property. The liberty of the citizen is the unique *end* of all laws. It is necessary that they all relate to it, either *directly*, as civil legislation, or *indirectly*, when they concern the government.[2]

In a footnote Sieyes added: 'This analysis is more exact than those that are usually made. People present liberty, property and security as the three ends of the social law; but these three goals are resolvable into each other (*rentrent l'un dans l'autre*).'[3]

These sentences may be said to express the unyielding core of Sieyes' ideas on the ends of the body politic throughout the revolutionary epoch. All his subsequent statements are in effect a development and deepening of this theme.

In the *Essay on Privileges* he stressed that 'liberty is anterior to every society, to every legislator.' Men unite in society, he went on, 'only in order to give their rights protection against the attempts of the wicked, and in order to devote themselves, under the shelter of this security, to a development of their moral and physical faculties which is more extensive, more energetic, and more fruitful in enjoyments. The legislator is created not to accord us our rights, but to protect them.'[4] These words express another characteristic Sieyesian theme: human rights have their springs in man's essential nature, they are not granted or accorded to him – yet at the same time the formation of a body politic represents a massive growth in the enjoyment of human rights.

In *What is the Third Estate?* the discussion is deepened again. Here Sieyes approached the subject of the ends of the state not by way of rights but by way of a discussion of the 'common will' that public institutions were created to express. He had already demonstrated in the main body of the work the form in which such a common will could be legitimately articulated, namely through the will of the majority expressing itself in a representative assembly. In the final chapter he looked at what the common will itself embodied, at its substance. 'What is the will of a nation?' he asked, and he replied:

> It is the resultant of individual wills, just as the nation is an assemblage of individuals. It is impossible to imagine a legitimate association the object of which is not the common security, the common liberty, in a word the public weal. . . . To say that the associates gather together to regulate the things that

> touch them in *common*, is to explain the sole motive which could bring the members to enter into an association. ... Three types of interest may be observed in the hearts of men: 1. That in which all citizens are alike; it denotes the just extent of the common interest. 2. That which links only some individuals together; such is the corporate interest. Finally, 3. That which isolates each citizen, in so far as each is thinking purely of himself; that is the private interest. The interest which links a man with all his fellow associates, is patently the *objective* of the will of all and that of the common assembly.[5]

The multiplicity and diversity of private interest, Sieyes added, would help to prevent them from dominating the national assembly, but the formation of corporations – and here he was clearly thinking of the great half-private, half-public corporate entities that existed in the *ancien régime* – would have to be banned to prevent their domination of the assembly, and for the same reason those who belonged to the corporate entity of the executive branch of government could not be allowed to be elected to the assembly.

A little later Sieyes returned again to the subject of the common interest, developing it slightly further:

> I imagine the law at the centre of a huge globe: all citizens without exception stand at the same distance on the circumference; all depend equally on the law, all offer it their liberty and property to protect; and that is what I call the *common rights* of the citizens, in which they are all alike. All these individuals are interacting with one another, trading and contracting amongst themselves, all under the common guarantee of the law. If in this general movement someone wishes to dominate the person of his neighbour or to usurp his property, the common law checks this attempt, but it does not hinder each, following his own natural or acquired faculties, and more or less favourable chances, from increasing his property by all that luck or more productive work can add to it, and it cannot without *exceeding* its legal place, raise or create for him in particular the happiness most suited to his tastes, and most worthy of desire. The law, in protecting the common rights of every citizen, protects each citizen in all that he can be until the moment when his efforts injure the rights of another.[6]

This citation is important because it points up the very close interconnection that existed in Sieyes' mind between the common will of the nation and the common rights of its members. The common will was the identical will of each and every citizen to enjoy and increase his liberty, that liberty which was his inherent and underived, or human right, and intimately connected with property and security.

The citation is important too because it indicates the point at which this common will to enjoy liberty and property might justly restrain and restrict the particular or private will to enjoy liberty – namely the point at which such a particular or private will injured the rights of others. In another section of *What is the Third Estate?* Sieyes expanded on this important matter in relation to property, explaining that by very definition property could not embrace or include a right to harm others:

> One must have a singular idea of *property* to confuse it with *public functions*, and to view without astonishment, in a country that is called monarchical, the sceptre broken into a thousand fragments, and the thieves transformed into legitimate proprietors. Surely people must see that under the undefined word

> *property* has slipped in something which is in reality the complete opposite of genuine propriety, for example, the *right* to harm others? Is there any possession, however long established that could legitimize such a disorder? I am not now talking of public functions, which plainly can never become the property of an individual nor be detached from sovereign duty; I am speaking of manifest usurpations of *common* liberty or property.[7]

Because Sieyes held property – in all its varied forms – in such high esteem it must not be imagined that he regarded it as an absolute right, untouchable by public authorities. For Sieyes there was emphatically 'no kind of liberty or right without limits. ... Political liberty had its limits like civil liberty.'[8] There 'could not be limitless liberty.'[9] It was part of his general doctrine that 'everything held together' in the social order, that particular bits of the body politic could not be detached and made into absolutes. Property was no exception: by very definition it was subject to limitations.

This brings us back to the *Deliberations* where, as already observed, Sieyes' concern to define the end of the body politic blended with his demand for a declaration of rights to be placed at the head of the constitution to be framed by the constituent assembly. The latter, wrote Sieyes, must not restrict itself to organizing a legislature. It was necessary also 'to indicate its *goal*, and to say to it: you will go there, and not elsewhere. This goal is indicated to it by a declaration of rights, and this in turn can be reduced to development of the principal points contained in the two words *liberty* and *property*.'[10]

Once the Constituent Assembly had been created Sieyes, at the request of the Constitutional Committee, proceeded to set out systematically his proposals for a declaration of rights, and it is to these proposals that we must now turn.

2 Sieyes' *Exposition of the rights of man and citizen*

Sieyes was not, of course, the only person to call for a declaration of rights early in 1789. The demand was widespread in the *cahiers*. Neither was he the only one who proceeded to draft such a declaration once the Constituent Assembly had been formed. As early as 19 June 1789 Target had proposed that the bureaux of the Assembly should start work on a declaration. On 9 July Mounier, in the name of the first Constitutional Committee, called for a declaration not only of rights of man, but of the principles of monarchy, the rights of the nation and the king, and the rights of the citizen. On 11 July Lafayette laid before the Assembly the first draft declaration of rights, and from this moment onwards a spate of such documents appeared. Sieyes' draft *Exposition of the rights of man and citizen* was read to the Constitutional Committee on 20 July and was published shortly afterwards. It achieved a wide circulation in France, being republished at least twice in slightly different forms, and a truncated version was also published in Brussels in August.[11]

Sieyes' draft must be distinguished from the famous *Declaration of the Rights of Man and Citizen* that was finally approved by the Constituent Assembly on 26 August. The latter was a composite work, the resultant of a complex of contending influences at work in the various committees of the Assembly and on the floor of the chamber. The influence of Sieyes' draft can be detected on only one of the seventeen articles – namely article seven concerning the rule of law.[12]

Despite its comparative lack of influence on the final text of the official Declaration, Sieyes' *Exposition* is of fundamental importance. First of all, it is the most systematic of all his published writings on the ordering of the state, and the least deflected by the political struggles of the day. Second, precisely because of its systematic quality it presents more of a challenge to the student of political theory than the more fortuitously composed official Declaration. It presents an unfolding argument, and not merely a succession of assertions. Lastly, of course, Sieyes' draft is of importance because the subject of human and civil rights continues to exercise men's minds to-day. His ideas have sufficient originality to make them of interest to those who discuss rights in our own time.

The *Exposition* presents the purpose of a declaration of rights briefly and pithily:

> The representatives of the French nation, exercising the functions of the constituent power, consider first of all that the object of every social union, and consequently of every political constitution, can be nothing other than to guarantee, to serve, and to extend the rights of man living in society; they believe therefore that it is necessary to begin by recognizing these rights. They think that it is good to expound them, and to proclaim them, so to speak, at the head of the constitution, not only in order to instruct the citizens in a matter of which no one ought to be ignorant, but to guide themselves by placing permanently before them the goal of their labours, and finally to provide the French people with a fixed yardstick that will enable them to judge and to reform political institutions which happen to deviate from their true destination.
>
> For this reason, the National Assembly recognizes and consecrates by a positive and solemn promulgation, the following *tableau of the rights of man and citizen*, as they appear to spring from their natural and social relationships.[13]

On one important point the *Exposition* differed from the earlier *Deliberations*. In the latter Sieyes – like many of his contemporaries – had been content to envisage a declaration of rights taking the form of a secular 'catechism'. In the former, however, he made plain at the outset that this was *not* the right way to proceed:

> There are two ways of presenting great truths to mankind. The first is to prescribe them like articles of faith; to commit them to the memory rather than to reason. Many people maintain that the law ought always to be of this character. However that may be, a *Declaration of the Rights of the Citizen* is not a succession of laws, but a succession of principles.
>
> The second way of presenting the truth is not to deprive it of its essential characteristics, reason and evidence. One only truly knows what one knows through reason. It is in this way that the representatives of the French in the eighteenth century ought to speak to their electors (*commettans*).[14]

The very title of Sieyes' draft – a 'reasoned exposition' – emphasizes the point made here. His aim was not to proclaim a list of rights, but to present an argument, a demonstration. When, at the end of his 'reasoned exposition', he set out a declaration of rights in the form of a numbered list of articles – varying in the different published texts between 32, 37 and 42 – he made it plain that he did so unwillingly. 'I have yielded to the councils of others', he wrote in a footnote, 'rather than followed my own opinion, in drawing up the following declaration, in detached maxims, after the style of those of the Americans.'[15] Even when we look at Sieyes' numbered list we find that it does not consist so much of a list of separate rights, as of a very compressed restatement of the chain of reasoning of which the main text of the *Exposition* is made up.

The guiding principles of Sieyes' approach to a declaration of rights are made clearer still in an important unpublished text by him, written in year III of the Republic, in which he looked back, not without a certain melancholy, at the significance of what he had tried to do in 1789 when he drafted the *Exposition.*[16]

In this unpublished text Sieyes began with a brief historical consideration of declarations of rights. The declarations or charters of rights of the past, he wrote, were essentially 'a *compromise* between masters and their rebellious subjects.' 'The general character common to all these declarations is always the *implicit recognition* of a seigneur, or suzerain, or master towards whom one is naturally obliged, and of certain oppressions which one is no longer prepared to tolerate in the future. Everything comes down to these words: "you promise not to renew this link in our chain".'

The American Revolution, Sieyes acknowledged, had marked a real innovation because it shook the yoke of the master or despot in and for itself.

> But the Americans envisaged the new authority that they were going to establish in the same way that governmental power had been envisaged up till then. They wanted to arm themselves against the oppression of authority; they declared their own rights; and they supposed that, everything then being settled, they could devote themselves in peace to their own affairs. The memory of the evils they had suffered, and those of which they had been most sensitive, guided in general the pens of those who drafted the *declaration of rights*.

If the American example were followed, Sieyes continued, declarations of rights would necessarily be different for each nation. The English would set out their own particular list, the Spanish another, and the Turks a third. Each would have their own grievances, reflecting the political struggles of their respective countries.

This, however, was not the proper mode of procedure for a people that had recovered its full sovereignty. It was 'ridiculous' for such a people to give itself a declaration of rights in any of the particular senses that had been discussed. It could no longer be a question of saying that either man or citizen would no longer bear such and such a chain; all chains had to be broken.

> The differences between the declarations of rights of all the peoples of the earth could not form part of its declaration ... it could only contain what was common to all, that which belongs to man and to citizen. On this supposition, a declaration of rights necessarily changes its whole spirit and character; it ceases to be a compromise, a transaction, the condition of a treaty, a contract, etc., between authority and authority. There is only *one* power, only *one* authority. When a man establishes an attorney for his affairs, he gives the attorney *instructions*, he gives the attorney a declaration of his *duties*; he does not amuse himself by saying: as for me, I wish to conserve intact such and such of my

> rights. That would be cowardly, miserable, ridiculous, etc., and in any case I challenge him to make a complete enumeration, or even one moderately good.

Here the crux of Sieyes' conception of a declaration can be seen: it was not a reservation of rights either by individuals against society, or by a particular society against its government. It was rather a positive guideline given by those who formed a political union or nation to the powers they constituted regarding the duties and obligations of government as such.

In the concluding words of his unpublished text Sieyes described the fate of his proposed declaration:

> I was full of these ideas when I composed my declaration of rights, and I did not envisage it in any of the earlier senses. I put myself at my ease, in complete *independence*. I wanted to construct the peristyle, the *preliminary* of the best political *constitution*; and this was the title I gave it. I proclaimed the *ends* and *means* of the social state, derived from the nature of man, from his *needs* and his *means*. To be sure, people scarcely understood me, and in order to get closer to public opinion, I was forced to add to the end of my declaration about forty articles in the American style, including the least objectionable elements of the kind of declarations about which I spoke earlier. I wanted to give *instructions* to our constituents, not *arbitrary wishes* such as a man might give to his attorney, or to his agent in private matters. I opened up the *natural laws* of the social state, and I said there is the *science* from which we have to draw in doing our work. The first page, to which no attention was paid, where I acknowledge and declare the tasks I am going to accomplish, appeared to them as a piece of *conventional ceremonial*, and, before I properly realized it, I saw, perhaps alone, the nudity, the vacuum, that its absence would leave. In my imagination I had hoped to render a great service, to raise first my colleagues and then the whole nation to a high level of political discourse. But all that was lost, not in terms of real effects, which is some consolation, but for the architecture of society.

This passage is crucial not least because it makes plain the kind of argument or demonstration that Sieyes elaborated in the *Exposition*. 'I opened up', he writes, 'the *natural laws* of the social state.' Sieyes was concerned in fact to reconstruct in a purely logical way the necessities of man's relationships with his fellow man, stripping away all that was contingent and merely empirical. Natural laws were not for him the inscrutable maxims of an inscrutable Deity, but the *rationale* inherent in human relationships. The logical recomposure of social life – and it has already been sufficiently stressed that this was the core of his theoretical method – was simultanously the exposure of natural law regarding human existence.

The 'social state', which was the way Sieyes usually described the object of his analysis and reconstruction in the *Exposition*, requires further elucidation. It did not mean society *before* it had established what is often called 'the state': that is to say, political institutions. It meant rather man united with his fellow men in a fully fledged social relationship which was *ipso facto* a political union with political institutions.

Now for the argument presented in the body of the *Exposition*. Three successive themes emerge in it. First of all there is a two-pronged argument designed to demonstrate that the social state is in no way a limitation or contraction of man's natural being, but rather a positive development and enhancement of it. Second, there is an examination of the specific ways the social state enhances man's condition. Lastly, there is an analysis of the public, constituted structures that form the indispensable means whereby the ends of the social state are achieved.

The opening argument begins in a characteristically Sieyesian manner. There is no grand rhetorical flourish about human liberty, but a remarkably down-to-earth prosaic proposition from which others are developed in quick succession:

> Man is subject, by his nature, to *needs*; but he also possesses, by his nature, the *means* to provide for them.
>
> He experiences, at every moment, the desire for well-being; but he has received an intelligence, a will and force: intelligence, to know; will, to resolve; and force, to execute a resolution.
>
> Thus well-being is the *goal* of man; his moral and physical faculties are his personal *means*: with them he can lay claim to or procure all the goods and external means which are necessary to him.
>
> Placed in the midst of *nature*, man gathers together his gifts; selects from amongst them; multiplies them; perfects them by his work while at the same time he learns to avoid and to forestall the things that can harm him; he protects himself, so to speak, against nature by the forces he has received from her; he even dares to struggle with her: his industry improves continuously, and the power of man, indefinite in its progress, can be seen to harness increasingly all the powers of nature to serve his needs.[17]

It is only at this point, after he has considered man placed in the midst of *nature*, that Sieyes considers man placed in the midst of his *fellow men*. Here, he writes, man feels himself beset by a 'mass of new relationships'. 'Other individuals appear necessarily either as *means* or *obstacles*.' If men regard one another as reciprocal means of welfare, all is well, 'they can occupy in peace the land, their common habitation, and march together in security towards their common goal.' If, however, they regard one another as obstacles, war soon results and the 'human species seems no more than a huge error on the part of nature.'[18] Thus two kinds of relationship between men are possible; those that arise from a state of war and are based on force, and those that arise freely from reciprocal utility.

Only the latter are, in Sieyes' view, legitimate. Why? In the *Exposition* he argues in the following manner:

> Two men, being equally men, have to an equal degree, all the rights which spring from human nature. Thus each man is proprietor of his person, or none is. Each man has the right to dispose of his means, or none has. Individual *means* are attached by nature to individual *needs*. He who is subject to needs ought therefore to dispose freely of the means. It is not only a right but a duty.
>
> There exist, it is true, great inequalities of means among men. Nature creates strong and weak; it accords to some an intelligence it withholds from others. It follows that there will be inequality of work, inequality of product, inequality of consumption and enjoyment amongst men; but it does not follow that there can be inequality of rights.
>
> All having an equal right, springing from the same origin, it follows that he who enters upon the right of another, exceeds the bounds of his own right; it follows that the right of each ought to be respected by the other, and that this

> right and duty cannot be other than reciprocal. Hence the right of the weak over the strong is the same as that of the strong over the weak. When the strong succeeds in oppressing the weak, it produces an effect but no obligation. Far from imposing a new duty on the weak, it revives in him the natural and imperishable duty of resisting oppression. . . .
>
> It is necessary therefore to dwell solely on the relations which can legitimately bind men to one another, that is, to those which arise from a real engagement.
>
> There is no engagement, if it is not founded upon the free will of the contractors. Hence there is no legitimate association unless it is established on a reciprocal voluntary and free contract on the part of the co-sociates.[19]

This is a good point at which to consider a little further Sieyes' assumptions about man in his original condition. The crux is that he does not simply posit man as running up against his fellow man, and having to come to some kind of arrangement with him; he posits him as being concerned to shape, channel, transform and master external nature, both by appropriating and working on it, and by developing and improving the faculties he possesses to transform and master it. Man is preoccupied simultaneously with nature and with other men. Sieyes' intellectual background, his long preoccupation not only with political theory in the narrow sense, but with political economy also, is vividly apparent here.

Man's double preoccupation gives Sieyes' argument a double underpinning: a utilitarian chain of reasoning runs alongside a moral one. Thus in seeking to master nature man is concerned in a very practical way with satisfying needs and achieving welfare, while in coming into contact with his fellow man a quite different factor comes into question, namely right. The social state, founded upon the reciprocal voluntary and free contract of the co-sociates, was for Sieyes the coming to fruition of man *both* as a subject of right *and* a seeker after welfare. On the one hand the social union represented an enormous accretion of man's powers to satisfy his needs. It was a combination of means for overcoming nature. On the other hand the social union enabled man's basic equality, his equality of right, to become far more secure. This is how Sieyes describes the development:

> It has been recognized earlier that men can do much for one another's happiness. Hence, a society founded upon reciprocal utility is really in line with the natural means that present themselves to man for the attainment of his goal. Hence this union is an advantage and not a sacrifice, and the social order is like a continuation, or a complement of the natural order. Thus even if all the sympathetic faculties of man did not lead him in a very real and powerful, though not yet enlightened way, to live in society, reason alone would do so.
>
> The object of the social union is the happiness of the associates. Man, we have said, proceeds constantly towards this end, and he certainly did not intend something different when he associated with his fellow men.
>
> Hence the social state does not tend to degrade or to debase men, but on the contrary to ennoble and perfect them.
>
> Hence society does not weaken or reduce the particular means which each individual brings to the association for his private utility; on the contrary it enlarges them; multiplies them by a greater development of the moral and physical faculties; increases them still further by the invaluable conjunction of labour and of public assistance; to such an extent that if the citizen pays subsequently a contribution to the public, it is only a kind of repayment; it is

but the slightest part of the profit and advantages that he receives from it; it is a putting-in-common, from which all derive the greatest benefit.[20]

From this accumulation of material benefits that the social state brings with it, Sieyes turns to the benefits that accrue in terms of the protection of right:

The social state does not establish an unjust inequality of rights alongside the natural inequality of means; on the contrary, it protects the equality of rights against the natural but harmful influence of the inequality of means. The law of society is not made in order to weaken the weak and to strengthen the strong; on the contrary it is concerned to shelter the weak from the undertakings of the strong; and, covering the universality of the citizens with its tutelary authority, it guarantees to all the fullness of their rights.

Hence man on entering society does not sacrifice a part of his liberty. Even outside the social bond no one has the right to harm another. This principle is true in whatever situation one posits the human species. Since the right to harm can never be a part of liberty, it is an error to think that one loses it in associating with one's fellow men.

Far from diminishing individual liberty, the social state extends it, and ensures its usage; it removes a mass of obstacles and dangers to which it was too much exposed under the sole guarantee of private force; and it entrusts it to the all-powerful protection of the whole association.

Thus, since in the social state man enlarges his moral and physical faculties, and escapes at the same time from the anxieties which accompany their usage, it is true to say that liberty is fuller and more complete in the social state, than it could ever be in the state which is called *natural*.[21]

It is clear then that for Sieyes the state was not a necessary evil but a positive good; its contractual character did *not* mean that it was not 'natural' to man in the sense of being a vital and immense enhancement both of his status as a free being, and of his ability to exercise his freedom. The difference between Sieyes and Locke here is worth noting.

The second theme of the *Exposition* consists of a more detailed demonstration of the way the state enhances right on the one hand and welfare or material happiness on the other. Sieyes unfolds the notion of right from the idea of man's ownership of himself:

Liberty exercises itself on *common* things and *owned* (*propres*) things.

The first right is ownership of one's *person*.

From this original right springs the ownership of *actions* and of *work*, for work is simply the useful employment of the faculties; it emanates patently from ownership of one's person and actions.

Ownership of external objects, or *real* property, is similarly only a consequence and an extension of personal property. If the air we breathe, the water we drink, the fruit we eat, are transformed into our own substances as a result of the voluntary or involuntary action of our bodies: so, in like manner, by operations that are analogous though more dependent on the will, I appropriate an object which belongs to no one and which I need, by work that modifies it and prepares it for my use.

My work was mine; it still is: the object on which I have applied it, which I have invested and penetrated with it, was mine like everyone else's; it was mine more than the others' because I enjoyed, more than the others, the right of first occupant. These conditions are sufficient to make this object my exclusive property. The social state adds to this, through the strength of a general

> agreement, a kind of legal consecration; and one has to assume this last act in order to give the word *property* the full meaning that we are accustomed to give it in our policed societies.[22]

Here we encounter, from a slightly different perspective, Sieyes' leading idea of a gradual solidification of man's rights as he passes from the natural to the social state. The germ of property is undoubtedly there before the social state, but it comes to full bloom in this state. Sieyes' account of property is incidentally tinged with the terminology of the Physiocrats (who spoke of *personal* property becoming *real* property and then *territorial* property) but differs from their theory in essence because he does not posit an 'absolute' right of property that pre-exists the social union.

The comment Sieyes makes immediately after this passage is also of great interest because it shows that he envisaged the possibility that certain forms of property might, *within* the social state, become of more concern to society than to the individual:

> *Territorial* properties make up the most important part of *real* property. In their present state, they relate less to personal need than to social need; their theory is different: this is not the place to present it.[23]

Unfortunately Sieyes did not leave us a theory of territorial property and social need. What we do have from his pen is a full discussion of the status and destiny of church property, and this discussion confirms that he believed that property could be modified by society in the interests of the whole community. His views on this matter will be discussed in a later chapter.[24]

Now to follow through a little further the account of the growth and articulation of man's original right that Sieyes presents in the *Exposition*:

> A man is free who has the assurance that he will not be troubled in the exercise of his personal property or in the usage of his real property. Thus every citizen has the right to stay, go, think, speak, write, publish, work, produce, keep, transport, exchange and consume, etc.
>
> The limits of individual liberty are placed only at the point at which they begin to harm the liberty of others. It rests with the law to recognize these limits and to indicate them.
>
> Beyond the law, everything is free for everyone: for the social union does not only have as its object the liberty of one or several individuals, but the liberty of all. A society in which one man would be more or less free than another would be unmistakably badly ordered: it would cease to be free: it would have to be reconstituted.[25]

Here the obverse side of Sieyes' doctrine of human rights can be recognized: while they are immeasurably *strengthened* and *extended* by the state, they are not in origin *granted* by the state. Man does not have as much free-dom as the law concedes; he is completely free unless and until the law imposes a limit.

Sieyes continues with a highly interesting comment on the right of reciprocal exchange or contract as it is exercised under the guarantee of the state:

> It seems at first sight, as if he who makes a contract loses a part of his freedom. It is more accurate to say that at the moment he contracts, far from being deprived of his liberty, he exercises it as it suits him. For every engagement

> is an exchange in which each side prefers what he receives to what he gives.
> While the engagement lasts, doubtless he must fulfil its obligations: the thing contracted is no longer at his disposal; and liberty, as we have said, never extends to the infraction of the rights of others. When a change of relationships has displaced the limits within which liberty can be exercised, liberty is no less complete, if the new position is solely the result of a choice that has been made. But here we touch upon the most difficult and delicate part of legislation. On the one hand, society no longer exists if engagements are not guaranteed by the law: on the other, liberty no longer exists, if every kind of engagement is guaranteed, or if personal service can be engaged for too long a period. The legislator will consult, on this matter, the nature of man, and he will strive to achieve the just mean.[26]

Once again it can be seen that Sieyes avoids a doctrinaire, absolutist position. The state exists to guarantee and extend the right of free exchange of contract, as an integral expression of human freedom. But Sieyes was well aware that under the guise of such free exchange or contract, positions of personal subjugation might reappear and congeal. The external form of free exchange must not blind the legislator to an abuse of its essence, and he must be ready to intervene to correct such abuse.

The logical implication of the guarantee which the state of society exists to provide for human rights is the possession of sufficient force. 'No right is completely assured, if it is not protected by a relatively irresistible force.'[27] More explicitly, Sieyes wrote that there were three types of dangers to which rights were exposed in such a state. The first were the actions of malevolent fellow citizens. The second were the attacks of public officials. The third were the attacks of foreign enemies. These demanded three different types of guarantee: a judicial system backed by sufficient force; a proper distinction and constitution of all public powers; and an army. On the difference between the first and last Sieyes was particularly insistent: there was a fundamental distinction to be drawn between the internal force required to ensure obedience to the law and the external force required to keep common enemies of the whole citizen body in check. Everything should be done to organize the state in such a way that the army could be used only against a foreign enemy.

> The internal order of the state ought therefore to be established in such a way that in no case and in no circumstance should recourse be necessary to the military power, except against a foreign enemy. It should thus be a basic and unimpeachable maxim that the soldier should never be used against the citizen. It is plain that we mean here by *soldier* a person engaged for a given time under the law of military discipline. In a wider sense, every citizen is a soldier, and, in a good state of society, the army *en commission* is only a detachment of the great national army.[28]

From the guarantee that the state gives to man as essentially a free being Sieyes passes on to the benefits that the state brings as a combination for material welfare:

> The advantages to be derived from the social state are not limited to the effective and complete protection of individual liberty; the citizens have a right too to all the benefits of the association. These benefits will multiply as the social order profits from the *lumières* that time, experience, and reflection will

give to public opinion. The art of producing all possible goods from the state of society is the first and most important of arts. An association combined for the greatest good of all would be the masterpiece of intelligence and virtue.

No one can fail to see that the members of society derive the greatest advantages from public properties, public works, etc.

It is well known that those citizens whom misfortune has rendered incapable of satisfying their needs have just rights to the help of their fellow-citizens, etc.

It is well known that nothing is more suited to perfect the human species, both morally and physically, than a good system of public education and instruction, etc.

It is well known that a nation forms relations of interest with other peoples that call for an ever-vigilant surveillance on its part, etc.

But a Declaration of Rights is not the right place for a list of all the benefits that a good constitution can procure for the people. It suffices here to say that the citizens in common have a right to all that the state can do in their favour.[29]

Sieyes therefore was by no means a protagonist of the 'nightwatchman state' that has so often been belaboured and caricatured and derided since his time in the name of 'social justice'. Not only did his concept of political union as a means of guaranteeing personal rights in society make room for the possibility of the state intervening to preserve the essence of personal right against distortion, but it was complemented and balanced by the idea of political union as a combination for the multiplication of benefits to those who shared in it. These ideas are incidentally embodied most clearly, not in the famous Declaration of Rights of 26 August, but in the less familiar first Title of the 1791 Constitution: the 'fundamental dispositions guaranteed by the Constitution'. Sieyes undoubtedly had a hand in drafting these.[30]

In the sections of the *Exposition* that have so far been described and examined Sieyes' emphasis was on the ends of political society. He wanted to show why it was established and what man gained from its establishment. In the last sections he turned to what he expressly called the 'public means' that were required to ensure that these ends were achieved. He provided a succinct account of what he meant by a 'constitution' and of the powers it organized. This is a subject that will be more appositely treated separately in the next chapter. Sieyes also recapitulated briefly his doctrine of the nation as the constituent power – something that was treated in chapter 3. Then he proceeded to give an account of the *political* rights of the citizen. It is this final theme that will be concentrated on here, for it rounds off the argument about rights contained in the earlier sections.

Sieyes himself made plain the way political rights were related to the rights that he had already defined:

Having exposed the *natural and civil rights* of the citizens, the plan we are following has brought us to recognize *political* rights.

The difference between these two sorts of rights consists in the fact that society is formed *for* the maintenance and development of natural and civil rights, while political rights are those *by* which society is formed and maintained. It would be better, for the sake of linguistic clarity, to call the first *passive* rights, and the second *active* rights.

All the inhabitants of a country ought to enjoy within it the *passive* rights of a citizen; all have a right to the protection of their person, of their property, of their liberty, etc.; but all do not have a right to take an active part in the formation of public powers: not all are *active* citizens. Women, at least in the present situation, children, foreigners, and those who contribute nothing to the support of the public establishment, ought not to exercise an active influence on the public weal (*la chose publique*). All may enjoy the advantages of society; but those alone who contribute to the public establishment can be likened to the true shareholders (*actionnaires*) of the great social enterprise. They alone are the true active citizens, the true members of the association.

The equality of political rights is a fundamental principle. It is sacred, like that of civil rights. From the inequality of political rights privileges soon emerge. A privilege consists either in a dispensation from a common responsibility or in the exclusive concession of a common good. Every privilege is hence unjust, odious and in contradiction with the real goal of society. The law being a common instrument, the work of a common will, it can only have as its object the general interest. *One* society can only have one common interest. It would be impossible to establish order, if one attempted to follow several opposed interests. The social order presupposes necessarily *unity* of purpose and *concentration* of means. Whenever the law establishes privileges society perishes, and the social pact is broken.[31]

Sieyes proceeds to hammer home this last point by arguing that while the actual decision concerning the form of the public establishment (that is, the constitution) must necessarily be allowed to be taken by a *majority*, this does not contradict the notion that the prior, fundamental pact that decides that *there should be* a public establishment must necessarily be conceived of as being a *unanimous* one. 'The choice of the means alone is delivered up to the majority.' This is Sieyes' doctrine of the state as a form of 'mediate unanimity' in which the underlying general will is 'formed by the will of the majority.' Sieyes' words on this important matter have been cited *in extenso* in chapter 3.[32]

Sieyes continued his *Exposition* by setting out in some detail the implications of the principle of the equality of political rights with regard to political representation, taxation, military service, and the carrying of arms.

No active citizen has more right than any other in the formation of the law; no class of citizens can have special representatives in the National Assembly, whether constituent or legislative, or in any primary Assembly; in a word representation must be *common* and *equal*.

To maintain a tutelary authority within and without, men and money are of course needed. Every citizen, without exception, must be ready to pay with his purse, and if need be with his person. The just measure of this double necessity, the proportion, method and employment of this double contribution, must be regulated to the liking of the mass (*généralité*) of the citizens, by their representatives.

No citizen has more right than any other to defend his life, his honour, or his property. Thus no public or private means of defense ought to be left exclusively to some rather than others. Hence the *carrying of arms*, beyond military functions and national exercises, should either be allowed to all or to nobody, without exception.[33]

Concluding his *Exposition*, Sieyes concentrated on the nature of public office, emphasizing that to hold such an office was not a right but rather a duty, and stressing again an idea that has already been encountered in another context, namely the ultimate inalienability of the national contituent will:

> No public mandatory, whatever his post within the different parts of the public establishment, exercises a power that belongs to him personally; it is the power of all. The latter has only been committed to him: it cannot be alienated, because the will is inalienable; the people are inalienable; the right of thinking, willing, and acting for oneself is inalienable; its exercise can only be committed to those who have our confidence, the essential character of such confidence is to be free. It is hence a major error to think that a public function can ever become the property of a man; it is a major error to envisage the exercise of a public power as a *right*; it is a *duty*. The officers of the nation are distinguished from other citizens only in having more duties; and do not think that in stating this truth we wish to diminish the character of the public man. What produces and justifies the regard and respect which we accord to men in public office is the idea of a great duty to be carried out and consequently of a great utility for others. None of these sentiments arise in free souls towards those who are distinguished solely by their rights, that is to say, those who awaken in us only the idea of their private interest.[34]

With this rousing passage the argument of the *Exposition* comes to an end. The text has been followed closely, not because it represents Sieyes' final opinion on every subject contained within it – some of his afterthoughts will be examined in the next section – but because it provides by far the best starting-point and framework for understanding his conception of the ends of the state. It is also a unique and original contribution to the debate on rights that took place at the end of the eighteenth century both in Europe and America. The most striking aspect of Sieyes' approach is that human rights are not abstracted and isolated and set over against society and the state, but are seen the whole time in the context of society and the state. The state's duty is to guarantee and develop human rights, but equally human rights are *only* guaranteed and developed through and within the state. It is a reciprocal relationship, rather than a stark confrontation, that Sieyes expounds.

3 Sieyes' later reformulations of his concepts of liberty and rights, and his attack on the Jacobin exaggeration of the notion of the common will

The emergence of what is perhaps best termed the democratic dictatorship of Robespierre and the Mountain in the years 1793 and 1794 drove Sieyes to think again about the overall ends of the state and the nature of rights. He restated his position in two significant works at this time, one of which he published, the other remaining unpublished.

The first is the short essay entitled *The benefits of liberty in the social state and the representative system* which was published in the *Journal of Social Instruction* on 8 June 1793, only a few days after the Mountain and the Sections of Paris had purged the Convention, and the Girondin group had been destroyed. It is a kind of last appeal to reason by Sieyes before the total ascendancy of the Jacobins. The second is the manuscript entitled *Bases of the social order or a reasoned series of some fundamental ideas concerning the social and political state* which was written by Sieyes in Year III of the Republic, and is to be found in the Sieyes Archives. Judging from the tone of the conclusion of this text, which is one of gloom rather than hope, it was probably composed at some time between September 1794 and March 1795. In addition to these two completed works there are some unpublished fragments of this period which provide a useful insight into the distinction between Sieyes' conception of liberty and the common will and that of Robespierre and his followers.

It will be recalled that in the *Exposition* Sieyes had described two convergent paths leading towards the establishment of the state. On the one hand man was engaged in an original struggle with nature, and other men were invaluable aids in this struggle. On the other hand man, in entering into relationships with his fellow men, was concerned that these relationships should be based on right, or on a respect for the freedom inherent in each. In his brief essay on *Liberty* Sieyes carried this discussion forward by distinguishing two basic meanings of liberty: *liberté d'indépendance* and *liberté de pouvoir*. His main concern was to demonstrate that when liberty was conceived, as it should be, in *both* these senses – which indeed start to merge at a certain point – then it led to the representative system of government. The contention that liberty was incompatible with a representative system of government, he believed, was based on a one-sided definition of liberty as 'independence'.

In the essay Sieyes began his analysis of liberty by observing that while liberty undoubtedly existed in man before the development of *science*, it could not be held to exist before the development of *reason*. 'Liberty, without reason, is the liberty of animals, it is not human liberty.'[35] In other words, man merely impelled by instinct and sensuous impulse was not free. Only when man reflected and broke out of his immersion in unconscious nature could the word freedom be properly applied.

But was freedom itself then merely a movement *away*, a *repulsion*? Sieyes' answer was unequivocal:

> If man was a being without needs, destined for permanent repose and a purely contemplative existence, then liberty for him would undoubtedly be nothing more than simple *independence* from all that could trouble his repose or attack his existence.
>
> This portrait is not ours; we are born with needs. Needs! there lies the prime mover of the human machine, the true origin of the rights of man, the creative principle of the arts, etc., etc.
>
> To beings moved by resurgent needs and possessed of active faculties, something else is required besides negative liberty. Action is necessary for men as well as repose. Thus even if we confine ourselves to liberty as independence, it is already a double thing; it cannot be seen as existing complete and ready made in man, for it includes not only the repulsion of the factors that trouble his *repose*, but those that impede his *action*.[36]

Sieyes says little more about liberty as independence at this point, except to note that the impediments to which it is customarily held to refer relate to the actions of other men: 'man is held to be free when he is not hindered by other men from exercising his will.'[37] That is to say liberty in this sense does not relate to the impediments of nature, or to the inadequacies of a man's own faculties. Sieyes said he was prepared to abide by this customary definition.

But what of the impediments of nature, and the inadequacies of man's own capacities? Could they simply be ignored when liberty was being discussed? Sieyes was convinced they could not. Alongside *liberté d'indépendance* or *liberté négative* there stood the no less important *liberté de pouvoir*, the capacity to satisfy, and the actual satisfaction of a man's needs. These were his words:

> Man needs to be free, not in order to enjoy a sterile freedom, but in order to exercise or employ his power, and to increase it more and more.
>
> What would be the use of his empire even over objects he could reach, if he had only a dearth of useful objects around him? What would be the use of power sufficient for everything he encountered, if he encountered little or nothing that was necessary to him?
>
> The great object of liberty is the increase of this power. The more it extends, the more we become free. Natural man, like social man, aspires ceaselessly to increase his means of action or his empire, as well as to get rid of the impediments to his action, or to increase his independence.
>
> In speaking of power over external objects, let us not forget a power which is no less important and useful, the power man exercises over himself, over his personal faculties; for it is above all the strength of his foresight, the richness of his combinations, the utility of his occupations, and the skilfulness of his work, which narrows or extends his empire in relation to his needs, and consequently, the sphere of his freedom.[38]

The conclusion that Sieyes draws from this analysis, and from his earlier analysis of liberty as independence, is that liberty in both its basic forms is not a static thing, but capable of expansion and contraction:

> I say that liberty, as we have taken it here, in its widest sense, is susceptible to growth and diminution; that man will be more or less free, to the extent that he acquires more or less power, more or less independence.[39]

The crucial question therefore becomes not: is human freedom, regarded as a static thing, infringed by the social state and the representative system? but: is human freedom expanded or contracted by the social state and the representative system? Sieyes – as might be expected – answered this last question by saying that freedom was expanded, and he borrowed several passages from the *Exposition* to describe the benefits that accrue to man by becoming part of a social and political unity. There is no need to repeat these passages here, it is possible to proceed directly to the part of his argument where he goes beyond the *Exposition*. Sieyes recognized that, even if freedom were regarded as expandable, and even if it were accepted that there were important ways in which freedom, in both its primary senses, was extended in the social and political state, it might still be objected that the dependencies that this state implied, in terms of submission to a multitude of regulations, made if difficult to decide whether there was an overall extension or an overall diminution. This drove him to a fresh analysis of freedom as independence, or more precisely of the concept of dependence. There was, he observed, 'confusion in this word.'

'Since nature has given us needs,' Sieyes went on,

> it has placed us under the necessity of satisfying them. Dependence, in this sense, has to be dismissed from the problem as from the response. It belongs to every epoch of the human species, before and after society.

> Man and all that surrounds him is organized or constituted in such a way that he finds himself generally obliged to employ a succession of means, like the steps of a ladder, if he is to arrive at his objective. The object that he wishes to procure appears at the end of a more or less extended chain of intermediary acts or operations. For example, if he is beset by hunger or thirst, etc., the distance that separates him from the spring requires a more or less painful journey on his part; if the fruit he sees is not within his reach, he needs a stick to get at it, or he has to climb the tree. There are a mass of similar examples both in the natural and in the social state. Let us call dependence on *ends*, the dependence one experiences regarding the things that are necessary for consumption, use or pleasure. Let us call dependence on *means*, the dependence one experiences regarding the acts, the trouble, the intermediary work, that are necessary to achieve one's ends.
>
> The needs of man being presupposed, is it desirable that he should find himself in a splendid independence of means and ends? Would that not be rather complete destitution? What! Without the double yoke of ends and means what need would you have of liberty? Remember that it is your abundance in this matter that constitutes your power, and that it is the untroubled exercise of your empire over means and ends that constitutes your true independence.[40]

At this point in his argument Sieyes interposed an interesting paragraph in which he recognized the purely factitious nature of many so-called 'human needs'. He seemed to bow for a moment in the direction of Rousseau, acknowledging that the real, natural man might come to be overlaid by false and unnatural social habits. What, he asked, is the answer to this problem? And he replied:

> The most important object of morality, and hence of instruction should be to recall man to simple and natural needs, and to habits and passions that weigh lightly, and are productive of happiness. No: I neither defend nor seek to conceal the innumerable evils that prejudices and unsocial vanities impose on servile generations. Let me appeal from ignorance to enlightenment, from error to philosophy; allow me to posit a tolerable social state, otherwise one must keep silent.[41]

After this brief aside, Sieyes pursued his exposition of the theory of dependency, and illuminated it with a homely image – something rather rare in his writings:

> Imagine two men surprised by a violent storm, both afflicted equally by the lack of shelter. An open hayloft and a ladder come into view. One of the men runs to the ladder, raises it, sets it against the wall, climbs up, and takes cover. The other, to avoid being dependent on the ladder, remains shivering with cold, exposed to all the discomforts of the storm. There you see the independence of the savage; there you see the liberty of social man; there you see dependency and independency of means. These ideas help us to seize the true character of submission to the laws.[42]

Sieyes broadened his theme outwards from this illustration:

> When I want something I seem to make a contract with myself concerning the means to obtain it. Our relations with our fellow men must be seen in a similar way.
>
> Others depend on their will as we do on ours. The common interest is to consider and treat one another reciprocally as means, and not as obstacles, to

> our happiness, for if the will of another person, by an indelible decree of nature, stands among the most powerful means that she offers to us for the achievement of our ends, the same voice teaches us that it is to the will of the other person that our will should address itself, and not to his weakness. The exercise of force dislocates all social relationships and those of humanity. We have only to experience ourselves to feel that man is a means of a more sensitive, more delicate kind than the rest of nature. When your will addresses itself to the will of your fellow man, it is as if you touch an echoing body: it responds with an equal demand. Proceed with caution, if you strike unison or one of the harmonic chords, agreement is certain: if you play badly the discord will be horrible.[43]

The proper way for men to relate is thus by way of free and reciprocal contracts, and the most important and precious contract is that which forms a social unity under law. Sieyes concludes:

> Submission to the laws belongs to the theory of contracts. Both of them, considered from the point of view of liberty, are examples of dependence on means. That is enough. Submission to the laws, far from restraining liberty becomes its most powerful means, its surest safeguard.
>
> We may now go back to the main question. Does liberty by itself lead to the social state? If you take liberty as meaning developments of power and even of independence, then, unless you wish to betray its interests, you must agree that the answer is: Yes.[44]

If we stand back from the essay on *Liberty* it can be seen that it builds on and deepens the argument that Sieyes developed in the *Exposition*. Instead of the state growing out of man's simultaneous drive to increase his well-being and to secure his liberty, it is now seen as growing out of man's drive to increase his liberty in the double sense of power and independence. It is no longer a question of liberty being balanced or contrasted with something else, but of two complementary aspects of liberty. Liberty has become explicitly what it always was implicitly in Sieyes' doctrine of ends, the master concept that embraces all the basic aspirations of man.

Perhaps the most original aspect of Sieyes' argument in the essay was his insistence that liberty was extended by man's power to *get things done* either through the utilization of non-human things, or through the utilization of other human beings by way of the division of labour, so long as the latter was achieved in a way that respected man's will. In an unpublished note of about the same time he expanded on this theme. 'Liberty', he wrote,

> often consists less in doing than in getting done (*moins à faire qu'à faire faire*). Some people ... regard political liberty as the continuous exercise of political rights, an uninterrupted concern with public affairs. If is not that. Liberty always consists in procuring the *greatest product* with the *least cost*, and in consequence in getting something done when the result will be less hardship and more enjoyment. But I say getting things done, and not simply letting things happen (*faire faire et non pas laisser faire*). Ignorant servitude is letting things happen; electionism or enlightened representationism is getting things done. Getting things done means commissioning to do, it is choosing the more expert, it is not commanding what one should do, for in that case what would be the point of the chosen experts being expert, and how could a prior command permit deliberation between the actors in the convention? It consists therefore

> solely in choosing experts, and changing them often so that if they go wrong their successors, elected precisely by those who complain of the error and can see things better, will be more capable of conciliating interests.[45]

This passage shows with particular clarity the link between Sieyes' concept of liberty and his concept of representative government.

When we turn to the third and last of the major texts in which Sieyes considered the end of political union, the *Bases of the Social Order*,[46] we find yet another deepening of the argument contained in the *Exposition*. Like the latter, it is a very succinct logical unfolding of the state – *une suite de verités* as Sieyes called it – but it is less finished and proportionately more concerned with institutions than the earlier work. The experience of the Terror is very apparent in the *Bases* and it was almost certainly responsible for the fact that in the discussion of the ends of the state Sieyes concentrated entirely on the protection and guarantee of the rights of the individual – or liberty as independence – and has little to say about the state as a promoter of liberty as power. In the Preface to the work he wrote expressly that he did not think it necessary to 'go back so far' in his logical deduction of the state as he had done in the *Exposition*. There he had begun by looking at man's needs and the means he has for satisfying them. Now, he writes, he will begin with a more obvious and immediate 'fact', namely that 'all men ought to be free.'

If it is narrower in focus than the *Exposition* the discussion of the ends of the state in the *Bases* represents nonetheless a real development of some of the arguments contained in the earlier work. The development may be summarized by saying that the rather sudden transposition of man with his natural rights into the social and political state which is described in the *Exposition* becomes a more realistic, gradual, step-by-step process in the *Bases*. In the *Exposition* Sieyes had been content to argue that a man is by nature the proprietor of his person and that this is his right; that if one man is a proprietor in this manner, then all men are equally so; that to infringe the right of another is to exceed one's own; and that therefore the right of each should be respected by the others, and right and duty should be reciprocal. The use of force is hence wrong, and the state must be established by mutual contract. In the *Bases* by contrast we find a less abstract and more convincing argument that reveals a progressive concretization of man's *natural* right into first, *positive* right, and then *civil* right, with *civil* right then being complemented and reinforced by *political* right. Sieyes' words require once again to be cited at some length, so as to reveal the tight interlocking thread that binds them together:

> Unions of human beings can only establish themselves on one or other of these bases: either man is free or he is a slave, either he belongs to himself or he is the property of another, either he governs himself according to his own will, or he obeys that of a master. Choose: you are going to constitute the state of war or the state of peace.
>
> If man is free, all are, that is to say all are inviolable proprietors of their person and their things. They ought to be able to use both without hindrance from others. All rights are contained in this personal and *real* property. In this state of liberty, man can only treat together voluntarily and by way of exchange. They recognize their respective rights, and through this reciprocal recognition, these rights which are at first purely natural, take on the character of positive

rights. Voluntary engagement is the principle of all positive obligation. By the side of right, *duty* is *born*. The correlative play of rights and duties is the soul of the social order.

The rights of man are hence anterior to everything. They are not lost on entering society; on the contrary the great object of the political association is to give them a stronger guarantee, by placing them under the protection of the community. But it is important not to forget that to protect rights is not the same as to create or grant them. When a tutelary authority is established in society it is not from the authority that rights flow, they do not have their source in the law. On the contrary both the law and the legislator and every public authority, have their source and their reason for existing in rights, they precede everything and everything is made to serve them. One cannot add to natural rights; one simply declares the consequences that flow from them in the midst of the new relationships in which man finds himself in the state of society.

The social state offers several guarantees to the exercise of rights. They reside in usage, custom and opinion as much as or more than in the laws. But because some of the inevitable jostlings that take place in the union will be severe and important, experience and reason teach the legislator to suppress these by penalties sufficient to prevent them. The law declares in advance offences of this nature, and commits their prosecution to penal justice, which is always tutelary of the good when it punishes the bad.

Beyond this the law facilitates and regulates the exercise of a mass of rights which are required by the common utility to be subjected to a kind of uniformity and publicity (*notoriété*). The right which everyone enjoys of having recourse to the guarantee of the law and the tutelary authority is properly speaking *civil right*. If one wishes to speak with precision, *mediate* right adds nothing to original rights, it is a natural consequence of them, as we have said in the preceding article. It is rather a *service* of guarantee and regularization in the exercise of natural rights, which embrace everything and for which everything exists – a fact that cannot be too often repeated, so great are the pretensions of public officials who exploit the confusion of language and seek to persuade the multitude that we have only retained those rights that the law permits or authorizes.

In order to conform to usage we speak of our rights as having become *civil* through the guarantee of the city although the law is far from being able to declare and guarantee all our rights. For the rest, the facts that can be cited against this are not derived from political order but from political disorder, and we are only concerned here with right. Our civil rights are the property of all the inhabitants of the city, and as such present no difficulty. The majority do not see beyond this, and in spite of the long experience of events, are always on the point of telling you: what need do we have of *political* rights provided we can freely enjoy our civil rights! Certainly these rights are the most important, but for that very reason they are in greater need of guarantee.

In the same way that the mutual recognition of natural rights rendered them positive; in the same say that they received a fresh guarantee by becoming civil; so I demand a third guarantee and this the most necessary of all. Up till now these different guarantees only protect those who enjoy them against other individuals who would disturb their enjoyment. But where is the guarantee against the powers established for the sake of protection, if the latter turn their relatively irresistible force against individual rights? It lies in the existence and exercise of political rights. Since man is free and obliges himself only by way of voluntary engagement, he must have the right to pronounce his political will, his civil will. The political association is assuredly the work of the associates. The law which is to oblige them cannot be other than the expression of the

> general will. I say further, the creation of the public establishment, and the constitution which organizes it, cannot be other than the product of this same will.[47]

Natural right, *positive* right, *civil* right, *political* right: this step-by-step articulation is unquestionably an advance upon the more abstract and abrupt reasoning of the *Exposition*. Man's rights and duties now become specific through a cumulative process of exchange or agreement with other men, beginning with recognition, rather than through some sudden insight into the necessity of reciprocity.

It remains only to add one further dimension of Sieyes' conception of the ends of the state. We have seen earlier that his idea of the 'common will' of the nation was that of the identical will of its members to enjoy liberty and property. In the rise of Robespierre and the creation of the Jacobin dictatorship he saw, not only an attack on the idea of representative government in the name of negative liberty – something which he had tried to counter in his essay on *Liberty* – he also saw men subjected ruthlessly to a grotesquely exaggerated conception of the 'common will'. In three of his unpublished notes we can catch a glimpse of his reaction to this second development. The first of them is entitled simply 'The end of the social state'. These are his words:

> The *end* of the political order is individual liberty, the private weal (*la chose privée*).
>
> Those people who think of it as an abstract thing, a public happiness that belongs to no one, deceive themselves. Almost all so-called republican systems go wrong on this point. For them the public weal is nothing but an abstract being, a superstition, an idol to which one offers victims. Mark well: the only real happiness is that of individuals.
>
> Ask Lycurgus [Robespierre's hero – and Rousseau's] what his aim was in founding the Spartan constitution. He wished to construct a state. Men were for him the stones for his building. For me it is the stone that is all, the end of all, and the building is at its service.[48]

Another fragment written about the same time is entitled: 'The basis and end of society is not *unity* of property':

> Democracy as it is commonly understood will only give a *minimum* of individual liberty. For it is the complete sacrifice of the individual to the public weal, that is to say, of the tangible being to the abstract being, etc.
>
> Public properties, we have said, are friends of equality. Without doubt. But everything in its due measure. If you show your dislike for private labour by depriving it of too great a capacity to produce, you will diminish labour and soon public properties will wither away as well as private ones. Because public properties are friends of equality, it is not necessary to make everything into public property. If you remove from labour, from industry, their natural quality, the spontaneous effort of a free being to attain an object hidden in its will, you will reduce the people a hundredfold. This type of democracy will be the hardest form of slavery, and the kind of life it will necessitate will be the saddest that ever existed on the globe. How many people confuse *democratic equality* with *unity of property*. The Jesuits in Paraguay attempted this kind of servitude, combining it with the pleasures of an aristocracy.[49]

A little later Sieyes expanded further on this theme, in a fragment entitled 'Basis and end of society: respect for individual liberty.' It ran as follows:

> The public order (*chose publique*) is made for the individual and not the individual for the public order. In other words the public order is not, as we have observed a hundred times, the total order, or the sum of everything private. ... Hence it is wrong to think of *work* in general as being a part of the public order, you should not distribute it, command it, direct it, or reward it as if it were a public function; you should not organize a body of farmers, another of ploughwrights, of carpenters, blacksmiths, masons, tailors, sailmakers, etc. A social organization of this kind is no longer the social state created to protect and to perfect *individual liberty*. It would amount to the sacrifice of the *end* to an absurdly monastic ordering of *means*. Leave to the individual, for whom all exists, his rights, his tastes, his industry, his particular genius.
>
> Why do all makers of plans have an involuntary tendency to monasticize people? It is because they are systematic spirits, and they wish to *unify* and *integrate*, instead of to *unite* [*aduner* – the word that Sieyes himself coined to describe the unification of the administrative and electoral structures of France that he proposed in 1789]. It is because they regard the individual as materials for a building, his individual liberty is nothing to them.[50]

These words form a fitting conclusion to this discussion of Sieyes' conception of the ends of the body politic. The common or general will which public institutions represented was not for him an all-absorbing, total will into which the individuals that made up the body politic were blended, it was rather the impartial will to secure and develop personal liberty; liberty being defined as at once independence, or a freedom to act guaranteed vis-à-vis others, and power, the capacity to act. By the same token Sieyes' liberalism – for this is the only word that can adequately define his position – was not of the crabbed, doctrinaire type that sees liberty as essentially the right of the individual 'not to be interfered with', insists on reducing the scope of public action to the barest minimum compatible with 'law and order', and thinks that the idea of 'positive liberty' is in some sense 'totalitarian'. Sieyes' vision was broader and deeper. He argued that personal liberty was something that could be expanded, and that public actions and public works could and should help in this work of expansion. At the same time he showed that it was *only* in the expansion of the liberty of individual human beings, and not in their subordination to some abstract, reified communal ideal that the ends of the body politic were realized. In his own words, 'the only real happiness is that of individuals'.

7 The means of the new state: the representative system

Un système représentatif pour la chose politique, analogue à celui qui existe partout pour les choses particulières, voilà ce qu'il faut, et l'on y trouvera réuni, sans mélange du mal, tout ce qu'il y a de bon dans la démocratie, dans l'aristocratie, et dans la monarchie. Quelle nécessité de n'habiter qu'un labyrinthe noir et douleureux, quand on peut avoir un maison claire et commode.

Sieyes, *Bases of the social order* (1794–5)

SIEYES called the establishment of the representative system the 'true object of the revolution'.[1] Of all the leading political theorists of the past he is pre-eminently the theorist of representation. The concept runs like a thread throughout his political writings. Hobbes, it is true, had given representation a key role in the construction of *Leviathan*, but he had not developed the idea very far. Locke's notion of representation was extremely undeveloped. Rousseau had condemned representation. Sieyes by contrast displayed the full richness of the idea for an understanding of the political order. The representative system for him denoted the whole concatenation of means by which the ends of the state were realized.

To grasp Sieyes' notion of the representative system we must be prepared to go beyond the rather narrow meaning that tends to be attached to the term representation in the context of politics to-day. 'The modern tendency', writes Friedrich, 'is to identify representation with election.'[2] A representative political system tends to be seen, in the first instance, as a system within which there is a legislative assembly elected by popular vote. Linked very closely to this equation of representation and voting is the idea of representation as a kind of 'mirroring' or 'reflection'. A representative system is said to be truly representative when those who are voted into the legislative assembly 'reflect' the composition, whether it be social, political, religious, ethnic or otherwise, of the society that elects. We have only to glance at a work such as Birch's, which is purportedly about the whole notion of representation, to realize how narrowly in practice the modern mind focuses on these two interlocking themes.[3]

It would be quite wrong to say that Sieyes' representative system bore no relation to the issue of electing a legislature. He was intensely concerned to secure an equitably elected legislature in France in 1789, and his complete recasting of the electoral and administrative boundaries of the country remains one of his most significant and long-lasting contributions to the revolutionary movement. But to him the creation of a properly elected legislature was only a part of the idea of a representative system which was much wider in its connotations. To understand this idea we must stand back a little from conventional usages.

Of course much of what has been said in previous chapters foreshadows the content of this one. It has been shown how, in his great revolutionary tracts of 1788–89, Sieyes used his analytical method to demonstrate that the nation as a union of individuals must exercise the constituent power to establish a government by proxy or procuration. It has been shown how he believed that a representative system of government was not a constriction but an extension of the idea of liberty. Lastly, it has been shown how his early study of political economy, and in particular of the division of labour in society, was one of the shaping influences that determined his fervent advocacy of the representative system. Now the various pieces must be brought together and the kernel of Sieyes' conception of the representative system must be indicated.

Such a task is not easy because of the very proliferation of his statements on the subject. There is no single text by him that can be taken as the basic one, to which the others are more or less appendices. For this reason it seems best to begin by throwing into relief the leading elements of his idea of the representative system, as they emerge from the totality of his writings, and then to look in more detail at some of his arguments and deductions.

There would appear to be four central components of Sieyes' representative system. The first and most basic refers to the original constitution of the public establishment. A system of government was representative when the nation or people who formed a political union, instead of themselves exercising the power of the union, embodied this power in a structure of offices that was distinct from the other activities of the citizenry, and staffed by only a fraction of the citizenry. Representation here meant the deliberate separation of public activities, or activities related to the community as a whole, from other – by definition, private – activities, through a process of institutionalization, and the entrustment of the exercise of these institutionalized powers to specialists. It signified a decision to allow a segment of the citizenry to carry out public duties 'on behalf of' the others. It was a particular expression of the process of division and combination of labour that took place whenever a society came into existence in place of a mere collection of individuals each doing everything for himself.

Sieyes contrasted a representative system in this sense with democracy, according to which the whole mass of the citizenry exercised directly the power of the union, where there was not, properly speaking, a distinct act of constitution, and where the separate embodiment of public power and its exercise by specialists was rejected. For him democracy, or direct self-government, was undoubtedly a legitimate form of government, indeed he saw it as the only other legitimate form besides the representative system, but it was wholly inferior to the latter in terms of rationality, and in terms of the liberty of its individual members. Therefore when it is said that the French Revolution formed part of the 'age of the democratic revolution', it must be remembered that for one of the leading protagonists of the French Revolution democracy was *not* the objective, but something that went beyond it.

It has to be stressed that representation, in this first sense of separation, institutionalization and specialization, did not refer solely to the legislative power. It referred to all public powers, or as Sieyes tended to define them, the power to 'will' on behalf of the community and the power to 'act' on behalf of the community. Both those who made laws and those who applied them thus merited the title 'representative' even if the law-applying power happened to be concentrated in one man. To Barnave, who argued that only those who 'willed' for the nation were representatives, and that the king was therefore not a representative, Sieyes replied that 'every man who exercises a public power, even in the executive order, is by this title a genuine representative of the people.'[4]

Sieyes' actions and words in the Revolution also make it clear that he did not think it essential for the constituent power of the nation, or the power that established the representative system, to be exercised directly by the nation. In a large state it became necessary for it too to be represented as well as the normal powers of law-making and law-application.[5] His chief emphasis was that the two – the constituent power and the constituted powers – should be kept strictly separate, and not (as in Rousseau's *Contrat social*) blended together. In practice, during the period from 1789 to 1791, and again from 1792 to 1795 this strict separation was not achieved.

The second major element of Sieyes' representative system was that all holders of representative office had to be elected by the people. This condition he thought so self-evident that he did not dwell on it at any length in his writings. In his first pamphlet, the *Views*, he remarked simply that the term representation 'necessarily carries with it the characteristic of free election on the part of those who are represented'[6] and this was always his opinion. There could, in other words, be no self-assumed representation of public powers; no one could claim to represent by hereditary right, or by their supposed insight into what was necessary or good for the people, or by direct commission from God. Only those who had been elected to constituted public office had the right to represent.

The one important moment when Sieyes compromised with this principle was when he accepted that royalty, under the 1791 Constitution which he helped to draft, should be 'delegated in a hereditary manner' to the ruling family. He did not deny that this was a derogation from the strict principle of representation and defended it on entirely practical grounds, as the least troublesome and divisive way of settling the issue in the historical circumstances.[7] The 'monarch' that he proposed in 1799 in his last constitutional scheme – the so-called Great Elector – was not hereditary but chosen by a special college.

This leads to another important aspect of Sieyes' principle of election. He did not mean by it that the occupants of all representative offices, legislative and executive, should be directly elected by the people. The legislative should be so elected, but it was in his view precisely one of the main public tasks of a monarch or single 'leader' of the nation to choose or select, from *amongst* persons chosen by the people, the holders of what is commonly called the executive power. Hence the title 'Great Elector'. Election from below thus did not preclude selection from above, as indeed it does not in the practice of western constitutional states to-day.

The third component of Sieyes' representative system was the idea that no elected occupant of representative office could be bound by an imperative mandate. Within the sphere of duty that the consititution mapped out for them representatives had to be free to deliberate and decide. This principle Sieyes enunciated vigorously not only with regard to the institutions that were constituted after 1789 – it is embedded in Article 7 of Title III of the 1791 Constitution – but also with regard to the Estates-General summoned in 1789 and the National Assembly that was formed out of the Estates-General. His arguments during this very early period were directed first at ensuring that the Third Estate would have sufficient independence to bring about the creation of the National Assembly, and then at ensuring that the National Assembly itself would have sufficient independence to proceed with the work of constitution-making.

They were also directed at defeating any move to transform France into a confederation of small democracies united by a congress of instructed delegates, and here, once again, the contrast with Rousseau is interesting. For a small country Rousseau had advocated direct democracy in the legislature, but for the large country of Poland he had proposed a federal structure with local diets sending 'nuncios' to a central diet. On the question of imperative mandates Rousseau had been strangely equivocal. On the one hand he argued that the 'nuncios' should do nothing contrary to the express will of their constituents, and should render account to them. They should be '*asservis à leurs instructions*'. On the other hand he appeared to view the central diet as fully sovereign, to see its voice as 'the voice of God on earth', and to regard each local diet as completely subordinate to it. The local diets could thus punish their 'nuncios', and even 'have their heads cut off', but they had to obey the centre 'fully, always, without exception, without protest'.[8] Sieyes' ideas are free from this bizarre ambiguity. He regarded the idea of punishing a deputy for his opinion as barbaric and, when made into a legal provision, an absurd contradiction.[9] He rejected the idea of instruction completely.

The fourth and final component of Sieyes' representative system was the idea that there should be separation and specialization of function *within* the public establishment itself. The power exercised on behalf of the community should be broken down into its separate elements, each of which would be entrusted to a specialized public office, and all, working together, would produce the public action. Sieyes' idea of specialized functions had little in common with the kind of separation of powers that Montesquieu envisaged, or that was embodied in the English constitution. It was not based on the separate representation of the different strata of society, or a legislature composed of king, lords and commoners. It had little in common with the idea of 'balance of power' or 'counterweight' that was so closely entwined with the English system, though not necessarily connected with the representation of different orders. It was, however, aimed at preventing the accumulation of represented power in one hand, and hence at defending freedom against tyranny or despotism.

Sieyes believed in the functional separation of public powers from the start of the Revolution. After his experience of the Jacobin dictatorship he emphasized it with renewed vigour. The weakness of his last constitutional proposals – those of 1799 – is paradoxically that he pushed the principle of separate function to an unrealistic extreme, creating a public structure that sinned against the very principle which he had espoused in his early years, namely that of simplicity.

These then are the four basic principles of Sieyes' representative system: the deliberate externalization and specialized exercise of the public powers of the community; the election of those who exercised public powers; the granting of the power to deliberate and decide to the holders of public office; and the specialization of functions within the public establishment. It is time now to look more closely at the way Sieyes himself developed these principles in the course of his life.

1 Sieyes' advocacy of representation in his early writings and at the start of the Revolution

One of the most remarkable aspects of Sieyes' concept of the representative system is that it does not seem to have been the result of a gradual process of illumination but to have sprung fully-fledged from his pen at a very early age. Already in his earliest unpublished notes dating from 1770–75 the main lines of his doctrine can be quite clearly seen. Thus, to take the most striking example, in an unpublished note which is firmly dated 1770, we find him mapping out the following schema of government.[10] First, there are a couple of typical short emphatic sentences: 'The *government* of the state of a large nation is necessarily representative. It is a *deposit confided to a certain number of public officers*.'

Then three forms of representation are distinguished:

1. *Honorific representation*, or the depository of honours, and of national majesty. = the king.
2. *Volitional representation*, or the depository of public wills
   Legislation = the senate.
3. *Active representation*, or the depository of public acts
   Administration = the commissioned agents of the public wills.

Following this Sieyes appended the pregnant sentence: 'The three forms of monarchy, aristocracy, and democracy, more or less modified, meet together in the true constitution.'

On a succeeding sheet Sieyes set out the reasons why the republics of ancient times were *not* representative. The first was their small size, and the second was that their '*citizens* were only those inhabitants who were wholly or in large part *disposable*', that is, who were endowed with sufficient leisure to be able to consider public affairs. The rest of the population were either slaves or foreigners to the 'social action'. In modern society, by contrast, there were no slaves, no vast chunk of the population excluded from citizenship. Our society stood on 'a wider, more humane basis'. Then Sieyes continued: 'It follows that government is necessarily representative, that it can only be a commission ... our states are [also] more advanced in the arts of production and commerce, divisions of labour within them are more pronounced and more developed, and government exercised by detachment is all the better because each profession exercised by a class of men who devote themselves exclusively to it is more productive.'

These last sentences reveal plainly that Sieyes' conception of representation was largely shaped by his study of political economy. In the earlier discussion of the influences on his thought it was particularly emphasized that his youthful intellectual wrestling with the doctrines of the Physiocrats and Turgot played a considerable part in impressing his mind with the merits of representation.

In the revolutionary tracts that he published in the winter of 1788–89 Sieyes demonstrated by a process of analysis that government by representation was the form of government demanded by reason. In the *Views* he mapped out, in the form of a hypothetical step-by-step reconstruction, the way in which a small original community, in which all the citizens directly participate in their own government, expands in numbers, subdivides into a multiplicity of democratic cantons sending delegates to a confederal meeting-place, and then, dissatisfied with this mode of public decision, establishes a genuinely representative form of central government. In *What is the Third Estate?* the process of logical reconstruction is slightly shorter: a small political union, exercising its common will directly, expands in numbers, and decides therefore to establish a 'government exercised by procuration'. Perhaps the most interesting aspect of the account in the latter text was Sieyes' observation that in establishing a representative government, the pre-existing community or nation only detaches a 'portion of the national will and consequently of power' to be exercised by some amongst them. 'The community does not strip itself of the right to will; that is its inalienable property; it can only commit the exercise of it.'[11] His reasoning on this occasion has already been set out in chapter 3.

In his revolutionary tracts Sieyes did not merely argue that the future form of government in France must logically be representative, he also affirmed that those who had been elected to the Estates-General, and in particular those who had been elected by the Third Estate, were not merely 'carriers of votes' or instructed delegates, but genuine representatives. Their function was not to bear the particular grievances of those who had elected them to a common meeting-place, and then to express them publicly to the king; it was to make manifest the common will of the nation on behalf of the nation. To fulfil this function they required the freedom to deliberate and decide. There could be no imperative mandates.

Sieyes defined the necessary powers that were implied in representation in the concluding section of the *Deliberations*, first published in February 1789. His words express the nub of this important matter with exemplary clarity:

> The body of representatives of a great people deliberates in the same way as a very small people completely assembled together in the public square. There is only one difference, which is that in the small people voting for themselves there resides the plenitude of rights and powers, whereas the mission of the assembly of representatives of a nation is limited by its object. The representatives only represent with regard to the task with which they have been entrusted. But within the sphere of their mission their powers are full and unlimited. It would

> be ridiculous for them to be entrusted with making the law on some subject and then to be refused the means or the freedom to make it well. Hence the phrase *plenary power* can be understood in two senses. Either it is the power to *do everything*, limited only by natural morality, a power that belongs solely to the nation itself; or it has to be understood as the right to *do the best one can* in relation to the objective that you have entrusted your deputies to fulfil. In the latter sense powers are equally unlimited, but they are so with regard to the *extent* of right within the same business, and not because they *extend* over all business, for example over such matters as go beyond the mission that you have accorded them. These distinctions will appear metaphysical, but it is essential nonetheless to grasp them because it can then be seen that the question of *limited* and *unlimited* powers is purely a matter of words. Powers are never limited; they either exist or do not exist. Beyond the object of my procuration I have no powers. Within the object of my procuration either you charge me with doing my best, as you would do yourself, in which case I am your *representative*; or you charge me solely with making manifest your opinions, in which case I am only a *carrier of votes*.[12]

In a footnote added at this point Sieyes observed that it would 'perhaps be better to make a distinction between *power* and *powers*. *Power* gives the right to deliberate and decide. *Powers* indicate the matters over which the right to deliberate etc. is exercised.'[13] He then turned to the proper aim and mode of work of an assembly of representatives, of the kind that he assumed the forthcoming assembly of the Estates General in May 1789 ought to be. The deputies in such an assembly could not be regarded as mere 'carriers of votes', their object was to produce a common will out of the multitude of individual wills:

> How could that be done if each voting individual could not change anything he had said? The members of a representative assembly ... gather in order to balance their opinions, to modify them, to purify some through others, and to extract finally from the *lumières* of all, a majority opinion, that is to say, the common will which makes the law. The mixing of individual wills, the kind of fermentation that they undergo in this operation, are necessary to produce the result that is desired. It is therefore essential that opinions should be able to concert, to yield, in a word to modify one another, for without this there is no longer a deliberative assembly but simply a *rendez-vous of couriers*, ready to depart after having delivered their dispatches.[14]

These passages express the kernel of Sieyes' argument that any form of imperative mandate imposed upon the members of a legislative assembly was completely incompatible with the basic principles of the representative system.

Sieyes' view of the representative status of the elected members of the Estates-General makes it all the more understandable why he was to be so intransigent on the matter once the Estates-General had been transformed, on the initiative of the Third Estate, into the Constituent or National Assembly. Early in July, after the recalcitrant members of the other two Estates had been instructed by the king to join the new Assembly, the issue of imperative mandates came to the fore, some of the new members having declared that they considered themselves bound by them. On 7 July Talleyrand presented a report on the issue, which proposed that all the electing bailiwicks should annul their imperative mandates. Sieyes went a stage further. He declared that a discussion of this matter was superfluous: the newly constituted Assembly consisted expressly of 'representatives' and this in itself meant that its deliberations could not be obstructed by instructions from outside. He proposed that the Assembly should make a brief statement asking those bailiwicks that had tied their elected members by imperative mandates 'to accord their deputies the freedom necessary for true representatives of the nation' and declaring that 'the French nation being always legitimately represented as a complete unity by the majority of its deputies, neither imperative mandates, nor the voluntary absence of some members, nor the protestations of the minority can ever halt its activity, or alter the freedom, or attenuate the force of its statutes, or finally restrain the limits of the places subjected to its legislative power, which extend essentially to every part of the French nation and its possessions.'[15] The Assembly voted in favour of Sieyes' opinion that there were no grounds for a debate, and issued a watered-down version of his proposed statement. The decision marked another important consolidation of the revolutionary movement.

2 Sieyes' advocacy of representation between 1789 and 1793

From the point of view of the political theorist the single most important statement by Sieyes on the subject of the representative system between the formation of the Constituent Assembly and the creation of the Jacobin dictatorship in 1793 was his *Speech on the royal veto*, delivered on 7 September 1789. It brings together his ideas on the subject in a forcible manner: the socio-economic rationale of representation; representation versus imperative mandates; representation versus democracy; and representation versus confederation. In many ways it is a curious speech, because it ranges over a far wider span of issues than its title would suggest. To understand its rather odd construction something must be said of its historical background.

Essentially there were two developments that Sieyes wished to combat in his speech in September. The first was the movement which is now usually referred to as the 'municipal revolution', which was sparked off in July by the overthrow of the old city government in Paris and the fall of the Bastille, and which led to the purging and refounding of municipal authorities throughout the length and breadth of France. The municipal revolution was a vigorous grass-roots movement that brought new men into power in the townships, men who saw themselves as no longer owing allegiance to the king but to the National Assembly. As such it represented a vast accession of strength to the revolutionary change that had taken place in Versailles in June. At the same time it represented a danger, for it threatened the very national unity in the name of which that revolutionary change had been made. In Lefebvre's words, 'centralization was destroyed; each municipality exercised absolute power not only over itself but over surrounding parishes; from the month of August onwards, the towns began to conclude pacts of mutual assistance, so that France was spontaneously transformed into a federation of communes.'[16] Neither were there writers lacking to give support and justification to this centrifugal, disintegrative process. Brissot in particular drew up a 'Declaration of the rights of Communes' and advocated, on the express analogy of the United States of

America, a kind of federal structure for France.[17] (Perhaps this is where the later accusation of 'federalism' launched at Brissot and the Girondins had its root.)

Here then was one danger that Sieyes wished to combat. The second danger was more directly connected with the constitution-making activities of the National Assembly. After it had finally agreed upon the Declaration of Rights that was to form the preamble to the constitution, the Assembly moved, at the end of August 1789, to a discussion of the first clauses of the constitution itself, as drafted by the Constitutional Committee. Amongst the proposals of the Committee the one that stirred up by far the most intensive debate was that of the royal power to veto legislative measures. It occupied the Assembly from 1 September to 7 September.

In this debate two opposing views quickly emerged. On the one hand there were those who wished the king, under the future constitution, to have an absolute veto on legislation. This group included Mounier, d'Antraigues, Maury, de Sèze, Clermont-Tonnerre and Mirabeau. Most of those who wanted an absolute veto also wanted a two-chamber legislature, and a legislative system akin to the one that was believed to exist in England, a system of 'counterforces'. They were the Anglophiles. Opposed to them was the much larger group who argued in favour of a suspensive veto for the king. This group included Salle, Pétion, Malouet, the Lameths, Grégoire, Rabaut Saint-Etienne, Goupil de Préfeln, and Dupont de Nemours. The suspensive veto was thus supported by both radicals and moderates, and this was undoubtedly one of the reasons why it finally carried the day. The important thing to note is that the bulk of the partisans of the suspensive veto defended it as a procedure for 'remedying the vices of the system of representation.'[18] It was argued that by means of the king's suspensive veto an appeal could be made, behind the back of an elected legislative assembly, to the people itself. The assumption was that representation was not a very trustworthy mode of discovering the legislative general will, and that it needed to be supplemented and guarded against by a system of direct consultation of the people amongst whom the general will *really* resided. As one of the Lameths put it: '*L'appel au peuple est le voeu général, et la Constitution doit donner au Roi le veto suspensif.*'[19]

Sieyes had no sympathy for the English system of 'counterforces'; the legislative will of one nation had to possess the essential quality of unity. There was no need to divide it against itself. At the same time, for reasons which will already have become apparent, he was bitterly opposed to the suggestion that representation was somehow a second-best solution; for him it was the only rational and logical mode of deciding upon laws. Therefore he opposed *both* the absolute *and* the suspensive vetos, and argued instead that the legislative will of the nation could lie nowhere else than in the majority will of the legislative body established by the constitution. In a famous phrase he stated that 'the *veto*, whether it is called suspensive or absolute, seems to me nothing other than an arbitrary order; I cannot see it as anything else than a *lettre-de-cachet* directed against the national will, against the whole nation.' Curiously perhaps, one of the few members of the Assembly whose viewpoint coincided with that of Sieyes on this occasion, was Robespierre.

The similarity of the threat posed by the municipal revolution and the proposed appeal to the people needs scarcely to be emphasized. Both threatened to reduce the legislative assembly of France to a mere agency of bodies outside it, whether these bodies were the towns or the local electoral assemblies of the people. This explains why Sieyes dwelt so long in his speech on the question of the representative status of a legislative assembly. It also explains why he urged that the organization of the electoral system and of local government ought to be decided upon before a decision was taken on the structure of the national legislative body and so-called '*appel au peuple*'. He wanted the unity of the French body politic, and the representative character of its national assembly to be unequivocally established before the organization of the central powers was settled. Sieyes failed to hold up the Assembly's decision on the veto or the structure of the legislature but his subsequent labours on the territorial reorganization of France were partially successful in countering the dangers to the unity of the French state.

We are now in a position to follow Sieyes' reasoning. He began his discussion of representation with a general statement about the dangers inherent in the federalizing tendency at work in the country:

> I am aware that by dint of distinctions on the one hand and confusion on the other the national will has come to be regarded as if it were something other than the will of the representatives of the nation; as if the nation could speak otherwise than through its representatives. Here false principles become extremely dangerous. Their only result is to cut, chop, and tear France into an infinity of small democracies, which then join together simply by the ties of a general confederation, rather as the thirteen or fourteen United States of America formed a confederation in a general Convention.
>
> This object deserves our closest attention. France must not be an assemblage of little nations, governing themselves separately as democracies; it is not a collection of states; it is a single *whole*, composed of integral parts; these parts must not enjoy separately a complete existence, because they are not merely united wholes, but parts forming but one whole. The difference is immense; it is of vital interest to us. All is lost if we allow ourselves to consider the municipalities that are being established, or the districts, or the provinces, as so many republics united solely by the ties of common force or protection. Instead of a general administration spreading out from a common centre and falling in a uniform manner on the furthest reaches of the empire; instead of a legislation formed out of the citizens coming together in an ascending scale that reaches up to the National Assembly, the sole authorized interpreter of the general will; instead of this will that descends once again with all the weight of an irresistible force on the very wills that have concurred to form it – instead of all this we will have nothing more than a kingdom bristling within with every kind of barrier, a chaos of local customs, regulations and prohibitions. This beautiful country will become odious to travellers and to its inhabitants. But it is not my intention to present to you the innumerable inconveniences that will overwhelm France if she should ever be transformed into a confederation of municipalities or provinces. That is not your plan, gentlemen: it suffices therefore to note that, if we do not take care, the principles that we appear to be adopting, aided already by far too influential circumstances, could well lead us to a political situation which is not what we are aiming at, and from which we would have considerable difficulty in escaping.[20]

A little later Sieyes entered more directly into the rationale of the representative system:

> Modern European peoples bear scarcely any resemblance to ancient ones. Amongst us it is a question solely of commerce, agriculture, manufacture, etc. The desire for wealth seems to make all the states of Europe into nothing other than immense workshops: much more thought is given in them to consumption and production than to happiness. Political systems too are to-day founded exclusively on work; the productive faculties of man are everything; we scarcely know how to make use of the moral faculties which could nevertheless become the most fruitful source of truer enjoyments. We are thus compelled to regard the greater part of humanity as nothing other than work machines (*machines de travail*). However you cannot refuse the status of citizen, and civil rights, to this uneducated multitude whom compulsory labour absorbs in its entirety. Since they must obey the law, just like you, they ought to participate, like you, in making it. This participation must be equal.
>
> It can be exercised in two ways. The citizens can give their confidence to some amongst them. Without alienating their rights, they commit their exercise. It is for the common utility that they nominate representatives more capable than themselves of knowing the general interest and of interpreting their own will in this respect.
>
> The other way of exercising one's right with regard to the formation of the law, is to concur directly in its making oneself. This direct concurrence is what characterizes true *democracy*. Mediate concurrence designates *representative government*. The difference between these two systems is enormous.
>
> The choice between these two methods of making the law is not in doubt amongst us.
>
> In the first place, the vast majority of our fellow citizens have neither sufficient education, nor sufficient leisure to want to occupy themselves directly with the laws that ought to govern France; their decision (*avis*) is thus to nominate representatives; and since it is the decision of the greater number, enlightened persons must submit to it like everyone else. When a society is formed, the decision of the majority, as you know, is the law for everyone.
>
> This reasoning, which is valid for the tiniest municipalities, becomes irresistible when one remembers that it is a question here of the laws to govern twenty-six million men. For I always maintain that France is not, and cannot be a *democracy*; it must not become a *federal state*, composed of a multitude of republics, united by some kind of political tie. France is and must be a *single whole*, subject throughout to a common legislation and a common administration. Since it is plain that five to six million active citizens, spread over more than twenty-five thousand square leagues cannot assemble together, it is incontestable that they can only aspire to a legislature by *representation*. Hence citizens who nominate representatives, renounce and must renounce the idea of making the law directly themselves. Hence they have no individual will to impose. They have full power and influence over the persons of their mandatories, but that is all. If they dictate their wills, it would no longer be a representative state but a democratic one.[21]

From here it was but a short step to a condemnation of imperative mandates:

> For a deputy there is, and there can be, no imperative mandate, or indeed positive will, except that of the national will. He need defer to the councils of those who directly elect him only in so far as these councils are in conformity with the national will. And where else can this will exist, where else can it be recognized except in the National Assembly itself? It is not by scrutinizing

> particular *cahiers*, if such exist, that he will discover the will of his electors. It is not a question here of conducting a democratic poll, but of proposing, listening, concerting, modifying his opinion, in a word of forming in common a common will.[22]

Perhaps the most interesting part of Sieyes' argument concerning imperative mandates on this occasion was his use of the analogy of a small democracy. Sieyes did not argue that in the representative system the imperative mandate typical of a small democracy had to be abandoned, but rather that even in a small democracy the imperative mandate did not exist:

> It is not on the evening before, each in his own house, that democrats dedicated to freedom form and fix their own opinions, so that they can then carry these opinions to the public square, with the reservation that, should it not prove possible to discover a common majority will from all these isolated opinions, they can return back home and start again in isolation. Let it be said immediately: this procedure for forming a common will would be absurd.[23]

In effect what Sieyes is saying here is that even in the smallest direct democracy an element of representation creeps unavoidably in because the citizens assembled in the public square, deliberating and making decisions together, are distinct from the citizens taken one by one in their own homes. The constitution of a representative system simply develops this seed of representation further. It does not remove from the individual the right to see his own personal will reflected in each law (for this did not exist even in the democratic polity) but it separates from the mass of the citizenry a mode of extracting a common will, namely an assembly operating by majority decision, that already existed in the democratic polity.

To insist on the imperative mandate within a representative system can thus only be called a 'democratic' demand if the aim is to break a country up into a congeries of small democratic states held together by a confederal tie. The imperative mandate is not an intrinsic part of democracy, but rather a means of external linkage *between* democracies. To insist on imperative mandates *per se*, in all situations, on the assumption that they are truly democratic, would be in reality to destroy all possibility of establishing a political unity. Carried to its logical conclusion one would be left with nothing more than individuals co-existing like monks in their cells. This is what Sieyes meant when he continued:

> It is useless for there to be a *decision* in the bailiwicks or the municipalities, or in each town or village house, for the ideas that I am fighting against lead to nothing other than this kind of political *Chartreuse*. Pretensions of this kind go beyond democracy. Decision belongs and can only belong to the nation assembled.[24]

The logical corollary of Sieyes' argument against imperative mandates was that those who were elected to the legislative assembly were not properly speaking representatives of their constituencies but of the whole nation. The districts that performed the work of electing members were not to be seen as distinct wholes which together made up the body politic, but rather as sub-divisions of the whole, created by the whole, that is to say by the nation as constituent power, in order to fulfil the specific task of choosing the members of the national legislative assembly. Sieyes had elaborated this point in his very earliest work, the *Views*. In his speech of 7 September he was briefer:

> The deputy of a bailiwick is chosen immediately by his bailiwick; but mediately, he is elected by the totality of bailiwicks. That is why every deputy is representative of the whole nation. Without that, there would be a political inequality that nothing could justify; and the minority could make law for the majority.[25]

The speech on the royal veto has been cited at some length because in it the various components of Sieyes' representative system can be seen as an interlocking unity. It may seem perhaps as if his comprehensive dismissal of the idea of transforming France into some kind of federal union of small states was somewhat peremptory so it is worth noting that in an unpublished paper that he wrote at about the same time he actually listed the disadvantages of small states.

The object of this paper was to clarify his proposals for the territorial redivison of France into 720 communes, and he began by picturing these communes as so many little independent republics. he then imagined someone proposing that they unite to form a single immense empire. Why make such a proposition? Why move from many small states to one big one? Sieyes suggested three principal reasons. First, experience showed that numerous neighbouring small states were always at war, and that their wars were all the more savage because of their close proximity. Second, much more abundant and more efficient public works were possible in large states, and such works were a powerful stimulus to the advancement of the sciences. Third, a large state was more capable of defending itself against outside attack than a small one, and alliances were not a sufficient alternative because they left room for intrigue between the participating states and outside states.[26]

It is clear from these words that, just as Sieyes did not regard representation as simply a technical requirement, made necessary by the size of a given country, so he did not think the size of a state was merely a contingent or accidental factor, of negligible interest when compared, say, with the need to have a purely democratic form of government. On the contrary the size of a state, its bigness, was of direct and vital relevance to its ability to carry out its functions as a state, namely the preservation of peace, the maintenance of welfare, and defence against attacks from without. It was not contingent but necessary for states to be large.

The unpublished paper to which reference has been made was the first draft of Sieyes' *Observations* on the plan for the territorial redivision of France that had been drawn up by the Constitutional Committee of the National Assembly, and for which he himself had been primarily responsible. The *Observations* were published in October 1789, and contain a general statement about representation which, although it overlaps to some extent with his speech in September, nevertheless expresses some interesting new elaborations:

> For those who consult reason rather than books it is evident that amongst men there can only be *one* legitimate government. It can manifest itself in *two* different forms.
>
> The members of a political association want either to rule themselves, or to

choose some of their number only to occupy themselves with the care and supervision that public needs demand.

In the first instance it is pure, I was going to say raw democracy, on the analogy of the raw materials and crude foodstuffs that nature has everywhere offered to man, but which man everywhere applies his industry to modify and prepare in order to make them suitable for his needs and enjoyment.

Men do not unite in political society in order to spend an idle life amongst pleasant pastimes; they have other things to do besides organizing games and fêtes. Nature has subjected us to the law of work. She has made the first advances to us, and then said: Do you wish to find enjoyment? Work. It is for a more assured, more abundant, more differentiated consumption, and hence to guarantee and progressively to perfect his work, that man is destined to unite with his fellow men. Reason, or at least experience, has said furthermore to man: you will succeed better in your occupations the more you learn to limit them. By concentrating all the faculties of your spirit on only one part of the totality of useful work, you will obtain a greater product with less hardship and less cost. Hence arises the division of labour, cause and effect of the growth of wealth and the improvement of human industry. The subject has been thoroughly developed in the work of Doctor [Adam] Smith. This division is to the common benefit of all members of society. It applies to political work as well as to every kind of productive work. The common interest, the improvement of the social state itself summon us to make government a distinct profession. Only the voice of superstition and tyranny attempts to push us further and urges us to cede to those who govern the inalienable right of making law. It is evident that if the ministers of the law could make it, they would be the masters; it is evident that the law ought to be the free work of those who ought to obey it, the clear and promulgated expression of their will.

Thus the purely democratic constitution becomes not only impossible in a large society; even in the smallest state it is much less appropriate for the needs of society, much less conducive to the objects of political union, than the *representative* constitution: such is the second legitimate form of government.[27]

Sieyes' reference to Adam Smith here should not deceive us into thinking that his ideas on representation derived from him. As his early notes show, and as he himself observed, he had developed his idea of a representative system before he read Smith's *Wealth of Nations*, though the latter doubtless reinforced his convictions.[28]

There is no need to dwell on Sieyes' other speeches and writings before the abolition of the monarchy in 1792. Suffice it to say that in this period, both in his unpublished notes and in his published statements – for example his polemics with Thomas Paine in 1791 – he defended the necessary representative role of a monarch. The key statement in the Constitution of 1791: 'The French constitution is representative: the representatives are the legislative body and the king' almost certainly came from his pen, along with many other passages and ideas. The king's flight to Varennes in June 1791 shattered his faith in Louis XVI and in the workability of the 1791 Constitution while Louis was king, but it does not appear to have made him into a republican in the sense of one who believes that monarchy is incompatible with a well constituted representative order.

Sieyes welcomed the removal of Louis XVI in 1792 but he heartily detested the democratic movement, spearheaded by the Mountain, the Paris Commune, the sections of Paris, and the Jacobin Clubs, which finally in 1793 attacked the representative institution of the National Convention and subjected it to the dictatorial rule of an oligarchy. This regime, although Sieyes did not himself use these terms, stood for the 'feudal' or 'false' democracy that he had castigated in 1789, a democracy which does not take the form of direct self-government, but of a group of citizens who identify themselves with the 'people' and think their rule legitimated simply by the act of self-identification. It was a dictatorship totally antithetical to the representative system.

Sieyes' opposition to this Second Revolution was expressed in his essay on *Liberty* which was examined in the previous chapter. 'I am grieved to see that people are trying to discredit the representative system in the very name of liberty', he wrote. 'It is a great evil. If they succeed we will start a most disastrous era for the human species.'[29] As we have seen his argument was that liberty, true liberty, rather than merely a fervour for independence, was not antithetical to the representative system but profoundly in accordance with it.

3 Sieyes' advocacy of representation 1794–99

The bitter experience of the Jacobin dictatorship is reflected in Sieyes' writings and speeches on the theme of representation after the fall of Robespierre in 1794. Needless to say, he reiterated his belief in the merits of representation and his scorn for democracy with renewed vigour, but fresh nuances are also visible in his advocacy, the fruit of the terrible setbacks that had occurred.

Two texts in particular express his thoughts on representation in the wake of the collapse of Robespierre's regime. The first is the important unpublished paper entitled *Bases of the social order* which was written either in the latter part of 1794 or early in 1795.[30] The second is the speech that Sieyes delivered in the National Convention on 20 July 1795, commenting on the new constitution that was being drafted. The texts overlap on a number of themes, so that the *Bases* can in a sense be seen as a preliminary to the second.

In the *Bases* Sieyes retraces the path from democracy, logically the first form of government, to representation in a way which will by now be familiar. There is, however, an interesting reference to Rousseau, and the advantages of representation vis-à-vis democracy are rather more systematically stated than before. These are the relevant passages:

> The division of labour, of professions, etc. is simply the representative system establishing itself spontaneously; it goes hand in hand with the progress of the society it animates; it is most favourable to the production of wealth, the convenience of exchange, and the general movement of business. It has seized hold of virtually all human activities. An unfortunate phrase of J[ean] J[acques Rousseau] stands alone in opposition to this unanimous agreement. 'The will', he says, 'cannot be represented.' Why not? It is not a question of the whole will of man, and there are numerous examples of individuals and powers who conduct business on this or that matter by way of procuration. Besides, in the social state with which we are concerned here, the person who refuses to submit to the contract made by his representative is free to leave the association.
>
> Far from constricting liberty, the representative system is favourable to it. 1. In crude democracy, passions are too much to the fore. 2. Because voting is not confined in such a system within a narrow sphere, by means of a limited

procuration, the constituent is confused with the constituted power. 3. The less enlightened majority, conscious of possessing all powers simultaneously, can abuse its strength and destroy everything at one stroke by subjugating the minority. 4. The necessity of remaining small in population, and insufficient in wealth, puts it at the mercy of all its neighbours. Unquestionably democracy is necessary in a good social system, but we will see below its place and employment.

This idea that representation is not democracy, and yet that there is an element of democracy in representation, was clearly a favourite one with Sieyes. In a note written well before the Revolution he had remarked briefly: 'Representation returns democracy to its proper usage.'[31] In a note written towards the end of his political career he was more eloquent:

> Democracy is a vast field of political fermentation and production. It is there that man yields all he can yield, and that the state gathers in all that it can gather in. The hothouse of monarchy cannot be compared to this harvest of a great territory.
>
> But the public establishment is not democracy, it is a body raised by democracy, on democracy for the public requirement. Democracy is in the citizens and their mass, but in the public establishment by contrast only *unity* and *organization* are possible.
>
> It is only in democracy that the public establishment stands on its base, on its true base; it stands on the whole territory, on *all* the citizens, and it rises to a point in order to organize itself.
>
> In the monarchy by contrast, the point is the base, the establishment is turned upside down, and the mass of the citizens is a body, a land apart. . . .
>
> Now tell me what is the idea of those who wish to democratize every political action within the body of the public establishment, and every civil or industrial action within the mass of the citizens? To democratize justice, the police, war, finance, etc. It is to democratize shoe-making, building etc.[32]

What exactly did Sieyes mean by his frequent assertions that democracy was the base of the representative system? The answer would seem to be twofold. First, he meant that the nation or people was the only legitimate constituent power of the public establishment. The latter was a body 'raised by democracy'. It is true that he believed that a large people or nation could only exercise the constituent power itself through representatives, but a least the nation would be the electing mass that chose such representatives. Second, he meant that the personnel who were to form and apply the national will within the public establishment had to be chosen by the mass of the citizens meeting in primary assemblies. In the *Bases* this second point is made with great clarity:

> The primary assemblies are the true foundation of the political state; they contain all the elements of it; they are composed of all the citizens who have the will and capacity to assist in it. To build the social edifice on another basis, is to lack one completely.
>
> Should the extent of territory and the population require an intermediary stage between them and the national assembly, electoral colleges can be temporarily formed, composed of delegates elected freely by the primary assemblies, and these colleges can send deputies to the central assembly. Whatever the population I would never recommend that there should be more than one intermediary stage, or that deputies should be nominated for too long a period. It is good for the legislature to be frequently refreshed by the democratic spirit.

In his great speech to the Convention on 20 July 1795[33] Sieyes ranged widely over the subject of representation. He began by distinguishing between a representative assembly and the deputies taken individually:

> We all know that there is only one political power in a society and that is the power of the association; but it is permissible to call improperly powers, in the plural, the different procurations that this single power gives to its diverse representatives. In the same way it is through abuse or pure politeness that we assume or are given individually the title of representatives. There is only one representative here and that is the body of the Convention, and beyond it there are as many representatives as there are kinds of political procurations given to bodies or individuals occupied with public functions. It is essential that all who exercise a political function for the people are its representatives if they are commissioned or usurpers if they are not.

Having made these distinctions Sieyes proceeded to expound once again the virtues of the representative system vis-à-vis the democratic one, referring back to the brief essay on *Liberty* that he published in 1793:

> Everything is representative in the social state. It is to be found everywhere in the private as in the public order; it is the mother of productive and commercial industry as of liberal and political progress. I would go further and say that it is identical with the very essence of social life.
>
> More than two years ago I undertook to demonstrate that the representative system was the means whereby we could bring ourselves to the highest point of liberty and prosperity that it was possible to enjoy.
>
> The friends of liberty of that time stopped the printing of my work after the first number. In their crass ignorance they thought that the representative system was incompatible with democracy – as if a building could be incompatible with its natural base. Or else they wanted to stop short at the base, doubtless imagining that the social state ought to condemn people to bivouac all their lives.
>
> I wished to prove that the people had everything to gain by putting into representation all the different kinds of power which go to make up the public establishment, reserving to themselves solely the power of entrusting every year sensible persons, known to themselves, to renew the retiring portion of their petitionary, legislative and communal representatives....
>
> But at that time, as even to-day, an extremely damaging error had taken hold, namely that the people ought only to delegate those powers that it cannot exercise itself. This so-called principle is supposed to be the safeguard of liberty. It is as if one set out to prove to citizens wishing to write to Bordeaux, for example, that they would preserve their liberty much better if they reserved the right of carrying the letters themselves, as they were quite capable of doing so – instead of conferring this task on that part of the public establishment that is responsible for it. Can this kind of faulty logic reveal genuine principles?

The principle that Sieyes attacked here, the principle that the people should delegate only those powers that it cannot exercise itself seems to have originated from Montesquieu.[34] Robespierre employed it in his definition of the democratic form of government that he favoured: 'Democracy is a form of government where the sovereign people, guided by laws which are its own work, does itself all that it can do well, and by deputies all that it cannot do itself.'[35]

Sieyes then turned to the problem of alienation through representation, recognizing that this was indeed a danger and arguing that the way to prevent it was to differentiate the representative institutions of the people, so that not all powers were accumulated in the hands of the same people. Needless to say, Sieyes had always recommended the separation or distinction of public powers as an intrinsic part of the representative system of government, but it was not until after his experience of the tremendous concentration of power that took place during Robespierre's ascendancy that he gave the matter particular prominence:

> It is indubitable that liberty is increased when one is represented in as many things as possible, while it is diminished when all the various representations accumulate in the hands of the same people. Look at the private realm and see if the freest man is not he who gets the most things done for him; while everyone agrees that the more a man accumulates representations in one and the same person the more he becomes dependent on him, so that eventually, if he concentrates all his powers in the same individual, he makes a kind of alienation of himself.
>
> Instead of binding the people to reserve for themselves the exercise of all the powers that it is in their interest to put into representation, it would be more useful and more just to say to them: take care not to entrust all your rights to the capacity of one single representative, distinguish carefully your different representative procurations, and ensure that the constitution does not allow any category of your representatives to go beyond the limits of its special procuration.

Sieyes' recommendations for the organization of the government in 1795, and again in 1799, reflected this change of emphasis. They embodied far more subdivisions than in the proposals he had made in 1789.

Sieyes next turned to destroy another misconception. The making of a political union did not mean that every right of every individual was put in common. One was not founding a monastery. He was attacking here, once again, the aims and practices of the Jacobin dictatorship. The Jacobins had not only emphasized over and over again the sovereign power of the people and the subordination of government to this power, they had also believed that the great final object of political union of the people was to bring about the moral rejuvenation of the members, to establish a 'republic of virtue'. In rejecting the Jacobin alternative Sieyes gave one of the earliest definitions of 'totalitarian democracy'. He called it (both in the *Bases* and in his speech of July 20 1795) the policy of *ré-totale* in place of *ré-publique*. This is the relevant passage of his speech:

> Unlimited powers are a monstrosity in politics, and a major error on the part of the French people. It will not commit such an error again in the future. You will tell it another important truth that is too often neglected amongst us, namely that it does not itself possess these powers, these unlimited powers, which its flatterers attribute to it. When a political association is formed it is not a question of putting in common all the rights that each individual brings into the society, or the whole power of the entire mass of individuals.
>
> One puts in common, under the name of the public or political power, only the minimum possible, and solely what is necessary to maintain each in his rights and duties. This portion of power falls far short of the exaggerated qualities which people tend to attribute to so-called sovereignty – and note that I am talking here about the sovereignty of the people, for if the thing exists

anywhere that is what it is. This word only makes such a huge impression on the imagination because the mind of the French, still full of royal superstitions, has made a virtue of endowing it with the whole legacy of pompous attributes and absolute powers that gave a glitter to usurped sovereignties. We have even seen the public, in its infinite largesse, become irritated because it could not endow it with more. People seemed to think, with a kind of patriotic pride, that if the sovereignty of great kings was so powerful and so terrible, then the sovereignty of a great people had to be something greater still.

As for me, I say that as people become more enlightened, and as we move further away from the time when people thought they *knew* when all they were doing was *wanting*, then sovereignty will retreat into its proper limits, for once again the sovereignty of the people is not unlimited, and systems which have been extolled and honoured, including the one to which people still think they have the greatest obligations [by which Sieyes meant the Jacobin Constitution of 1793] will appear simply as monkish conceptions, misguided plans of *ré-totale* rather than of *ré-publique*, as destructive of liberty as they are ruinous of both the public and the private weal.

In the *Bases* Sieyes had also turned his fire against Robespierre and Saint-Just's idea of creating special 'institutions' to 'moralize' the people. In his address to the Convention on 26 February 1794 Saint-Just had said:

In a monarchy, there is only a government; in a republic there are also institutions, either to restrain morals or to halt the corruption of laws or men. A state in which such institutions are lacking is only an illusory republic; and as each understands by his liberty the independence of his passions and avarice, the spirit of conquest and egoism establishes itself amongst the citizens, and the private idea that each makes of his liberty, according to his interest, produces the slavery of all.... *We lack the institutions which are the soul of the republic.*[36]

This is Sieyes' response to such an idea in the *Bases*:

Pedants and fools preach for what they call beautiful *institutions*. They prostrate themselves before Lycurgus, St Benedict, Ignatius de Loyola, the order of the clergy, above all the order of the nobility, etc., without considering that superfluous wheels can only impede the movement of a machine, and that to institute a people or a class of men for particular purposes is to sacrifice the general end to dangerous redundancies. In a well-ordered state there is no need for other institutions than those of the establishment reduced to its *minimum*. Leave all the rest to the exercise of private rights.

There was another danger to which Sieyes turned his attention during the course of 1795. From his early reflections on politics onwards he had always seen what he called the 'disposable class' (*classe disponible*) as being peculiarly suited to occupy public office. He had pointed out in 1789 that within the Third Estate there were considerable numbers of this class: men who were sufficiently well-off 'to receive a liberal education, cultivate their reason, and in short interest themselves in public affairs.' They were eminently qualified to be 'good representatives of the nation.'[37] His electoral proposals in that year (which will be looked at more closely in the next chapter) seem to have been designed in part to 'winnow out' such civic-minded persons, and to give them political rights.

In an important note written in 1795 he reflected further on the 'disposable class viewed politically.'[38] He now saw certain possible dangers in their dominance:

> One of the effects of the representative system of politics is to place each kind of function in the hands of *experts*. The talents, knowledge, moral and physical habits, in sum the kinds of dexterity and intrigue that are so to speak the [?indecipherable] of apprenticeship which is necessary or good in order to handle public affairs must in every country belong almost exclusively to the *disposable* class. In other words to that which can live without work.
>
> If this is accepted, the nobility, while it existed, the owners of land above a certain size, *rentiers* living off permanent or life funds, heads of manufacture, merchant families, etc. have more aptitude for guiding public affairs, and sooner or later the disposable class will take possession not only of the government but of the popular representation also.
>
> Hence sooner or later fortune leads to power. *inde mali labes.*
>
> The spirit of legislation can counterbalance this tendency but sooner or later this class will finish by controlling the spirit of legislation. I was therefore right to distinguish certain *fundamental* articles [Sieyes is here referring to Title I of the 1791 Constitution] which legislation cannot touch any more than the Constitution. If you have within your disposable class a particular order of men who think themselves noble and different from you, having interests that are distinct and opposed to the common interests, take care not to let them dominate, or rival, or even exist *en masse* within your disposable class. If this class thinks of itself as equal with you, then you have need only of constitutional and fundamental forces to prevent it from usurping the empire, but if it thinks itself unequal, if it lays claim to *nobility*, it will agitate and intrigue and behave illegally until either it is overthrown, or you will have lost your liberty founded on equality of rights.

Sieyes thus was alive to the dangers of moneyed *caste rule* developing out of the specialization of politics which was characteristic of the representative system of politics. His cure for it was a good constitution, and safeguards to the constitution, together with constant watchfulness to prevent a sense of exclusivity and superiority growing up within the class of men whose talents and upbringing gave them a special advantage in pursuing a public career.

From the summer of 1795 through to the making of the *coup d'état* of 18 Brumaire in 1799 Sieyes was silent on the fundamental issues of the proper constitution of the state. Not until after the *coup* did he divulge his ideas once again and they were fortunately transcribed by Boulay de la Meurthe. In typical terse fashion Sieyes prefaced his detailed plans for the organization of the government with some remarks on his favourite theme:

> Crude democracy is absurd.
>
> Even were it possible, the representative system is far superior, alone capable of allowing true liberty to flourish and to ameliorate the human species.
>
> Democracy, basis of the representative system and of the public establishment.
>
> Government raised on this base is necessarily representative and ought not to resemble this base – a representative republic.
>
> The representative regime is not solely necessitated by the extent of territory and the number of inhabitants. In all cases, even in that of the smallest territory, the people has everything to gain by putting into representation all the powers that make up the public establishment.
>
> Even the warmest partisans of crude democracy have no intention of establishing it in the executive, administrative and judicial branches; they want it

> solely in the legislative order. It is hence a question of putting the legislative function into representation as well, for it is this that basically distinguishes the representative regime from pure democracy.
>
> In this [i.e. the representative] system the citizen loses the right that he derives from the mass of his co-associates and retains no more than *his right as individual associate*. From that moment there is no longer political equality between the citizen-as-individual and the citizen-as-representative. It is the difference between the mass and the individual.
>
> There are two kinds of representation, that which is attached to the *individual* representative, and that which is attached to the *body itself* of which he is a member.
>
> The individual representative has the right to busy himself, to petition, to speak, to vote on behalf of the mass: the representative body has the right to judge and decide.[39]

It was Sieyes' final statement on the representative system.

4 Conclusion

Throughout his political career, from 1789 to 1799, Sieyes remained loyal to the idea of the representative system, a system that he had originally conceived and espoused nearly twenty years before the Revolution occurred, and which he progressively refined and developed during the revolutionary epoch. He saw the establishment of this system as the true object of the Revolution, and he regarded the Second Revolution that took place in 1792–93 as running completely counter to it. The point at issue was not that he favoured a monarchical element in government while Robespierre and his colleagues were republican, or that he favoured a more restrictive form of suffrage than Robespierre and his colleagues. The differences went far deeper than this. For Sieyes the leaders of the Jacobin dictatorship did not understand the meaning or value the benefits of political representation. Far from being 'republican' they did not understand what the 'public thing' embodied in a true republic was.

From the speeches and brochures that have been cited in this chapter it is evident that Sieyes believed that there were only two legitimate forms of state: democracy, by which he meant a political unity in which all the citizens assembled together and decided by majority vote on the public weal, and a representative system, by which he meant the deliberate externalization and specialization of the power of the body politic, election to public office, the granting of the power to deliberate and decide to those elected to public offices, and the distinction and specialization of functions within the public establishment.

Sieyes saw the representative system as infinitely superior to the democratic one, yet he always recognized that the two systems grew from the same stem, and that there was a democratic element within the representative system – as there was a monarchical and an aristocratic element. It has been shown that this democratic element consisted in the people being the constituent power of the public establishment in the representative system, a power they exercised either directly or by electing a constituent assembly, and in the people electing the holders of the representative offices established by the constitution. The aristocratic element consisted in the fact that only a minority of the citizens were elected to representative office. The monarchic element consisted in the necessity of having an office within the representative establishment consisting of one person taking decisions.

The arguments that Sieyes used to demonstrate the justness and utility of the representative system vis-à-vis a democratic one were manifold. His views on the socio-economic factors that favoured the creation of a representative system may perhaps be summed up by saying that in modern societies he saw (a) a vast enlargement of the circle of inhabitants who counted as citizens, (b) the emergence, as a result of the intensification of the division of labour, of a large number of citizens who were neither willing nor able to occupy themselves continuously with political matters, as the democratic system required, and (c) the emergence of a new 'disposable class', by which he meant a substantial number of citizens whose wealth gave them the education and leisure to occupy themselves continuously with public affairs. All these developments within modern society favoured the adoption of a representative system in which some citizens were elected to carry out political functions on behalf of the others.

Not surprisingly Sieyes also used the argument that the large size of a people or territory made a representative system necessary, but he never used this argument alone, and he always maintained that the large size of modern states was not a contingent or fortuitous thing but was required for optimum economic production and defence. The large size that made representation necessary was itself necessary. Moreover Sieyes maintained that even in small states representation was preferable to democracy.

Sieyes' perception that even the purest democratic regime contained within itself a germ of representation, and his observation that even the most fervent advocates of democracy (perhaps he had Rousseau in mind) did not go so far as to recommend that it be adopted in the executive or judicial branches of government, may be seen as auxiliary arguments for the representative system. The latter, in other words, did not so much negate democracy as draw out and expand features that were already present in it.

Far more important than all these arguments was Sieyes' contention that the representative system was a rational method of expanding individual liberty. It was rational in the sense that it consisted in the deliberate definition of the ends of the body politic and of the means that were best suited to achieve these ends. Democracy tended to lump everything together – the constituent and constituted powers, the public and private person, the whole mass of the public powers – into one undifferentiated unity. It was indiscriminate, or as Sieyes put it, 'crude', or 'raw', like a primary product of nature unrefined by human art.

Representation was an expansion of liberty because, as we have seen, liberty was not for Sieyes merely a jealous independence of the power of others, it was power over one's environment enhanced by 'getting things done' by and through others, rather than trying to do everything oneself. To put political power into representation was precisely such an enhancement. It did not mean resignation or complacency or disinterest, but organized effectiveness.

Sieyes was aware of the danger that representation could become alienation, but he rejected Rousseau's assertion that representation of the will, as distinct from representation of the power that executed the will, was *in itself* alienation. Sieyes argued instead that representation of the will, both of individuals and of corporate entities, was perfectly legitimate and happened all the time. Political representation only became alienation in two ways. First, it did so if the nation as constituent power entrusted its *whole* will to the government it established. This, however, was not, in Sieyes' view, the object of political constitutions. Indeed he argued that whether or not the continued existence of the national constituent will was provided for in a constitution, the nation retained the right to reassert it if its government strayed from the path of legitimacy. To this extent he believed that the national will was 'inalienable'.

The other way in which political representation might become alienation was if all representative offices accumulated in the hands of the same people. The way to cure this, however, was not by less representation, but by taking greater care to separate or differentiate the various component functions of the public establishment.

The third way in which alienation might occur was through the development of the 'disposable class' into a moneyed caste. To counter this Sieyes pinned his faith on a good constitution with strong built-in safeguards, and a constant vigilance to prevent the caste sense of inequality, or of 'different peoples', breaking the underlying sense of *one* people.

8 The basis of the representative system: the redivision of France

La France ne doit point être un assemblage de petites nations, qui se gouverneroient séparément en démocraties; elle n'est point une colléction d'états; elle est *un tout* unique, composé de parties intégrantes; ces parties ne doivent point avoir séparément une existence complète, parce qu'elles ne sont point des tous simplement unis, mais des parties ne formant qu'un seul tout. Cette différence est grande; elle nous intéresse essentiellement.

Sieyes, *Speech on the royal veto* (1789)

TO SIEYES ABOVE ALL OTHERS belonged the responsibility for the redivision of France into eighty-three departments, subdivided into districts and cantons, that was accomplished in 1790. His ideas formed the core of the proposals that were presented to the National Assembly by the Constitutional Committee on this matter. He himself had no doubt about his role. When asked long after if he had been the principal author of the division of France into departments he replied proudly: '*Le principal! mieux que celà, le seul!*'[1]

Too often Sieyes' plan for the territorial redivision of France is seen in a vacuum, as the more or less arbitrary creation of a rationalizing mentality with an itch to make everything neat and tidy. How quintessentially French and Cartesian, we exclaim, it all seems! Why could he not have left the old historic provinces of France untouched instead of carving them all up with the aid of a ruler and set-square?

To understand Sieyes' plan it has to be seen in the context of his own experiences before the Revolution and, even more importantly, in the context of his main aim of creating a representative system and of the dangers that threatened the achievement of this aim in the autumn of 1789.

Of the first of these factors it need only be said that Sieyes was familiar with the plans, some of them partially executed, for reshaping the local administration of France that were made in the last years of the *ancien régime* by Turgot, Necker and Calonne. He had been a member in 1787–88 of the Provincial Assembly of Orléans, one of the new bodies that Calonne had established in his efforts at reform, and he had had the opportunity then to reflect on the way the organization of local administration and its relationship with central government could be improved. The idea of 'departments' appears in some of the schemes he studied at this time.[2]

How did territorial redivision fit in with his idea of a representative system? Clearly there were two main reasons why the system required redivision. The first was electoral. A future representative legislative assembly had to rise up from the nation as a single association of individuals, and not from a mélange of corporate bodies differing widely in size and shape. The second reason was administrative. The laws passed by a future government representative of the nation had to fall upon, or be applied to, the nation as one single association. There could not be different ways of executing the laws in different parts of the country, and still less could the application of national laws be at the discretion of local unities, as if these were the partners in some loose federal tie. Sieyes often made an analogy, sometimes in his speeches and writings, and sometimes in sketched diagrams, between the dynamics of a representative system, and a circular movement in which powers 'ascended' from the people and then 'descended' on them again.[3] The territorial redivision of France related to the starting-point and end-point of this process: it aimed to ensure that they were both the same, namely the nation. Sieyes invented a new word to describe this objective: *adunation*. Later he was to contrast this idea with the far more radical efforts at creating unity that the Jacobins attempted. They, he wrote, wished to *unifier*, *intégrer* instead of *aduner*.[4]

In his pre-revolutionary tracts Sieyes argued the case for territorial redivision primarily on the grounds of creating electoral uniformity. In the *Views*, it is true, he wrote that: 'Thousands of reasons urge the necessity of subjecting the surface of France to a new division, without regard to the ancient boundaries of provinces and bailiwicks. ... In making a new creation is it necessary to adopt ancient forms, foreign or even contrary to its object? Is it an indifferent matter to want to melt down the diverse peoples of France into a single people, and the diverse provinces into a single empire?'[5] The main substance of his argument was, however, the need to create new, uniform electoral subdivisions, without regard to existing administrative or judicial divisions.

The first thing required in order to create a new 'legislative constitution' for France, Sieyes maintained in the *Views*, was 'to establish a good national representation'.[6] To this end he mapped out a hypothetical electoral system with its base in the 'totality of parishes', rising up through 'arrondissements' of several parishes, to 'provinces' that would send deputies directly to the national legislature. At the same time he warned against an undue multiplication of the intermediary degrees of election. 'Every legislature continually needs to be refreshed by the democratic spirit; it is therefore necessary for it not to be placed at too great a distance from the first electors.'[7] It was an idea he was often to repeat.

This pyramidal structure, consisting of successive tiers rising from small local assemblies to a central legislature, was typical of all Sieyes' later electoral schemes. It was not so much a foreshadowing of present-day electoral systems as a rationalization and democratization of the way elections were conducted in the *ancien régime*.

The argument put forward in the *Views* was repeated in the *Deliberations*, except that the electoral tiers became 'parishes', 'cantons', 'provinces', and somewhat surprisingly, 'the national Senate', and the need to divide the land into 'equal spaces everywhere except at the frontiers of the kingdom' was specifically emphasized.[8] Sieyes also hinted at the idea that other factors, besides the principal one of population, should determine the number of deputies elected by each new unit.

Once the Revolution occurred, and the Constituent Assembly came into being and set to work to make a constitution, the early ideas that Sieyes had outlined on territorial redivision developed and crystallized with extraordinary speed. The most important landmark was his little tract entitled *Some constitutional ideas applicable to Paris in July* 1789, in which the kernel of the later departmental and municipal organization adopted by the Constituent Assembly can already be seen. Sieyes read this tract to the Committee of Sixteen – the committee established by the new municipality of Paris on 25 June 1789 to discuss the constitution of the city's government – a few days after its formation, though it was not published until September. Clearly it has to be seen against the background of the turbulent events in Paris and the provinces that occurred in July. As the last chapter noted, the overthrow of the old municipal government in the capital and the storming of the Bastille were the signal for the start of a municipal revolution throughout the length and breadth of France, a movement that threw into question the whole administrative unity of the country. This revolution explains why, in his first discussion of territorial redivision after the formation of the Constituent Assembly, Sieyes was as much concerned with redrawing the map of France for administrative purposes as he was with redrawing it for electoral purposes. The two ends now converge.

The most striking feature of Sieyes' proposals in July was their scope. The problems facing Paris were placed in the context of what he called in the opening paragraph 'our constitutional plan for the whole kingdom'. More precisely, Paris was considered according to two perspectives: first, as an integral part of a restructured national electoral system and a restructured national administrative system for the whole country, and secondly, as a municipality with its own local concerns, or as a body 'to a certain degree independent' of the overall national government framework. Sieyes spent by far the greater time on the first of these two perspectives.

To demonstrate the position of Paris within the national electoral system Sieyes outlined his plan for the latter. It followed on from his pre-revolutionary ideas, but with much greater detail and precision. At the base of the system stood 'cantons', measuring two leagues by two, each the seat of a 'primary assembly' or 'comitia' (*comice*) in which all the 'active citizens' were to meet together. In the more populous cantons there would have to be more than one primary assembly. The first task of the primary assemblies in the cantons was to draw up lists of persons from amongst their midst whom they considered to be eligible for all the higher levels of representation up to the national level. Their second task was to elect the members of the electoral assemblies that were immediately superior to them, the assemblies of the 'communes' or 'cities'. There were to be 720 of these, each consisting of nine cantons, and each measuring approximately 6 leagues by 6.

The communal assemblies would in turn elect from the 'lists of eligibility' the members of the assemblies at the next level, that of the 'province' or 'department' – the latter word occurring for the first time in Sieyes' terminology. There were to be 80 provinces – 81 if, as Sieyes argued, Paris was given a special position amongst French towns and accorded the status both of a province and a commune – and each province would embrace nine communes, and measure approximately 18 by 18 leagues. The provincial assemblies would elect from the lists of eligibility the 720 members of the national legislature. All the representative assemblies, up to the national level, would be renewable by a third each year.

Such, in bare outline, was the pyramidal electoral structure that Sieyes proposed in his July tract. Some of the complexities must now be examined. Who were the 'active citizens'? Sieyes thought that in the circumstances of his own day the right to participate in electing should be restricted to men who were French or had become French citizens; who had been resident in the relevant electoral area for at least a year; who were not minors; who paid taxes; and who made a small 'voluntary' or 'civic' contribution amounting to three livres a year. He believed, in other words, that one had not only to meet formal or mechanical criteria but also to give evidence of public spiritedness in order to earn the right to vote in the primary assemblies. Those who earned this right were 'active' citizens. To earn the right to be considered for a place on the lists of eligibility required further evidence: for this the voluntary tribute was raised to twelve livres.

In the future, when a system of national education and 'new interests' had improved the population, Sieyes envisaged more searching tests of 'active citizenship'. It would be necessary, he suggested, to demonstrate a knowledge of social affairs; to show that one was not unfitted for all work 'since work is the true foundation of all society'; and to pay the voluntary tribute at least twice. In other words Sieyes was looking not only for public spiritedness but also ability.

A further complication of Sieyes' system, and one that is even more surprising at first sight, is that he did not want representation in the various assemblies to be a function only of population. He was not solely concerned to ensure that each active citizen would have roughly the same proportional share in voting a national deputy into office. He believed representation at all levels of the system should be a function of several elements. First of all there would be the invariable territorial element: each canton, each commune, and each province would be entitled to a certain fixed number of deputies simply *qua* territorial unit. This fixed number would then be increased in proportion to the citizen population of the area, and the relative amount of compulsory and voluntary taxation paid by the area. For example, of the 720 deputies in the national legislature, Sieyes estimated that 240 would be sent by the provinces on the fixed basis of 3 deputies per province; 160 would reflect the relative population of the provinces; 160 would reflect the relative level of compulsory taxation; and 160 would reflect the relative level of voluntary contributions. This idea of an electoral system based on a 'composite ratio of several elements' had already been suggested in the *Deliberations*; now we find it worked out in detail.

So much for the new rational electoral system, and the new territorial divisions that Sieyes thought were essential to it. His proposed new system of local administration was based on the same territorial framework. While the primary assemblies in the cantons would simply meet to vote and then disband, the intermediary electoral assemblies – the communal and the provincial – were to be permanent bodies carrying out administrative functions. The most interesting feature here was the dual function that Sieyes proposed for the commune. On the one hand the commune was to be a part of the municipal order, and had to be organized as such. In this guise it was a whole that was 'to a certain degree independent'. That is to say, it was concerned with its own specific local affairs which were separate from those of the nation. On the other hand the commune was a part of the national administrative framework. In this guise, Sieyes stressed, the communes 'are more than *confederated states*; they are true, integral and essential parts of *one and the same whole*. This observation is important so that one never compares us with the United States of America.'

It is worth noting too that Sieyes' communes were large representative bodies and not small directly self-governing entities. 'We have no intention whatever', he wrote at the start of his tract, 'of subjecting the national government, nor even the tiniest municipal governments, to the democratic regime.'

The two particular areas that Sieyes earmarked for the communes and provinces as parts of the national administrative order were taxes and the militia, which he saw them administering under the control of the national legislature. Money and the military, the 'twin forces of every society', Sieyes argued, were too important to be placed wholly in the hands of the executive; they belonged to what he called 'legislative administration'. The various assemblies would not actually command the force or spend the fiscal revenue, but they would, in Sieyes' words, 'create the combinations of *money* and *force* for public needs, and then deliver them over to the [executive] heads to expend for national and municipal service.' The communal and provincial assemblies would each have to establish two 'directories', or small committees, to watch over these areas.

Sieyes also wanted the representative assemblies of the commune and province to perform certain electoral tasks in the administrative field. They were to draw up lists of those eligible for administrative office in the same way that the primary assemblies at cantonal level would draw up lists of those eligible to represent them. The king would have the discretion to nominate officers from the lists of administrative eligibility.

Paris, in Sieyes' view, deserved to be placed in a special category. Because of its size and importance, it could not be classified simply as a commune. Instead it would have to be elevated to the rank of a province, and to be subdivided in the same way as the latter. Only the names would be different: while the normal province would be divided into communes and cantons, Paris would be divided into districts and quarters. At the same time Paris belonged to the municipal order; it was a municipality with its own particular affairs to govern. It therefore would have to have its own distinct legislature and administrative departments for municipal purposes. In sum, Paris would combine the features of a province with the municipal features of a commune.

We have spent considerable time on the pamphlet *Some constitutional ideas applicable to Paris in July 1789* because although it is by no means the clearest of Sieyes' writings it contains nearly all the leading concepts that distinguish his ideas on the organization of elections and of local government, the concepts namely of tiers of electoral assemblies, active citizenship, lists of eligibility, representation weighted to take account of other things besides population, departments as administrative bodies, and the large representative commune with its twin functions, municipal and national.

Before proceeding to enquire how far these ideas were destined to be transformed into law, it is worth pausing for a moment to ask if Sieyes' conviction that the old territorial division of France had to be replaced by something completely new was justified. Why did he not attempt to make use of existing structures, and were his arguments for not doing so valid?

Sieyes himself put forward three closely related justifications for his policy of a fresh start. The first was the incoherence of the existing structures. The second was the newness of the idea of a proportionately elected legislature, and the desirability of giving this new idea a fresh form, instead of simply appending it to structures that were designed for a different purpose. Last but not least he thought it was necessary to break down the existing, historically evolved divisions because they obstructed the political expression of one nation.

To assess the validity of these arguments it is necessary to look, if only briefly, at the territorial divisions of France on the eve of the Revolution. There was, of course, no territorial unit specifically designed for electoral purposes. When it was decided to hold the Estates-General in 1789 the unit chosen as the general basis for the election was the bailiwick or seneschalty or, in other words, the unit for judicial administration.

When the local governmental structures of the *ancien régime* are examined as a whole, they reveal an incoherence that was in no way the invention of rationalists such as Sieyes. Armand Brette, whose short book on the subject, published in 1907, remains a classic, demonstrated the difficulty of finding any system at all in the units that existed.[9] There were, it is true, the three great administrative divisions of *pays d'élections*, *pays d'Etats*, and *pays conquis*, that appear constantly in the decisions of government. But, as Brette found, when one tried to find exactly where these three broad divisions began and ended one was led into inextricable difficulties. The concept of the 'province' Brette found even vaguer. However much individual provinces might coincide with administrative boundaries, they were emphatically not, as such, units of administration. Indeed Brette believed that the use of the word 'province' was so indiscriminate in the eighteenth century that no precise meaning could be ascribed to it, except in the ecclesiastical context.

It is interesting that in his search for a reliable guide to the local governmental divisions of what he called the *obscur domaine de l'ancienne France* Brette finally settled on the distinction made at the start of the report presented to the National Assembly on 29 September 1789 on the territorial reorganization of France, which may well have come from the pen of Sieyes himself! The passage reads:

> The kingdom is split up into as many different divisions as there are different types of regime or power: into Dioceses in the *ecclesiastical* context; into Governments in the *military* context; into Generalities in the *administrative* context; into Bailiwicks in the *judicial* context.[10]

Taking these four lines of division as his guide Brette proceeded to show how very complex was the pattern they revealed. The four categories were markedly different from one another. Brette estimated that there were 136 French dioceses in the country in 1789, with which were mingled 20 foreign ones. There were, he calculated, 40 military governments, 31 generalities, and well over 400 bailiwicks. Within the categories there were great differences in size, imprecision about boundaries, and variations in the kind of powers exercised. There is no need here to enter into the details of this confusion; suffice it to say that its extent makes Tocqueville's contention that France under the *ancien régime* enjoyed the same kind of centralization as that which existed in the mid-nineteenth century highly questionable.[11]

If the territorial divisions of France for the purpose of local government presented a muddled and sometimes even indecipherable picture, the divisions that separated the people in terms of their customs, their loyalties, their sense of historical rights, were deep and significant. Brette's rejection of the province as a unit of administration must not be equated with its non-existence as a historical-geographical entity. Brittany, Normandy, Flanders, Alsace, Lorraine, Dauphiné, Languedoc, Provence, and so on, may have coincided only haphazardly, or not at all, with the governments and generalities that made up the structure of local government, but they exercised nonetheless a strong influence over the minds and emotions of their inhabitants.

In part the provinces could be defined purely in cultural terms, as embodying sharp differences in the way the people of France spoke, dressed, built, worshipped and so on. But the provinces also had a political dimension. Several of them, chiefly those on the borders of the country, which had become parts of the monarchy at a comparatively late date, retained their ancient Estates, together with a pronounced sense of their own ancient political rights. They did not see themselves as being ruled in a uniform way by the French king, but rather as having made an original treaty or bargain with the king in which they retained their own special position and powers. Their Estates provided an important channel for the expression and assertion of these privileges. The twelve provincial Parlements, which exercised their rights as sovereign courts over areas that coincided for the most part with historic provinces, were also highly important channels for the assertion of the rights of the provinces.

The strength of provincial particularism as a political force can be seen vividly during the period from 1787 to 1789 in the resistance that was mounted to the introduction of provincial assemblies and in the movement that took place in certain provinces to revive their ancient Estates. The *cahiers de doléances* that were drafted as a result of the summoning of the Estates-General also provide ample evidence of the attachment of the people of the various parts of France to their provinces.

Pétion's powerful tract, *Avis aux Français*, that was published anonymously in 1788, provides a good, though at the same time strongly critical, picture of the strength of provincial divisions at that time. It is significant that he placed provincial divisions, or divisions between '*corps*', alongside divisions of social status, or divisions between '*classes*', as two of the chief banes of France, that a revolution must sweep away.

> The nation is a vast body whose dispersed members are not united by any political tie, and this lack of harmony leaves it without force or movement. On

the contrary, constantly reviving germs of hatred and jealousy foment perpetual divisions between the organized bodies (*corps*) and the different classes of the citizens.

It has been easier to unite the dispersed parts of the vast territory which today forms France by means of conquests, alliances and treaties, than it has been to draw together and unify the laws, customs, and spirit of the inhabitants who lived under the various governments.

Far more is needed for this character of uniformity to spread through the various provinces of the kingdom; and a stranger who travelled through Gascony and Limousin, without knowing that these two countries (*pays*) were under the same rule, would scarcely believe it. There are several cantons where French is neither spoken nor understood; there are some where the way of living and dressing is very different; where usages and customs bear no resemblance to one another; where good manners and luxury have not penetrated.

All the provinces that have been recently allied or conquered have retained privileges and franchises by means of capitulations and treaties; each of them, from that time on, has particular rights that it pushes to the fore; each isolates its cause from the common cause; each has less force with which to combat the activities of sovereigns; they furnish the means by which all of them are oppressed. The provinces thus damage both their own defence and the general defence.

That is not all; the nation is split into three great divisions, the clergy, the nobility, the third estate.[12]

Undoubtedly Sieyes would have agreed with the position that Pétion takes here. Time and again he reiterated the need to undercut provincial particularism and to create a new system of territorial subdivisions expressive of national unity. It is found in the early writings when he was concerned primarily with establishing a new electoral system. For example in the *Deliberations* he wrote:

It is only by effacing the boundaries of the provinces that it will be possible to destroy all these local privileges, which were usefully claimed when we were without a constitution, and which will continue to be upheld by the provinces even when they will have become no more than obstacles to the establishment of social *unity*. ... [The] representative assemblies, once they are established everywhere will oppose an irresistible force of reason and interest tied to the national interest against the old claims of the *pays d'état*. I know of no more prompt and powerful means of peacefully making all the parts of France into a single body, and all the peoples who divide it into a single nation.[13]

Several months later, after the proposals for the territorial redivision of France on which he had worked had been presented to the National Assembly, he made the same point again, and simultaneously expressed cogently and concisely all the other arguments which he was wont to put forward in favour of breaking with the past and redrawing the map *de novo*:

For a long time I have sensed the need to divide the surface of France afresh. If we let this occasion pass, it will never return, and the provinces will keep their *esprit de corps*, their privileges, their pretentions, their jealousies, for ever. France will never achieve the political *adunation* that is necessary to make but *one* people ruled by the same laws and under the same forms of administration. Without a new, more equal and better arranged division, how will it be possible to determine the just degree of influence that all the parts of the kingdom may

> rightfully claim? Furthermore, which of the four or five divisions that exist at present ought to be chosen? The governments, dioceses, bailiwicks, and generalities are all of different sizes and have different boundaries. None of these divisions may rightfully claim to have the priority. Finally, the establishment of a good representation is something both new and important enough to be given its own territorial base, one that is more equal and more in keeping with the spirit of the new constitution.[14]

Here Sieyes' case for a radical change can be seen in a nutshell, and the pages above have tried to show that his argument was based on the realities of the situation, and not merely on rationalizing zeal. In a sense it may be said that his redrawing of the map of France did for the ancient regional antagonisms and rivalries of France what his creation of the National Assembly did for the ancient social antagonisms and rivalries. They were complementary aspects of the emergence of one nation under one law which lay at the heart of the Revolution.

Now to return to Sieyes' actual proposals for the new electoral and administrative areas of France. It has been shown how his ideas crystallized in his tract *Some constitutional ideas applicable to Paris in July 1789*. Soon after this, on the famous night of 4 August, the National Assembly decreed that the privileges of the provinces and towns were to be abolished, and cleared the way for further reorganization. During the first week of September the debate on the royal veto took place, in which Sieyes argued strongly that a decision about the organization of the municipalities and provinces should be made before any decision about vetos or 'appeals to the people'. He was still worried by the centrifugal forces that had been unleashed by the municipal revolution, and he called for the establishment of a committee forthwith to draft a plan for the localities which would ensure that France would still form 'a *whole* uniformly subordinated to a common legislation and administration'.

Sieyes' proposal was not accepted. Shortly afterwards, with the defeat of its plans for a two-chamber parliament and an absolute royal veto, the first Constitutional Committee resigned and a new one was formed. Sieyes had not been a party to these plans and he retained his seat on the new Committee. At the end of the month, on 29 September, a report was presented in its name to the Assembly, making proposals for a new electoral system, the establishment of administrative assemblies, and the formation of new municipalities. The report was presented by Thouret, but the evidence of contemporaries, and of Sieyes himself, and indeed the content of the report, make it plain that Sieyes was primarily responsible for it. This is not to say that it included all his ideas. Some of his favourite schemes – most notably his proposals for 'lists of eligibility' and a 'civic' contribution – did not find acceptance with the Committee. This in turn helps to explain why, on 2 October, Sieyes produced his own *Observations* on the report of the Constitutional Committee. In part the *Observations* provide a fuller exposition of the reasoning behind the committee's proposals, but in part their object is to present some of the ideas that Sieyes believed ought to have been included in the proposals but were not. The tone of the *Observations* is, for Sieyes, remarkably genial. One feels that he was basically pleased with the way things were going.

A summary of the proposals contained in the Committee's report reveals the extent of Sieyes' influence. As regards the electoral and administrative systems, the aim was 'to found the double edifice of the national representation, and municipal and provincial administration, on the same bases.' These bases were to be provided by three new territorial units into which the country was to be divided. First there were to be 80 departments, each of about 324 square leagues, spreading out from Paris across the country. Paris itself was to form the eighty-first department. The departments were each to be divided into 9 'great communes', making 720 communes overall, each measuring 36 square leagues. Each commune was in turn to be divided into 9 cantons, making 6480 cantons overall, each of 4 square leagues.

The process of election to the national legislature was to proceed upwards from primary assemblies, bringing together the 'active citizens' of each canton, which would elect deputies to communal assemblies, which would elect deputies to departmental assemblies, which would finally elect the 720 deputies that made up the national legislature. To be an active citizen the following qualifications were required: (1) to be born, or be a naturalized Frenchman; (2) to have reached majority; (3) to be domiciled in the canton for at least a year; (4) to pay direct taxes to the local value of 3 days work; (5) not to be, for the moment, in a servile condition, that is in 'personal relations too incompatible with the independence necessary for the exercise of political rights'. In order to be eligible for election to the communal or departmental assemblies it was necessary to have paid in direct taxes at least the local value of ten days work. To be eligible for the National Assembly it was necessary to have paid direct taxes to the value of a mark of silver. While the number of deputies chosen at the lowest or primary level was to be a function of population, the number chosen at the communal and departmental levels was to be adjusted so as to be proportional to the territory, population and fiscal contribution of each unit.

For administrative purposes there were to be permanent, elected, assemblies at the departmental and communal levels, each assembly being divided into a council, or general assembly, and a smaller directorate. The administrative assemblies would be elected in the same way as the electoral assemblies for the same areas. The departmental assembly would number 54, the communal 26, and their members would be renewed by one-half every two years. The report stressed particularly that these local administrative assemblies were the agents of the central administrative power:

> Subordinated directly to the king, as supreme administrator, they [i.e. the local administrative assemblies] will receive his orders, transmit them, ensure they are executed, and conform to them. This direct subjection of the administrative assemblies to the head of general administration is necessary: without it there would soon be neither exactness nor uniformity in the executive regime, and the monarchical government that the nation has just confirmed would degenerate into democracies in the interior of the provinces.

Finally we come to the municipal order. Here the report proposed that the 720 great communes – which, were to be units both for electoral and administrative purposes – should also be constituted as municipal bodies. The municipalities that were actually existing in each town, burgh, parish or community, under the name of *Hôtels-de-ville, Mairies, Echevinats, Consulats* or some other name, were thus to be abolished, and their constituencies merged into bigger units. The report justified this radical change in the following way:

> Instead of attenuating the vigour of the nation by dividing the people into little corporations, in which every generous feeling is stifled by that of impotence, create large aggregations of citizens united by ties of habit, confident and strong in this union; enlarge the spheres where the first civic attachments are formed; and in this way the *community* interest, which is so close to individual interest, and so susceptible to the influence of local notabilities when its means are weak and its object too limited, will draw closer to the public spirit by acquiring greater power and elevation.

What exactly was the field of activity of the municipalities? The report distinguished it sharply from the national electoral and administrative functions of the other bodies. Municipal authority was essentially separate, local and particular:

> The municipal regime, limited exclusively to the care of the particular and so-to-speak private affairs of each municipal area, cannot enter into any relation either with the national representative system, or the system of general administration. The communes being the first units in the representative order that ascends to the legislature, and the last in the executive order which descends and finishes with them, each municipality is nothing but a simple, individual, constantly governed whole within the state; and these separate wholes, independent of one another, and never able to incorporate together, cannot be the component elements of any of the governing powers.

Each municipality would have its own little legislative assembly and its mayor, both elected by the primary assemblies. Each municipality would concern itself with such things as local police, health and safety, minor roads, the management and expenditure of municipal revenues, improvement projects, and so on. The municipal government would have its seat in the main town of the commune, with subordinate agencies or bureaux in the parishes and smaller towns.

The general outline of the Constitutional Committee's scheme for a national electoral system, a national system of local administration, and a new municipal order, will now be plain, and there can be little doubt that its leading features came from Sieyes. Certain of the ideas that he put forward in July are, as we mentioned earlier, missing from the September report. There are no lists of eligibility and no 'voluntary' or 'civic' contributions. There are also some changes of emphasis. In July Sieyes had spent considerable time arguing that the local administrative assemblies should exercise control over the raising of taxes and of the militia, under the overall supervision of the national legislature. In September the emphasis is very much on the strict subordination of the local administrative assemblies to the king. This change of emphasis is perhaps explicable in terms of the changed circumstances. In July the fate of the national Revolution still hung in the balance and there was every reason to assert the powers of the newly constituted legislature vis-à-vis the king. By September this was not so obviously the case while the disintegrating effects of the municipal revolution had become even more apparent. It was now both possible and necessary to assert explicitly the principle of central royal control.

Before enquiring into the fate of the Constitutional Committee's proposals, it is worth reflecting for a moment on two of the more puzzling aspects of Sieyes' vision of electoral, administrative and municipal reform that were incorporated into them. One is the distinction between 'active' and 'passive' citizens, which has already been touched upon, but deserves further discussion. The other is the idea of making territory and fiscal contributions play a part in determining representation alongside population. How are these positions to be reconciled with Sieyes' frequently reiterated principle that political rights belong to individuals and must be held equally?

In his *Observations* on the report of the Committee Sieyes makes some remarks which help us to understand and to resolve these apparent contradictions. There is for example a fairly long passage in which he presents the rationale of his notion of the 'active' citizen, and estimates their numbers. It is worth citing the passage *in extenso*, as this is an area where preconceived notions can easily lead to gross misconceptions of Sieyes' position:

> In the present state of customs, opinions and human institutions, women are to be found inheriting crowns, and yet, by a bizarre contradiction, they are nowhere permitted to be counted as active citizens – as if it were not sane policy always to increase more and more the proportional number of true citizens, or as if it were impossible for a woman ever to be of utility to the public weal. Following a prejudice which does not even allow doubt on this question, we are hence forced to discount at least half the total population. Twenty-six million souls [Sieyes was of course writing of the contemporary population of France] are reduced, by this act alone, to twelve million five hundred. It is now necessary to make a further deduction, namely of children, who form a third of the total population, and of young people below the age of 21, who amount to a sixth: already there are only about six million individuals left. But can one regard as citizens those who are beggars or voluntary vagabonds, or those who have no fixed abode, or those finally who are attached in *servile* dependence, not to some form of work, but to the arbitrary will of a master? Amongst the ancients, the state of slavery purified in a way the free classes. All the citizens were capable of exercising their political rights. Every free man was an active citizen. Amongst us, it is a matter of pride that the basis of the association is wider; principles are more humane; we are all equally under the protection of the law; and that is good politics. But precisely because the *civiciat* or the order of citizens embraces every level of the social edifice, it follows that the lower classes, those who have least of all, are far more estranged by their intelligence and sentiments from the interests of the association than the least esteemed citizens of the ancient free states. There remains, thus amongst us, a class of men who are citizens by right, but never in fact. Doubtless it is up to the constitution, and up to good laws progressively to reduce this class to the smallest number possible. It is nonetheless true that there are men who may be perfectly sound in a physical sense, but to whom all social ideas are remote, and who are hence not in a position to take an active part in the public weal. They should not be personally discriminated against: but who would dare to consider it wrong that they should be excluded to some extent, not, it must be repeated, from legal protection and public aid, but from the exercise of political rights? This exercise could be made to depend on a positive criterion which would be a direct voluntary contribution of a specific amount. The Committee has not dared to

> propose such a thing to the Assembly; it has restricted itself to a direct forced contribution to the local value of three working days.
>
> If the time is not yet ripe for the general establishment of a voluntary and *civic* payment, it is nonetheless difficult not to feel that such a free gift could provide great help in a good constitution, as it could be of infinite use in defending it to some extent from dangerous influences in a situation where there is not yet a system of national education.
>
> Those then are the considerations which cause our remaining six million individuals to be reduced to only four million, four hundred thousand; which is a sixth of the total population; this ratio is generally accepted by the most respected political arithmeticians.[15]

This passage conveys clearly Sieyes' position on the subject of 'active' citizenship. It should be noted straightaway that the distinction between 'active' and 'passive' citizenship is with us still to-day, and is unlikely to disappear even in the most democratic states. As Sieyes rightly observed: 'In every country the law has fixed certain qualifications, without which one can neither be a voter, nor be eligible for office.'[16] For example, while to-day foreign residents or visitors are generally accorded the protection of the civil laws of the state they are in, they are not generally accorded the right to vote in the elections of that state. Similarly every state makes the acquisition of the right to vote by its own nationals dependent on reaching a certain age. Passive citizenship is still an everyday fact.

Sieyes of course lagged behind the practice of most modern states in placing women in the category of passive citizens, but he made it quite clear that this was an unwilling concession to prevailing practices, and not something of which he approved. Given the length of time that it took to accord women the suffrage in France and elsewhere his outlook was progressive. On top of this he thought roughly a quarter of the adult male population of France did not possess the necessary qualities to vote. While he believed that only taxpayers should vote he did not think that the right way to ensure a responsible suffrage was to make it dependent on a certain level of tax payments. Rather he believed that it should depend on a person's willingness to make a small financial contribution to the common fund. Moreover he believed that future laws should reduce the number of 'passive' citizens to the smallest possible, and he was a strong protagonist of the establishment of a system of national education – one of the obvious ways of achieving this end.

Seen as a whole Sieyes' views are not those of a man determined at all costs to exclude the lower strata of society from the suffrage, and to reserve it for those with substantial property. On the contrary, they are the views of one who believed that the exercise of the most elementary political right called for certain moral and intellectual qualities, that not everyone in the society of his own day possessed these qualities, but that they ought to be encouraged to acquire them. It is noteworthy that he envisaged a young person's reception into a primary assembly, when he reached voting age, as not merely an act of registration, but as a definite occasion. 'This act, when it comes to be recognized how much a man's moral qualities can contribute to his happiness, will be for the families of new citizens, and even for the primary assembly itself, a day of rejoicing, a *jour de fête*.'[17] This idea, not endorsed by the Committee, was taken up by Sieyes' friend Mirabeau in the Constituent Assembly. On 28 October 1789 he secured the adoption of a proviso whereby the primary assemblies, on a given day, would conduct a ceremony in which all the men of the district who had attained the age of twenty-one would be sworn-in and inscribed as electors. It must have been one of the first fêtes to be established by the Revolution.

When we pass from the right to vote to eligibility for election then the charge that Sieyes sought to entrench the wealthy in power becomes slightly more plausible. It will be remembered that he called for a higher contribution to the common fund in order to be considered eligible. There can be little doubt that he believed that persons from the *classe disponible* would come to occupy the leading offices in the public order, and by *classe disponible* he meant those with a certain amount of property which freed them from the constant necessity of work.[18] However there is nothing in Sieyes' writings to suggest that he supported the Constitutional Committee's proposal (which was to cause a considerable outcry) that eligibility for the National Assembly should depend on paying direct taxes to the value of a mark of silver. Neither did he anywhere assert that wealth as such qualified one for public office. Wealth or a sufficiency of means was for him crucial in permitting one to look beyond one's own immediate pressing concerns, to take a broader view, to educate oneself in public affairs, to discern the public good. Always his emphasis was on civic mindedness, enlightenment and responsibility and not on furthering the interests of the rich.

Like voting qualifications 'tests' for eligibility to the national legislature are still with us. Candidates, at least in the western democracies, usually have to be pre-selected by one of a number of political parties, in order to have a reasonable chance of success, while legal provisions for deposits are designed to discourage 'frivolous' candidates from standing. It is against these alternatives that Sieyes' ideas on the subject have to be seen, and not in a vacuum. The factor that is most conspicuously missing in all his electoral schemes is any premonition that political parties might come to take over the function of *organizing* the process of election, and thus make his own schemes unnecessary.

This leads on to the second puzzling aspect of Sieyes' ideas, as reflected in the proposals of the Constitutional Committee, namely his conviction that representation in the departmental assemblies, and in the national legislature itself, should not be simply a function of numbers, but should be balanced to take account of the territory and fiscal contribution of the areas from which the various deputies were drawn. Needless to say, his proposals here should not be compared with some ideal modern situation where only numbers count, and each individual's vote has exactly equal weight, for this is rarely the case in practice. What is interesting is that Sieyes did not merely believe that some deviation from this principle was inevitable on purely practical or pragmatic grounds, but positively recommended it. How is his position on this matter to be reconciled with his belief that political rights should be equal between citizen and citizen? Clapham thought his concept of balanced representation was 'Whiggish', while Bastid thought it showed him deviating from the main lines of his own theory.[19] Is the charge of incoherence justified?

Sieyes' ideas on this subject can perhaps be made clearer if his overall conception of the structure of the state is recalled. The logical basis of the state, according to his theory, was the nation or people as a compacted community of equal individuals. However as he himself seems to have recognized, it is difficult logically to conceive how an immense nation could come together to form a political unity without any prior connections amongst and between its members. Hence in the *Views*, the first of his published works to be written, Sieyes posited certain prior stages in the making of a large nation. He posited a small original community growing in size and then dividing into a multiplicity of small communities held together by a loose federal tie. He then posited these communities becoming dissatisfied with this loose structure and transforming themselves into a single united state based directly on the individuals who made it up.

Sieyes' step-by-step reconstruction of the large state helps us to understand his doctrine of balanced representation, because he seems to have regarded his 'great communes', on which he placed so much emphasis in his plans for election, local administration and municipal organization, as being the counterpart of the communities that pre-existed the formation of the large nation. To be sure it was their destiny to become parts of a larger whole, but they still retained, *qua* municipalities, a portion of their prior independence. As real corporate entities their particular configuration (territory and wealth) deserved to be taken into account, alongside that of numbers, in the representative structure of the country.

Sieyes, it may be argued, did not see a contradiction between his demand for equal political rights for individuals and relative political rights for the great communes – 'the true unities or political elements of the French Empire', as the report of the Constitutional Committee surprisingly called them. The two could be blended without destroying one another. On the specific issue of the unequal representation of wealth, the report expressly denied that there was a conflict of principle:

> The ratio of tax contributions undoubtedly counts for nothing when it is a question of comparing the political rights of one individual to another, for otherwise personal equality would be destroyed, and an aristocracy of wealth would form. But this inconvenience disappears completely when the ratio of tax contributions is considered solely in relation to great masses, and purely from province to province. It serves then to balance fairly the reciprocal rights of cities, without compromising the personal rights of citizens.

This argument was further elaborated in the *Observations*, from which a few passages may be cited:

> Political inequality between citizens is the most serious social malady. If it were to become established within the communes, within these first elements of the great society, the constitution would sin in principle, it would soon alter. ... This fear need not be entertained when it is a question of comparing the communes and *a fortiori* the departments with one another. One can and one should then take cognizance of the difference in the tax contribution. ... Those who find it extraordinary that one should pay attention to territory are asked to note that although the area of the communes and departments ought to be as nearly equal as possible, there can nevertheless be a considerable difference

> between the smallest and largest department. That of the isle of Corsica is more extensive than all those of France; it will be almost double some of them. . . . A kind of equilibrium is necessary in politics, between all the members of the association.[20]

The report of the Constitutional Committee on the territorial reorganization of France was debated during the last three months of 1789. Parts of it were accepted, parts modified, and parts rejected. On 11 November the Assembly decided in favour of a redivision of the kingdom into about 80 departments. The number was finally fixed at 83. Concomitantly the old provincial estates were at first suspended and then swept away. Sieyes' ideas here won a striking and lasting victory. As Rabaut Saint-Etienne wrote: 'We had no longer any provinces: nay the very word *province* has disappeared from our vocabulary.'[21]

On the other hand Sieyes' notion of the 'great commune' – the linchpin in many ways of his whole system – was not accepted. It was replaced by the 'district' which although it had similiar functions to the great commune in the national administrative hierarchy, had no function in the electoral hierarchy, and above all had no function as a municipality. In a spirit totally at variance with Sieyes' ideas the Assembly decreed on 12 November that there should be a municipality in every 'town, village, parish or rural community'. In this respect the disintegrative tendencies of the municipal revolution were not reversed but actually confirmed. Another serious deviation from the Sieyesian principles enshrined in the report of 29 September was the failure to ensure that the local organs of national administration were unequivocally and strictly subordinate to the king.

Sieyes' pyramidal system of election and his distinction between 'active' and 'passive' citizens were accepted by the Assembly, though the electoral process was simplified by cutting out the intermediary rung between the primary and the departmental assemblies. In the final heated debates on the constitution in August 1791, the original wealth qualifications were also altered. The un-Sieyesian provision regarding the mark of silver was dropped, but new property qualifications, equally un-Sieyesian, were introduced for those who wished to be nominated as members of the departmental electoral assemblies.

Although therefore the territorial redivision of France that took place in 1789–90 can be counted as one of Sieyes' greatest achievements it must not be supposed that it entirely reflected his ideas or that he was unequivocally happy about the way it turned out. On the contrary, the failure of the Assembly to give full and unconditional support to his plan for *adunation* seems to have created a bitterness within him that outweighed any pleasure in its partial implementation.

9 Organizing the powers of central government

Divisez, pour empêcher le despotisme; centralisez, pour éviter l'anarchie.

Sieyes, *Opinion on the draft constitution* (1795)

THE TERRITORIAL REDIVISON of France, embodying as it did a complete refashioning of the electoral system and of the organization of local government, provided the substructure of Sieyes' representative system. Now it is time to examine the superstructure: the organization of public powers at the centre. The very idea of the representative system implied, as already shown, the division and combination of such powers. How exactly did Sieyes envisage this division and combination in the constitutional proposals that he put forward during the revolutionary epoch?

Edmund Burke, in a celebrated passage written in 1796, lampooned Sieyes as the quintessential constitution-monger for all seasons:

> Abbé Sieyes has whole nests of pigeon-holes full of constitutions ready made, ticketed, sorted, and numbered; suited to every season and every fancy; some with the top of the pattern at the bottom, and some with the bottom at the top; some plain, some flowered; some distinguished for their simplicity, others for their complexity; some of blood colour; some of *boue de Paris*; some with directories, others without a direction; some with councils of elders, and councils of youngsters; some without any council at all. Some where the electors choose the representatives; others where the representatives choose the electors. Some in long coats, and some in short cloaks; some with pantaloons, some without breeches. Some with five-shilling qualifications; some totally unqualified. So that no constitution-fancier may go unsuited from his shop, provided he loves a pattern of pillage, oppression, arbitrary imprisonment, confiscation, exile, revolutionary judgement, and legalized premeditated murder, in any shapes into which they can be put.[1]

It is an inspired vignette which has undoubtedly left a lasting impression on the Anglo-Saxon mind, and which perfectly transfixes a recurrent type of blinkered political fool. But is it a fair picture of Sieyes? It has already been sufficiently emphasized that the latter had a tremendously practical turn of mind which Burke, consciously or unconsciously, left entirely out of his account. There is no need to dwell on this aspect again. Let us consider simply Sieyes' ideas for the constitution of the central government. Was he endlessly and irresponsibly concocting alternative paper schemes?

His writings, published and unpublished, suggest that there was a strong underlying continuity in his ideas on the reorganization of government, a continuity that stretched back to his early days as a student in Paris, and forward to his constitutional plans after the *coup* of 18 Brumaire. They also indicate that there was a major shift of emphasis in his ideas after the experience of the Jacobin Terror, that is to say from about 1794 onwards. This experience did not mark an absolute break in Sieyes' way of thought, but it brought to the fore a number of new elements in his vision of the properly constituted government.

Looking at the revolutionary decade as a whole therefore it appears necessary to draw only one main line of division between Sieyes' constitutional ideas. On the one hand there are the ideas he propagated and defended between 1789 and 1791 and which are reflected to a significant extent in the short-lived but nevertheless epoch-making 1791 Constitution. On the other hand are the ideas that he developed in the aftermath of Robespierre's overthrow, which are brilliantly expressed in two speeches that he delivered to the National Convention in the summer of 1795, and which, in modified form, re-emerge in the constitutional proposals made by him after 18 Brumaire, and are partially incorporated in the Constitution of the Year VIII. These two phases in his ideas will be examined successively below.

1 Sieyes' ideas on the constitution of central government 1789–91

Certain general aspects of Sieyes' conception of government deserve to be recalled at the outset. He rejected entirely the old classification of governments as either monarchy, aristocracy or democracy, depending on the number of those who ruled. This division, he wrote, was 'like an *anatomy* of man which said that some men wore long clothes, others short, and others nothing.'[2] In other words it was a flat, empirical distinction that told one nothing about the essence of government. For Sieyes there were only two authentic forms of government: democracy and the representative system, of which the latter was infinitely superior to the former. Other, non-genuine forms of government Sieyes tended to lump together as being either 'brigandage' or 'theocracy'. By the first he clearly meant a system of naked force. By the second he meant not merely 'divine right' monarchy, but all those systems in which a nation was subjected to men who claimed to derive their authority from some abstracted idea, whether it was 'nature' or 'God' or 'absolute reason' or the 'needs of the people', rather than from the occupation of public offices constituted by the nation.

A genuine system of government was thus, for Sieyes, the creation of the people or nation as a compacted unity. The division between the constituent power of the people, which amidst a large people took the form of an elected constituent assembly, and the constituted powers was for him fundamental. It was a 'separation of powers' at least as important as any separation of powers that took place within the public establishment. A further feature of the representative system that Sieyes often emphasized was that it combined within itself the best features of monarchy, aristocracy and democracy. It was, in other words, a 'mixture', but one that was quite different from the so-called 'mixed' or 'balanced' constitution that the admirers of the English system revered.

These principles provide the background to Sieyes' more detailed proposals regarding the organization of the central government between 1789 and 1791. As in so many other areas most of his leading ideas can be found in his first pre-revolutionary pamphlet, the *Views*, which was composed in the autumn of 1788 and published early in 1789. Its words provide a useful basis for the analysis that follows.

Typically Sieyes began his discussion of the future form of government in the *Views* with a question: what is a constitution?[3] His answer was that it was an organization of public functions to achieve a common end. It had two 'essential parts'. The first was the 'legislative power' and the second the 'active power'. The two he argued should be kept distinct:

> Actors and legislators should no more be confused in the body politic than head and hands in the body of the individual. If he who watches over the execution of the law can also make it, he will do so in accordance with his own particular interest. The citizens will remain defenceless, and society will degenerate into servitude.[4]

This distinction between the 'legislative' and 'active' powers was typical of all Sieyes' early pronouncements on government. He saw the distinction as corresponding in the public sphere to the distinction between the will of an individual, consisting of his deliberation and decision upon a course of action, and the same individual's power to implement the course of action that he had decided upon. Precisely the same distinction can be found in Rousseau's discussion of government,[5] though Rousseau's constant distinction between the will (or the law) as something inherently general, and the act (or execution) as being inherently particular is not typical of Sieyes' writings, and reflects a different cast of mind.[6]

This leads to a further important characteristic of Sieyes' early vision of government. Although he called for the separation of the legislative and active powers, and although he always maintained that the legislative came first, both logically and in order of importance, in the public establishment, he did not for that reason diminish or belittle the active power. He did not see the latter merely as the subordinate commissioned servant of the former carrying out its orders in a more or less automatic way. He did not, unlike so many of his colleagues in the Constituent Assembly, deny a representative character to the wielders of the active power. He did not deem it unnecessary, as for example Thomas Paine did, to give any detailed account of the active power and its functions. On the contrary he always accorded it as much attention as the legislative power in his writings.

In a note written at the end of 1789 he stressed that:

> It is not enough for a people to know how to form and express its *common will* by representatives of its choice, it is also essential that the common will can be *applied* to all the instances for which it makes law. The charge of applying the law, authority, and force sufficient to ensure that this application is done with equity, and obeyed without resistance: such are the characters, such is the essence of the executive power.[7]

It must be remembered that Sieyes, in his youth, immersed himself not only in the writings of those, like Rousseau, who were concerned first and foremost with the legitimacy of government, but also in those of men, like Turgot, for example, and the Physiocrats, who were concerned not only with legitimacy but with creating an *effective* government for France. He was an intellectual heir of the administrative reformers of the *ancien régime*, as well as of those who sought to change that regime into a rightful one. Here is one seed of his particular concept of the separation of powers, which differs markedly from those who saw it as meaning little more than a supreme legislative assembly on the one hand and its subordinate executive servant on the other.

It is plain from the *Views* and from Sieyes' other early writings that he saw the legislative power, in a representative system, as being properly invested in a single elected assembly that carried out, in microcosm, precisely the same function as the assembly of all the citizens in a democratic polity. A representative legislative assembly was thus a forum of open discussion, out of which, by a majority decision, the common will of a nation was formed. The nature and the purpose of such discussion he described as follows:

> In all these deliberations [of a representative assembly] there is as it were a problem to be solved, namely to discover in a given case what the general interest prescribes. When the discussion begins it is impossible to tell what direction it will take in order to arrive surely at this discovery. Clearly the general interest does not exist except *via* the interest of someone; it is the particular interest which is common to the greatest number of voters. Hence the need for a contest of opinions. What appears to you as a muddle, a confusion designed to throw everything into obscurity, is the indispensable prelude to enlightenment. All particular interests must be allowed to jostle and collide with one another, to outbid one another in seizing the question and pushing it, as far as each can, towards a particular goal. In the course of this trial useful opinions separate from those that are harmful; the latter fall away, while the others continue to assert themselves and to balance one another until, modified and purified by their reciprocal efforts, they finally come together and fuse into a single opinion, just as in the physical universe a single and more powerful force can be seen to result from a mass of opposed ones.[8]

The full benefit of open discussion, Sieyes continued, could only be obtained by giving the members of the assembly absolute freedom to express their opinions. There could be no prosecution, still less punishment of them for anything they might say. Licence or excess could only begin at the moment when the internal order of the assembly could suffer from it.[9]

Sieyes' justification of public debate bears a resemblance to some of Rousseau's ideas in the *Contrat social*, notably his contention that when 'the pluses and minuses which cancel each other out' are taken away from individual wills, 'the sum of the difference is the general will.'[10] But Sieyes went much further than Rousseau in his endorsement of the merits of discussion. Rousseau believed that the 'greater harmony that reigns in the public assemblies, the more, in other words, that public opinion approaches unanimity, the more the general will is dominant; whereas long debates, dissensions and disturbances bespeak the ascendance of particular interests and the decline of the state.'[11] Sieyes did not share the suspicion of the clash of particular opinions. Rousseau, moreover, when (in the case of Poland) he conceded the possibility of a representative legislative assembly argued that the deputies could be punished by those who sent them. For Sieyes, as has been noted elsewhere, such punishment was not merely an 'absurd contradiction in the law' but a 'barbarism'.[12]

The first essential for a properly constituted legislative assembly, Sieyes argued in the *Views*, was that it should be based on a uniform system of election proportional to the population. His detailed ideas on this subject were examined in the last chapter. He also thought that deputies should be elected for a relatively short period (three years in the *Views*) and that there should be a rotating system of election, a third of the deputies being renewed at a time. This idea was not incorporated in the 1791 Constitution, but it was included in that of 1795. The legislative assembly should be permanent, any idea of it being summoned only at certain fixed intervals belonging either to 'French chatter or alleged English profundity.'[13] The assembly itself should decide on adjournments. It would also have full responsibility for fixing and raising taxes, but would exercise this responsibility in conjunction with the various regional assemblies that Sieyes envisaged in his plans for local government reorganization.

One of Sieyes' favourite ideas, between 1789 and 1791, was that the single legislative assembly which he favoured should be able to subdivide into 'sections' or 'chambers' in order to deliberate upon a given issue more thoroughly, though it would always decide by way of an overall majority vote. This was his answer to those who believed that a single-chamber legislature would be too precipitate in its behaviour. The idea makes its appearance for the first time in the *Views*.[14]

So much for Sieyes' conception of the organization of the legislative power. What of the 'active power'? In the *Views* Sieyes was conspicuously silent on the position of the king and referred only scathingly and obliquely to the king's ministers. He contented himself with a survey of some of the 'branches of the active constitution'[15] – notably the judiciary and education – clearly believing that a future constituent assembly should start as soon as possible to construct them on a fresh basis, independently of the ministers, and should eventually take in hand the reconstitution of the ministerial power itself.

The overall shape of Sieyes' early constitutional ideas is visible in the *Views* but there are some gaps that require to be filled in. One was his firm rejection from the start of the English constitutional model, which has been touched upon but needs further elucidation. His tract *What is the Third Estate?* provides perhaps the best basis for this.

Why did Sieyes reject the English model of a 'balanced constitution' in which king, lords and commons together made up the legislature? There were several reasons. First, and most superficially, he did not think that imitation was the proper way to go about reforming one's own institutions. A given people must do things for itself. More than this, the French should aim at being an example for other countries.[16] Sieyes was always intensely nationalist in this sense. Second, he thought that the division into orders that existed in France went far deeper than in England. In particular the status of the nobility was quite different in the two countries. 'In England there are no privileged nobles except those who are accorded a part of the legislative power. All other citizens are blended in the same interest: there are no privileges making them into distinct orders.'[17] In France it was quite different. There the creation of an upper chamber on the model of the House of Lords would consecrate a very profound civil division. The nation – which already had a genuine existence in England[18] – would be stifled at birth in France if an English kind of political structure was adopted. But Sieyes added that he was not attacking the concept of a division of the legislative assembly as such. 'I have only attacked distinct *chambers* in so far as they are distinct *orders*. Separate these two ideas and I would be the first to call for three completely equal chambers, each composed of a third of the great national deputation.'[19] This of course was his idea of a single legislature dividing into separate units for the purposes of deliberation, to which allusion has already been made.

Deeper than his objections to the English system on factual, empirical grounds, lay Sieyes' scepticism about the idea that a constitution consisted essentially in the establishment of a 'balance'. Once the people emerged as the constituent power of the government what was it that they needed to establish a balance *against*? Would not 'all the importance that one attaches to-day to the *balance* of powers collapse along with the order of things which alone renders it necessary?'[20] Was not the English constitution essentially a negative thing?

> I do not deny that the English constitution is an astonishing work for the time in which it was contrived. However, despite the fact that any Frenchman who does not prostrate himself before it is all too likely to be mocked, I will dare to say that I see in it, not the simplicity of good order, but rather a scaffolding of precautions against disorder ... it is quite in the ordinary course of events that extremely complicated machines precede real progress in the social art just as in every other art; its triumph likewise will be to produce greater effects by simple means.[21]

A constitution for Sieyes was thus not basically a negative thing, braking or restraining something that pre-existed it. This did not mean that it should not contain precautionary elements, but that these were not its sole or primary rationale. Its primary purpose was to create something that achieved the positive end of the body politic. An idea of his priorities can be deduced from the definition of a constitution in his *Exposition of the rights of man and citizen* that he drafted at the end of July 1789:

> The Constitution embraces simultaneously:
> The formation and internal organization of the different public powers,
> Their necessary correspondence and their reciprocal independence,
> And finally, the political precautions with which it is wise to enclose them, so that they are always useful and are never able to become dangerous.
> Such is the true meaning of the word Constitution; it relates to the entirety (*ensemble*) and the separation of public powers.[22]

A constitution for Sieyes was thus a positive creation, with safety measures attached, rather than a braking device. Checks and balances, mutual vetoes, did not express its essence.

A second gap in his early pre-revolutionary writings on the structure of government was of course that there was little or no discussion of the way the 'legislative' and 'active' powers were linked together, and in particular no discussion of the role of the king. It was not until September 1789, when the debates took place on the first proposals for a constitution – proposals that had been drafted by Mounier and his friends and sought to establish a system similar to the English one – that Sieyes made his ideas on these subjects clearer. His speech on the royal veto, delivered on 7 September, not only opposed the proposals of the Anglophiles, and probably contributed to their ultimate rejection by the Constituent Assembly, but gave an indication of Sieyes' own alternative to them.

The status that Sieyes accorded the king in this speech is an interesting one. The quality, he said, that was most appropriate to the person of the king, was that of 'head of the nation' (*chef de la nation*) or 'first citizen' (*premier citoyen*). In a footnote attached to the text of his speech he explained more fully what he meant by this:

> The king is citizen of all the municipalities; he alone is the first citizen; all the others are equal. Even in the sequence of *committed* powers, the executive power is not the first: thus it is not as the trustee of this power that the king is superior to all. I consider the *first citizen* as the natural *overseer* (*surveillant*), for the nation, of the executive power. I identify the king with the nation; together, they make common cause against the errors and undertakings of the ministry.[23]

In the main text of his speech he stressed the oneness of nation and king:

> In fact the prince, the head of the nation, can only be one with it; if you separate them for a moment, if you give him a different interest, a distinct interest, from that moment you debase the royal majesty. For it is all too clear that an interest different from the nation can never be on the same level with it, that, in a nation, everything gives way, and must give way, before it.
>
> Thus the king can never be separated, even in theory, from the nation whose whole majesty he represents. When the nation pronounces its will, the king pronounces it concomitantly. Everywhere he is the head; everywhere he presides; but all his acts presuppose him present in the midst of you. Finally, here alone can his legislative rights be exercised.[24]

One final statement rounds out Sieyes' concept of the monarch as first citizen:

> The king, considered as an individual, is reduced to his individual will; when seen in this capacity he is entitled only to vote in one of the primary assemblies, where every citizen is allowed to vote. The king, considered as *first citizen*, as *head of the nation*, is deemed representative of the nation in the whole hierarchy of assemblies, right up to the National Assembly. In all he has the right to vote; in all he may preside; in all he is legally the first, because there can be no such thing as a first citizen except through the law. But in none can his vote be equal to *two*.[25]

Sieyes dwelt at some length on this last point. As soon as one allowed any differential voting rights in the various assemblies, as soon as one allowed one man's vote to count for more than another, then the way was open to allowing one man to exercise the whole legislative power on his own. The king's vote could therefore count only as one.

The distinctive feature of Sieyes' conception of monarchy was that the king was a genuine *representative* of the nation. The king represented the 'majesty' of the nation. He participated in the legislative power, presiding over the activities of the legislative assembly, and voting like any other member in it. At the same time he was the overseer, on behalf of the nation, of the executive power. He was thus the linchpin, the hyphen – to borrow Bagehot's metaphor – between the legislative and executive powers.

Where does this conception of monarchy come from? Surprisingly perhaps it can be traced to Rousseau, not the Rousseau of the *Contrat social* but the Rousseau of the *Considérations sur le Gouvernment de Pologne*. In this work Rousseau argued, not that kingship in Poland should be abolished, but that it should be transformed so that the *chef d'une nation* was no longer the natural enemy of liberty but its defendant. He argued in particular that kingship should not be hereditary, so that kings would have no temptation to usurp power in order to pass it on to their sons. 'It is thus that the leader (*chef*) of the nation will become, no longer the born enemy of it, but the first citizen.'[26]

He continued:

> He [i.e. the king] will have little immediate and direct force to act by himself; but he will exercise much authority, surveillance and inspection, in order to contain each to his own duty, and to guide the government to its proper end. The presidency of the Diet, the Senate, and all [political] bodies, a severe examination of the conduct of everyone in a public position, an intense concern to maintain justice and integrity in all the courts, to conserve order and tranquility within the state, and to give it a good standing externally, the command of armies in time of war, useful establishments in time of peace – these are the duties which are particularly attached to the office of king, and which will keep him busy enough should he wish to carry them out himself. For once the details of administration have been entrusted to ministers established for that purpose, it ought to be a crime for a king of Poland to entrust any of his own to favourites . . . . Along such lines the equilibrium and balance of the powers that make up the legislation and administration ought to be established.[27]

The resemblance between Rousseau's conception of kingship and Sieyes' is striking. There is another interesting connection between the two men on the subject of monarchy. Sieyes was fond of a particular quotation from Pliny which read: 'If we have a prince it is in order to save ourselves from having a master.' He took it expressly from Rousseau's *Discours sur l'inégalité*.[28] The quotation is particularly pertinent to the events of 18 Brumaire. Sieyes, before the *coup*, seems to have been looking for a German 'prince' to become a constitutional monarch of France. In the event Napoleon seized all the reins of government and Sieyes, recognizing the fact, is said to have remarked to his friends: 'Gentlemen, you have a master!'[29]

To return to Sieyes' speech of 7 September 1789. Its main theme was of course the question whether, under the new constitution, the king should possess a veto, either absolute or suspensive, on legislation. Sieyes' answer was categorically to deny that the king should have any veto power at all. Even if he was considered, in the conventional way, as the trustee of the executive power, he should have no such power. Individual wills were the only legitimate elements in the formation of the general legislative will and the execution of the law came after its formation. For these reasons the executive power could claim no right to play an integral part in the making of laws. As the right to veto laws was virtually the same as a right to make them, it was plain that the executive power could not possess it. Sieyes went so far as to say that its exercise, in any form, by the executive power, was nothing but a *lettre de cachet* directed against the national will. The most the executive could do was to give advice on laws.

What of the king in his role as first citizen? Could he not legitimately claim a right of veto? After all, Sieyes himself argued that the king, as first citizen, had the right to vote in all the various representative assemblies. Sieyes' answer to this was that the exercise of an absolute veto over nationally sanctioned legislation by a particular will of any kind was an absurdity, not worthy even of discussion. However, the idea of allowing a second examination of such legislation, of permitting a suspensive veto on the work of a legislative assembly, did merit consideration.

Sieyes argued that it was necessary to examine this problem first in relation to matters affecting the constitution, and then in relation to ordinary legislation. In England, where there was no distinction between the constituent power and the legislative power, the king necessarily held a veto because the parliament might attack his very position in the constitution. In France, however, this danger was impossible because the constituent and legislative powers had been separated. This meant that if the constituted powers began to encroach upon one another's very existence, or fundamental rights, then an appeal could be made back to the constituent power for a resolution of the issue. A special convocation of the constituent power, therefore, made the exercise of a veto by any or all the constituted powers on constitutional matters redundant.

Sieyes then considered the utility of a suspensive veto with regard not to constitutional matters, but to ordinary legislation. It was often argued that such a veto was necessary in order to lessen the danger that the legislative assembly might act precipitately or unwisely. Sieyes accepted the logic of this: the danger did exist. The real question was: what was the best method of preventing or mitigating it? In Sieyes' view the most effective solution lay in his cherished idea of a single legislative assembly dividing into two or three sections, in order to deliberate more fully upon a given issue. This, he argued, would have the same effect as a suspensive veto without requiring that such a veto was given to any particular person. Hence if one of the sections judged it necessary to prolong its deliberations this would be the same, in effect, as a suspensive veto; if all sections finished their discussions quickly it would indicate that there was no need for such a veto. The final decision, of course, would have to be taken by counting individual heads, and not by treating the section as units.

Sieyes, in sum, thought that the suspensive veto was best exercised *within* the national legislative assembly itself, rather than by some body standing outside it. 'The first person who, in mechanics, made use of the *regulator*, took care not to place it outside the machine whose precipitate movements he wanted to moderate.' The king, as head of the nation, or first citizen, would have the same opportunity to influence the assembly's veto as he would to influence its law-making in general, but no more.

The speech on the royal veto of September 1789 crystallized Sieyes' ideas on the interaction of the constituted powers and showed that for him monarchy or kingship was a necessary part of the public establishment. The nation did not only require to be represented in an assembly, it required a leader, a head, a single person to represent its majesty, presiding over its legislative representation and supervising the execution of its laws. Such a monarch was far from being a ruler by divine right, or by some kind of paternal right, he was a rational element in a representative mechanism deliberately established by the nation. But could he be representative if he was not elected to office? Sieyes' answer to this objection will be seen in a moment.

In the *Observations* of October 1789 Sieyes returned briefly to the subject of kingship. In a curious, compressed passage he defined two types of monarchy, 'simple' and 'double'.[30] According to the first there would be no intermediary between the legislature and the ministers responsible for the main executive departments. The ministers would be little 'kings' in their own domains. According to the second there would be a monarch superior in rank to the various ministers, and who would nominate them. He would not be responsible to the legislature, but his ministers would. This second concept corresponds to Sieyes' favoured idea of the king as 'first citizen' and '*surveillant*'.

Sieyes' unpublished notes on '*le prince*', which are dated 1789–91, further substantiate and amplify the concept of monarchy already sketched.[31] On one sheet he defined the prince as 'the representative of the *social unity* vis-a-vis foreign powers; the representative of the *national primacy* internally; [and] electorality within the order of subordinate action.' By the latter of course he meant that the prince would choose the ministers. He stressed that the prince was '*irresponsable, inviolable*', and that such offences as he might commit were a matter for the constituent power and not for the ordinary legislative power. Part of the royal function was to discourage the ambitions of demagogues.

It is clear from these notes that Sieyes was also tinkering during this period with a system of choosing the king by lot. He emphasized that it would not be for the legislature to nominate him as this would destroy the separation of powers. The king should be appointed for life. In one highly interesting fragment which appears to be quite late (i.e. probably 1791) he envisages 'choice by lot' being effected by 'the hazard of birth', thus bringing a constituted hereditary monarch very close to a constituted 'chosen', if not actually elected, one. This fragment helps us to understand his willingness to accept the hereditary principle embodied in the 1791 Constitution, a willingness that he also expressed in his polemics with Thomas Paine. The hereditary principle in the monarchical context did not have the same meaning as in the aristocratic context.

The polemics with Paine arose in the immediate aftermath of Louis XVI's disastrous flight to Varennes in June 1791. There can be no doubt that this action completely destroyed Sieyes' belief in the ability of Louis XVI to fulfil the office that the 1791 Constitution allotted to him. Louis would have to go. He was no longer worthy of being a 'representative' of the nation. But at the same time Sieyes clearly saw no reason to join the republican (in the sense of the anti-monarchical) movement that now began to raise its head in France. What was needed was a new king, not no king at all.

In a letter to the *Moniteur* published on 6 July 1791 Sieyes attempted to refute the rumour that he was turning towards republicanism.

> It is not because of any fondness for old customs, or because of any superstitious royalist feelings, that I prefer monarchy. I prefer it because I consider it demonstrable that there is more liberty for the citizen under a monarchy than in a republic. It seems to me puerile to decide on any other grounds. The best social regime, in my opinion, is that in which not one, or only a few, but all enjoy peacefully the greatest possible extent of freedom. If I find this characteristic in a monarchical state then it is clear that I must seek it above all others. Such is the secret of my principles and my authentic profession of faith.

Perhaps, Sieyes added, he might have the opportunity in the near future of debating the issue more fully with those who believed in a republic. This opportunity came in fact very quickly, because Thomas Paine read his letter and wrote to him immediately, defending republicanism and declaring his total opposition to the 'whole hell of monarchy'. The one substantive point Paine made in his letter was to define republicanism:

> I do not understand by republicanism the thing that carries this name in Holland and some Italian states. I understand simply a government by representation; a government founded on the principle of the declaration of rights; principles with which several parts of the French constitution are in contradiction. The French and American declarations of rights are but one and the same thing in principle and almost in expression; and that is the republicanism that I undertake to defend against what is called monarchy and aristocracy.[32]

Sieyes in his response to this in the *Moniteur* of 16 July was extremely measured. Against Paine, he argued that the concept of government by representation was much wider than that of republican government. All good government was representative, he agreed, but there were many ways of combining and organizing representative institutions, and it was not enough simply to equate one system of representation with the whole concept. There was no need to start by saying 'I understand by republicanism good government, and by monarchy bad: stand up and defend yourself.' And he added, not without irony, that one 'could not ascribe language of this sort to an intelligent man like M. Paine.'

Where then lay the difference between representative government organized in a monarchical way and representative government organized as a republic? Sieyes distinguished them as follows:

> If you organize all political action, or what you are pleased to call the executive power, so that it culminates in an executive council deliberating by majority vote, which is nominated by the people or by the national assembly, then you have a republic.
>
> If on the other hand you put responsible heads in charge of the various so-called ministerial departments (which ought to be better defined than they are), and if those heads are independent of each other, but dependent for their ministerial life on an individual of superior rank, representing the stable unity of government, or, what amounts to the same thing, on a national monarchy charged with appointing and dismissing, in the name of the people, the chief

executive heads, and of exercising various other functions useful to the public, but of such a nature that his irresponsibility cannot create dangers – then you have a monarchy.

It can be seen that the question resolves itself almost entirely into how the government is headed. What monarchists wish to do by means of individual unity, republicans want to do by a collective body. I do not accuse the latter of being insensitive to the need for unity of action; I do not deny that such unity can be established through a senate or supreme executive council; but I do think it will be badly constituted in a variety of ways. I think that unity of action requires, if it is not to lose any of the advantages that it provides, to be inseparable from individual unity, *etc.*

Thus according to our system the government is composed of a head monarch, who is elector and irresponsible, and six responsible monarchs who are appointed by him, and who act in his name. Below these are the directors of departments, etc.

According to the other system the executive is headed by a council or senate nominated either by the departments or by the legislative assembly. Beneath are the departmental administrators, etc.

Those who like to give abstract notions a pictorial form can visualize monarchic government finishing in a point and republican government in a platform. But the advantages we attribute to one form rather than the other are of such importance that we ought not to feel bound by a simple image ... the distinctive character of the two systems [is] ... the difference between a responsible individual decision contained by an irresponsible electing will, and a majority decision discharged from all legal responsibility.

It might seem from these words as if Sieyes never considered himself a 'republican' or called himself a supporter of a 'republic'. That would be to misrepresent his position. As he observed at the end of his reply to Paine the word 'republican' could also be used in a wider sense to denote those who saw the 'public thing' as quite distinct from the 'private thing'. In this sense he *did* regard himself as a republican, and thought that it was quite possible to believe in a monarchic rather than a polyarchic government without ceasing to be republican. (Here of course he was once again in accord with Rousseau's viewpoint.) In fact Sieyes tended throughout his life to use the word republic more often in the broad sense, and to see himself as a protagonist of such a regime.

But could a hereditary monarch be reconciled with the idea of representation? Sieyes addressed himself to the problem in his reply to Paine. He began by saying 'without equivocation, that according to good theory it is false that hereditary transmission of a public office, of any sort, can ever be reconciled with the rules of genuine representation.' Then he continued:

Heredity, in this sense, is as much an affront to principle as it is an outrage upon society. But let us examine the history of elective monarchies and principalities. Is there one in which the elective mode is not worse than the hereditary mode? Who would be foolish enough to dare to blame the National Assembly, to reproach it for having lacked courage? What else could they have done two years ago? They were basically men much like many others, that is, they judged what was being offered by what they knew, and judged what was possible by what had already happened. Even if they had been able now to enter into an examination of the problem, was there any choice between an absurd but peaceful system of heredity and an equally absurd system of election, often

> accompanied by civil war? To-day, it is true, we have become more accustomed to the elective mode; reflection has led to the realization that it is susceptible of a great variety of combinations. There is certainly one which is highly appropriate to the first public function. It seems to me to unite all the advantages of heredity without its inconveniences, and all the advantages of election without its dangers. However I am far from believing that the circumstances are favourable for changing the enacted constitution on this point, and I am very happy to indicate strongly my opinion on this subject.

Sieyes then preferred, basically, some form of elected or chosen monarch, but was not prepared to divulge the form of election or choice that he had concocted, and was prepared for the time being to abide by the hereditary mode on purely pragmatic or practical grounds. Later, after the fall of the Bourbons, he proceeded with his idea of a non-hereditary monarch and the 'Great Elector' was the result. Unfortunately his idea was destined never to become a reality because of Napoleon's vehement opposition.

Sieyes' ideal of government in the early years of the Revolution thus took the form of a nationally constituted parliamentary-cum-monarchical regime. The parliament was to be permanent and unicameral but with the possibility of subdividing for the purposes of deliberation. Its membership was to be elected on a uniform, proportional basis, and to be renewable by thirds. Its function was essentially to be a public forum of discussion in which laws would be made. A monarch, not responsible to the parliament, but answerable like all public institutions to the constituent power, and representative of the majesty of the nation, was to supervise the execution of the laws made by the parliament but not actually to take part in such execution. He was in effect to reign, but not to govern. He was not to possess any kind of veto power. He was, however, to choose the executive ministers who were to be responsible to parliament.

Sieyes' ideas about the organization of the central government, like many of his other ideas, were to be reflected in the 1791 Constitution on which he worked so assiduously in the successive Constitutional Committees of the Constitutional Assembly. In fact there is more of him than of any other single individual in this Constitution. Article 7 of the Declaration of Rights, much of the First Title setting out the 'fundamental dispositions guaranteed by the Constitution', much of the Second Title concerning the territorial division of the kingdom, many of the electoral provisions in the Third Title, for example the idea of 'active citizens' and the rejection of imperative mandates, as well as the provision for departmental administration, can be attributed directly to him.[33] Perhaps most important of all, he must be held to have been primarily responsible for the key sentence referring to the public powers: 'The Nation, from whom alone all the Powers emanate, cannot exercise them except by delegation. The French Constitution is representative: the representatives are the Legislative Body and the king.' Apart from this there are many provisions in the 1791 Constitution, for example the stipulation that there should be a single, permanent legislative chamber, which Sieyes clearly favoured but which were so widely held that it would be wrong to suggest that they originated from him. Finally there are the provisions which do not reflect his ideas, or which were decided, quite independently of him, by debates in the Constituent Assembly.

Overall his influence can be said to have been pervasive, and perhaps he was partly right when he implied that the 1791 Constitution had been largely 'dictated' by himself to his colleagues in the Constitutional Committee.[34] It may of course be said that all the labour that he expended on this Constitution was in vain for it lasted no more than a year. This is to forget that several of the provisions, in particular those relating to the territorial division of France, embodied lasting changes. More importantly it overlooks the fact that the 1791 Constitution, the first European constitution to be based unequivocally on the nation as constituent power, was of profound significance as a model for subsequent European constitutions. It influenced the shape of constitutions throughout the nineteenth century in a vast number of countries. Indeed, certain of the stipulations of principle made for the first time in 1791 are to be found little changed in the constitutions of the present day.[35] Sieyes' work was by no means in vain.

2 Sieyes' ideas on the constitution of central government 1794–99

Sieyes' defence of constitutional monarchy against Paine's republicanism in July 1791 was followed by a long period during which he remained conspicuously silent on the issue of the proper organization of central government. The collapse of the 1791 Constitution in 1792 did not draw from his pen a proposal for a new system. He advised the Girondin group in the National Convention, but their constitutional proposals, presented early in 1793, were not drafted by him, and certainly did not reflect his ideas. His theoretical essay on *Liberty*, published in June 1793, defended the representative system against those who decried it in the name of liberty, but did not attempt to prescribe a structure of governmental powers. He had nothing whatever to do with the Jacobin Constitution of 1793 and derided it as being no more than a 'table of contents'.[36]

Not until the fall of Robespierre in 1794 did he once again address himself to the problem of governmental organization. His unpublished papers, and in particular the memorandum entitled *Bases of the social order* which was written probably late in 1794 or early in 1795, show him rethinking the main issues in the light of the experience of the Jacobin dictatorship. He did not sit on the Committee that drafted the 1795 Constitution but he did give the Committee his views, and in July and August he delivered two major speeches in the National Convention on the proposed new system. The changes that he recommended in these speeches were not accepted, and the Constitution that established the Directorate only reflected his ideas in a peripheral manner.

During the Directorate Sieyes remained silent on the question of governmental organization, and even during the summer and autumn of 1799 when he was plotting against the regime he did not divulge the kind of constitutional structure that he was seeking to establish in its place. Not until after he had successfully engineered the *coup* of 18 Brumaire did he reveal his plans and seek to incorporate them in the new constitution. Napoleon, however, had his own ideas on government, and Sieyes' final efforts to provide France with an authentic regime, based on the principles of the representative system, were unsuccessful. The Constitution of the Year VIII bears only the blurred imprint of his mind.

The ideas Sieyes put forward in 1799 proceed along the same line as those he expressed in 1794–95 and they will be considered in conjunction here. The line deviates significantly from the one he pursued in 1789–91, though its goal remains the establishment of the representative system. In the period after 1794 Sieyes took the idea of separation of powers to new lengths. He was also concerned to build into the public establishment institutions that would 'conserve' the achievements of the Revolution against possible overthrow. Not only the making of a new regime, but also its preservation had become his aim. For these reasons his later proposals have a far greater complexity than his earlier ones.

In the *Bases* Sieyes announced one of the main changes in his ideas with remarkable abruptness. 'The legislative power', he wrote, 'is not confined to a single chamber of deputies. It has been felt necessary to divide it itself into three parts. The head of state, the senate, and the chamber of deputies: none of these three branches can call itself separately the legislative body, none can deem itself the legislator, or the legislative representation. These qualities are indivisible and only pertain to the reunion of all three.'

This sudden abandonment of his old ideas did not mean that Sieyes was returning to the English idea of a mixed constitution. All his statements from this time onward show rather that he had become convinced of the necessity of representing separately legislative initiative and legislative decision. Almost certainly his reading of James Harrington helped him to arrive at this idea of separating organs of proposal from organs of decision.[37] Their precise relationship will become apparent in a moment.

The *Bases* are interesting too because they reveal Sieyes for the first time confronting the idea of sovereignty. Although in the early years of the Revolution he had constantly referred to the people or nation as the constituent power he had very rarely referred to the 'sovereignty of the people' and the notion of sovereignty is conspicuously infrequent in his writings. In this he differed markedly from other revolutionary writers. However, in the *Bases* he felt obliged to pose the question 'what is *sovereignty*?' He replied:

> Do those who associate together [in a political union] pool and represent the totality of their forces and resources? Certainly not. Hence sovereignty in the sense of a supreme power that dominates and embraces everything does not exist. It does not rest in the mass of public functionaries taken as a whole; and if the constitution separates the various powers, and if each of them is limited to its own particular mission and cannot go beyond it without usurpation and crime – where is the gigantic idea of sovereignty to be assigned? It is clear that the terms supreme or sovereign authority can only be understood to signify the final decision of several special authorities whose judgement allows of no appeal.

In his speech to the Convention in July 1795 Sieyes touched again on the subject of sovereignty. He observed that it was not possible to conceive of it except as being 'of the people'. At the same time he strongly objected to the idea that it was a boundless power, such a thing being a 'monstrosity in politics'.

What then was Sieyes' doctrine of sovereignty? Taking all his scattered statements into account, it may perhaps be paraphrased as follows. Full sovereignty 'belonged' to the people. It was the original national will to create a public establishment to secure individual liberty. In creating such an establishment the nation could either exercise the powers concerned directly, or (as Sieyes advocated) it could detach a part of its will and exercise public power by way of representation. But in creating a representative system the nation always retained the right of re-constituting the public establishment should the latter degenerate into despotism or anarchy. Sovereignty in this second sense signified the continuity of the nation as constituent power behind all the vicissitudes of established representative government. Finally, within the established system, when it was working in accordance with its mission and purpose, sovereignty could be taken to signify the ultimate power of decision accorded by the constitution to particular authorities. What Sieyes stressed was that in none of these senses was sovereignty a limitless power to do anything and everything – it was always geared to a specific end.

One final excerpt from the *Bases* is worth citing because it has such close links with Sieyes' final constitutional plans after the *coup* of 18 Brumaire. Towards the end of the memorandum he referred expressly to the 'permanent and peaceful nomination of the Great Elector'. What did he mean by this? He explained: 'Resolve this great problem: How to procure within a state all the advantages of the *election* of a head without becoming a prey to all its inconveniences, and all the advantages of *heredity* without its immeasurable dangers? Only then will your constitution carry within itself the principle of its own conservation.' In these words can be seen the line of continuity that runs from Sieyes' polemics with Paine in 1791 through to his proposal to institute a 'Great Elector' in 1799.

In the speeches that Sieyes delivered to the Convention on 20 July and 5 August 1795 respectively an echo of the *Bases* can be heard in several places, though he refrained entirely from making a proposal for establishing a single head of state, and appears to have accepted the prevailing opinion at that time in favour of a collective or collegiate executive.

What was the theme of these two speeches? On the one hand they contain a powerful reassertion of the principle of representation coupled with a denunciation of the principles of the Jacobin dictatorship and of 'unlimited' sovereignty. On the other they provide a new and striking formulation of Sieyes' concept of the separation or differentiation of powers. Finally, they contain four major proposals for the reform of the draft constitution. The reassertion of representation has already been discussed in an earlier chapter. Attention will be concentrated here on Sieyes' more specific organizational proposals.

His reformulation of the concept of division of powers occupied the start of his first speech. The heart of the operation of constitution-making, he said, lay in the organization of the public establishment, something that could be settled in about fifty articles, rather than two or three hundred. (The completed constitution was to have 377 articles.) The prime task was to find a middle way between the complete unity of public powers and their complete division, or between despotism and anarchy. Unity had to be combined with division. There were two ways of doing this. The first was that of 'counterweight' or 'equilibrium', or in other words, the English system. The second was that of 'conjunction' or 'organized unity'. It was the latter that Sieyes favoured. It was the logical expression of the representative system.

Sieyes proceeded to differentiate his system of 'organized unity' from that of 'counterweight'. The latter consisted basically in creating two or three representative bodies each of which exercised the *same* function. Its logic was the following. First of all a representative body was created which exercised all the powers of government. Fear of this immense concentration of power then led to the creation of a second body of representatives exercising the same bundle of functions, but balancing the first. In this way government by single action (*action unique*), or despotism, was fended off. Such a system did not necessarily require upper houses consisting of nobles or clergy. The American example showed that it could be created without these antiquated forms of social hierarchy. The essence lay in countervailing bodies each exercising the same function.

The weakness of this system was shown by the fact – and here Sieyes had the English example in mind – that in practice despotism (*action unique*) reasserted itself by way of intrigue and corruption. What was the famous English party of opposition, he asked, except 'the disgraced ante-chamber of the king, constantly occupied with intriguing and babbling against the ante-chamber in service, in order to enter once again into the profits of the house?' These developments were not accidental. If you attached two independent horses to the carriage of state, it needed a royal coachman to make them move forward in the same direction.

Sieyes proceeded to argue that his concept of 'organized unity' or 'unity of action' in the public power meant neither counterweight nor despotism. Unity of action meant the convergence of several different, specialized actions in one and the same end. Unlike the system of counterweight it did not give two or three heads to one and the same body so that each could counteract the other, but rather separated out a number of different faculties within a single head in such a way that together, in combination, they produced a single action. This was the true, the natural way forward both for France and for other countries too. It was dictated by the *art social*.

Sieyes acknowledged that the draft constitution embodied certain worthwhile ideas: 'it moves further along the true path than any other.' He referred in particular to the idea of placing the power of legislative proposal in one chamber – the so-called Council of Five Hundred – and the power of legislative decision in another – the Senate. This was precisely the kind of *functional* division of powers of which he approved. He also referred to the tentative effort to separate the executive power into its two principal parts, by which he can only have meant the division between the so-called Executive Directory, a five-man body that the new constitution placed at the heart of the executive power, and the ministers that the Directory appointed and revoked.

However, despite these good features, Sieyes believed there was a lack of harmony and coherence in the draft plan as a whole. It was at this point that he began to make his own concrete proposals. They were four in number. The least radical affected the Council of Five Hundred, the law-proposing chamber of the proposed new two-chambered legislature. Sieyes wanted it to be transformed into a smaller body, which he called the 'tribune of the French people'. Like the Council, the tribune would be a law-proposing body, and its specific role would be to articulate the concrete, ever-changing needs and demands of the people at large.

More radical were Sieyes' recommendations regarding the 'government', which he saw as a second law-proposing body set over and against the 'tribune'. He began by saying that he had studied the draft constitution but had not been able to find the government anywhere! The time, however, was past when 'the government was considered an antipopular institution'. All parts of the public establishment were 'for the people', and this included the government. 'If the contrary opinion were to prevail again, it would be equivalent to having neither law, nor representation, nor any public establishment.' The government thus had to be 'put in representation' alongside the other institutions. It had to be given a guaranteed position vis-à-vis the tribune of the people. At the same time the government ought not to be confused with the executive power:

> I know that my demand that the government be put into representation in the upper part of the central establishment and opposite the tribune, will appear so shocking at first sight, but, let us be clear, I do not confuse the *executive power* with the *government*. On the contrary I consider the separation of these two powers, in a republic, as one of those ideas that still belong to the progress of science. It is time to reveal its importance and to do it justice.
>
> The executive power is all *action*, the government is all *thought*. The latter admits of *deliberation*, while the former excludes it at all levels in its hierarchy without exception. But since our task is to clarify ideas, and to bring greater precision into the language, permit me to comment that the term executive power is not a good choice as a description of the major part of the official service of the law.
>
> Who executes the law? Those who observe it. In the first place the citizens, each in that which concerns him (this is the major part of the execution of the law). In the second place all the public officials, each in the function or employment with which he is charged. All law can be classified under one or other of these heads. It is in this sense that protective laws are distinguished from directive laws. The first are executed by the citizens; the others by public officials. When non-execution or resistance occurs in one or other category, then a portion of official power is set in motion to determine or force execution on the part of those who contest or resist it. Be that as it may, the executive power, in the sense of the power exercised by the organizers of the action of the law, ought to be separated from the government which is exclusively concerned with three major areas:
>
> 1. The government in the upper part of the central establishment is a *jury of proposition*.
>
> 2. Once the law has been promulgated and thus *put into execution*, the government reappears at the threshold of the lower part of the central establishment in the role of *jury of execution* ...

3. Finally the government is the *procurator of execution* and in this guise nominates the executive power or the chief organizers and directors of the official service of the law.

The first and third functions of government are largely self-explanatory. The government both proposes laws and appoints executive ministers. If the word 'jury' seems odd, we must remember Sieyes' deep respect for the English jury system, which he wished to be adopted in the French judicial structure. (It was the one English institution he admired.) As he grew older the 'jury idea' expanded beyond the original judicial role that he assigned to it and permeated much of his political thinking too. He made it plain later in his address that he envisaged the government as a body of representatives consisting of seven persons, whose meetings would not be public.

By the phrase *jury of execution* Sieyes meant simply that the government would be the place where implementing legislation would be drafted, in the form of *arrêtes* and regulations. It would be a kind of *législature d'exécution*. He recognized that such activity would have to be closely watched to prevent abuse of power.

Sieyes argued that the great merit of his proposal for separating the government from the executive power, and placing it in overall charge of the executive power, was that it would shield the executive from the attacks of the legislature, and allow it to carry out its duties in peace and security, without having constantly to defend itself. The executive power, he explained,

> takes on an appearance, acquires a certainty, a promptness of action, and a security unknown until now. It is no longer, as in systems of equilibrium, a weight in the legislative scales that counterbalances the weight of the representatives of the people, for in the first place every public functionary is representative of the people within the scope of his mission, and secondly, we consider the executive power, not as a counterweight, but as the continuation and complement of the social will, since it is charged with completing its action by realizing it, and since it is charged with ensuring everywhere the faithful and certain execution of the law.

What of the government's function as an initiator of legislation, as Sieyes put it graphically, as a 'workshop' of legislative proposals? According to his scheme legislative proposals were to spring from two sources. On the one hand they were to come upwards from the tribune and to reflect the concrete needs and demands of the people at large, and on the other they were to flow downwards from the government and to reflect the needs of the government. In his typically terse way Sieyes summarized the logic of this idea:

> Where is the necessity or actuality of a law to be recognized? In the feeling of need.
>
> Well, have I not identified need in its proper place? In the governed and the governors. . . .
>
> Can you conceive of two better *workshops of proposition*?
>
> What else is there besides them? Nothing.

But who was to decide upon the proposals emanating from the government and the tribune? Here we come to the third of Sieyes' recommendations. To judge on all legislative proposals, but without possessing the power to make such proposals itself, there would be a separate body of representatives, larger in number than the tribune, and meeting in a single chamber. This would be the legislature proper, which Sieyes called the 'true central point, the supreme regulator of all the parts of the public establishment.' It would, as he himself observed, be rather like a court, listening to the case for legislation being proposed and argued by two litigants, namely the tribune and the government, and pronouncing the 'national judgement' upon their propositions. Sieyes suggested that the legislature might be composed of the 'three great industries that make up the movement and life of a prosperous society, namely rural industry, urban industry, and the ubiquitous one which has for its object the culture of man', but he did not press this extraordinary point, which bears little relationship to any of his other statements on the organization of government.

In his proposals of 1795, then, Sieyes was more concerned than before to distinguish and separate the specialized functions that went to make up the totality of the public establishment. There was to be a separate representation of the needs of the people, a separate representation of government, a separate representation to arbitrate and decide on legislative proposals, and a separate representation of execution. All these bodies would ideally interlock to produce the 'unity of action' he sought. He empahsized that one of the main reasons for the careful differentiation of powers was to canalize and to tame the ferocious passions that – as the previous four years had shown – could break to the surface and swamp the political mechanism. Separation of government and executive power would, he argued, put an end to the 'permanent civil war between the popular representation and the executive' that arose in systems of equilibrium. Separation of tribune, government and legislation could help to prevent the re-establishment of the empire of demagoguery, or another eruption of popular anti-governmental passions. But could it not be argued that his installation of a kind of constant legal contest between tribune and government might itself exacerbate passions and divide the country rather than unite it? Sieyes recognized the force of this kind of objection to his proposals and attempted to answer it in the conclusion of his first speech:

> In truth it is unjust to attribute the existence of a disorder to the person who labours to cure it . . . . The existence of two parties similar or analogous to those that are known elsewhere under the names of the ministerial party and the party of opposition is inseparable from any kind of representative system. Let us be honest, they are to be found everywhere, whatever the form of government. In a single chamber they might develop with too much fury perhaps. They will develop with greater brilliance and less danger in the deliberative assemblies of a truly free republic. These two parties, using the right to speak and to write to the fullest extent, take on the character of combatants in the state of nature if there is no recognized superior above them. They are forced to confine themselves to the role of advocates as soon as there is an authority competent to decide between them.

In other words Sieyes believed his legislature, standing over and above the tribune and government, would transform the potentially explosive and destructive struggle between government and opposition into a more dignified contest, rather as the often bitter hostility between parties to a legal dispute is transmuted into the more benign contest of advocates at the bar.

Beyond the tribune, government and legislature Sieyes proposed the establishment of a 'constitutional jury'. This was his fourth major recommendation, which he elaborated in his second speech, delivered on 5 August 1795.

Why was a constitutional jury needed? Sieyes' answer was almost peremptory:

> How can the forethought of the legislator be reconciled with the idea of a constitution abandoned to itself, so to speak, at the moment of its birth? A constitution is a body of obligatory laws or it is nothing; if it is a body of laws, then where is the guardian or magistracy of this code to be found? This question has to be answered. An omission in such a matter in relation to the civil order would be as inconceivable as it would be ridiculous. Why allow it in the political order? Laws of whatever kind presuppose the possibility of infraction, and a real need to secure their observation.

Hence the necessity of a constitutional jury. What exactly would be its functions? Once again Sieyes was admirably concise:

> I want the constitutional jury to perform three tasks. 1. To act as faithful guardian of the constitutional trust. 2. To busy itself, safe from the influence of baneful passions, with all opinions which could help to perfect the constitution. 3. Lastly, to support civil liberty with a source of natural equity on those serious occasions when the tutelary law [*loi tutélaire*] has neglected to provide its just guarantee. In other words I consider the constitutional jury 1. as a court of appeal in the constitutional order, 2. as a workshop for proposing such amendments to the constitution as the course of time demands, and finally 3. as a reserve of natural jurisdiction for the gaps in positive jurisdiction.

Sieyes devoted the remainder of his speech to an elaboration of these three functions. As a constitutional court he envisaged the jury possessing jurisdiction over the acts of the legislature and the electoral assemblies. It would not make judgements on its own initiative, but would wait for cases to come before it. The legislative assemblies and private individuals would possess the right of appealing to the jury, but Sieyes was reluctant to accord this right to the electoral bodies, remarking significantly that 'anything that might nourish the permanence of the primary assemblies' was to be avoided. Once again we can see the impact of the Jacobin era. He would probably have granted the government too the right of appeal – at least in the sense that he conceived the government – but he deliberately refrained from making a recommendation regarding the executive organ proposed in the draft constitution.

Turning to the role of the jury as an amending mechanism Sieyes developed an interesting two-sided argument in favour of his scheme. On the one hand he maintained that every constitution should have the capacity to evolve, but on the other he was strongly opposed to the idea of reconvening the constituent power at fixed intervals. The principle of 'a periodic and total reproduction' of the constitution was completely antithetic to the very idea of a constitution, which implied fixity. The 'periodic return of a convention would be a real calamity.'

Deploying his arguments against the automatic summoning of the constituent power, Sieyes delivered some passages which have a certain irony when we consider his stance in 1789. A political constitution, he said, is connected 'with the nation that remains, rather than with the particular generation that passes, and with the needs of human nature, common to all, rather than with individual differences.' In a longer passage he sounded positively Burkean:

> You would rightly be terrified of a project which tended to establish the permanence of the constituent power. It would be the same as not having a constitution at all. It would lose, along with every principle of stability, those sentiments of love and veneration which free peoples above all should bestow upon it, because these feelings are incompatible with the idea of changeability that would inevitably cling to it. No law has more need of a kind of immutability than a constitution. Ideally it should have almost the great and terrible character of necessity that marks the laws that govern the universe, if human industry could be as skilful and powerful as the hand of the eternal mechanic who has organized nature. A work from the hand of man needs to remain open to the progress of his reason and experience.

This was the problem: how to ensure immutability *plus* openness to the future. Sieyes believed his constitutional jury provided the answer. It embodied the principle, not of abrupt or total change, or of permanent change, but of the progressive improvement of what existed. It would not have the power directly to alter the constitution, but simply that of making proposals for its amendment in the light of the changing needs and requirements and insights of the times. More concretely, Sieyes proposed that every tenth year after 1800 the jury should publish a *cahier* or project for the amelioration of the constitution. The primary assemblies would then vote to decide whether the project should be considered by the constituent power. If they decided in the affirmative, the legislature would be transformed temporarily into the constituent power and would be at liberty to accept or reject the jury's proposals, either as a whole or in part, though it would not have the power to amend them or to propose its own alternatives. Seen as a whole, it was a realistic and judicious scheme to permit gradual constitutional evolution.

Of the third function of the jury – that of being a supreme court of equity – little need be said, for the notion is self-evident. Sieyes envisaged only a small proportion of the jury sitting in this capacity. The main objective of the court would be to ensure that individual liberty – which, as he repeated over and again, was the final end of the whole political order – should not be indiscriminately sacrificed to the letter of the positive laws, but that the possibility should exist of having recourse to the original and eternal natural law. Indeed he said that the equity court formed by the constitutional jury would be nothing less than a 'tribunal of the rights of man'. That was the 'true name of the moral and political instrument that I recommend you to establish, for everything relates to the rights of man.'

In concluding, Sieyes mapped out briefly the way he thought the constitutional jury should be composed and selected. It would consist of 108 members, a third of whom would be renewed each year. The jury itself would choose its new members from the retiring members of the legislative assemblies. The original selection of the jury would be done by the Convention; members would be drawn from the 'constituent, legislative and conventional assemblies.'

Sieyes' 1795 speeches have been dwelt on because they reveal him at the very height of his powers. They are in many respects extraordinarily prescient. Take for example his idea of the 'government' being an element in the public establishment which cannot be simply subsumed under the category of 'legislative' or 'executive', but has its own independent, pivotal position pointing in both ways simultaneously. Is not this the reality of the constitutional structures of the modern western world? And is it not still ignored in many works on politics that continue unthinkingly to use the old simple division of legislative and executive? Again, his idea of a separate assembly sitting in judgement on the competing legislative proposals of government and opposition may seem a very strained application of the jury idea, but if we place his government and opposition *within* the assembly, then do we not find once more the reality of many parliamentary structures in the modern western world? And do not his proposals for a constitutional court – for this is what his 'constitutional jury' amounts to – match anything that was being said at the time in America on this subject in terms of clarity, precision and logic?

None of Sieyes' proposals were accepted by the Convention and the constitution that was finally adopted on 22 August 1795 remained an amalgam of a two-chamber legislature with a five man executive – the Executive Directory. Its patent objective was to ward off extreme democracy on the one hand and monarchy on the other. As has been seen it is wrong to think that it was totally at variance with Sieyes' ideas: some of its ingredients, such as that of a functionally divided legislature, and the renewal by thirds of its members, actually coincided with them. His views on it are perhaps best summarized in the patronising, but not wholly hostile comment that he made when the Constitutional Committee approached him for the second time for his views. 'This work is not bad,' he said. 'Taken all in all, and compared with existing constitutions, there is perhaps not one that is as good as this. But there are nonetheless many observations to make and it is not yet what is required.'[38]

Four years later, in 1799, Sieyes was to become convinced that the time was ripe to change the Directorial regime, and his manoeuvrings led finally to the *coup* of 18 Brumaire. It is time now to consider his last constitutional proposals, the ones that he put forward in the wake of this *coup*, and to see how far they show a continuity with those of 1795.

Fortunately the original text of the constitutional proposals that Sieyes dictated to Boulay de la Meurthe in the last days of Brumaire has been rediscovered, and the manuscript now rests in the Sieyes Archives. It contains on the title pages some explanatory words written in Sieyes' own hand.

> Constitutional observations dictated to citizen Boulay (de la Meurthe), member of the Legislative Committee of the Five Hundred, in the last days of Brumaire in the year VIII, and which he returned to me after having them transcribed. . . . '*Note*. Nothing is more incomplete and faulty than this hastily dictated outline.'

There then follows a sentence written obviously at a much later date:

> It was according to these ideas that the constitution was constructed, a constitution successively adopted with apparent satisfaction, then changed, increasingly altered, and finally abolished.[39]

The text itself, which is short and contains numerous insertions in Sieyes' hand, does indeed give the impression of having been dictated in haste. It is curiously unbalanced. It begins with some 'observations' on the merits of the representative system which have been reproduced *in extenso* earlier. It proceeds to enunciate certain 'principles', the first and most important of which reads:

> No one should be invested with a function unless he has the confidence of those over whom he exercises it, but also, in a representative government, no functionary ought to be *nominated* by those on whom his authority will weigh.

There then follows a detailed discussion of the way in which these principles are to be implemented by a suitably constructed electoral system. In essence Sieyes recommended the adoption of the 'lists of eligibility' that he had originally proposed in 1789 but which had at that time been rejected. In fact he wanted lists of those considered eligible for public office to be drawn up by the citizens at large, and public officers to be selected from these lists.

After this Sieyes described in some detail the powers of the government properly so-called, which he placed in the hands of two Consuls, and the executive power that the government supervised. This is followed by a substantial section on the body called by Sieyes the 'College of Conservators' (*Collège des Conservateurs*) and the text ends abruptly with a short statement about the status and powers of the so-called 'Great Elector' (*Grand Electeur*). What is conspicuously missing from the account is any detailed discussion of the various legislative assemblies and the way they were to interact. They are mentioned in the course of discussing the electoral mechanism but not considered directly.

When one considers the overall structure of the government the proposals of 1799 can be seen to grow out of the speeches of 1795, just as these in turn grew out of the unpublished *Bases*. There are some striking innovations, but the underlying thrust of the ideas is recognizably similar. This can be seen if Sieyes' conception of government is examined. In the Brumaire text, as in 1795, Sieyes distinguished the government carefully from the executive power proper. But in 1799 he wished the principle of separation of powers to be taken yet one stage further and to be applied *within* the government itself. Governmental powers were now to be divided between two Consuls, one of whom would be responsible for internal government and the other for foreign affairs. The sphere of competence of the Consul for foreign affairs embraced relations with other governments, the army and navy, and the colonies; the sphere of competence of the Consul for internal affairs embraced police, justice, the 'interior properly so-called', and finance. Sieyes envisaged each Consul presiding over a Council of State or cabinet, the Council for foreign affairs being necessarily smaller and more secret than that for internal affairs.

The powers of the Consuls and their Councils, within their different spheres, were broadly similar to the powers that Sieyes accorded to the government in 1795. They would be able to place legislative proposals before the legislative assembly; they would be the authoritative interpreters of laws once made, whenever the various ministers under them requested an interpretation; they would make regulations to govern the actions of public officials; and they would hear cases of a purely administrative nature raised by lower officials or citizens against ministers (by way of a special court). They would, in other words, stand between legislation and execution proper, pointing in both directions simultaneously.

Beneath the Consuls and their Councils stood the ministers, each in charge of their respective departments. They formed the executive power proper. 'It is thus that the division of powers should be understood, namely as a division from top to bottom following the natural order, in such a way that no link in the chain can move out of place.' Sieyes now envisaged fourteen ministries in all, four of them concerned with external affairs, the rest with internal law, order and services. Beneath them again were the departmental agencies, which Sieyes described as being simply '*bureaux de transmission*' both downwards and upwards between central and local government; and below them stood the administrative offices of the 'great communes' which for Sieyes were always the appropriate unit at the base of the local government system. Here at the communal level, said Sieyes, were '*la véritable administration et les véritables administrateurs*.' Once again his infinite capacity for logical and terminological subdivision can be seen at work.

Turning from the executive to the legislative side of the public establishment we find that, as in 1795, Sieyes did not accord the government a monopoly of the law-proposing power. It was to be shared by it and another body which he called the *tribune de pétition*, a body composed of as many members as there were departments. The government (i.e. the Consuls and their Councils) and the tribune would thus each present and argue the case for legislative measures, while the final decision on legislation would be taken by a separate legislative assembly consisting of 300 members. The similarity between this tripartite system of legislative proposition and decision and that of 1795 is patent.

Two further organs of the public establishment remain to be considered: the Great Elector and the College of Conservators. At first sight they appear to be radically new features in Sieyes' constitutional ideas, but the idea of the Great Elector was already present in the *Bases* of 1794–95, and was really the culmination of Sieyes' long search for some kind of elected constitutional monarch, while the College of Conservators grew out of the constitutional court or jury that he had proposed to the Convention in 1795.

Let us look more closely at the position of the Great Elector. His most important constitutional power was to appoint and to dismiss the government (i.e. the Consuls). He also chose the leading holders of executive office, though not, it seems, the members of the Councils of State, who were to be selected by the Consuls. The Great Elector's appointments to governmental and executive office were made from the so-called 'national list' of eligible candidates, of which more in a moment.

Sieyes' overall intentions in establishing this particular form of electing power are best expressed in his own telegrammatic words:

> He [i.e. the Great Elector] is not a king, for he would need subjects for that. Government and execution take place under his name, and account is rendered to him. He supervises but he does not govern. His signature is affixed by a clerk. He is not responsible.
>
> He represents the national majesty abroad and at home and, as the people do not exercise any executive right, so he himself does not exercise any. He is

represented by his ministers. *He transmits movement to the executive machine and gives it unity*. Being independent and placed above particular passions and the interest of factions, he *chooses* and *dismisses* the government and the ministers, etc., under the sole influence of his reason and properly ascertained public opinion. He forestalls or neutralizes, by his existence alone, all dangerous ambition on the part of the government or of any other citizen.

With regard to foreigners he represents the nation and guarantees it against their influence.

He watches over the government in the hands of the Consuls, decides disputes about competence that arise between them, and maintains harmony.

The basic structure of legislative, governmental and executive powers according to Sieyes' constitutional proposals of 1799 will now be clear. It remains to examine the final component in his scheme, the College of Conservators. This is how Sieyes described it:

> In all states sufficiently constituted to preserve their existence there exists in the public establishment, and above all at the highest level of this establishment, a moral power which, through its influence on habits (*moeurs*), minds (*esprit*), and even fashions (*modes*), keeps all the various movements within a specified sphere and prevents the vagaries of disordered ambitions.
>
> In monarchies, this power lies in the monarch, the princes of the blood, the grandees of the crown. In the ancient republics it lay in a hereditary-aristocratic mass.
>
> But in overthrowing the vicious scaffolding to which time and experience had attached a kind of public service, it is essential to look for ways of providing this service, for without it a national need goes unsatisfied and the public order suffers.
>
> It is in the College of Conservators that we wish to place this great influence of habit, virtue, service, names and even property.

To play its part effectively, Sieyes argued, the College would have to be as independent as possible of all the other organs of public power. It must have no motive for joining any of these powers to overthrow the established order. To this end he proposed that it should be endowed with its own sources of income, in the form of landed estates specially set aside by public decree. Such estates would enable each member of the College to enjoy a handsome salary. He continued:

> This will be called oligarchy. I reply that it is the only way of putting a brake on the natural oligarchy of riches in every large and wealthy republic, and also of destroying the old aristocratic influence and making it pass over in its entirety to the side of the republic.

It may seem from this as if the College of Conservators was simply a kind of constituted social establishment – an 'order' even – acting by way of example to preserve the *status quo*. But the College had more tangible powers. In the first place it had a crucial electoral role. It could not, of course, appoint the governmental or executive officers: that was the preserve of the Great Elector. Beyond this, however, the College's electoral prerogatives were formidable. To understand them it must be remembered that the electoral system proposed by Sieyes in 1799 was a peculiar one. Profoundly worried – as Boulay informs us – by the divisive effects of a system of election in which a mass of local assemblies chose the representative of the nation, Sieyes decided that while 'confidence must come from below' the actual selection of those who were to represent the nation as a whole must come from a single national body. This single electoral power was to be the College of Conservators.[40]

Briefly, the system was to work as follows. The citizens of each commune would draw up lists of eligible candidates for local and national office. These lists would be progressively thinned out as they progressed upwards from the communal assemblies to the departmental assemblies. The College of Conservators would be responsible for determining the final 'national list' from the names that were sent forward by the departmental assemblies. This final 'national list' would consist of 5400 names, and from it the national office-holders would be selected. The College of Conservators would itself select the members of the two legislative assemblies, the tribune and the legislature. It would also nominate the Great Elector, who would in turn nominate government and executive office-holders. All the 'lists of eligibility' would be revised annually.

A word now needs to be said of the composition of the College of Conservators itself. It would have a hundred members, each of whom would be appointed for life. Once appointed a member could neither retain, solicit nor obtain any other office, even if he tendered his resignation. Membership, as Boulay remarked, was a 'kind of perpetual consecration to the public weal.'[41] Eighty of the hundred members would be selected by the College itself from the 'national list' and would always be replaced from this source. The remaining twenty seats would be kept vacant to be filled as and when necessary by nomination. This right of nomination represented another vital power of the College, because any public office-holder so nominated, including the Great Elector, could not refuse membership, and was compelled to lay down his office. This was the famous right of 'absorption' which Sieyes said embodied all that was good in the ancient practice of ostracism. Once again it was intended as a brake on all dangerous extremism.

The remaining attributes of the College, Sieyes observed briefly, were indicated in the speech that he gave on the constitutional jury of 1795. From this and other remarks by him we can assume that in addition to its functions, the College was to be a constitutional court, a workshop for constitutional amendments, and a court of equity.

Such was the substance of Sieyes' final proposals for the organization of France's government. Their most conspicuous characteristics are probably caution and complexity. The principle of differentiating powers has been taken to an extreme. Sieyes' cherished idea of election from below combined with nomination from above serves only to make the machinery even more cumbrous. If Sieyes' early preference for simplicity in constitutional matters is recalled, the baroque elaboration of his final vision is highly ironic.

Why did it develop? The answer that has been suggested here is that from the time of the Jacobin dictatorship onwards he felt the need not merely to construct a system of government that incorporated the basic principles of the Revolution, but at the same time to protect such a structure against overthrow by either demagogic or reactionary forces. In the course of developing his scheme of government to meet this need he threw out some ideas that were, taken individually, excellent. His concept of a constitutional court was one, his distinction between 'government' and 'executive' was another, and his development of the notion of a monarch or president who 'supervises but does not govern' was a third. But in the end the 'will to subdivide' seems to have got the better of his judgement and to have produced a structure which suffered from precisely the defect that he had, in the early years, detected and castigated in the English system of government, the defect of being at heart a 'scaffolding of precautions against disorder.'

This criticism does not mean that Burke was right in seeing Sieyes as an irresponsible concocter of harebrained paper schemes of government. Sieyes' final plan may have been extremely cumbersome but there was nothing arbitrary or mercurial about his way of thinking.

On the contrary, there was a tenacity of mind and purpose, a determination to think things through to the end, that was remarkable. Rather than constantly manufacturing different schemes he may be said to have proposed only two: a first and more simple representative system that was largely realized in the 1791 Constitution, and a second and more complex representative system that evolved gradually into the schema of 1799.

It remains only to examine how far this final schema was embodied in the Constitution of the Year VIII, that established the Consulate. In the course of drafting Sieyes' ideas suffered a sea-change. Napoleon had no wish to be relegated to the position of the Great Elector, and said so forcibly. For him the real substance of power was what mattered. Hence in the final text the office of Great Elector was not to be found. His place was taken by a First Consul, Napoleon, armed with the full panoply of governmental power, and assisted by two other Consuls who had advisory rights only. Sieyes' College of Conservators was retained under the name of the Conservative Senate, but it lost all power to appoint or dismiss the holders of government office. Similarly Sieyes' idea of a functionally differentiated two-chamber legislature was accepted, but his *tribune de pétition* – now called the *Tribunat* – lost the important power of proposing laws. This now belonged entirely to the government. The idea of electing a legislative assembly indirectly, through 'lists of eligibility', was retained, though it was destined never to be put into practice. In sum the outer face of Sieyes' system was visible but the inner workings had been drastically altered. In the succeeding years the alterations were to be taken yet further, as Bonaparte tightened his autocratic grip on government, and the representative system was transformed into a military empire.

10 The church, education, the press, justice and the army

Le grand interêt de l'Etat réside dans les propriétés, et non dans tel ou tel propriétaire.

Sieyes' *Summary observations on ecclesiastical goods* (1789)

SIEYES' REPRESENTATIVE SYSTEM was by definition a system in which state and society were distinct. Representation meant the specialization of the public establishment, its separation from private activities and associations. In contrast to the *ancien régime* it meant a system where 'public functions' and 'private works' were distinguished from one another. In contrast to the Jacobin regime it meant the creation of a *ré-publique* and not the creation of a *ré-totale* where private and public, society and the political realm, became totally identified. To be sure, a single united nation or people stood at the base of the *ré-publique*, but unity in and for itself, unity *à l'outrance*, a complete politicization of the nation, was not the purpose for which the nation came into being.

The question remains: given the separation of public and private, how far could and should the responsibilities of the public establishment extend? Where did Sieyes envisage the boundary running between public and private? In chapter 6 this question was treated in broad terms. The present chapter will try to answer it in a more specific manner by looking at certain policy areas on which Sieyes expressed an opinion during the revolutionary epoch, in particular the policy of the new regime towards the church and its property, towards education, and towards the liberty of the press. In the concluding section Sieyes' proposals for the organization of the judiciary, the police and the army will be discussed. They round off his plans for the complete structural reorganization of government.

1 The church, education and the press

The position that Sieyes adopted in August 1789 on the issue of the disposal of the property and income of the church, and in particular his views on the correct way of dealing with tithes, caused the first major setback in his career as a leader of the Revolution. They brought down on his head a torrent of abuse. When the revolutionary movement swept up against the edifice of the church then the 'priest Sieyes' – or so it seemed to many – forgot his revolutionary principles and rallied to the support of the order in which he had made his career. While others wished to sweep away, peremptorily and *in toto*, the odious feudal privileges of the nobility and the clergy, he wished to stay the process and to introduce a system of redemption for tithes.

Sieyes was not only attacked in his own day for his attitude towards church property. To-day his position has been attacked again, not because it reflected his warmth of feeling for the church, but because it represented a narrow endeavour to bolster up the exploitative property relationship of the *ancien régime*, a conservative policy designed to favour the 'rich classes' against the poor, and a blinkered legalistic attitude that maintained property could never be tampered with, and that showed no appreciation of underlying economic necessities.[1]

What is the truth on this matter? The best place to begin is probably the moment when the controversy broke. First we will examine Sieyes' short speech on tithes, delivered on 10 August 1789.[2] At root he was arguing that the National Assembly should hold to its original decision, made on the famous night of 4 August, that tithes should be redeemed, and that it should not follow the more radical policy which had subsequently come to the fore, of abolishing them without any compensation. Tithes, Sieyes argued, did not belong to the proprietors of the land subject to them, therefore the proprietors had no right simply to appropriate them. *'Prenez-garde, Messieurs, que l'avarice ne se masque sous l'apparence du zèle'*.[3] This was Sieyes' message. Sacrifices 'ought to be made for the national interest, for the relief of the people, and not for the private interest of the landed proprietors, that is to say of the classes that were in general the most prosperous in society.' This is what he meant by his ringing slogan: 'They wish to be free, but they do not know how to be just.'[4]

In the statement he attached to this speech, when it was published, Sieyes developed his theme further. He knew all the arguments against tithe, he said, but because 'the tithe is a veritable scourge for agriculture, because it is more essential to free the land from this charge than from any other, and because redemption of tithe can be used more usefully and more equally than tithe itself, I see no reason for making a present of about seventy millions in rent to the landed proprietors.'[5] 'I look,' he said, 'for what has been done for the people in this great operation, and I cannot find anything. But I can see perfectly the advantage to the rich. It is calculated in proportion to wealth, so that the richer one is the more one gains. I have also heard someone thank the Assembly for having, by this decree alone, increased his revenue by thirty thousand livres.'[6]

It had been argued, Sieyes continued, that suppression of tithes helped tenant farmers. This was an error. In general the benefits of any reduction in tax or charges on land accrued to the proprietor, and the larger proprietors would not become more efficient cultivators because their revenues increased by a tenth. The small proprietors, who cultivated their own lands, Sieyes argued, 'certainly deserved more attention.'[7] According to his scheme of redemption, he said, they could have been helped by a rebate provided by the parish, graded in accordance with the paucity of their means.

In his *Summary observations on ecclesiastical goods*, published at the same time as his speech, Sieyes' argument broadened yet further. Once again he firmly rebutted the thesis put forward by those in favour of peremptory abolition of tithe, that the goods that the clergy claimed to own had merely been 'leased' to them by the nation, that the nation, long ago, had 'despoiled itself' in favour of ecclesiastics and could now summarily rectify this error. The clergy, as a moral body, was in Sieyes' view the genuine proprietor of all the donations and foundations that had been granted to it in perpetuity. Like all goods the church's properties were *in* in the nation, in the sense that they had to contribute to the public purse, but it was not true to say that the nation 'owned' them.[8]

Legislation simply to take away the goods of one class of citizen and to give them to another was also far removed from the aims and object of a constituent assembly. 'It is to reform and modify public powers that the nation delegates the exercise of its constituent power, and not to displace properties.'[9] Then Sieyes cited certain principles from his earlier essay, the *Views*. 'When principles are consulted, the guarantee of property is found to be the goal of all legislation. How could one imagine that the legislator could steal it from one. It exists only to protect it. ... Add to this that the legislator represents the common will of the nation, it acts by general laws, never by private (*particuliers*) acts of authority. It cannot despoil some to protect others, and its procuration, however extensive, cannot authorize it to crush one class of citizens in order to relieve the others.'[10]

Did all this mean that, in Sieyes' view, nothing could be done to alter the status and property of the clergy? Not at all. The clergy, as Sieyes repeatedly stressed, had been endowed with its property in order to perform a public service; unlike the nobility, it was not merely a personal order, but also a genuine public profession.[11] As he made plain in one of his other tracts the heart of this profession lay in conducting the religious worship of the bulk of the people, providing education, and caring for the poor.[12] The clergy thus formed part of the totality of political bodies that made up the government. As such it fell within the scope of the National Assembly's concerns and activities. In his *Summary observations* Sieyes specified three ways in which the Assembly might legitimately alter the clergy's position. It might simply disband the clergy as a moral body, because it had no further use for it, and wished to constitute the public service differently. In other words the Assembly could abolish the owner of church lands and goods, and hence enter into possession of them itself; though Sieyes insisted that it would have to wait for the life tenants of church property to die off before it could legitimately appropriate their property. Then, secondly, the Assembly could legitimately take steps to ensure that the income from church property was effectively directed towards the public service for which it was intended. This was no breach of property rights. Finally, and perhaps most significantly, the Assembly could legitimately extinguish *with compensation* property that was harmful to the public good. Sieyes' words on this crucial theme are worth quoting directly:

> I attribute to the law the right to determine which properties deserve to be extinguished by way of compensation because they come into conflict with the public good. But this is a general rule that applies to every class of society. As soon as any property is deemed harmful to the public weal *(chose)* it ought to be suppressed with compensation to the proprietor, either by mutual agreement or following a rule fixed by the law itself. The tithe, for example, which I regard as the heaviest and most oppressive charge on land for agriculture, can and ought

> to be redeemed as has just been proposed in the session of 4 August. But one cannot, if one retains any idea of justice and logic, conclude from these truths that ecclesiastical goods belong to the nation and not to the clergy and that one can simply take them, contenting oneself with providing the clergy, in some way or other, with suitable salaries.[13]

Sieyes concluded his pamphlet by launching an attack on the idea that the wealthy, idle, private landed proprietor was somehow a more worthy and more useful person in society than those who – like the clergy – possessed lands on condition that they performed a public service. 'An exaggerated opinion presents the free proprietors as the most important class in the state,' he wrote.

> It is more exact to say that they are, generally speaking, the most fortunate citizens. That is what distinguishes them from others and not some alleged superiority over all other classes. The great interest of the state rests in properties and not in this or that proprietor. For the land to be productive, good cultivators are required, and considerable advances. The idle consumer of the *produit net* is not, whatever one says, the most essential cause of reproduction, because work and advances would undoubtedly continue to take place, even if the consumer ceased to be idle. What is important for the state is thus that the land is well cultivated and pays a heavy proportional tax. ... However, such is the prejudice reigning in most heads that a great proprietor, fully preoccupied with his private enjoyments, considers himself quite simply as more important than anyone else, as the precious object for whose benefit the whole political machine moves, and for whom all classes of citizen, whom he calls his employees (*salariés*), ought to work and move. How many errors have to be corrected before one can have a good constitution![14]

Here Sieyes is plainly criticizing the doctrine inculcated by the Physiocrats that the status of the great landed proprietors ought to be the *meilleur état socialement possible*.[15] But his words – and the other statements by him that have been cited – enable us to form a balanced picture of his conception of property. There can be no doubt that for him the great end of the public establishment was to implement the common will of all the individuals who made up the nation for liberty, property and security: three concepts that were resolvable into each other.[16] For this reason he believed that it was absurd to give the public authorities the right to take away a person's property at will, and without compensation. For this reason too he believed that it was absurd to think of the public establishment as a mechanism for gratifying the possessive appetites of one group or class of people at the expense of another, and doubly absurd to think of it as a mechanism for favouring the richer classes against the mass of the people. The public establishment was concerned to sustain properties, or property in general, not with giving absolute protection to the position of this or that proprietor. Furthermore, if the property rights of this or that proprietor came into conflict with the common will, or the public good of the nation, then it was quite legitimate for such particular rights to be modified, or extinguished with compensation, in the name of the public good.

In his anonymously published, undated *Opinion of a deputy on the clergy* (which probably appeared early in 1790) Sieyes turned from critique to construction. What ought to be done with the clergy? It was time, he wrote, for the

National Assembly to make up its mind on this matter. In his view the clergy should be dissolved both as an order and as a corporation. It should become expressly and exclusively a public profession, salaried by the state, responsible for the three areas of public service for which it had been originally endowed: religious worship, education and the care of the poor. The property it owned as a corporation should be converted to the financing of the new public system. The district ought to be the basic unit of administration for worship, education and poor relief, under the supervision of the department.

Sieyes took it for granted that, as far as religious worship was concerned, the new structure would remain Roman Catholic in essence, though he stressed that religious liberty must be respected. Moreover he envisaged that teaching and the relief of the poor would be undertaken almost wholly by lay people rather than by priests, and that indeed lay people ought one day to be permitted to preach. Roman Catholic bishops and archbishops, albeit reduced in numbers, would continue to supervise the strictly religious side of the new public service, and would ordain priests.

This was essentially the scheme that Sieyes elaborated more fully in his *Draft of a provisional decree on the clergy*, published in February 1790. The introduction contained a spirited attack on the anti-clerical passions of the Assembly, written in Sieyes' best polemical style. It took the form of a 'speech' or 'conversation' that was supposed to have occurred shortly after the abolition of tithes on 11 August 1789. Sieyes' main point was that the Revolution had taken place initially by the simultaneous working of reason in many heads, rather than by Machiavellian intrigues, and that only by holding fast to reason could it be carried through successfully. The Assembly must not descend to the level of petty personal grievances; it must keep to the high ground of general laws. Institutions, orders and practices must be abolished or reformed, but persons must be respected. 'Treat persons with tact and respect, for societies exist for persons. It is necessary to repress disorders, to destroy abuses, to crush despotism and aristocracy once and for all. Get rid of the thing, but respect the individuals; because if the one object of the social state is not the happiness of individuals I no longer know what the social state is.'[17]

In the case of the clergy, the proper sequence of reform should have been to abolish it as a corporation and *then* to have decided what to do with its wealth, for a defunct body could scarcely have made objections. Tithes could then have been looked at from the view both of agriculture and of the national treasury. It was his firm opinion, wrote Sieyes, that 'after people had been made free, the means must be found of freeing the land,' but this liberation must take place slowly, without violating property 'this first principle of the social order, this god of all legislation.'[18] Then he launched into a direct attack on the anticlericalism of the Assembly:

> [A]re you going to suffer little hateful passions to take possession of your souls and to soil with immorality and injustice the most beautiful of revolutions? Are you going to quit the role of legislators to reveal yourselves as what? *Anti-priests*? Can you not forget for a moment this animosity against the clergy, which I do not deny exists, since I have the sad privilege of being the only one amongst you to be its victim? Is it for us to harbour the opinions that reign on

> this matter in the streets, cafés, and salons of Paris? Ought we to uphold that bourgeois jealousy which torments the inhabitants of little towns against M. *le Chanoine* or M. *le Bénéficier*? The miseries of the private man are not suitable to guide us in our calling. The clergy, like all the great bodies of the state, must be taken *en masse*. We must say, we must at least know what it ought to be, before attacking what it is. Let us aim at a constitution, at the restoration of finance. Once again: be legislators. Soon enough you will again become simple individuals, able to exercise your hatreds, your scorn, your private vengeances, and there is surely no need to reproach yourselves one day for having diverted the greatest and most respectable of all powers in order to satisfy private passions.[19]

The projected decree, which followed this lively introduction, envisaged a total reformation of the ecclesiastical establishment, taking place over a period of ten years. All ecclesiastical corporations were to be abolished, but the basic Catholic hierarchy of bishops, curates and vicars was to be retained. The clergy would be salaried by the state from funds provided by the erstwhile goods of the church. These funds would also be used to finance a double 'national foundation', one for the poor and the other for public instruction. Any surplus income from the disposal of church goods could be put to meet the other pressing needs of the state.

The administration of the new triple public service of religious worship, poor relief and education would be based on the district. No citizen could henceforth be employed in the ecclesiastical profession without the authorization of the municipality and district, and ordinations made by authorities or outside France would no longer be recognized, but this did not apply to the existing priesthood, who could continue to serve. Sieyes left the mode of appointing priests open, saying simply that the Assembly would have to decide on the 'conditions of eligibility and the mode of election' to be established.[20] Vows of lifelong celibacy were described as anti-social and condemned, and henceforth priests were not to wear their special costume outside the performance of their specific religious duties. Much of the project was taken up with the transitional arrangements for the existing recipients of an ecclesiastical revenue. All existing church foundations for the provision of poor relief and of education would continue to exist, until it was decided how they would be taken over and run by the civil authorities.

Sieyes' unpublished writings at this time round out his published proposals. He was, it appears, planning to write a tract entitled *Qu'est-ce que le clergé?* to follow his *Qu'est-ce que le Tiers état?* but this was destined never to appear.[21] He also presented his views to the Ecclesiastical Committee of the Constituent Assembly and the draft of his speech is preserved amongst his papers. It is clear from this that Sieyes took a very cool, utilitarian view of the future organization of the clergy. He was not seeking to reinvigorate the Roman Catholic faith by placing it on a purer and more authentic basis. Rather he started from the simple, incontrovertible, empirical fact that the bulk of the population shared the same religious beliefs and observed the same public rituals and that therefore there was a case for making the organization of the Roman Catholic faith a part of the public establishment. But he stressed that this ordering must be purely external and political and not internal and religious. The feelings of a man towards the divinity, the heart of religion, were not susceptible to legal regulation.

Under the new organization, he argued, the clergy should be the least costly, and the least numerous possible. Their organization should follow as closely as possible the new administrative divisions of the kingdom. Vicars should be elected by the primary assemblies; curés by districts. There should be only six bishops: one each for Paris, Nantes, Bordeaux, Marseilles, Lyons and Nancy. They would be peripatetic, and would be chosen by the king from names presented by the departments within their dioceses. The clergy would have a certain administrative and legal autonomy, but – to prevent the development of a dangerous *esprit de corps* – the Ecclesiastic Committee of the National Assembly would exercise overall supervision.

It is clear from these proposals that Sieyes' vision of the future organization of the clergy in France did not differ in any significant way from the Civil Constitution of the Clergy that was presented to the Constituent Assembly in May 1790 and passed by it on 12 July of that year. The details may not have been the same but the leading idea of a civil or external reordering of the Roman Catholic Church on a national basis, corresponding to the new administrative structures, and incorporating election at all levels, was basically the same.

Why then, by the early months of 1791, had Sieyes become resolutely opposed to the Civil Constitution of the Clergy? And why did he, later in that same year, call for its abandonment? The answer can only be that he disagreed fundamentally with those who saw in the Civil Constitution – despite its neutral wording – a means of bringing about a religious renewal, and those who were prepared (for whatever motive) to impose the new system on the existing clergy with all the fury and intolerance of religious bigotry. It is significant that Sieyes nowhere proposed that the clergy should be compelled to take public oaths of loyalty to the new political and religious constitutions, and it was the enforcement of these oaths on the clergy that stirred up the religious strife that began in France in the latter part of 1790.

Sieyes' attack is revealed in a passage of his speech to the Constituent Assembly on 7 May 1771. Here he remarked pointedly that the Departmental Directorates of France – Sieyes was at that time a leading member of the Departmental Directorate of Paris – had no desire to share the sentiments of the Ecclesiastical Committee of the Assembly 'or to be more exact, of that part of the Ecclesiastical Committee who seem to have seen in the Revolution simply a superb occasion to advance the theological importance of Port-Royal and to bring about at last the apotheosis of Jansenius on the tomb of his enemies.' Here he was striking out at such men as Camus and Treilhard, who had taken a leading part in the framing of the Civil Constitution and who were inspired by a zeal to bring France back to the pure discipline of the early Christian Church. Their attitude explains Sieyes' observation, in one of his unpublished notes, that the 'first mistake of the Assembly is to have made a religious constitution for the clergy.'[22]

Sieyes' speech of 7 May 1791 was directly occasioned by the conflict aroused by the imposition of the Civil Constitution. In April of that year religious disturbances in Paris reached a peak with the flagellation of several hundred nuns for having chosen to hear mass from priests who had not taken the oath. These troubles, together with a letter from the king to the Directorate of the Department calling for measures to restore order, impelled Sieyes and the other members of the Directorate to take action. The decree that was issued by the Department on 11 April was his work. It caused an immediate outcry and came before the National Assembly on 18 April, when Sieyes expounded and defended it, article by article.[23] Basically the decree aimed at two things: to establish a system of policing for the national churches to ensure they were used only by the publicly salaried clergy attached to them, and to set out the conditions for conducting religious worship in private houses and buildings. The purpose of these conditions was not to limit private worship, but to ensure that it was adequately protected against any interference. In Sieyes' words the Department 'has done nothing else than say to those who hide "you are not persecuted", and to the intolerant and fanatical "you will not persecute".'

The decree was attacked both on grounds of content and because it was deemed to go beyond the legitimate sphere of action of a departmental authority. Talleyrand presented a report on it in the name of the Constitutional Committee, but Sieyes found this too equivocal and justified the Department's action in his vigorous speech of 7 May 1791.

In this speech Sieyes attacked with ferocious irony the arguments of those who maintained that between the principle of religious liberty enshrined in the Declaration of Rights and its actual exercise there was a huge gulf, and that the Department therefore did wrong to protect those who continued to practise the 'old religion'.[24] How, asked Sieyes, could there be liberty *en principe* but no liberty *en conséquence*? It was absurd to think of the National Assembly unlocking a little bit of liberty here and a little bit there when it thought it was appropriate. Such liberty *ne valait pas la Révolution*. It was not the legislator but the citizen who held the key to his own liberty; the legislator's task was solely to prevent the liberty of the citizen from harming that of others. 'There is no particular law that fixes the length of our coats or the cut of our hair: the liberty we enjoy in this sphere derives from the most general principle, namely that beyond the law all is permitted, and that the law only concerns itself with actions which harm the right of another.' It was this principle that had to be applied in the case of religious liberty.

What of the argument that the action of the Department had exceeded its powers and had tended towards administrative anarchy and the establishment of a *fédération républicaine*? It was strange indeed to find the man who had trenchantly attacked the tendency towards federalism in 1789 being himself accused of it two years later – and Sieyes made the point pungently. Then he turned the weapon against those who had used it. There were, he said, two certain ways of turning France into a federal republic. The first was to endow the country with an unco-ordinated and unnecessarily cumbersome form of administration: the kind of system that was in fact developing despite Sieyes' early efforts. The second was to take the path to anarchy. There were again two ways of producing such anarchy: 'the disobedience of the administered, facilitated, favoured, and authorized by the insufficiency of a legal force, or by uncertainty regarding its action, and the bizarre idea entertained by many idle people that they are entitled by their very existence, without any other commission, to share actively in all political functions.' That is to say the threat posed by executive and administrative weakness, and the threat posed by democratic pretensions. Sieyes ended with a ringing call for more action, energy and efficiency on the part of the public authorities.

Sieyes' speech helped to persuade the Assembly to pass a decree (on the same day, 7 May 1791) which endorsed the Department's action, acknowledging that it was inspired by the same principles as those which the Assembly itself had recognized in the Declaration of Rights. As Aulard observed, the Assembly actually went further than the Department: it declared that the fact of not having taken the oath could not be brought up against any priest who presented himself in a parish church, chapel-of-ease or national oratory. Aulard concluded: 'It is evident that liberty of worship was rather wrenched from the men of the Revolution than granted by them of their free will. The Constituents recognized it in the decree of 7 May 1791, with a bad grace and many precautions and restrictions, but it was actually recognized, and it was a great step towards secularization.'[25]

Important as the decree of 7 May was as a landmark in the evolution of liberty of worship, it did not end the religious strife in France. Towards the end of 1791 Sieyes, who had now become a private citizen again, the Constituent Assembly having dissolved, made one last unavailing effort to stem the disturbances. The draft law 'to put an end to religious troubles' that was published anonymously in the *Chronique de Paris* on the 18 November that year undoubtedly came from Sieyes' pen and represented the ultimate evolution of his ideas on the religious issue. It was short and radical. The individual oath imposed on priests was to be suppressed. The Civil Constitution of the Clergy was to be abrogated. Priests were no longer to be public functionaries, but were to become a private profession like any other. The legislature was to cease to play a role in organizing the religion of the citizens, and each individual was to 'enjoy completely the right recognized and guaranteed to him by the first section of the constitution, *to elect or choose the ministers of his confession*.'

As a private profession, the priesthood were to be subject to certain regulatory laws, in the same way as medicine, pharmacy and so on. Priests would have to register with the municipal authority of the area in which they intended to practise, and would have to furnish a 'civil caution' at the same time. This would take the form of a written statement by a third party to the effect that the applicant was not tainted by the *maladie de fanatisme*, backed up by a thousand *écu* deposit, forfeitable each time the applicant directly or indirectly disturbed the free exercise of any religion or belief. Stern punishments were envisaged by Sieyes for those acting as religious ministers without registration, and indeed for all disturbances of public order by persons of any profession, under pretext of religion.

Between 1789 and 1791, then, Sieyes' attitude towards the organization of the church and state underwent a transformation. Initially, on purely empirical grounds – the bulk of the population observed Roman Catholic rites – he favoured the external restructuring of the organization of the existing church, bringing it into accord with the other organizational changes that had occurred. There was to be a state church, Roman Catholic in content, based on the new territorial divisions, with freedom of worship for non-Catholics. The passion and intolerance with which many sought to impose this new structure and the bitter divisions it caused, led Sieyes to abandon the idea and to advocate instead the separation of church and state, and a system of equally guaranteed freedom of religious worship. In fact, if we refer back to the ideas that he expressed before the Revolution on the subject of religion, it was probably this idea of equally guaranteed freedom of worship that he always, at heart, favoured the most.[26]

Let us now turn to Sieyes' views on education. In his earliest revolutionary tract, the *Views*, written in the middle of 1788, Sieyes had particularly stressed the need for the forthcoming Estates-General to take action to create a system of public instruction; it was, he said, a 'powerful and essential means of prosperity, liberty, improvement and happiness.'[27] As has been shown, his plans for the disposal of church property were intimately linked to the creation and financing of a public system of education and of aid to the poor. He was not concerned only with freeing the individual from the unnecessary restraints laid upon him under the *ancien régime*, he also wished to reshape the welfare institutions of the *ancien régime* so that they became more effective and equitable.

It may well have been Sieyes who composed the paragraphs concerning education and poor relief in the first Title of the 1791 Constitution:

> A general establishment of Public Assistance will be created and organized, to bring up abandoned children, give relief to the disabled poor, and to provide work for able-bodied poor people who cannot obtain it.
>
> A system of Public Instruction will be created and organized, which will be common to all citizens, free as regards the education that is indispensable for everyone, and ordered in a hierarchy of establishments that will be related to the division of the kingdom. National fêtes will be established to preserve the memory of the French Revolution, sustain fraternity between the citizens, and attach them to the Constitution, the Fatherland, and the laws.

As we shall see, Sieyes was rather keen on fêtes.

In the early years of the Revolution Sieyes was heavily engaged in the central problems of constitution-making and had neither the time nor the inclination to express himself on educational matters. It was not until after the fall of the monarchy and the summoning of the National Convention in 1792 that he turned his attention to them. On 13 October 1792 he was appointed a member of the Convention's Committee of Public Instruction but resigned from it soon afterwards. Then on 28 February 1793 he rejoined the Committee, and in May became its president. Finally on 26 June 1793 his plan for the establishment of a system of national instruction was presented to the Convention by Lakanal.

Sieyes' absorption in the problem of education at this particular juncture was the reverse of his withdrawal on to the sidelines of the bitter struggle between the Girondins and the Mountain that was raging within the Convention. Initially an adviser of the Girondins, he had, it appears, lost faith in them by the early months of 1793, and decided that the only useful outlet for his energies was the relatively uncontroversial one of education.

His plan was not, of course, the first to appear during the revolutionary period. Talleyrand's report on public instruction presented in September 1791, the plan published under Mirabeau's name in the same year, Condorcet's proposals to the Legislative Assembly in April 1792 on behalf of the Committee of Public Instruction, as well as other projects, less prominent, that appeared before the Convention, were the forerunners of Sieyes' plan, and several more were to appear after it.

The core of Sieyes' proposed system was the provision of free education for all children between the ages of six and thirteen through a network of national schools to be established on the basis of one school per thousand inhabitants, amounting to a total of some 24,000 national schools.[28] The right of citizens to establish private schools and courses at all levels was in no way restricted. Overall supervision of the new public educational structure was to be in the hands of a central ministerial committee attached to, and under the direct authority of, the executive council of the Republic, while beneath this there was to be a network of *bureaux d'inspection* attached to the administrative machinery at district level.

Sieyes believed that, for the moment at any rate, higher education could be left to be taken care of by private institutions, bolstered by state subsidies. These subsidies would serve on the one hand to maintain libraries and museums and to encourage scientific research and achievement, and on the other to assist the children of poor parents to proceed to higher learning. Later, in more propitious circumstances, the state could do more in this field. Sieyes' plan (Article XLVII) envisaged the central committee making proposals in the future for the establishment of *lycées*, *instituts*, bodies for the teaching of arts and professions, and so on.

The most striking and surprising feature of Sieyes' scheme was the elaborate proposals for the establishment of public fêtes at the cantonal, district and departmental levels, and in the capital. There were to be forty such fêtes, the largest proportion of them (fifteen) to be held in the cantons. They were designed to celebrate natural phenomena, such as the changing seasons, the stages of human life and human achievements, and the great events of the French Revolution. There was even to be a 'national theatre' in each canton where people could engage in military exercises, dance, music and gymnastics, and where the standard of public fêtes could be enhanced.

Why did Sieyes place such emphasis on the establishment of public fêtes? If one looks closely at his reasoning on this matter one can see that the fêtes follow on from his idea that the units that stood at the basis of the representative system, the primary assemblies, should be more than merely bits of electoral machinery, or geographical entities. He wanted them to be genuine little communities. Thus in his early proposals for an electoral system he had envisaged that the first reception of a young man into a primary assembly as an 'active' citizen should be a *jour de fête*.[29]

The educational fêtes represent a further development of this idea. Men need to meet together, Sieyes wrote, and churches fulfilled this need in the past. It was in the countryside that the need was greatest and that was why the largest proportion of the public fêtes were to be held in the cantons. Unfortunately, Sieyes went on,

> the cantons provide only a confused and degenerate idea of the primary unions or *primariats*. The legislators of 1789 were invited [i.e. by Sieyes himself] to consider the primary assemblies as so many political families, equal components of the great national family, whose common affairs were to be directed by way of representation. This simple and fecund idea gives an image of every people that wishes and undertakes to be free.
>
> The *assimilation* of men is the first precondition of the social state, in the same way that the *adunation* of political families is the first precondition of the great national reunion, in a people that is *one*.[30]

The fêtes, then, formed part of the 'art of assimilating men in their first political environment, the primary assemblies.' They were *'un des moyens les plus propres à rapprocher les hommes, à les moraliser, à les policer'*.[31] From an unpublished note we can assume that this idea of socialization or moralization came to Sieyes primarily from Holbach, and in particular from the latter's book *Ethocratie*.[32] Like Holbach, Sieyes did not believe that correct laws and properly modelled constitutions were everything: customs and habits, everything that is summed up in the word *moeurs,* were also crucial. Above all there had to be a real *sentiment* of belonging together, of forming one people, if the representative system, based on the *idea* of this one people, was to work.

The fêtes were also necessary to give people a respite from daily toil. It took but little reflection, Sieyes wrote, to see that such holidays were to the advantage above all of those sections of the people that did the heaviest forms of work.

Sieyes appended to his proposals some general reflections on education which are worth noting briefly. He stressed in particular that the legislator was concerned with the framework within which instruction was conducted, and not with instruction itself. The legislator was like an architect building an aqueduct; he did not make the water that flowed along it. The water, the *canal de l'instruction,* was the province of *savants* and *gens instruits*.

Secondly, in a way that is surprisingly modern, Sieyes conceived of public instruction as a very broad concept indeed. It was broad in the sense that he believed it ought to embrace the whole man. Education hitherto had been predominantly literary, the new national education should be 'literary, intellectual, physical, moral and industrial' (Article XXI). But it was broad too in the sense that it ought not be conceived purely as the education undergone in youth. Instruction, he wrote, was a much more comprehensive concept than education; it did not stop when one had reached maturity. 'Men of all ages ought to receive the uninterrupted, albeit freer, assistance of national instruction, which lends itself to all common needs and interests, but above all to the great interest of the public weal.'[33] Instruction was a continuous, lifelong process.

Before it was discussed in the Convention, Sieyes' educational plan was presented to the Club of the Réunion, and then crudely attacked by Hassenfratz in the Jacobin Club. As a result the Committee of Public Instruction thought it advisable to make some alterations to the text. Ten of the forty fêtes were suppressed. The central committee was taken from its position directly under the executive council and placed under a committee of the legislative assembly. Various other small changes were made.

Commenting on these changes Sieyes remarked that he did not particularly mind the reduction in the number of fêtes but was sorry to see the *Fête des animaux compagnons de l'homme* disappear. The mere mention of this fête in the discussion of the proposals had evidently caused an outburst of disapproval. 'What is this *fête des animaux*?' people cried. To which the Rapporteur (presumably Lakanal) had replied: *'Mes amis, c'est la vôtre'*. It was the kind of quip that Sieyes relished. The objectors plainly thought the proposal smacked of materialism and idolatry, whereas Sieyes thought of it merely as involving friendly rural contests to award prizes to the best farm animals. To those who detected materialism in it, he countered ironically: 'we have too important business on our hands to-day to go back fifty years and to take up once again the blissful pursuits of the Jesuits, Capucins and others.'[34] So much for the Jacobins.

In similar vein he ridiculed those who had attacked his central committee because it was 'aristocratic'. One of his passages deserves to be cited because it expresses succinctly the core of his response to this kind of criticism:

> It is not the plurality of office holders that creates aristocracy, for if this were so then virtually all the new constitution would be aristocratic. It is not the exercise of offices which have been judged necessary and delegated, that creates aristocracy, for if this were so then there would scarcely be a public officer who would dare to do his duty. Aristocracy consists in the usurpation of power, in the exercise of an authority which does not come from the people, and is not conferred upon you within constitutional rules. Is there anything like this in the Committee's plan?[35]

The discussion on Sieyes' project opened in the Convention on 15 July 1793. The Mountain was now in control and so it was a foregone conclusion that his proposals would quickly be condemned to limbo. What is interesting is that it was Robespierre himself who took the initiative in pushing into the foreground a rival plan, by Michel Lepelletier, that was given pride of place.

The speech in which Robespierre presented Lepelletier's ideas to the Convention provides an excellent opportunity to indicate the gulf that separated the educational ideas of the Mountain and the Jacobins from those of Sieyes.[36] The latter had called for education to be broadened, so as to encompass all aspects of life, literary, intellectual, physical, moral and industrial. Robespierre, however, wanted education to encompass the whole man in a far more fundamental sense than this. He wanted what he called a system of 'public institutions' to stand at the base of all public instruction. The system would be implemented by 'houses of institution' scattered throughout town and countryside, each housing four hundred to six hundred pupils.

It would be compulsory for every child in the nation to be sent to such establishments, boys between the ages of five and twelve, and girls between the ages of five and eleven. They would be separated from their families during this period, and be brought up in common, wearing the same clothes, eating the same food, receiving the same teaching and care. Every moment of every day of their lives would be strictly regulated and supervised. 'In public institution ... the totality of the existence of the child belongs to us; the material, so to speak, never leaves the mould; no external object intrudes to deform the modification you give him.'[37]

Austerity and discipline would be the themes of this total moulding. The pupils would be toughened to privation, sleep on hard beds, eat frugally and wear coarse clothing. Moreover they would not only undergo basic formal education but would be actively engaged in farming and manufacture. The houses of instruction would be at the same time 'workshops', which would partly support themselves from their own output, and add to the annual manufacturing output of the Republic. Taxes on the rich of each area would provide the other main means of support.

The purpose of this system of public institution was, in Robespierre's words, to bring about an 'entire regeneration', 'to create a new people'.[38] By it all the components of the Republic would be thrown into a republican mould. 'There, all treated equally, fed equally, clothed equally, taught equally, equality will be for the young pupils not a specious theory but a continually effective practice. In this way a new race will be formed, strong, hard-working, regulated, disciplined, and separated by an inseparable barrier from all impure contact with the prejudices of our antiquated species.'[39]

The difference between the mentality of 1789 and the mentality of 1793–94, or between the First Revolution and the Second could scarcely be more vividly illustrated than in this contrast between the educational plans of Sieyes and those of Robespierre.

It is time to look finally at Sieyes' ideas on the freedom of the press. He expressed these most fully in January 1790 when he proposed to the Constituent Assembly that a law should be passed 'against offences committed by way of printing and by the publication of writings and engravings.'[40] His proposed law was a response to the removal of almost all restraints on the expression of opinion which had taken place in the course of 1789, and which, in the view of many, had led to a dangerously irresponsible press.

Sieyes' law was intended to be a provisional one, to be replaced by something more complete later on. Nevertheless with characteristic modesty, he announced that 'even in its state of imperfection' it 'appears to us to be the best of its kind to exist anywhere in the world.'

There is no need to make an exhaustive survey of its contents. Suffice it to say that it was divided into three parts, the first defining the offences and the penalties for them, the second defining the notion of responsibility for the offences, and the last the procedure for investigating and judging them. Offensive publications included works inciting citizens to oppose by force the execution of the laws, to use violence, and to use illegal means to redress their grievances; works containing imputations injurious to the person of the king; and works written with the patent intention of offending *bonnes moeurs*. Provision was also made for bringing accusations of crime levelled at private persons within reasonable bounds, and for preventing breach of copyright. The most important feature of the adjudicating mechanism was the use of juries to decide upon questions of fact, once an ordinary judge had decided that a *prima facie* case existed. Juries were of course one of Sieyes' favourite legal, and indeed political, devices.

Once again it is Sieyes' preliminary statement of the principles involved in the law that is of most interest to-day. As in the case of religious liberty, so in the case of press freedom, his emphasis was that public laws did not accord or grant freedom, but only regulated freedom's scope. Freedom was *a priori*:

> It is not by virtue of a law that citizens think, speak, write and publish their thoughts: it is by virtue of their natural rights. ... Printing it is true could only arise in the social state, but if the social state, by facilitating man's invention by useful instruments, extends the usage of liberty, it does not mean that this or that usage can ever be regarded as a gift of the law. The law is not a master gratuitously according benefits. In itself liberty embraces all that is not another's. The law is only there to prevent it from losing its way. It is solely a protective institution, formed by the very same liberty anterior to everything, and for which everything exists in the social order.
>
> But at the same time, if we want the law effectively to protect the liberty of the citizen, it must be able to check the attacks that can be made on it. It ought, therefore, to indicate, in the naturally free actions of each individual, the point beyond which they could become harmful to the rights of another. At that point it ought to place signals, establish limits, prohibit infringements and punish the foolhardy who dare to disobey. Such are the proper tutelary functions of the law.
>
> The liberty of the press, like all liberties, ought therefore to have legal limits.

Such were the basic principles of Sieyes' proposals. Much of the rest of his preliminary observations consisted simply of a paean to the tremendous enhancement of man's powers of communication brought about by the invention of printing, and of the benefits brought about by the free interchange of ideas. Within this enthusiastic outburst lurked an attack on those who looked back wistfully to the republics of classical antiquity:

> Printing has changed the fate of Europe; it will change the face of the world. I consider it a new faculty added to the most beautiful faculties of man; through it liberty ceases to be confined to little republican aggregations; it expands over kingdoms, over empires. Printing is for the immensity of space what the voice of the orator was for the public square of Athens and Rome; through it the thought of the man of genius carries simultaneously everywhere, it strikes so to speak the ear of the whole human race. ... Philosophers and publicists have been too quick to discourage us, proclaiming that liberty can only belong to small peoples. They could not read the future except in the past; and when a new cause of perfectibility was thrown into the world and gave hint of prodigious changes amongst men, they never looked for what could or ought to happen except in the past. Let us raise our hopes higher, and realize that the most extensive territory, that the largest population, that everything lends itself to liberty.

Sieyes' modest attempt to restrain the licence of the press provoked a furious response from the journals of both right and left. Marat's *Ami du Peuple* claimed that it contained 'bases destructive of all liberty' and was a 'pendant of martial law': absurd exaggerations typical of Marat's style. The *Révolutions de Paris* regarded the idea of placing legal limits on liberty as 'enigmatic' and concluded that 'one should not speak of putting limits on liberty; these words represent ideas which contradict one another' – another fatal misconception.[41] The Constituent Assembly did not even deign to discuss Sieyes' draft. And so the licence continued through 1790 and 1791 with every extreme opinion, however unsubstantiated or libellous, given free rein. The seeds of the wild movements that brought Robespierre and the Jacobins to power in 1793 were sown in this way. The only crumb of satisfaction for Sieyes must have been the provision (inserted by him?) in the 1791 Constitution for a jury system to decide if a given publication had contravened the boundaries of freedom that it laid down.

3 The organization of justice, the police and the army

This concluding section will look at the remaining sectors of the public establishment on which Sieyes voiced his opinion during the revolutionary epoch. Amongst his prodigious activities during the year 1789 he found time to draft a plan for a new organization of justice and police for the whole country. The plan was composed in September, but because it ran counter to the trend of opinion in the Constitutional Committee Sieyes held it back and did not make it public until March 1790.[42] By then reform of the law had come to the fore in the Constituent Assembly's agenda, and Sieyes clearly hoped to influence its deliberations. Contrary to his usual custom he did not preface his plan with a statement of principles. He restricted himself to emphasizing that his proposal was concerned with the 'organization of judicial machinery and not a general system of justice.' Constitution-making was properly concerned with the former; subsequent legislation could provide the latter, in the shape of a police code and judicial code. Always in Sieyes one find this careful distinction between the structure of the public powers and the content of their activity.

Apart from this, all that exists are the bare bones of a draft decree, consisting of 176 articles. The organization it proposes is not difficult to grasp. The bodies that were to be responsible for the twin functions of justice and police were to be based on the new electoral and administrative divisions of the country that were being created. At the bottom level each primary assembly would choose annually from amongst its members a lieutenant of police and a lieutenant of justice or justice of the peace (*juge de paix*) to be responsible for its own particular area. In the larger municipalities bureaux of police and justice would be set up, bringing together the officers of the various primary assemblies that existed within their boundaries.

Above this, in the capital town of each department, there would be a court of twelve judges, to be chosen by the electoral body of the department in such a way that there would always be one judge from each district. These judges would remain in office unless their removal was positively voted for in an annual *scrutin d'épreuve,* or unless they were guilty of misdemeanour. The departmental court would be subdivided into one criminal and two civil chambers, with provision made for the regular holding of assizes. Alongside the courts there would be a high chamber of general police in the capital town of each department, to be composed of three members of the directorate of each department and the president of the criminal chamber. There would also be chambers of police in each district.

Central to Sieyes' proposals was the provision that all judicial cases, whether civil or criminal, and whether held in an assize court or at the central court of a department, would be decided by means of a jury. Juries would be chosen from a list of eligible persons (such lists were a favourite Sieyesian device that has already been noted in other contexts) to be drawn up by the electoral body of each department from the active citizens in all the primary assemblies of the department. In particularly complex or difficult cases, Sieyes envisaged that two members of the jury would join with the judge to form a *conseil d'instruction* to analyse and to set out clearly all questions of fact and right, the remainder of the jury forming the *conseil de décision*. He recognized that while this work of analysis and decision was relatively straightforward in criminal cases, it was often extremely difficult in civil ones, nevertheless he held that the process in both was fundamentally similar: first, to establish the truth regarding the fact whether real or personal, then to determine where the fact was contrary to the law, finally to determine who was responsible and who should incur the penalty or make the reparation demanded by the law. Judge and council of instruction should therefore, he wrote, not become 'discouraged' but should recognize 'that the present decree submits all questions, without exception, questions of fact, questions of right, questions that are a mixture of fact and right, to the successive decisions of the jury, and that the essential thing is to adopt the correct path, that leads in the surest way, by a good series of questions, to the just conclusion of the matter.' It was thus the task of the judge and the council of instruction to pose the absolute minimum of relevant questions to the jury for its decision, the judge regarding himself 'as a director of justice, charged by the law with getting justice done, rather than as a judge according to the old order of things, charged with rendering justice himself.' If the name 'judge' was retained it was because it was up to him to pronounce judgement and hence to be in this sense the organ of the law.

Four types of case were recognized by Sieyes as presenting special problems and needing special treatment: disputes within one and the same family, disputes and requests for justice in commercial matters, offences by public officers in the course of their duties, and disputes over fiscal matters. The most interesting category here is probably the third, that of 'political offences'. To try these – in the first instance – Sieyes envisaged all three chambers of the departmental court coming together in a 'grand committee'.

Finally Sieyes described the crowning organization of justice at the national level. Here he envisaged a National Court consisting of 83 *grands juges de France*, one chosen by the electoral body of each department. Their security of tenure would be the same as that of the departmental judges. The National Court would be divided into four high chambers. The first of these, the *grand conseil de police*, would have general supervision over the police of the kingdom. The *grand conseil de revision* would hear appeals against judgements made at the departmental level, and be responsible for maintaining unity in the judicial procedures of the country. The *tribunal politique* would be the appeal court for all offences by public officials or bodies including those by judges and courts at the departmental level. The only exemptions would be for ministers, other executive heads, and the judges of the National Court itself, whose cases would be heard by the National Court in its entirety. Finally, the *tribunal des crimes d'Etat* would hear cases involving an attack on the constitution, the state, or the person of the king. It would always use a grand or 'national jury' consisting of one parliamentary deputy from each department. Ministers, other executive heads, and the judges of the National Court could only be brought before it following a decision to this effect by the National Assembly.

Such in broad outline was the system of justice and police that Sieyes envisaged in 1789 and 1790. Although enthusiastically endorsed by some deputies, it met with strong opposition from the lawyers in the National Assembly, and its central proposal, for the use of juries in both criminal and civil matters, was rejected. In the 1791 Constitution juries were retained only for criminal cases.

It is time finally to look at Sieyes' views on military matters. Talleyrand was fond of telling the story that Sieyes conceived the idea of the formation of a people's militia, or 'National Guards' – which became a reality in July 1789 – well before the Revolution. He did so, Talleyrand maintained, as a result of an act of brutality that he had witnessed in Paris.[43] Lord Brougham, a long time after the Revolution, was assured by both Carnot and Talleyrand that Sieyes had been the originator of the Guards.[44] There is happily one document amongst Sieyes' unpublished papers which lends credence to these assertions. It is a paper, clearly written before the Estates-General met in May 1789, which calls on the forthcoming Assembly to dismantle, as a preliminary to the drafting of the Constitution, the threefold instrument of despotism: the muzzling of the press, the blind and unlimited obedience of the military, and *lettres de cachet*.[45] Sieyes expressly mentioned in this paper the need for a 'National Guard'. It is yet one more example of his pervasive influence at the start of the Revolution.

During 1789 and the years immediately following, his unpublished notes show him ruminating on the organization of the army, though it is difficult to date his observations precisely. One clear theme that emerges – which is reflected in his tract on *The Rights of man and citizen* – is his conviction that a standing, specialized army was necessary in order to deal with foreign dangers, but that it must be kept quite distinct from the militia, attached to each district, which would be responsible for maintaining internal order. Naturally, in time of acute danger the internal militia would defend the country and prevent its invasion, but normally the two would be separate. To prevent the standing army from becoming oppressive it would be necessary to ensure that it was 'of the people' and 'had the same spirit as the people,' in a word to 'de-aristocratize' it, and Sieyes spent considerable time on the details of recruitment, pay and the maintenance of morale in the professional armed forces, stressing that competitive merit must be the sole criterion for advancement.[46]

Not until early in 1793, however, did Sieyes make a detailed public statement on military matters. It took the form of a report to the National Convention on the organization of the Ministry of War. His involvement in this matter came about as follows. When he was elected to the National Convention in

September 1792 Sieyes appears to have decided to keep out of the limelight and to limit his public work to serving on committees. In October he was appointed a member of the Constitutional Committee, *inter alia,* and when at the start of January 1793 the Convention decided, in view of the critical external conditions of the country, to establish a Committee of General Defence, Sieyes was seconded from the Constitutional Committee to serve on it. On 9 January he and two others were assigned the task of making proposals for the reorganization of the Ministry of War. Four days later Sieyes presented a report to the Committee on this subject, and on 25 January it came before the Convention as a whole.

One can only be amazed at the speed with which Sieyes plunged into this new area of activity and produced a report on it. One can sympathize too with the note which he wrote on his personal dossier on the subject: '*Je fus forcé de m'en occuper mais j'en étais incapable. Je jettais à tout hazard quelques idées d'ensemble mais sans rien prétendre et sachant bien que j'étais hors du technique de la chose.*'[47]

Despite his understandable sense of inadequacy, Sieyes' report bears all the hallmarks of clarity and system that distinguish his others, and it opens with a statement that is quintessentially Sieyesian, however much it may have also served as a bold front, covering his lack of detailed study of the subject in question:

> It is not in the national or royal Almanack, or even in the chaos of ministerial legislation, that we have been able to discover a single notion that is remotely correct or philosophically analysed of the great terrible part of the public service that bears the name of the *Department of War*. Here, as elsewhere, the legislator who wishes to carry out his duty of studying his subject directly, or of penetrating into its parts, is soon forced to renounce the vain assistance of routine. He gets straight to his objective by referring back *to the nature of things,* a kind of primary school that is fortunately impossible to close, and that has always responded to those who consult it attentively and in good faith, and one that, in my opinion, will long be the best source of legislative lessons.[48]

Following this radical method Sieyes argued that three things were needed for the servicing of war: 'certain elements, their combination, and direction.' The Ministry of War was thus responsible for the furnishing of men and material; their civil administration; and their military direction. To which Sieyes added a further activity that became necessary in time of war, namely the sphere of command of the general in the field, a sphere of command that inevitably included vast areas of discretionary activity.

The substance of the report dealt with these four areas in turn. As regards the first, the furnishing of men and material, Sieyes argued that it was essential to establish what he called an *économat national,* or a central procurement agency for all the provisions necessary for war: arms, munitions, horses, forage, wood, hemp, copper, etc. As the name suggested, the *économat* was to be not an administrative body, but an agency for purchase and supply which might also, in the course of its duty, direct the state workshops responsible for war supplies; though Sieyes remarked in passing that it would be more economic if private industry played a larger part, and the state a smaller part, in this kind of manufacture. He envisaged the *économat* as consisting of fifteen *commissaires* and a secretary general, and argued that it should be placed under the control and supervision of the Executive Council of the Republic (the supreme executive authority following the deposal of Louis XVI) and of individual ministers authorized by the Council. It was not appropriate for it to be under the direct supervision of the legislature.

Turning to the structure of the Ministry of War itself Sieyes' argument was that the fundamental line of organizational division lay between the administrative functions and the function of military direction. Other distinctions, such as that between material and personnel, were secondary to this. The single minister responsible for war should therefore have beneath him two heads, an administrator and a director. There should be no question of them all meeting together in council and taking decisions by majority vote: this was 'always a capital error at the executive level', though public opinion seemed to favour it. The minister's task of co-ordination would be aided if he had a small bureau of four to six *conseillers-inspecteurs* at his disposal and under his responsibility. This bureau would provide the *point central* where administration and direction would meet. Sieyes stressed that the popular suspicion of ministers, characteristic of both the *ancien régime* and the 'four years agony of the royalty', had no place in the new republican order. The Minister of War should have another small council at his disposal to help him keep abreast of the work of the legislature in so far as it affected his department, to help him investigate any weaknesses in his department, and to assist him in the drafting of memoranda.

Finally Sieyes turned to the tricky problem of the wartime general in the field, and the kind of power and authority that should be accorded to him. Once again he began with principles:

> I see an army as the military representation of the Republic, and the Ministry of War as a house permanently set up by the constitution, and assigned to the army to satisfy continuously all its needs, to follow it in all its movements, and to enable it to concentrate on nothing except fighting. The Tartars or Tatars, and the wandering Arabs can go to war *en corps de nation,* and completely *democratically*. For us, fixed by culture, arts, and the division of labour on the land we inhabit, it is impossible to quit the representative system even in order to fight; which is not to deny however that when we are attacked in our own homes, representation comes to be mixed with a little democracy.
>
> The army, or the Republic *ambulante et militaire,* is forced, at the risk of being unable to perform its task and to provide for its own security, to submit to a veritable temporary dictatorship. Thus because it exists for one end only and is organized as a whole, it necessarily requires at its head a kind of dictator in the shape of its general.

If, Sieyes continued, the economic or administrative services of the Ministry of War failed to function effectively, and, more especially, if the army left French soil and became engaged in action far afield, then the dictatorial powers of the general were bound to grow, and to extend into economic and administrative areas, as well as purely military ones. The problem hence was to moderate this kind of *dictature impératoriale* (how closely Napoleon is foreshadowed here!) by establishing some sort of liaison between the general and the Ministry of War. But how was this to be done?

Sieyes' solution, in brief, was that, alongside the 'ambulatory' military representation of the Republic, there should exist an 'ambulatory' representative of the Ministry of War. In other words, attached to the general in the field there should always be at least three *adjoints généraux,* one representing the administrative wing of the Ministry of War, the other its directive wing, and the third its economic side or the *économat.* The powers of the *adjoints* could vary, depending on the situation of the army in question, but they would form, with the general, a kind of miniature Ministry of War in the field. When the army moved into foreign territory, then this miniature ministry would become more formally organized into what Sieyes called a *véritable ministère du dehors,* with powers rivalling and indeed possibly surpassing those of the ministry at home.

Caught in the crossfire of the political passions of the hour, Sieyes' proposals – lucid, impersonal, and systematic – stood little chance of success. In the debate in the Convention two committed Montagnards, Saint-Just and Fabre d'Eglantine, attacked it at the outset.[49] Saint-Just wanted the War Ministry to be directly responsible to the Convention and not to the Executive Council. Fabre d'Eglantine wanted the furnishing of war supplies to be carried out by the local communes and not by the *économat national.* He thought that Sieyes' plan 'like all the institutions of the *ancien régime,* assumed that the people were wicked and the administrators virtuous.' Jean De Bry, usually regarded as a Girondin, supported his proposals, but Buzot, another Girondin, attacked them, arguing that Sieyes, instead of concentrating in an impersonal way on matters of organization, should have directed his fire against the Minister of War – Pache – himself. Lamarque, a Montagnard, again wanted the Convention rather than the Executive Council to wield the supervisory power over the War Ministry. He proposed that commissars should be sent out by the Convention internally and externally to accompany and supervise the armies (here we can see the later concept of *représentants en mission* foreshadowed). Barbaroux, a Girondin, supported Sieyes, but Salle, another Girondin, launched a wild barrage of criticisms against it. Robespierre promptly recommended that Salle's speech be printed, and the debate was over. Sieyes' plan, which was also attacked in the Jacobin Club, sank into oblivion, and Barère's was adopted in its place.

The fact that Sieyes was attacked on this occasion not only by Montagnard deputies, but by Girondins too – the group that he had advised during the early months of the Convention – probably persuaded him to withdraw even further on to the sidelines of the power struggle, and to devote himself to educational matters.

This survey of Sieyes' views on the judiciary, the police and military matters concludes our study of his political ideas as a whole. It may seem arbitrary to exclude from the study any discussion of his ideas on foreign policy, but the latter because of its very nature is more susceptible to narrative treatment than to the more analytical approach that has been adopted in this work. Suffice it to say that in this area Sieyes' ideas were distinguished by the same grandeur of vision that marked his constitutional ideas, combined with a very firm attachment to the concrete reality of the French national interest.

Conclusion: Sieyes' position in the history of political thought

Mad[e]. says that his Writings and Opinions will form in Politics a New Era as that of Newton in Phisics.

Madame de Staël, referring to Sieyes (1791), reported by Gouverneur Morris in his *Diary of the French Revolution,* ed. B.C. Davenport (1939), II, 107.

THIS STUDY HAS, it is hoped, revealed the full scope of Sieyes' political ideas and shown how they interlock to form a system. It has tried to alter the conventional image of him as the author of a single brilliant revolutionary tract which made a momentary impact on the course of the French Revolution. It has also sought to correct the view that sees his ideas as merely a bridge to the extreme doctrines of Robespierre and the Jacobins. It has argued instead that Sieyes articulated a remarkably complete and consistent liberal political philosophy, one that embraced both a theory of revolution and a theory of constitutional construction. The theory of revolution was put into practice in a strikingly exact way in June 1789, and the theory of constitutional construction exercised a strong influence on the work of the revolutionaries up until 1791, and then made a further impact in 1799 as Sieyes and his colleagues strove to bring the Revolution back on to its original course. The fact that Sieyes' liberal philosophy was never fully implemented during the revolutionary epoch does not detract from its grandeur and prescience. It remains the most coherent expression of the ideals of 1789, and the tragedy that unfolded in the years after 1789 cannot be fully appreciated unless its main principles are understood.

It remains to assess Sieyes' place in the history of political thought. Taking the long view, what was his contribution? Three particular achievements stand out. First, he transformed the modern theory of the state that had gradually been developing in the wake of the Reformation, that is to say the theory of the state as the creation of a social contract, into a practicable, realizable idea. Embedded in the modern abstract doctrine of the social contract lay the idea that the form of government of a given state had to be decided upon by the people, acting by majority, if the form of government was to be legitimate. This idea is latent in Hobbes' doctrine of the instituted commonwealth in *Leviathan,* in Locke's doctrine of the original compact in the *Second Treatise of Government,* and in Rousseau's account of the institution of government in his *Contrat social* – even if Rousseau confused the government-founding power of the people with the ordinary legislative power. Sieyes made this idea into a tangible objective of policy through his concept of the nation as the constituent power of the public establishment. He urged the Third Estate of France in 1789 to recognize themselves as such a nation and he showed them what this meant in practicable terms, namely the establishment in place of the Estates-General of an extraordinary national constituent assembly.

To be sure, the idea of the nation as constituent power had broken through into reality in the American Revolution. But in America the idea had 'developed unclearly, gradually and sporadically'[1] in the period from the Declaration of Independence of 1776 to the making of the Pennsylvania Constitution of 1790. It had developed so to speak under the shadow of an act of rebellion by thirteen colonies against a far-distant imperial power. In France by contrast the conflict lay from the start within one and the same territorial state. There Sieyes articulated the doctrine of the nation as the constituent power in a clear unequivocal manner at the very outset of the crisis, and the implementation of the doctrine in a sense *was* the Revolution.

Sieyes thus brought the idea of the social contract down to earth. He helped to realize the classic modern theory of the state. This leads on to his second major contribution, which was to link the idea of the nation as constituent power with a concrete economic and social movement, namely the development of the Third Estate in France. Throughout this study it has been emphasized that Sieyes was not only a theorist of political form and structures, he was also profoundly interested in what to-day would be called 'economics', in fact he was a participant in the movement of ideas which, in the second half of the eighteenth century, laid the foundations of the modern science of economics. Even before the publication of Adam Smith's work, *The Wealth of Nations,* the young Sieyes had come to the conclusion – against the Physiocrats – that labour was the true source of wealth.

Sieyes expressly linked the revolutionary idea of the nation as constituent power with the growing economic and social significance of the Third Estate. The fact that the latter had become a vast self-subsistent combination of labour, capable of performing all the useful work, public and private, that was required in a rationally ordered body politic, was the solid basis that guaranteed the realization of the new political order.

Sieyes' identification of revolutionary principles with an economic and social development marks him off sharply from the writers of the French Enlightenment who had preceded him. He was not, like them, content to propose or to outline political reforms in the hope that someone, somewhere, might transform these reforms into reality. He had indeed little interest in presenting theories of right order in and for themselves. He was always equally interested in the possibility of implementation. Because he saw in the social forces of the day the underpinning for a mutation in the political order he was a truly revolutionary theorist, and not, like so many of his predecessors, simply a theorist from whom revolutionary consequences might be drawn.

In this context it is worth mentioning a further factor that differentiated Sieyes from his Enlightenment predecessors and which has been stressed in this study. His cast of mind was different from that which gave the French Enlightenment its typical character. He reacted against the naturalism and materialism that permeated the epistemological, moral, economic and political writings that he read so avidly as a young student. Sieyes was, in the philosophical sense of the word, an idealist, that is to say he emphasized the active spirit within man which distinguishes itself from what is natural and shapes and masters it. His idealist philosophy influenced his doctrine of revolutionary practice in the same way that French revolutionary practice in turn influenced the development of philosophical idealism in other thinkers.

Sieyes' third great achievement was to demonstrate the full political significance of the idea of representation. Here he went well beyond Hobbes, Locke and Rousseau, and also well beyond Burke – who is often regarded in the English-speaking world as having said the final word on representation in his speech to the electors of Bristol in 1774.

Sieyes' advocacy of representation deserves to be recognized once more as a major turning-point in the history of political thought. Too often, contemporary political theory treats representation as a relatively minor offshoot of the issue of democracy. Democracy is assumed to be the touchstone of all that is desirable in a political system and immense energy is devoted either to demonstrating that present political systems are in fact a species of democracy, or that they are not a species of democracy but should and could become so.

Sieyes did not see representation as a minor offshoot of the issue of democracy. He saw representation as a principle as rational as that of democracy, indeed more so. It was for him virtually identical with the notion of a rightly constituted political order. Representation, or more precisely the representative system, necessarily included an element of democracy, but equally it included an element of aristocracy and monarchy; in fact it was the transcendence of this ancient crude tripartite mode of classifying governments. For Sieyes the only defensible alternative to the representative system was pure democracy, but pure democracy suffered from immense drawbacks, and in any case contained within itself an ineradicable element of representation. For Sieyes the aim of the French Revolution was not to create a fully-fledged democracy but to create a fully-fledged representative system.

The crux of Sieyes' doctrine of representation was that no one had an inherent right to rule other people. Given that rule was necessary in order to enable human beings to secure and expand their freedom, and given that pure democracy or the identity of rulers and ruled was an incredibly crude and ineffective method of rule, Sieyes argued that legitimate rule must be indirect rule. The people must first create a system of public offices to represent their common or general will, and then must choose persons to fill such offices. Only those who ruled by virtue of being elected to nationally constituted public office could claim legitimacy.

The prime enemy of representative rule was, in Sieyes' eyes, caste rule, a system in which a particular group laid claim to an inherent and exclusive right to rule others. In pure democracy people ruled themselves directly. In caste rule or 'false democracy' some people ruled other people directly. In both instances the right to direct rule was asserted as against the indirect, roundabout form of rule typical of the representative system. It is only necessary to recall the large number of states in the modern world in which small groups or parties lay claim to an inherent and exclusive right to rule others – usually by virtue of their quality as the 'vanguard' of the masses – to realize that the caste enemy which Sieyes denounced at the end of the eighteenth century is still with us to-day. Against this false form of democracy his advocacy of a national revolution to establish a representative system of government retains all its original force.

The antithesis that lay at the root of Sieyes' revolutionary doctrine was not that of one class versus another but of the nation, which was by definition a combination of classes, versus the caste, which was a class claiming an inherent and exclusive right to rule. He was not seeking merely to change the ruling personnel but to change the quality of rule itself. This did not mean that he ignored class differences. It has been shown that he believed that the presence within the nascent nation of France in 1789 of what he called 'disposable' classes – by which he meant people of some property and education, who were freed from the immediate necessity of earning a living by economic work and hence were available to carry out the political or public work that the representative system required – strengthened the position of the nation in its revolutionary endeavours. Sieyes clearly believed that men of property and education both should and would be chosen by the electorate to occupy representative offices under the new system. He did not think that they should be chosen because they would voice the interest of money or capital, but because leisure and education would enable them to get a clearer view of the overall, public interest of the nation, than people who were wholly immersed in a particular, private kind of work.

Sieyes did not believe that people necessarily and inevitably sought to further their own particular interests to the exclusion of everything else. His whole campaign for revolutionary change in 1789 was based on the premiss that people could look beyond their own particular self-interest and raise themselves to the level of principle by the use of reason, and on this issue he was surely right. Even Marx acknowledged that in 1789 the leaders of the French Revolution expressed the interests of the whole people and not only their own interests – and he contrasted their broad vision with the narrow outlook of the Prussian bourgeoisie in 1848, who, he said, had sunk to little more than an 'estate'.[2]

But if Sieyes believed that people could look beyond their particular interests, he did not naively believe that they could always be relied upon to do so. It was in his view the task of a well-made constitution to ensure that the propertied and educated class did not become and did not think of themselves as a caste with an inherent and exclusive right to rule others, and that the members of this class who were chosen to occupy public office did not regard it merely as an opportunity to further the sectional interests of their own class. The idea of one national community, of the equality of civil rights, and of the duty of public representatives to serve the people as a whole, had to be firmly entrenched by constitutional law, and this law itself had to be protected (as Sieyes came to see in 1795) by a special constitutional court. Sieyes also recognized the importance of fostering a sentiment of 'belonging together' amongst the people; his plans for a system of free national education included a whole range of national and local fêtes aimed precisely at this. It is an aspect of his thought which is usually ignored.

On the crucial matter of the suffrage Sieyes' views have been described in detail in this study. Certainly he accepted that the voting right would have to be – and indeed would always have to be, in whatever state – restricted. Certainly the restrictions he envisaged were far tighter than in most modern states. But he never believed that the kind of restrictions that he accepted as necessary at the end of the eighteenth century ought to be made permanent. He thought it self-evident that the circle of voters would have to be progressively widened, as absurd prejudices – such as that against female suffrage – fell away, and as a national system of education began to take effect.

Sieyes' conception of individual liberty – the final end of the properly constituted state – was linked to his conception of representative government. Interestingly he did not accept the view so strongly advocated to-day, that true liberty was negative liberty, or liberty as independence. Liberty for him was independence *and* the positive power to do or to achieve things. It was as an expression or extension of positive liberty that he justified the representative system. Moreover Sieyes expressly rejected the doctrine of *laisser faire* that originated with Gournay and the Physiocrats and became the shibboleth of a certain type of liberal in the nineteenth and twentieth centuries. For Sieyes positive action by public authorities was not to be shunned *a priori*; it could well help to achieve the overall end of the state. In a word, Sieyes' liberalism was not based on a narrow reverence for the automatic mechanism of the market but on a deeper reverence for man's nature as a free being and his capacity to develop and expand his freedom. It was a nobler, grander vision of liberalism than that which has regrettably so often been expressed in Europe since his day.

This account of Sieyes' achievements should not be taken to imply that his ideas were always logical, coherent and wise. Like everyone he was fallible. Perhaps the greatest defect in his thinking, which we can see with the privileged clarity of hindsight, was his underestimation of the dangers involved in his demand for a complete break with existing structures, or the dangers of revolution-making. A revolution is a kind of war. To make a revolution, as Sieyes' own writings demonstrate, is actively to divide a society into friends and enemies, the good and rational on one side, the evil and irrational on the other. It is paradoxically an acknowledgement of the strength of the irrational and evil in history by the upholders of the rational and good – this paradox can also be seen in Sieyes' writings. Unfortunately war, once declared, develops its own momentum and can easily break free from the rational guidelines and goals within which its originators sought to channel it. The hostile feelings generated by the struggle intensify, the goals of the struggle degenerate into dogmatic slogans. This progression is not inevitable, but it is always a possibility, and it can be seen taking place in the French Revolution. Sieyes seems not to have grasped its possibility and in the event he paid a heavy penalty for his lack of foresight.

There were other deficiencies in his reasoning. He had a tendency towards over-subtlety or over-cleverness. The elaborate and unrealistic structures he proposed in 1799 are the best illustration of this. He had a tendency to become obsessed with a concept and to drive it to an extreme. The most obvious example is his fascination with the idea of the jury, which he began to see as a formula applicable at all levels of government. Good ideas were unnecessarily obscured as a result. He also failed to foresee the development of the political party as a means of organizing elections.

Now we may turn from Sieyes' achievements and failures to the influence of his ideas on later generations. A detailed examination of the impact of his writings would clearly require a further study, so the discussion must necessarily concentrate on the broad overall pattern. Three main areas of influence can be distinguished. First, there is the influence that Sieyes exercised through his positive, creative works in the early years of the French Revolution, and in particular through the 1791 Constitution which he, more than any other individual, helped to shape. This constitution only lasted a short time, but as the first European embodiment of the idea of a nationally constituted representative government it marked a very real turning-point in European political history. For example, it provided the working basis for the French Constitutional Charter of 1814, as well as for both versions of the Dutch Basic Law of 1814 and 1815. It was the prototype for the Spanish Constitution of 1812 and for the Norwegian Constitution of 1814. According to Gillisen, 10 per cent of the Belgian Constitution of 1831 was derived directly from it (and a further 40 per cent from the Dutch Basic Law of 1815) and the Belgian Constitution in turn exercised an influence on subsequent constitutions in Spain, Greece, Rumania and Luxemburg, Italy, Prussia and the Netherlands.[3]

To-day one need only look at the West German Basic Law of 1949 to find provisions that could almost have come from Sieyes' pen. Article 20, paragraph 2 reads: 'All state power emanates from the people. It is exercised by the people through votes and referenda, and through special organs of legislation, the executive power and the administration of justice.' The Spanish Constitution of 1978 reads (Article 1, paragraphs 2 and 3): 'National sovereignty is vested in the Spanish people, from whom emanate the powers of the State. The political form of the Spanish State is that of a Parliamentary Monarchy.' Once again the words are reminiscent of Sieyes even if, as we have seen, he was chary of using the word 'sovereignty' in place of the term 'constituent power'. It is interesting too that in France the establishment of a Constitutional Council in 1958 marked a belated step towards the realization of the 'constitutional jury' that Sieyes had proposed in 1795. In sum, Sieyes' vision of the nationally constituted representative system has entered into the lifeblood of European constitutionalism.

The second way in which Sieyes exercised an influence lay in the transmission of his liberal philosophy to other political thinkers of standing. Here the most prominent example is that of Benjamin Constant. He more than anyone else deserves to be called Sieyes' spiritual heir – despite the fact that he died before the long-lived Abbé. Constant (like Madame de Staël) knew Sieyes and held his political ideas in high esteem. His own political writings often have a strong echo of Sieyes in them, without being imitative. His celebrated essay *De la liberté des anciens comparée à celle des modernes,* which was first delivered as a speech in 1819, deserves to be compared with Sieyes' essay on liberty, as well as with some of Sieyes' other reflections on the reasons why, in the modern world, the representative system has become a necessity. The arguments of the two men were by no means identical, but there is nonetheless a marked similarity in their outlook. Constant was, as it were, a more scholarly Sieyes, keeping the standard of the representative system aloft through the Napoleonic era and the Restoration.

It is tempting to see some link between Sieyes' political ideas and those of Kant, particularly as the two men nearly came into direct communication, and shared an idealist philosophical outlook.[4] Certainly there are some striking similarities in the general results of their political theories. Kant, for example, wrote in *Die Metaphysik der Sitten* that: 'any true republic ... is and cannot be anything other than a *representative system* of the people. ...'[5] But the more one looks at Kant's meagrely developed doctrine of representation, and indeed at his political theory as a whole, the more one is led to see them as forming an autonomous growth, distinct in temper and emphasis from Sieyes' reasoning.

Of the great English liberal writers only Lord Acton seems to have been fully familiar with Sieyes' works and to have held him in high regard. He wrote: 'In the little band of true theorists, composed of Harrington and Locke, Rousseau and Jefferson, Hamilton and Mill, the rank of Sieyes is very far from being the lowest.'[6] On another occasion he said that had he had the time he 'would have tried to explain the connection between the doctrine of Adam Smith, that labour is the original source of all wealth, and the conclusion that the producers of wealth virtually compose the nation, by which Sieyes subverted historic France.'[7] Hopefully the present study has implemented Acton's unfulfilled aim.

The third and last way in which Sieyes influenced posterity was through his doctrine of revolution. In particular his doctrine helped to shape Marx's theory of revolution. To understand this it has to be recalled that the young Marx busied himself intensively with the history of the French Revolution during the early 1840s. That he became familiar with Sieyes' tract *What is the Third Estate?* at this time can be taken for granted. The first reference to it in his writings appears in October 1842.[8] The second comes in 1845 when he observed that 'Proudhon's work *Qu'est-ce que la propriété?* has the same importance for modern national economy as Sieyes' work *Qu'est-ce que le Tiers état?* for modern politics'.[9] Marx referred to Sieyes' work again in later writings, albeit fleetingly.

The influence of Sieyes on Marx's revolutionary theory is encapsulated most strikingly in the sentence in the *Communist Manifesto* which reads: 'Since the proletariat must first of all acquire political supremacy, must rise to be the national class, must constitute itself as the nation, it is itself still national, though not in the sense of the bourgeoisie.'[10] The parallel with Sieyes' appeal to the Third Estate is patent.

The link between the two men's ideas is, however, more fully revealed in Marx's essay entitled *Zur Kritik des Hegelschen Rechtsphilosophie,* written late in 1843, which is also the essay in which the two main components of his revolutionary theory, namely the proletariat on the one hand and the idea of human emancipation on the other, came together for the first time. In this essay, Marx argued that the time had come for the radical critique of religion and philosophy which had been developed in Germany to resolve itself into practice. But was, he asked, Germany capable of practice *à la hauteur des principes*? Could it, in other words, make a revolution? To make a revolution it was not only necessary to have a radical theory, there had also to be a 'material base', or concrete social needs. 'It does not suffice for thought to press towards realization, reality must itself pass towards thought.'[11] For a *political* revolution to occur, he went on, it was necessary for there to be a class which identified itself with and was widely felt and recognized to be the 'general representative' of society against another class that embodied all that was wrong with society. Marx referred here expressly to the French Revolution, and it is clear that this was the inspiration of his theory – though his use of the words 'class' and 'estate' interchangeably when referring to it represents a very serious confusion.

The crux of Marx's argument was that in Germany a situation similar to that of 1789 was not present. On the one hand there was no class ruthless enough to be the 'negative representative' of society. On the other there was no estate that possessed 'that breadth of soul which identifies itself, if only momentarily, with the soul of the people – that genius for inspiring material force towards political power, that revolutionary boldness which flings at its adversary the defiant words: '*I am nothing, and I must be everything!*'[12] Here Sieyes' doctrine, which one senses had been in the back of Marx's mind throughout, becomes finally apparent.

Classes in Germany, Marx continued, were narrow, egotistic, and jealous of one another. Hence no *political* revolution could be expected, but only one more radical which would bring about a 'universal emancipation', or a complete dissolution of existing society, and which would not be the result of any generous impulses, but of the harsh, direct pressure of oppressive necessity. There *was* a material base for such a total revolution, Marx concluded. It lay in the proletariat. German radical theory which aimed at a general, 'human emancipation' thus had its necessary material counterpart in a social class. The German revolution was not going to be a political revolution led by a class or estate that genuinely represented society as a whole, it was going to be a revolution to emancipate humanity led by a class condemned to increasing misery and oppression.

The connection and the contrast between Sieyes' ideas and those of Marx is evident in this argument. Both men believed that a revolution was a yoking together of an interest with an idea. In Sieyes' case the 'interest' was that of an estate, a combination of classes that had grown in numbers and wealth and now did all the economic and most of the public work in society. It had become 'everything' in economic and social terms and for this reason wanted a greater share in political power. The 'idea' was that of the nation as the constituent power of the body politic. For Marx by contrast the 'interest' was that of the proletariat, which was a single class condemned to become nothing, indeed to be the suffering embodiment of all the woes of humanity. Because it was condemned to total degradation the proletariat would, Marx believed, seek to become 'everything', to redeem humanity from all its woes. The 'idea' to which it would be driven would be that of the reintegration of mankind into one unmediated unity. To use Sieyes' own words, Marx wanted 're-total', while he wanted 're-public'.

When Sieyes' achievements and influences in the realm of political thought are considered as a whole it can be seen that he stands as a landmark, a point of reference that cannot be ignored. He takes one line of development to a triumphant conclusion and simultaneously opens a new era. To Benjamin Constant he was 'one of the most profound writers, one of the strongest minds, and one of the most energetic powers that have acted upon our century'.[13] To-day his ideas are still alive. Sieyes was a master spirit of the age of the French Revolution.

Notes

NOTE Place of publication is London unless otherwise indicated. For full details of Sieyes' works referred to in abbreviated form in the notes, see pp. 9–15 above.

Introduction: the life, works and significance of the Abbé Sieyes

1. Anonymous, *The Revolutionary Plutarch* (1806) I, 102n.
2. Camille Desmoulins, *Correspondance inédite* (Paris, 1836).
3. A. Mathiez, 'Sieys ou Sieyes', *Annales révolutionnaires*, I (1908), 346; A. Mathiez, 'L'Orthographe du nom Sieys', *Annales historiques de la Révolution française*, II (1925), 487, 583; H. Calvet, 'Sieys ou Sieyes', *Annales historiques de la Révolution française*, X (1933), 538.
4. See, for example, his signatures to the original and amended motion of 15 June 1789 in 284 AP 4.1, and the attribution of his own name to the text *Opinion d'un deputé sur le clergé*, 284 AP 18.2. For archival references, see the end of the ntroduction.
5. Sainte-Beuve, Notes de lecture, in R. Fayolle, *Sainte-Beuve et la XVIIIe siècle ou comment les révolutions arrivent* (Paris, 1972), 394.
6. *Notice*, 166. Details of Sieyes' works will be found at the end of the Introduction.
7. J.H. Clapham, *The Abbé Sieyes* (1912).
8. P. Bastid, *Sieyes et sa pensée* (Paris, 2nd edn, 1970). In the second edition Bastid incorporated the results of his study of Sieyes' rediscovered papers.
9. Sainte-Beuve, *Causeries du lundi* (Paris, n.d.), VIII, 346.
10. Lord Acton, *Lectures on the French Revolution*, ed. J.N. Figgis and R.V. Laurence (1910), 159.
11. A.M. Headlam-Morley, *The New Democratic Constitutions of Europe* (1929), 31.
12. J.L. Talmon, *The Origins of Totalitarian Democracy* (1961), 70.
13. Emmanuel Sieyes, *Qu'est-ce que le Tiers état?*, ed. R. Zapperi (Geneva, 1970).
14. 284 AP 5.1.
15. Particularly his essays in the *Deutsch–Französischen Jahrbüchern* (1843–44), 'Zur Judenfrage' and 'Zur Kritik der Hegelschen Rechtsphilosophie: Einleitung'.

1 Sieyes' mode of thought: a general perspective

1. *Views*, 2, 29; *What is the Third Estate?*, 173, 175.
2. *What is the Third Estate?*, 151.
3. *Ibid.*, 175.
4. *Views*, 46.
5. *Essay on Privileges*, 1.
6. See the account of the evolution of his ideas in M. Göhring, *Rabaut Saint-Etienne. Ein Kämpfer an der Wende zweier Epochen* (Berlin, 1935).

7. *Views*, 1.
8. *Ibid.*, 31n.
9. *What is the Third Estate?*, 132, 149–50. His discussion of Calonne's experiment with provincial assemblies (153–5) may also be termed 'historical'.
10. *Ibid.*, 199.
11. *Views*, 148–9.
12. 284 AP 17.2. In an undated letter to Clément de Ris Sieyes wrote of Servan, the author of *Reflexions sur les états provinciaux*, that he was 'la seule tête, où j'ai trouvé un peu de *combinaison*, ce qui ne dit pas qu'il soit beaucoup plus avancé que les autres.' The letter appears to have been written shortly after the publication of Sieyes' *Essay*. Sieyes also had some respect for Cérutti, whom he cites in *What is the Third Estate?*, 155.
13. *What is the Third Estate?*, 145.
14. *Ibid.*, 151.
15. *Ibid.*
16. *Ibid.*, 201.
17. *Ibid.*, 212.
18. *Views*, title-page and 1.
19. *Ibid.*, 8.
20. 285 AP 5.1.
21. Mallet du Pan, cited by Sainte-Beuve, *Causeries du lundi*, V, 205.
22. A. Rivarol, *Oeuvres choisies*, ed. M. De Lescure (Paris, 1880), II, 269–70n.
23. M.J. de Chénier, *Tableau historique de l'état et des progrès de le littérature française depuis 1789* (Paris, 1816), 56.
24. W. von Humboldt, *Gesammelte Schriften* (Berlin, 1903–18), XIV, 422.
25. *What is the Third Estate?*, 157.
26. *Views*, 1–2.
27. *What is the Third Estate?*, 175–6.
28. *Views*, 29–31.
29. *Ibid.*, 32–3.
30. *Ibid.*, 40.
31. *Ibid.*
32. 284 AP 2.3.
33. *Notice*, 165.
34. *What is the Third Estate?*, 178.
35. *Opinion on the constitutional jury* (1795).
36. *Views*, 38.
37. *Ibid.*, 36.
38. *Essay on Privileges*, 6n.
39. *Liberty*, 45.
40. 284 AP 2.3. The word 'one' has been emphasized in making the translation in order to convey Sieyes' meaning clearly.
41. Turgot, *Eloge de Gournay*, in *Oeuvres*, ed. E. Daire (Paris, 1844), I, 287.
42. The *Journal de la Société de 1789* has recently (1982) been reprinted by EDHIS, Paris.
43. On Condorcet's concept of 'social mathematics' see especially K.M. Baker, *Condorcet: From Natural Philosophy to Social Mathematics* (Chicago, 1975).
44. *Prospectus*, 1–2.
45. *Rights of man and citizen*, 4–15. The 'notables' were the second Assembly of Notables, convened in November 1788; the *Parlement* of Paris decided in September 1788 in favour of retaining the old form of the Estates-General.
46. *What is the Third Estate?*, 216–17.
47. P.L. Roederer, *Oeuvres* (Paris, 1853–9) IV, 204.
48. *What is the Third Estate?*, 213, 216.

49. 284 AP 1.2.
50. *Ibid.*, 2.3.
51. *Prospectus*, 3.
52. *Ibid.*
53. *Liberty*, 38–9.
54. 284 AP 2.3.
55. *Ibid.*, 5.1.
56. *Opinion on the draft constitution* (1795).
57. 284 AP 2.3.
58. *Ibid.*
59. *Ibid.*
60. *Essay on Privileges*, 24.
61. *Notice*, 168.
62. *Moniteur*, 14 March 1791.
63. 284 AP 2.2. Sixth section: 'Sur Dieu Ultramètre et sur la fibre religieuse de l'homme, 1780.'

2 The influences on Sieyes' thought

1. A. Néton, *Sieyes (1748–1836), d'après des documents inédits* (Paris, 1900), 118.
2. G. Pariset, 'Sieyes et Spinoza', *Revue de synthèse historique, 12* (1906), 309ff.
3. J.H. Clapham, *The Abbé Sieyes* (1912), 24, 31.
4. S.B. Liljegren (ed.), *Theodore Lesueur, A French draft constitution of 1792 modelled on James Harrington's Oceana* (Lund, 1932); D. Trevor, 'Some sources of the constitutional theory of the Abbé Sieyes: Harrington and Spinoza', *Politica* (London School of Economic and Political Science), 2 (1935), 325–469.
5. P. Bastid, *Sieyes et sa pensée* (Paris, 2nd edn, 1970), Part 2, chap. 1, *passim.*
6. R. Zapperi, Introduction to Sieyes' *Qu'est-ce que le Tiers état?* (Geneva, 1970), see especially 19, 50, 52, 56, 57.
7. J. Roels, *Le concept de représentation politique au dixhuitième siècle* (Louvain, 1969), 155.
8. E. Schmitt, *Repräsentation und Revolution. Eine Untersuchung zur Genesis der kontinentalen Theorie und Praxis parlamentarischer Repräsentation aus der Herrschaftspraxis des Ancien Regime in Frankreich (1760–89)* (Munich, 1969), 114–29.
9. 284 AP 18.1. (= *Le Courrier belge*, 30 July 1836); his remark that 'On ne sait véritablement que ce qu'on sait avec sa raison' is in his *Rights of man and citizen*, 3.
10. E. Dumont, *Souvenirs sur Mirabeau* (Paris, 1832), 64. The reference to ordering books from Paris is in 284 AP 17.2.
11. 284 AP 1.3.
12. *Notice*, 164.
13. Dumont, *Souvenirs*, 64–5.
14. K.E. Oelsner, *Bruchstücke aus den Papieren eines Augenzeugen und unparteiischen Beobachters der Französischen Revolution* (n.p., Leipzig, 1794), 187.
15. 284 AP 5.3 (first section).
16. *Ibid.*, 2.2.
17. W. von Humboldt, *Gesammelte Schriften* (Berlin, 1903–18), XIV, 485, 492, and more especially Humboldt's letter to Schiller of 23 June 1798 in *Neue Briefe Wilhelm von Humboldts an Schiller*, ed. F.C. Ebrard (Berlin, 1911), 221–3.
18. Sainte-Beuve, *Portraits littéraires* (Paris, n.d.), I, 178.
19. Condillac, *Traité des sensations*, Introd.

20. Condillac, *Extrait raisonné du Traité des sensations, Précis de la quatrième partie.*
21. Condillac, *Traité des sensations*, first Part, chapter 6.
22. 284 AP 2.1.
23. *Ibid.*, 2.3.
24. *Ibid.*, 5.3.
25. *Ibid.*
26. *Ibid.*
27. *Ibid.*
28. *Opinion on the constitutional jury* (1795).
29. Condillac, *Traité des systèmes.*
30. Condillac, *La Logique*, Part II.
31. 284 AP 5.3.
32. See Condillac's *Cours d'études pour l'instruction du Prince de Parme*, Book III.
33. Condillac, *Traité des sensations*, fourth Part.
34. *Notice*, 165–6.
35. 284 AP 2.10.
36. *Ibid.*, 2.15 (first *cahier*).
37. *Ibid.*, 2.3 (first section).
38. *Ibid.*, 2.7 (other schemes can be found in this dossier).
39. Baudeau, *Première introduction à la philosophie économique*, chapter 1, parts VI and VII. This work was republished in *Physiocrates*, ed. E. Daire (Paris, 1846), II, 656ff.
40. 284 AP 3.2.
41. Sieyes' views on property will be discussed more fully in chapters 6 and 10.
42. This was the definition he gave in *What is the Third Estate?*, 143–4.
43. See section XV of Turgot's work where he defines the 'disposable class' as that of the proprietors, 'the only one which, not being bound by the need for subsistence to one particular kind of work, may be employed to meet the general needs of the society, for example in war and the administration of justice, whether through personal service, or through the payment of a part of its revenue with which the state or the society may hire men to discharge these functions.'
44. 284 AP 3.1 (third section).
45. *Ibid.*, 2.15. Sieyes accused Condillac of going about his work as an 'homme de lettres' rather than an 'homme de génie'.
46. See, for example, the passage cited below, p. 141.
47. 284 AP 2.13. 'Travail'.
48. *Ibid.*, 5.3 (second section).
49. *Essay on Privileges*, 24.
50. 284 AP 4.1.
51. Sainte-Beuve, *Portraits littéraires*, II, 184.
52. See F.J.L. Meyer's account of his encounter with Sieyes in *Fragmente aus Paris im IV^{ten} Jahr der Französischen republik* (Hamburg, 1797) where he notices 'Voltaire's schlecht gearbeitetes Profil von Wachs' hanging behind Sieyes' armchair.
53. 284 AP 2.3 (first section).
54. *What is the Third Estate?*, 196n.
55. *De l'Esprit des lois*, XI, chapter 6. Sieyes objected to the principle that the people should only do through representatives what it could not do itself. See below, p. 141.
56. 284 AP 2.3 (third section).
57. *Bases of the social order*, *ibid.*, 5.1.
58. *Ibid.*, 2.3.
59. *Ibid.*, 4.7, and again *ibid.*, 5.2. 'Ayons un prince pour nous sauver du péril d'avoir un maître.'

60. Dumont, *Souvenirs*, 64–5. One of the most curious echoes of Rousseau comes in Sieyes' *Deliberations* where he twice uses the word 'nonces' for the deputies to be elected to the Estates-General, the same word that Rousseau uses in his representative scheme for Poland.
61. 284 AP 5.1.
62. *Notice*, 266–7.
63. 284 AP 5.1.
64. This account is based on the *Discours sur l'inégalité*.
65. See especially his *Profession de foi du vicaire savoyard*.
66. *Contrat social*, I, chapter 3.
67. 284 AP 5.1.
68. *Ibid.*
69. Lakanal, *Eloge de Rousseau*, cited by R. Barny, 'Rousseau dans la Révolution', *Dix-huitième siècle*, VI (1974), 97.
70. Barny, *op. cit.*
71. *Opinion on the draft constitution* (1795).
72. Schmitt, *Repräsentation und Revolution*, 114–29. For the evidence of Holbach's authorship see *The Encyclopédie of Diderot and D'Alembert*, ed. J. Lough (Cambridge, 1954), XIV–XV.
73. 284 AP 2.3.
74. Chastellux, *De la Félicité publique* (Paris, 1822), 101–2.
75. 284 AP 2.3.
76. *Ibid.*, 5.1 (first section).
77. Liljegren, *Lesueur*.
78. Clapham, *Sieyes*, 31–2.

3 The revolutionary principle: the nation repossesses itself

1. *Views*, 4.
2. *Ibid.*, 147.
3. See, for example, *What is the Third Estate?*, 157, 195; *Deliberations*, 25, 28, 30.
4. *What is the Third Estate?*, 132, 157.
5. *Essay on Privileges*, 4.
6. *What is the Third Estate?*, 128. From Lord Acton onwards the significance of this brief passage has been grossly exaggerated, and Sieyes has been regarded as holding some kind of 'racial' theory of history. See Lord Acton, *Lectures on the French Revolution*, ed. J.N. Figgis and R.V. Laurence (London, 1910), 160.
7. *What is the Third Estate?*, 140.
8. *Ibid.*, 198.
9. *Ibid.*, 154, 169, 170, 199; *Deliberations*, 44.
10. *What is the Third Estate?*, 208.
11. *Ibid.*, 178.
12. *Views*, 14–15.
13. *Ibid.*, 25–6.
14. *Ibid.*, 16.
15. *Ibid.*, 15, 16.
16. *Ibid.*, 16–17.
17. *What is the Third Estate?*, 178.
18. *Ibid.*
19. *Views*, 17–18.
20. *What is the Third Estate?*, 188.
21. *Ibid.*, 201.

22. *Rights of man and citizen*, 38–9.
23. *Views*, 20–1.
24. *Ibid.*, 21.
25. *Ibid.*, 22n.
26. *Ibid.*, 23–4.
27. *What is the Third Estate?*, 178–9.
28. *Ibid.*, 157n.
29. *Ibid.*, 181n.
30. *Ibid.*, 180–1.
31. *Ibid.*, 181–2.
32. *Ibid.*, 182.
33. *Ibid.*, 182–3.
34. *Ibid.*, 184.
35. *Ibid.*
36. *Ibid.*
37. *Ibid.*, chapter 1, title.
38. *Ibid.*, 121.
39. *Ibid.*, 122.
40. *Views*, 81.
41. *Notice*, 170.
42. *Deliberations*, 24.
43. K. Marx, *Die Frühschriften*, ed. S. Landshut (Stuttgart, 1968), 361.
44. *Ibid.*, 223.
45. *Ibid.*, 218.
46. *What is the Third Estate?*, 135 ('les trois articles qui forment la réclamation du Tiers sont insuffisans.'); 137 ('l'insuffisance des trois demandes du Tiers'); 144 ('la timide insuffisance de cette réclamation'); 149 ('la trop modeste demande du Tiers').
47. *Ibid.*, 119.
48. *Ibid.*, 130.
49. *Ibid.*, 149–50.
50. *Ibid.*, 196.
51. *Essay on Privileges*, 17n.
52. *What is the Third Estate?*, 195.
53. *Ibid.*, 122.
54. *Ibid.*, 143.
55. *Ibid.*, 156.
56. *Ibid.*, 134–5.
57. *Ibid.*, 198.
58. *Ibid.*, 147.
59. *Ibid.*, 201.
60. *Essay on Privileges*, 1–2.
61. *Ibid.*, 2.
62. *Ibid.*, 3.
63. *What is the Third Estate?*, 128.
64. *Ibid.*, 161. See also 137: 'pour appartenir véritablement au Tiers.'; 217: 'la véritable nation.'
65. *Ibid.*, 129.
66. *Ibid.*, 135–6.
67. *Ibid.*, 130.
68. *Ibid.*, 137.

4 The enemy: the nobility as the embodiment of caste-rule

1. K. Marx, *Die Frühschriften*, ed. S. Landshut (Stuttgart, 1968), 220.
2. *What is the Third Estate?*, 143n.

3. See *What is the Third Estate?* and the *Essay on Privileges, passim.*
4. *What is the Third Estate?*, 147–8n.
5. *Ibid.*, 125n.
6. *Ibid.*, 211.
7. *Ibid.*, 125.
8. *Ibid.*, 168.
9. *Essay on Privileges*, 4.
10. *Ibid.*, 6n.
11. *Ibid.*, 8 and n.
12. *Ibid.*, 18.
13. See above, p. 80.
14. *What is the Third Estate?*, 123.
15. *Ibid.*, 125.
16. *Ibid.*, 164.
17. *Essay on Privileges*, 18–20.
18. *Ibid.*, 24.
19. *What is the Third Estate?*, 132.
20. *Essay on Privileges*, 11–12n. Bernard Cherin (1718–85) was the leading authority of his day on the genealogy of the nobility. His advice and judgement on matters of personal status and descent were sought not only by the great noble families but by Louis XV and Louis XVI. For example, he was designated to adjudicate the proofs of nobility required from those seeking commissions in the armed forces by the Ordinance of 22 May, 1781.
21. *Ibid.*, 13.
22. *Ibid.*, 14.
23. *Ibid.*, 13n.
24. *Ibid.*, 15.
25. *Ibid.*, 17n.
26. *Ibid.*, 16.
27. *Opinion on the draft constitution* (1795).
28. *What is the Third Estate?*, 196n.
29. Marx, *Frühschriften*, 50.

5 The revolutionary act: June 1789

1. *What is the Third Estate?*, 158.
2. *Ibid.*, 133.
3. *Ibid.*, 184.
4. *Ibid.*, 185.
5. *Ibid.*
6. *Ibid.*, 187.
7. *Ibid.*, 190.
8. *Ibid.*, 197.
9. *Ibid.*, 201.
10. *Ibid.*, 202.
11. *Ibid.*
12. *Ibid.*
13. *Ibid.*, 203.
14. *Ibid.*, 203.
15. *Ibid.*, 203–4.
16. 284 AP 4.1.
17. *Rights of man and citizen*, 17–18.
18. *Ibid.*, 19n.

19. *Draft decree on the clergy*, 3–4.
20. *Notice*, 273–4.

6 The ends of the new state: securing and furthuring personal liberty

1. *Deliberations*, 38.
2. *Views*, 11.
3. *Ibid.*, 11n.
4. *Essay on Privileges*, 2.
5. *What is the Third Estate?*, 204–6.
6. *Ibid.*, 209.
7. *Ibid.*, 141–2n.
8. *Ibid.*, 139.
9. *Ibid.*, 144. Compare his statement in the *Deliberations*: 'For no power can be arbitrary, all must know limits, or they are monstrosities in politics (28).' And in his *Opinion on the constitution of 1795*: 'Limitless powers are a monstrosity in politics.'
10. *Deliberations*, 38.
11. *Plan de la Constitution ... Par Mr. l'Ab ... S ...* Brussels, 8 August 1789. It contains 32 articles. A copy is in the British Museum.
12. See B. Schickhardt, *Die Erklärung der Menschen- und Bürgerrechte von 1789–91 in den Debatten der National versammlung* (Berlin, 1931). This is the most thorough and useful analysis of the origins of the Declaration of 26 August 1789.
13. *Rights of man and citizen*, 19–20.
14. *Ibid.*, 3.
15. *Ibid.*, 41n.
16. 284 AP 5.1 (fifth section). 'Fausses déclarations'.
17. *Rights of man and citizen*, 20–1.
18. *Ibid.*, 21.
19. *Ibid.*, 22–3.
20. *Ibid.*, 23–5.
21. *Ibid.*, 25–6.
22. *Ibid.*, 26–7.
23. *Ibid.*, 27.
24. See below, p. 195–8.
25. *Rights of man and citizen*, 27–8.
26. *Ibid.*, 28–9.
27. *Ibid.*, 29.
28. *Ibid.*, 31–2.
29. *Ibid.*, 32–3.
30. See below, p. 195–8.
31. *Rights of man and citizen*, 36–8.
32. See above, p. 74–5.
33. *Rights of man and citizen*, 39. The concept of 'active' citizenship is discussed more fully below, p. 162–3.
34. *Rights of man and citizen*, 39–40.
35. *Liberty*, 34–5.
36. *Ibid.*, 35.
37. *Ibid.*, 36.
38. *Ibid.*, 36–7.
39. *Ibid.*, 39.

40. *Ibid.*, 43–5.
41. *Ibid.*, 45.
42. *Ibid.*, 46.
43. *Ibid.*, 46–7.
44. *Ibid.*, 48.
45. 284 AP 5.1.
46. *Ibid.*
47. *Ibid.*
48. *Ibid.*
49. *Ibid.*
50. *Ibid.*

7 The means of the new state: the representative system

1. *Notice*, 176.
2. C.J. Friedrich, *Constitutional Government and Democracy* (Waltham, Mass., 1968), 279.
3. A.H. Birch, *Representation* (1971).
4. 284 AP 4.5.
5. *Rights of man and citizen*, 36.
6. *Views*, 153.
7. See particularly his reply to Thomas Paine, 16 July 1791.
8. Rousseau, *Considérations sur le Gouvernement de Pologne*, chapter 7.
9. *Views*, 103.
10. 284 AP 3.2.
11. *What is the Third Estate?*, 179.
12. *Deliberations*, 60–2.
13. *Ibid.*, 62n.
14. *Ibid.*, 62–3.
15. *Arch. parl.*, VIII, 207.
16. G. Lefebvre, *La Révolution française* (Paris, 1957), 137.
17. Brissot endorsed the American example in a speech delivered on 21 July 1789. His *Déclaration des droits des Communes* was printed in the *Patriote français*, 14–15 August, 1789, and later in a separate brochure. See S. Lacroix, *Actes de la commune de Paris pendant la Révolution* (Paris, 1894–1909), I, 292–3, 382–4.
18. H. Grange, 'Le débat sur le veto à l'Assemblée constituante', *Dix-huitième siècle*, I (1969), 118.
19. *Arch. parl.*, VIII, 552.
20. *Speech on the royal veto*, 7–9.
21. *Ibid.*, 11–14.
22. *Ibid.*, 14–15.
23. *Ibid.*, 15.
24. *Ibid.*, 16.
25. *Ibid.*, 4–5.
26. 284 AP 4.2.
27. *Observations*, 33–5.
28. See above, p. 56.
29. *Liberty*, 33.
30. 284 AP 5.1.
31. 284 AP 3.2 (first section).
32. 284 AP 5.2.
33. *Moniteur*, XXV, 291–7.
34. Montesquieu, *De l'Esprit des lois*, XI, chapter 6. See above, p. 59.

35. Robespierre, 'Rapport sur les principes de morale politique', in *Discours et Rapports à la Convention*, ed. M. Bouloiseau (Paris, 1965), 214.
36. Saint-Just, *Oeuvres choisies*, ed. D. Mascolo (Paris, 1968), 191. See also Robespierre's educational proposals below, pp. 207–8, which Sieyes may well have had in mind.
37. *What is the Third Estate?*, 143–4.
38. 284 AP 5.1 (fourth section). Written probably in 1795.
39. *Constitutional observations dictated to citizen Boulay*, 284 AP 5.2.

8 The basis of the representative system: the redivision of France

1. F.A. Mignet, 'Notice historique sur la vie et les travaux de M. le comte Sieyes', in *Notices et mémoires* (Paris, 1843), I, 12.
2. 284 AP 7.5.
3. For example in his *Opinion on the draft constitution* (1795).
4. The word *adunation* occurs in the *Observations* (October 1789), 2, 18. The contrast with the Jacobin concept occurs in 284 AP 5.1.
5. *Views*, 131–3n.
6. *Ibid.*, 128.
7. *Ibid.*, 131.
8. *Deliberations*, 42–3.
9. A. Brette, *Les limites et les divisions territoriales de la France en 1789* (Paris, 1907).
10. *Ibid.*, 84.
11. Alexis de Tocqueville, *L'Ancien Régime et la Révolution.*
12. J. Pétion, *Avis aux Français*, in *Oeuvres* (Paris, Year I), II, 67–8.
13. *Deliberations*, 43–4.
14. *Observations*, 2.
15. *Ibid.*, 19–22.
16. *What is the Third Estate?*, 139.
17. *Observations*, 23.
18. See the discussion above, p. 146–7.
19. J.H. Clapham, *The Abbé Sieyes* (1912), 263; P. Bastid, *Sieyes et sa pensée* (Paris, 1970), 411.
20. *Observations*, 38.
21. P.J. Rabaut [Saint-Etienne], *The History of the Revolution in France*, trans. J. White (1793), 166.

9 Organizing the powers of central government

1. E. Burke, *Works* (1890–7), V, 142–3.
2. 284 AP 4.2.
3. *Views*, 116.
4. *Ibid.*, 119.
5. Rousseau, *Contrat social*, III, chapter 1.
6. In the *Views* Sieyes remarks that the legislature must act by 'general laws' and not by 'particular acts of authority' (73) but this is a distinction between public and private, not between the legislative and executive.
7. 284 AP 4.5.
8. *Views*, 94.
9. *Ibid.*, 103.

10. *Contrat social*, II, 3.
11. *Ibid.*, IV, 2.
12. See above, p. 131.
13. *Views*, 135.
14. *Ibid.*, 89.
15. *Ibid.*, 121.
16. *What is the Third Estate?*, 175.
17. *Ibid.*, 167.
18. 'Il n'y a en Angleterre qu'un seul ordre, la nation.' *Ibid.*, 167n.
19. *Ibid.*, 170.
20. *Ibid.*, 172n.
21. *Ibid.*, 172–3.
22. *Rights of man and citizen*, 34.
23. *Speech on the royal veto*, 2n.
24. *Ibid.*, 2–3.
25. *Ibid.*, 5.
26. *Considérations sur le Gouvernement de Pologne*, 465.
27. *Ibid.*, 465–6.
28. 284 AP 4.7. The quotation comes from the second part of Rousseau's *Discours*.
29. J. Fouché, *Mémoires* (Paris, 1824), 1, 147.
30. *Observations*, 36–7.
31. 284 AP 4.7.
32. Paine's letter is prefixed to Sieyes' reply to it in the *Moniteur*, 16 July 1791.
33. In chapter 6 it was observed that some of the ideas contained in Sieyes' *Exposition of the rights of man and citizen* appear in the First Title of the 1791 Constitution. In one of his later unpublished notes (284 AP 5.1) Sieyes wrote that he had been right to distinguish certain articles of legislation as 'articles *fondamentaux*' which the legislature could not touch. This surely refers to the First Title of the 1791 Constitution. The other derivations are more obvious.
34. He implied this to Wilhelm von Humboldt. See his *Gesammelte Schriften* (Berlin, 1903–18), 14, 469. Also at the end of Sieyes' *Bases of the social order* he states that the *faiseurs* in the constituent Assembly in 1789 and 1790 were caught napping and were 'reduits à recevoir sous dictée ce qu'on voulut bien leur apprendre,' 284 AP 5.1.
35. The influence of the 1791 Constitution is discussed further in the Conclusion.
36. K.E. Oelsner, *Exposé historique des écrits de Sieyes* (n.p., Year VIII), 84.
37. See above, p. 67.
38. L.M. de Larevellière-Lépeaux, *Mémoires* (Paris, 1895), I, 239–40.
39. 284 AP 5.2.
40. Boulay de la Meurthe, *Théorie constitutionnelle de Sieyes. Constitution de l'an VIII* (Paris, 1836), 36.
41. *Ibid.*

10 The church, education, the press, justice and the army

1. See R. Zapperi's introduction to his edition of Sieyes' *Qu'est-ce que le Tiers état?* (Geneva, 1970), and his article, 'Sieyes et l'abolition de la féodalité en 1789', *Annales historiques de la Révolution française*,' *44* (1972), 321–51.
2. The text of this speech, with an introduction, in printed together with Sieyes' *Summary observations on ecclesiastical goods* in a single brochure published soon after the speech was delivered. See items 9 and 10 in the bibliography of Sieyes' works.
3. Introduction to speech on tithes, 42.

4. *Ibid.*, 41; *Summary observations*, 14, 24.
5. Introduction to speech on tithes, 33–4.
6. *Ibid.*, 39.
7. *Ibid.*, 40.
8. *Summary observations*, 3.
9. *Ibid.*, 9.
10. *Ibid.*, 5–6.
11. See his remarks on the clergy in *What is the Third Estate?*, 124–5n.
12. *Opinion on the clergy*, 2.
13. *Summary observations*, 18–19.
14. *Ibid.*, 25–6.
15. Mercier de la Rivière, *L'Ordre naturel et essentiel des sociétés politiques*, ed. E. Depitre (Paris, 1910), 17.
16. See above, p. 106.
17. *Draft for a decree*, 6.
18. *Ibid.*, 9.
19. *Ibid.*, 14–15.
20. *Ibid.*, 27.
21. 284 AP 4.9. The following discussion is based on this dossier.
22. *Ibid.*
23. See item 20 in the bibliography of Sieyes' works.
24. See item 21 in the bibliography of Sieyes' works.
25. A. Aulard, *Christianity and the French Revolution* trans. Lady Frazer (1927), 77.
26. See above, p. 35.
27. *Views*, 125.
28. This account is based on the text of Sieyes' plan published in the *Journal d'instruction sociale*, June–July 1793. See item 29 in the bibliography of Sieyes' works.
29. See above, p. 163–4.
30. *Journal d'instruction sociale*, 146.
31. *Ibid.*, 147.
32. 284 AP 5.1 (eleventh section).
33. *Journal d'instruction sociale*, 83.
34. *Ibid.*, 151.
35. *Ibid.*, 155.
36. The speech was delivered on 13 July 1793. The text used is Robespierre, *Textes choisis*, ed. J. Poperen (Paris, 1973), II, 157–8.
37. *Ibid.*, 174.
38. *Ibid.*, 159.
39. *Ibid.*, 184.
40. Report presented on 20 January 1790. See item 15 in the bibliography of Sieyes' works.
41. Extracts from both responses are reprinted in L.G. Wickham Legg (ed.), *Select Documents illustrative of the History of the French Revolution* (Oxford, 1905), I, 194–5.
42. See item 18 in the bibliography of Sieyes' works.
43. E. Colmache, *Reminiscences of Prince Talleyrand*, ed. Mme. Colmache (1848) I, 240–2, and F.A.M. Mignet, 'Notice historique sur la vie et les travaux de M. le comte Sieyes', in *Notices et mémoires* (Paris, 1843), I, 4.
44. Lord Brougham, *Historical Sketches of Statesmen who flourished in the time of George III*, Third Series (1845), I, 137.
45. 284 AP 4.11. It was probably written about the same time as the *Deliberations* which also calls for immediate protection against the 'blind and unlimited obedience of the military' and for immediate action to secure the freedom to write

and publish, though not for a National Guard. *Deliberations*, 41.

46. 284 AP 4.11. 'Des rapports de la Constitution de l'armée avec la liberté.'
47. 284 AP 9.3.
48. Report presented to the Committee of General Defence on 13 January 1793. See item 26 in bibliography of Sieyes' works.
49. See the report of the debate in *Archives Parlementaires*, LVII, 738–48, and LVIII, 34–44, and in P.J.B. Buchez and P.C. Roux, *Histoire parlementaire de la Révolution française* (Paris, 1834–8), XXIII, 407–15, 420–8.

Conclusion: Sieyes' position in the history of political thought

1. R.R. Palmer, *The Age of the Democratic Revolution*, I, *The Challenge* (Princeton, 1959), 216.
2. Karl Marx, *Neue Rheinische Zeitung*, 15 December 1848, in Karl Marx and Friedrich Engels, *Werke* (Berlin, 1959–70), VI, 107–8. See also Marx's earlier characterization of the French bourgeoisie to which reference is made in n.12 below.
3. J. Gilissen, 'Die belgische Verfassung von 1831 – ihr Ursprung und ihr Einfluss', in W. Conze (ed.), *Beiträge zur deutschen und belgischen Verfassungsgeschichte in 19 Jahrhundert* (Stuttgart, 1967), 38–69. See also J. Hawgood, *Modern Constitutions since 1787* (1939), 51–3.
4. How close Kant came to entering into correspondence with Sieyes is indicated by a letter from him to A.L. Théremin dated 9 March 1796, which is in the Sieyes Archives (284 AP 17.8). It is assessed by A. Ruiz, 'Neues über Kant und Sieyes', *Kant–Studien*, *68* (1977), 446–53.
5. H. Reiss (ed.), *Kant's Political Writings* (Cambridge, 1970), 163.
6. Lord Acton, *Historical Essays and Studies*, ed. J.N. Figgis and R.V. Laurence (1907), 492.
7. Lord Acton, *History of Freedom and other Essays*, ed. J.N. Figgis and R.V. Laurence (1907), 57.
8. Marx-Engels, *Werke*, I, 106.
9. *Ibid.*, II, 33.
10. Karl Marx, *Die Frühschriften*, ed. S. Landshut (Stuttgart, 1968), 545.
11. *Ibid.*, 218.
12. *Ibid.*, 221. The same contrast between the French and the German class situation was made by Marx in 1848. See n.2 above.
13. Benjamin Constant, 'Souvenirs historiques', *Revue de Paris*, XVI (1830), 103.

Bibliography

1 Sieyes' published and unpublished writings

A comprehensive list of the main published writings and speeches of the Abbé Sieyes will be found in the final section of the Introduction to this study. Only some of his minor public interventions during the period from 1789 to 1799, which are of negligible significance for the development of his political thought, have been omitted. The list specifies the editions of his works that have been used in the study, and provides full references to the *Moniteur* and the *Archives Parlementaires*, in which many of his writings and speeches appear.

Sieyes' unpublished writings, together with his personal papers, form the Sieyes Archives, and are lodged in the National Archives in Paris. A description of the unpublished writings will also be found in the final section of the Introduction, as well as an explanation of the system of references. A full inventory of the unpublished writings is provided by A. Marquant, *Les Archives Sieyes* (Paris, 1970).

The only collected edition of Sieyes' political writings was published in German in 1796: *Emmanuel Sieyes, Politische Schriften vollständig gesammelt von dem deutschen Ubersetzer nebst zwei Vorreden uber Sieyes Lebensgeschichte, seine politische Rolle, seinem Charakter, seine Schriften etc.* (n.p., Leipzig). The translator was J.G. Ebel. The two prefaces were written by K.E. Oelsner. The first contains an extremely valuable discussion by Oelsner of Sieyes' life and works. The second is a German version of the *Notice sur la vie de Sieyes* (see item 31 in the list of Sieyes' published writings). As Oelsner makes clear in the second preface, both the *Notice* itself, and the German version of it were put together by him in June 1794 from manuscript notes by Sieyes. Recently the publishing company EDHIS of Paris has announced that it is planning to produce a new collected edition of Sieyes' works.

The two speeches that Sieyes delivered on constitutional matters in 1795 were republished in *Les discours de Sieyes dans les débats constitutionnels de l'an III (2 et 18 thermidor)*, ed. P. Bastid (Paris, 1939).

A German edition of some of Sieyes' early tracts was published in 1975: *Emmanuel Joseph Sieyes, Politische Schriften, 1788–1790*, ed. E. Schmitt and R. Reichardt (Darmstadt). The book contains an excellent bibliography of secondary material on Sieyes.

Sieyes' most famous tract has been translated into English by M. Blondel: *Emmanuel Joseph Sieyes, What is the Third Estate?*, ed. S.E. Finer (London, 1963).

To avoid misunderstanding it should be added that the *Mémoire sur le rachat des droits féodaux declarés rachetables par l'arrêté de l'Assemblée nationale* is not by him but by the comte d'Antraigues. On this see R. Zapperi, 'Sieyes et l'abolition de la féodalité en 1789', *Annales historiques de la Révolution française*, XLIV (1972), 321–51.

2 Works by Sieyes' predecessors and contemporaries which influenced the development of his political ideas

The vast range of Sieyes' reading has been indicated in chapter 2 and it does not seem necessary to list all the works with which he was familiar. Such a list would amount virtually to a bibliography of the Enlightenment. It may, however, be helpful to specify the editions which have been used for some of the more significant works discussed. For Condillac's writings the edition used is Georges Le Roy's *Oeuvres philosophiques* (Paris, 1947–51), 3 vols. For the Physiocrats and Turgot, Eugène Daire's *Collection des principaux économistes* (Paris, Part 2, 1846; Parts 3 and 4, 1844) is still useful, particularly for the lesser known Physiocrats such as the Abbé Baudeau. Daire does not, however, provide a full version of Mercier de la Rivière's *L'Ordre naturel et essentiel des sociétés politiques*, and for this the edition by E. Depitre (Paris, 1910) has been used. Gustave Schelle's edition of Turgot's works (Paris, 1913–23), 5 vols, complements that of Daire, while R.L. Meek's volume *Turgot on Progress, Sociology and Economics* (Cambridge, 1973) contains English translations of some of the main texts. The two-volume study published by the Institut National d'Etudes Démographiques entitled *François Quesnay et la Physiocratie* (Paris, 1958), includes not only Quesnay's works but also a collection of essays on him and a comprehensive bibliography. Finally, for Montesquieu and Rousseau the complete editions of their works published by the Gallimard Press, Paris, in the Bibliothèque de la Pléiade have been used.

3 Works on Sieyes' ideas by his contemporaries

As one of the main actors in the revolutionary epoch Sieyes is mentioned in a great number of contemporary writings. Bailly, Barère, Barras, Lafayette, Napoleon, Talleyrand, Lord Broughham – to mention only some of the better known names – provide accounts of his character and activities in their memoirs and papers. The number of contemporary writings that focus on his ideas and their origin is, however, relatively small. The following list indicates the most significant:

Anonymous, *Des Opinions politiques du citoyen Sieyes et de son vie comme homme politique* (Paris, Year VIII), 280 pp. Although this work continues to be ascribed to K.E. Oelsner it is clearly not by him, as Alfred Stern pointed out in 'Sieyes et la constitution de l'an III', *La Révolution française, 19* (1900), 375–9. The work is rather wooden in style and consists largely of extended extracts from Sieyes' writings.

Antoine Boulay de la Meurthe, *Théorie constitutionnelle de Sieyes. Constitution de l'an VIII* (Paris, 1836). This work by a close friend of Sieyes remains indispensable. The 'constitutional observations' dictated by Sieyes to Boulay in 1799, from which the latter quotes in his book, are now to be found in the Sieyes Archives 284 AP 5, Dossier 2, 7.

Benjamin Constant, 'Souvenirs historiques à l'occasion de l'ouvrage de M. Bignon', *Revue de Paris*, XI (1830), 115–25; XVI (1830), 102–12, 221–33. These three letters of reminiscence were written by Constant in the last year of his life, and reveal the high esteem he had for Sieyes. They have been partly reprinted by A. Aulard in 'Sieyes et Talleyrand d'après Benjamin Constant et Barras', *La Révolution française*, LXXIII (1920), 289–314.

Etienne Dumont, *Souvenirs sur Mirabeau* (Paris, 1832). Contains some interesting fragments on Sieyes.

Friedrich von Gentz, 'Darstellung und Vergleichung einiger politischen Constitutions – Systeme die von dem Grundsatze der Theilung der Macht ausgehen, *Neue Deutsche*

Monatsschrift (Oct. 1795), 75–157. Analyses Sieyes' constitutional proposals of 1795.

Wilhelm von Humboldt, *Gesammelte Schriften*, ed. Königlich Preussischen Akademie der Wissenschaften (Berlin, 1903–18), 15 vols. Vol. 14 contains Humboldt's journal of his stay in Paris in 1797–98 and describes his frequent meetings and conversations with Sieyes.

—— *Neue Briefe Wilhelm von Humboldts an Schiller 1796–1803*, ed. F.C. Ebrard (Berlin, 1911). Contains a letter to Schiller with a masterly delineation of Sieyes' character and philosophical position.

Konrad Englebert Oelsner, Prefaces to the two-volume German edition of Sieyes' works (see the section on Sieyes' writings above), I pp. iii–cxvi, II, pp. iii–lxviii.

——*Exposé historique des écrits de Sieyes, tiré au nombre de 25 exemplaires aux frais de l'auteur* (n.p., year VIII). This anonymous work is essentially a French version of Oelsner's Preface to vol. I of the German edition of Sieyes' works.

——*Bruchstücke aus den Papieren eines Augenzeugen und unparteiischen Beobachters der Französischen Revolution* (n.p. Leipzig, 1794). Scattered references to Sieyes.

——'Über Sieyes', *Klio*, I (1796), 1–16, 127–66.

Pierre-Louis Roederer, *Oeuvres de Comte P.-L. Roederer*, ed. Baron A.M. Roederer (Paris, 1853–59), 8 vols. Roederer was probably Sieyes' closest friend and his works contain many references to him and his writings.

4 Subsequent works devoted to Sieyes and his ideas

Lord Acton, *Lectures on the French Revolution*, ed. J.N. Figgis and R.V. Laurence (London, 1910). Lecture XI is devoted to Sieyes and the Constitution Civile.

M. Adler-Bresse, *Sieyes et le monde allemand* (Lille, 1977), 2 vols.

A. Aulard, *Les Orateurs de l'Assemblée constituante* (Paris, 1882). Chapter VI is devoted to Sieyes.

P. Bastid, *Sieyes et sa pensée* (Paris, 1970). The standard French text on Sieyes, first published in 1939, and revised and enlarged in 1970 to take account of Sieyes' rediscovered papers.

E. de Beauverger, *Etude sur Sieyes* (Batignolles, 1851).

A.A. Bigeon, *Sieyes, l'homme, le constituant* (Paris, 1893).

O. Brandt, 'Untersuchungen zu Sieyes', *Historische Zeitschrift*, CXXVI (1922), 410–35.

J.J. Chevallier, *Les Grandes Oeuvres politiques de Machiavel à nos jours* (Paris, 1962). A section (pp. 174–84) is devoted to Sieyes.

J.H. Clapham, *The Abbé Sieyes* (London, 1912).

Y. Koung, *Théorie constitutionelle de Sieyes* (Paris, 1934).

G. Lefebvre, *Etudes sur la Révolution française* (Paris, 1954). Contains a discussion of Bastid's work on Sieyes, pp. 99–105.

S.B. Liljegren (ed.), *Theodore Lesueur: A French draft constitution of 1792 modelled on James Harrington's Oceana* (Lund, 1932). Discusses the relationship of Harrington and Sieyes, pp. 44–79.

L. Madelin, *The Revolutionaries (1789–1799)*, trans. R.J.S. Curtis (London, 1930). Contains a chapter on Sieyes, pp. 284–314.

F.A.M. Mignet, 'Notice historique sur la vie et les travaux de M. le comte Sieyes, in *Notices et mémoires* (Paris, 1843), I, 1–27.

B. Mirkine-Guetzievitch, 'L'Abbé Sieyes', *La Révolution française*, new series, XIV (1936), 229–36.

A. Néton, *Sieyes (1748–1836), d'après des documents inédits* (Paris, 1900). The standard work in French before Bastid.

G. Pariset, 'Sieyes et Spinoza', *Revue de synthèse historique*, XII (1906), 309–20. A strained attempt to demonstrate an affiliation between the two thinkers.

J. Roels, 'La notion de représentation chez l'abbé Sieyes', *Revue generale belge*, XCIX (1963), 87–105.

Sainte-Beuve, *Causeries du lundi*, V (Paris, n.d.). Contains Sainte-Beuve's masterly essay on Sieyes, pp. 189–216. Sainte-Beuve was able to make use of Sieyes' unpublished writings before they disappeared in the course of the nineteenth century.

E. Schmitt, 'Sieyes', in H. Maier (ed.), *Klassiker des politischen Denkens*, II (Munich, 1968), 135–60. Schmitt has done more than anyone else in recent years to rehabilitate Sieyes as a political theorist.

A. Stern, 'Sieyes et la constitution de l'an III', *La Révolution française*, XXXIX (1900), 375–9.

J.M. Thompson, *Leaders of the French Revolution* (Oxford, 1962). Contains an essay on Sieyes, pp. 2–16.

D. Trevor, 'Some sources of the constitutional thought of the Abbé Sieyes: Harrington and Spinoza', in *Politica* (London School of Economics and Political Science), II (1935), 325–469.

G.G. Van Deusen, *Sieyes: his life and nationalism* (New York, 1932, repr, 1970). Van Deusen was the first to draw attention to the relationship between Wilhelm von Humboldt and Sieyes.

R. Zapperi, 'Sieyes et l'abolition de la feodalité en 1789', *Annales historiques de la Révolution française*, XLIV (1972), 321–51.

Mention should also be made here of the various introductory essays to editions of Sieyes' *Qu'est-ce que le Tiers état?* notably those by E. Champion (1888), O. Brandt (in his German edition of 1924), P. Campbell (in S.E. Finer's English edition of 1963) and R. Zapperi (1970).

5 Other works consulted

Anonymous, *The Revolutionary Plutarch* (London, 1806), I.

Lord Acton, *Historical Essays and Studies*, ed. J.N. Figgis and R.V. Laurence (London, 1907).

—— *History of Freedom and other Essays*, ed. J.N. Figgis and R.V. Laurence (London, 1907).

A. Aulard, *Histoire politique de la Révolution française* (Paris, 1921).

—— *Christianity and the French Revolution*, trans. Lady Frazer (London, 1927).

K.M. Baker, *Condorcet: From Natural Philosophy to Social Mathematics* (Chicago, 1975).

R. Barny, 'Rousseau dans la Révolution', *Dix-huitième siècle*, VI (1974), 59–98.

C.L. Becker, *The Heavenly City of the Eighteenth Century Philosophers* (Yale, 1967).

K. von Beyme, *Die verfassungebende Gewalt des Volkes* (Tübingen, 1968).

A.H. Birch, *Representation* (London, 1971).

A. Brette, *Les limites et les divisions territoriales de la France en 1789* (Paris, 1907).

P.J.B. Buchez and P.C. Roux, *Histoire parlementaire de la Révolution française* (Paris, 1834–8), 40 vols.

Edmund Burke, *Works* (London, 1890–97), 8 vols.

L. Cahen, *Condorcet et la Révolution française* (Paris, 1904).

E. Carcassonne, *Montesquieu et le problème de la constitution française* (Paris, 1927).

J.A.J. Cérutti, *Oeuvres diverses* (Paris, 1792), 3 vols.

M.J. de Chénier, *Tableau historique de l'état et des progrès de la littérature française depuis 1789* (Paris, 1816).

W.F. Church (ed.), *The Influence of the Enlightenment on the French Revolution* (Boston, 1964).
A. Cobban, *Rousseau and the Modern State* (London, 1968).
—— *Aspects of the French Revolution* (St Albans, 1973).
E. Colmache, *Reminiscences of Prince Talleyrand*, ed. Mme. Colmache (London, 1848), 2 vols.
Condorcet, *Oeuvres*, ed. A. Condorcet O'Connor and M.F. Arago (Paris, 1847–49), 12 vols.
Benjamin Constant, *De la Liberté chez les Modernes. Ecrits politiques*, ed. M. Gauchet (Paris, 1980).
R. Darnton, *Mesmerism and the end of the Enlightenment in France* (Cambridge, Mass., 1968).
K. Deinet, *Konrad Engelbert Oelsner und die Französische Revolution* (Munich, 1981).
Camille Desmoulins, *Correspondance inédite de Camille Desmoulins* (pub. M. Matton, Paris, 1836).
W. Doyle, *Origins of the French Revolution* (Oxford, 1980).
L. Ducros, *French Society in the Eighteenth Century* (London, 1926).
J. Egret, *The French Prerevolution 1787–1788*, trans. W.D. Camp (Chicago, 1977).
R. Fayolle, *Sainte-Beuve et le XVIIIe siècle ou comment les révolutions arrivent* (Paris, 1972).
M. Forsyth, 'Thomas Hobbes and the constituent power of the people', *Political Studies*, XXXIX, 191–203.
J. Fouché, *Mémoires* (Paris, 1824), 2 vols.
C.J. Friedrich, *Constitutional Government and Democracy* (Waltham, Mass., 1968).
F. Furet, *Interpreting the French Revolution*, trans. E. Foster (Cambridge, 1981).
F. Furet and D. Richet, *The French Revolution*, trans. S. Hardman (London, 1970).
M.B. Garrett, *The Estates General of 1789. The Problem of Composition and Organization* (New York, 1935).
P. Gay, *The Enlightenment: an Interpretation. The Rise of Modern Paganism* (London, 1967).
J. Gilissen, 'Die belgische Verfassung von 1831 – ihr Ursprung und ihr Einfluss', in W. Conze (ed.), *Beiträge zur deutschen und belgischen Verfassungsgeschichte in 19 Jahrhundert* (Stuttgart, 1967), 38–69.
J. Godechot, *Les Constitutions de la France depuis 1789* (Paris, 1970).
M. Göhring, *Weg und Sieg der Modernen Staatsidee in Frankreich* (Tübingen, 1947).
—— Rabaut Saint-Etienne, *Ein Kämpfer an der Wende zweier Epochen* (Berlin, 1935).
H. Grange, 'Le débat sur le veto à l'Assemblée constituant, *Dix-huitième siècle*, I (1969), 107–21.
B. Groethuysen, *Philosophie de la Révolution française* (Paris, 1956).
D. Gwyn, *The Meaning of the Separation of Powers* (New Orleans, 1965).
N. Hampson, *The Enlightenment* (London, 1968).
—— *Will and Circumstance: Montesquieu, Rousseau and the French Revolution* (London, 1983).
J. Hawgood, *Modern Constitutions since 1787* (London, 1939).
A. Headlam-Morley, *The New Democratic Constitutions of Europe* (Oxford, 1929).
H. Hintze, *Staatseinheit und föderalismus im alten Frankreich und in der Revolution* (Berlin, 1928).
Immanuel Kant, *Kant's Political Writings*, ed. H. Reiss (Cambridge, 1970).
I.F. Knight, *The Geometric Spirit: the Abbé de Condillac and the French Enlightenment* (New Haven, 1968).
S. Lacroix, *Actes de la commune de Paris pendant la Révolution* (Paris, 1894–1909), 15 vols.
L.M. de Larevellière-Lépeaux, *Mémoires* (Paris, 1895), 3 vols.
A. Latreille, *L'Eglise catholique et la Révolution française* (Paris, 1946–50), 2 vols.

E. Lebègue, *Thouret (1746–1794)* (Paris, 1910).
G. Lefebvre, *La Révolution française* (Paris, 1956).
R. Lefèvre, *Condillac, ou la joie de vivre* (Seghers, 1966).
L.G. Wickham Legg (ed.), *Select Documents illustrative of the History of the French Revolution* (Oxford, 1905), 2 vols.
E. Lemberg, *Nationalismus* (Hamburg, 1964), 2 vols.
K. Loewenstein, *Volk und Parlament nach der Staatstheorie der französischen Nationalversammlung von 1789* (Munich, 1922).
J. Lough (ed.), *The Encyclopédie of Diderot and D'Alembert* (Cambridge, 1954).
Kingsley Martin, *French Liberal Thought in the Eighteenth Century*, ed. J.P. Mayer (London, 1954).
Karl Marx, *Die Frühschriften*, ed. S. Landshut (Stuttgart, 1968).
—— and Friedrich Engels, *Werke* (Berlin, 1959–70), 41 vols.
A. Mathiez, 'La Révolution française et la théorie de la dictature', *Revue historique*, CLXI (1929), 304–15.
H. Michel, *L'Idée de l'état* (Paris, 1898, repr. Aalen, 1973).
F.A.M. Mignet, *Histoire de la Révolution française depuis 1789 jusqu'en 1814* (Brussels, 1824).
D. Mornet, *La Pensée française au dix-huitième siècle* (Paris, 1969).
—— *Les Origines intellectuelles de la Révolution française* (Paris, 1933).
C. Müller, *Das Imperative und Freie Mandat* (Leiden, 1966).
P. Naville, *D'Holbach* (Paris, 1943).
Thomas Paine, *The Rights of Man*, ed. A. Seldon (London, 1966).
R.R. Palmer, *The Age of the Democratic Revolution*, I: *The Challenge* (Princeton, 1959), II: *The Struggle* (Princeton, 1964).
J. Pétion, *Oeuvres* (Paris, Year I), 3 Vols.
F. Picavet, *Les Idéologues* (Paris, 1891).
Rabaut Saint-Etienne, *Oeuvres*, ed. Collin de Plancy (Paris, 1826), 2 vols.
H. Rausch (ed.), *Zur Theorie und Geschichte der Repräsentation und Repräsentativverfassung* (Darmstadt, 1968).
R. Redslob, *Die Staatstheorien der französischen Nationalversammlung von 1789* (Leipzig, 1912).
S. Riemer, *Die Staatsanschauung des Grafen d'Antraigues in seiner Denkschrift über die Generalstände* (Berlin, 1934).
A. Rivarol, *Oeuvres choisies*, ed. M. De Lescure (Paris, 1880), 2 vols.
Robespierre, *Oeuvres complètes* (Paris, 1910–67), 10 vols.
—— *Textes choisis*, ed. J. Poperen (Paris, 1974), 3 vols.
—— *Discours et Rapports à la Convention*, ed. M. Bouloiseau (Paris, 1965).
J. Roels, *Le concept de représentation politique au dix-huitième siècle* (Louvain, 1969).
—— *La notion de représentation chez Roederer* (Heule, 1968).
M. Roustan, *The Pioneers of the French Revolution*, trans. F. Whyte (London, 1926).
G. Rudé, *Interpretations of the French Revolution*, Historical Association Pamphlet No. 47 (London, 1961).
Sainte-Beuve, *Causeries du lundi* (Paris, n.d.), 16 vols.
—— *Portraits littéraires* (Paris, n.d.), 3 vols.
Saint-Just, *Oeuvres choisies*, ed. J. Gratien (Paris, 1968).
B. Schickhardt, *Die Erklärung der Menschen- und Bürgerrechte von 1789–91 in den Debatten der Nationalversammlung* (Berlin, 1931).
C. Schmitt, *Verfassungslehre* (Berlin, 1928, repr. 1965).
E. Schmitt, *Repräsentation und Revolution* (Munich, 1969).
—— 'Repraesentatio in toto und repraesentatio singulariter. Zur Frage nach dem Zusammenbruch des französischen Ancien Regime und der Durchsetzung moderner parlamentarischer Theorie und Praxis im Jahr 1789', *Historische Zeitschrift*, CCXIII (1971), 529–76.

H. Sée, *Les Idées politiques en France au dix-huitième siècle* (Paris, 1920).
L. Silberstein, *Lemercier de la Rivière und seine Politische Ideen* (Berlin, 1928).
Madame de Staël, 'Considérations sur les principaux événements de la Révolution française', in *Oeuvres complètes de Mme la Baronne de Staël* (Paris, 1819–21), vols 12–14.
Lorenz von Stein, *Geschichte der sozialen Bewegung in Frankreich von 1789 bis auf unsere Tage* (Hildesheim, 1959, original edition 1921), 3 vols.
D. Sternberger, *Nicht alle Staatsgewalt geht vom Volke aus* (Stuttgart, 1971).
J.L. Talmon, *The Origins of Totalitarian Democracy* (London, 1961).
E. Thompson, *Popular Sovereignty and the French Constituent Assembly 1789–1791* (Manchester, 1952).
Alexis de Tocqueville, *L'Ancien Régime et la Révolution* (Paris, 1953), 2 vols.
M. Troper, *La Séparation des pouvoirs et l'histoire constitutionelle française* (Paris, 1973).
T. Tsatsos, *Zur Geschichte und Kritik der Lehre von der Gewaltenteilung* (Heidelberg, 1968).
C. Vereker, *Eighteenth-century Optimism* (Liverpool, 1967).
M.J.C. Vile, *Constitutionalism and the Separation of Powers* (Oxford, 1967).
E. Zweig, *Die Lehre vom Pouvoir Constituant* (Tübingen, 1909).

Index